Fundamentals of
Physiological
Psychology

Fundamentals of Physiological Psychology

Richard L. Bruce
University of Alaska, Anchorage

HOLT, RINEHART AND WINSTON New York Chicago San Francisco Atlanta
Dallas Montreal Toronto London Sydney

Library of Congress Cataloging in Publication Data

Bruce, Richard Loren, 1938–
    Fundamentals of physiological psychology.

    Includes bibliographies and index.
    1. Psychology, Physiological. I. Title.
QP360.B78   152   76-25484
ISBN 0-03-002841-8

Acknowledgments

For permission to reprint from copyrighted materials the author is indebted to the following:

American Association for the Advancement of Science for Figure 23.6 from Binkley, S.: "Pineal function in sparrows: Circadian rhythm and temperature." *Science, 174*:311–314, October 15, 1971. Copyright © 1971 by the American Association for the Advancement of Science. Figure 11.1 from Bodian, D.: "The generalized vertebrate neuron." *Science, 137*:323–326, August 3, 1962. Copyright © 1962 by the American Association for the Advancement of Science. Figure 21.4 from Heston, L. L.: "The genetics of schizophrenic and schizoid disease." *Science, 167*:249–256, January 16, 1970. Copyright © 1970 by the American Association for the Advancement of Science. Reprinted by permission.
American Institute of Physics for Figure 16.4 from Davis, H. et al.: "Acoustic trauma in the guinea pig." *Journal of the Acoustical Society of America, 25,* 1953.
American Medical Association for Figure 16.7 from Bunch, C. C.: "Age variations in auditory acuity." *Archives of Otolaryngology, 9*:634, 1929. Copyright © 1929 by the American Medical Association.

(Continued on p. 397)

Preface

My involvement with the field of physiological psychology follows a circuitous route. I have always been interested in animal behavior (including the human species), and after several false starts discovered that experimental psychology allowed me to dabble in my interest and receive academic credit as well. The approach at that time was to study the stimulus-response characteristics of the intact animal. The behaving organism was considered a "black box" which should be left inviolate. In keeping with this approach, I avoided taking formal classes in biology, a decision I have regretted many times.

A growing impatience with the intrinsic limitations of obtaining definitive answers by means of a "black box" approach, combined with a fortuitous encounter with a stimulating graduate instructor, made me suddenly aware of the vistas available for understanding the mechanisms inside the box. In most cases, the instigating "question" which needed to be answered was a behavioral one. In order to understand the behavior, I found it necessary to exert considerable effort to acquire the biological knowledge I had missed. It was my intention while writing the text to make it an introduction to this fascinating world of knowledge. The biological facts and terminology have been selected according to their applicability to understanding behavior. This book is an attempt to present the known (or suspected) mechanisms that might account for the responses of organisms to their environment.

I have assumed no necessary prior biological or psychological knowledge, although it would be a formidable undertaking to try to become acquainted with both spheres in a single course! Terminology is extremely important to understanding the material. When an important term is introduced in the text, it appears in boldface type and is defined in the glossary-index. These terms are usually presented in a definitional sentence in the flow of the text. Thus, boldfaced terms are assumed to be part of the reader's working vocabulary in the material that follows. The chapters are intended to be self-contained and sequentially cumulative; however, sometimes the order of introduction may not make sense to the reader. In these cases, other chapters in the same part may fill in the missing gaps. In addition, each part begins with a list of alternate references that may be turned to for clarification. Although the book is wide-ranging in the variety of concepts discussed, it is in no way a comprehensive or encyclopedic text. It is, quite frankly, meant to pique the curiosity of the student about a world of knowledge at an earlier stage than I was when I discovered it. If the reader is challenged to go beyond the discussions here, I have succeeded. For students whose only contact with physiological psychology is this text, I have tried to make the coverage as representative as I could.

It is almost embarrassing to take the credit for authorship, for this book owes its existence to many individuals who contributed support at various critical stages. My contribution appears to be that of dogged perseverance. Although I am responsible for the organization and phraseology of the text, many specific parts are the result of assimilating the fruits of interaction with others more clever than I. I wish that I had compiled a specific list; however, lacking that, the following acknowledgments must suffice.

First, the publishing team at Holt, Rinehart and Winston has provided all the support I could possibly expect. The book has emerged through a process of nurture, review, editing, translating, creating, and coordinating by many individuals, many of whom I do not know in spite of the inconveniences I created for them. Despite my occasional protests at the time, the text is better for their efforts. The practice of borrowing illustrations from other publications has also been most helpful to this project, and specific acknowledgments to these sources are provided elsewhere.

On a more personal level, many people have contributed to the project through their tolerance and/or encouragement. The following have been particularly instrumental:

Merle Meyer and Tom Law, who were crucial teachers in my educational development.

Joel S. Milner of Western Carolina University, Gary Greenberg of Wichita State University, Gary Schaumberg of Cerritos College, Thomas R. Scott of the University of Delaware, and Neil Fashbaugh of Cabrillo College, who reviewed the manuscript at various stages and offered helpful suggestions.

The students in my physiological psychology courses at Claremont Men's College, Los Angeles State College (now University), and the University of Alaska, Anchorage, who provided valuable feedback as the course evolved into a text—Ben Newkirk at CMC and Don Wasson and Don Gustafson at L.A. State, particularly.

My friends in the Psychology Department here in Anchorage, who not only played the reinforcement game, but did it well enough to get me to finish the manuscript. The cumulative graph is still on my office wall.

Karen Christensen, who converted my mangled rough draft into a coherent document. In addition to typing, Karen provided much needed spelling, punctuation, language, and concept improvements along with timely encouragement.

Gin Rountree, who tackled the nitty-gritty details which are an absolute must for the sake of the book but provide such a low reward-cost ratio. Ginny held the act together when things got discouraging and was instrumental in the development of many of the finished features. She was the "silent partner" in the project.

Finally, the members of my family—my wife Sally, and Karyn, Marian, and Linda, who sustained the project in many ways, not the least of which was giving up many weekends we should have been out enjoying Alaska.

R.L.B.

Anchorage, Alaska
October 1976

Contents

Fundamentals of Physiological Psychology

Part

I

Introduction

One way to approach a new discipline is to identify some of the basic concepts that are central to it. Physiological psychology represents a combination of the worlds of biological science and behavioral science. The common denominator is the study of the structures and functions of the brain in order to understand why people behave as they do. The assumption is that as we learn more about the mechanisms of the nervous system, we will be able to explain and predict an increasing proportion of human behavior.

Speculation regarding the internal events that cause an individual's behavior has been almost universal in history. Art, philosophy, science, religion, and the occult have all offered their own solutions to this problem. The so-called mind-body question represents early philosophical attempts to resolve the relationship. With increasing scientific investigation, however, we find that such explanations become more limited and restricted in scope. Thus, instead of dealing with the entire body, a physiological psychologist is likely to focus on a specific bodily structure and attempt to determine its particular function in the entire panoply of human behavior. This structural-functional relationship is the theme that pervades this text. Physiological psychologists assume an organic explanation for behavior. The key to understanding the nature of human beings is to understand the internal mechanisms that structure them.

The contemporary status of any discipline is the product of an historical sequence of thoughts and ideas leading to the present. Theories are constantly proposed which are then tested by observation. Scientific progress is accomplished through this close interaction between technology and ideas. The refinement of a theoretical statement or an improvement in observational technique may lead to new vistas of knowledge. The continuing process of redefining, accumulating, and summarizing knowledge is basic to all sciences. In this ongoing process, many earlier ideas are replaced with new ones. Yet even though the earlier notions may be displaced or found erroneous, they often have an indelible effect on the progress of the science. Some theories that are found to be wrong lead to exciting new data which contribute a significant advance. For example, the alchemists' attempts to convert base metals into gold led to discovery of the basic principles of chemical reactions. Other ideas appear to be so compelling that they actually impede progress. For example, the therapeutic value of various oriental practices such as acupuncture or meditation was greeted with skepticism because of a "scientific conviction" that they were not effective. At any point in time, including the present, a science consists of an increasingly large body of "facts" which are established by testing "convictions" or "hunches."

In many ways, then, the study of the history of a science is an exercise in understanding the obsolete. Most of the early concepts are erroneous, not complete enough, or merely amusing. On the other hand, these early ideas have determined to a large extent the character of the science as it exists today. Being aware of some of the major historical trends and highlights helps in understanding many contemporary characteristics. Such a background also provides us with a perspective for evaluating present "facts." The study of the brain and behavior is accelerating. Much of the material in this text will constitute the "amusing early concepts" for future physiological psychologists.

A major hindrance to understanding an unfamiliar discipline is the "jargon" of the new area. Learning the vocabulary of a science can be a frustrating task because different words are demanded for seemingly inconsequential differences. Often it seems that the same thing could be said as well or better in everyday English. There are obvious cases when this is true, yet the working vocabulary of a discipline is also established by a constant selection process. New terms are introduced for the purpose of precision, to capture a specific concept that is different from all others. If the concept constitutes a significant part of the discipline, then usage of its descriptive term is established. If the term applies to something that is trivial or ambiguous, it will not survive the process of selection. Thus, the vocabulary of physiological psychology tells us which concepts are important in the study of the nervous system. If the difference between two descriptive terms seems confusing, it would be a good investment to spend some time trying to understand what distinguishes the concepts the terms describe. The distinction very likely has value in giving us a clear picture of some aspect of a physiological mechanism.

The methodology of science provides valuable clues to the characteristics of the science. The study of the relationship between the brain and behavior involves a comparison of the structures and the related functions. There are only a limited number of ways such a comparison can be accomplished. Unfortunately, no single method is universally superior to the rest. Each provides useful information but is also subject to error. By interrelating the observations obtained by two or more of these methods, it is possible to focus fairly sharply on the actual relationship between the physiological event and its behavioral result.

The chapters in Part I introduce some of the basic dimensions of physiological psychology. The historical development of the field, the vocabulary used by physiological psychologists, and the methods that are used for data collection all contribute to a description of the discipline.

SUGGESTED READINGS

An introductory text such as this one suffers from two exasperating tendencies. First, it oversimplifies the material and often stops short of the level desired by the reader. Second, and simultaneously, it overcomplicates by using examples and/or language that do not effectively communicate to the reader. In the hope that they will be used for the former and not the latter reason, supplementary sources are provided for each part section of this text.

Historical Trends

There are undoubtedly comprehensive medical history books that trace the development of physiological thought. The following sources provide a briefer sketch as related to understanding behavior.

Boring, E. G. *A history of experimental psychology*. New York: Appleton, 1950.
Chaplin, J. P. & Krawiec, T. S. *Systems and theories of psychology*. New York: Holt, Rinehart and Winston, 1960.
Wolman, B. B. *Contemporary theories and systems in psychology*. New York: Harper & Row, 1960.

Introductory Physiological Psychology Texts

The following sources provide an alternative presentation of the basic material.

Beatty J. *Introduction to physiological psychology*. Monterey, Calif.: Brooks/Cole, 1975.
Deagle, J. *Study guide and workbook—physiological psychology*. Englewood Cliffs, N.J.: Prentice-Hall, 1973.
Isaacson, R. L., Douglas, R. J., Lubar, J. F. & Schmaltz, L. W. *A primer of physiological psychology*. New York: Harper & Row, 1971.

Leukel, F. *Introduction to physiological psychology* (2d ed.). St. Louis: Mosby, 1972.

Schwartz, M. *Physiological psychology*. New York: Appleton, 1973.

Teyler, T. J. *A primer of psychobiology: Brain and behavior*. San Francisco: Freeman, 1975.

Thompson, R. F. *Introduction to biopsychology*. San Francisco: Albion, 1973.

Wooldridge, D. E. *The machinery of the brain*. New York: McGraw-Hill, 1963.

Advanced Physiological Texts

The sources listed below provide a more comprehensive coverage of the topic. Considerable attention is given to research results. The strict adherence to empirical results adds considerable precision to the generalized statements in an introductory text. It also multiplies the number of items to be learned and the incidence of conflicting data. As one becomes more involved in any field, the less simple are the answers.

Altman, J. *Organic foundations of animal behavior*. New York: Holt, Rinehart and Winston, 1966.

Deutsch, J. A. & Deutsch, D. *Physiological psychology*. Homewood, Ill.: Dorsey, 1966.

Grossman, S. P. *A textbook of physiological psychology*. New York: Wiley, 1967.

Grossman, S. P. *Essentials of physiological psychology*. New York: Wiley, 1973.

Milner, P. *Physiological psychology*. New York: Holt, Rinehart and Winston, 1970.

Morgan, C. T. *Physiological psychology* (3d ed.). New York: McGraw-Hill, 1965.

Smith, C. U. M. *The brain: Towards an understanding*. New York: Putnam's, 1970.

Thompson, R. F. *Foundations of physiological psychology*. New York: Harper & Row, 1967.

Laboratory Manuals

Laboratory experience is invaluable to understanding the descriptive phrases and illustrations in a textbook. Even if there is no laboratory available, reading about the techniques, equipment, and procedures adds to an appreciation of the topic.

Brown, P. B., Maxfield, B. W. & Moruff, H. *Electronics for neurobiologists*. Cambridge, Mass.: MIT Press, 1973.

Hart, B. J. *Experimental neuropsychology*. San Francisco: Freeman, 1969.

Sidowski, J. B. *Experimental methods and instrumentation in psychology*. New York: McGraw-Hill, 1966.

Skinner, J. E. *Neuroscience: A laboratory manual*. Philadelphia: Saunders, 1971.

Webster, W. G. *Principles of research methodology in physiological psychology*. New York: Harper & Row, 1975.

Zucker, M. H. *Electronic circuits for the behavioral and biomedical sciences*. San Francisco: Freeman, 1969.

Edited Readings

Experimental observation is the foundation stone of the science of physiological psychology. There are many professional journals which communicate experimental activities to other scientists. Research articles that have unusual impact on the field are collected into books of readings. While the writing style is aimed at a professional audience, the editor's selection usually guarantees that the effort to attain this level will be rewarding.

Landaur, T. K. (Ed.) *Readings in physiological psychology*. New York: McGraw-Hill, 1967.

Lubar, J. F. (Ed.) *A first reader in physiological psychology*. New York: Harper & Row, 1972.

McGaugh, J. L., Weinberger, N. M. & Whalen, R. E. (Eds.) *Psychobiology*. San Francisco: Freeman, 1966.

Strange, J. R. & Foster, R. (Eds.) *Readings in physiological psychology*. Belmont, Calif.: Wadsworth, 1966.

Thompson, R. F. (Ed.). *Physiological psychology*. San Francisco: Freeman, 1971.

Professional References

Research journals are the primary source of information for the active worker in physiological psychology. Due to the "information explosion," however, the range of expertise is frequently concentrated and relatively narrow. The following sources are frequently used as a "data bank" when the scientist must extend his or her area of immediate knowledge. The level of writing assumes considerable understanding of the field and even then is often difficult.

Field, J., Magoun, H. W. & Hall, V. E. (Eds.). *Handbook of physiology*. (Vols. 1, 2, 3.) Washington, D.C.: American Physiological Society, 1959, 1960.

Kling, J. W. & Riggs, L. A. *Woodworth & Schlossberg's experimental psychology* (3d ed.). New York: Holt, Rinehart and Winston, 1971.

Osgood, C. E. *Method and theory in experimental psychology*. New York: Oxford, 1953.

Quarton, G. C., Melnechuk, T. & Schmitt, F. O. *The neurosciences: A study program*. New York: Rockefeller University Press, 1967.

Schmitt, F. O. *The neurosciences: Second study program*. New York: Rockefeller University Press, 1970.

Schmitt, F. O. & Worden, F. G. *The neurosciences: Third study program*. Cambridge, Mass.: MIT Press, 1974.

Stevens, S. S. *Handbook of experimental psychology*. New York: Wiley, 1951.

Chapter

1

A Brief History

A basic question regarding the nature of human beings involves relating the physiological structures and the psychological experience. Death presents a problem to the individual's concept of—and wish for—immortality. The notion of self-determination and freedom is confronted by persons who must endure the inevitable limitations imposed by the traumatic effects of brain injuries, diseases, and birth defects. The emergence of the scientific method for exploring the physical world states that human behavior has a cause and that the mechanisms within the body must explain the behavior. Understanding this relationship is the long-term goal of physiological psychology, but the ability to correct or improve the action of the bodily mechanisms provides important short-term gains.

Although humans have probably always thought about these kinds of questions, the earliest systematized statements concerning mental activity and human behavior are to be found in the writings of the Greek philosophers. One of the enduring problems of physiological psychology, that of the relationship between mind and body, and the search for the "seat of the soul," was one of the earliest philosophical questions raised by the Greeks. As long ago as the fourth century B.C., Plato made an arbitrary separation between the mind and the body. In his philosophical system, the realm of the mind consisted only of ideas, while the body's domain was made up of physical sensations and movements. This separation of mind and body offered a convenient solution to a number of philosophical problems, such as the obvious mortality of the body and the belief in the immortality of the mind or soul. The mind-body separation also provided a logical line of demarcation—one that may be traced to the present—between the spheres of influence of science and religion.

Aristotle, whose life overlapped Plato's, did not share his predecessor's commitment to the mind-body separation. He observed that the body seemed to respond to the dictates of the mind and thus to be somewhat governed by the mind's psychic powers. Aristotle speculated that the locus of the interaction—the "seat of the soul"—was in the heart. Although this idea was discredited by modern neurophysiologists, a heritage of Aristotle's speculations lingers in the sense that the heart remains the traditional symbol of love and affection.

In a way, the search for the "seat of the soul" is what physiological psychology is all about. Physiological psychology is still attempting to identify and explain the mechanisms that account for thought and action, even though the terminology has grown in sophistication from earlier references to "animal spirits" and "nervous fluids." Theories concerning changes that occur in the nervous system when learning occurs are theories concerning interactions between the mind and the body.

FROM THE EARLY GREEKS TO THE RENAISSANCE

In many ways, Aristotle was so complete a scientist that he impeded subsequent development of scientific thought. He made innumerable observations of natural phenomena, collected samples of plants and animals from foreign countries, conducted dissections, and catalogued all of this accumulation of knowledge into a comprehensive and authoritative written collection.

During both the Dark Ages and the Middle Ages, with the Church paramount in all aspects of society, "truth" was sought through divine revelation or along certain dogmatic organizational principles (such as through the "magic" number seven, which was thought to be the "perfect" number). Since a magnificent collection of natural facts existed in written form, largely inherited from Aristotle, it was assumed that all knowledge appropriate for human consideration had already been gained, and during these centuries, natural observation and experimentation were neglected or rejected. With the Renaissance came adoption of the modern model for science. Basic to this approach is the collection of empirical observations and facts into a systematic body of knowledge, which is then used as a guide for further fact finding.

Most early speculation about physiological mechanisms that might account for sensation, movement, and thought was based on a hydraulic model. The movement of fluids through hollow tubes was understood, and this principle was employed to explain behavior. Aristotle knew about the arteries and veins connecting the heart with all parts of the body and proposed that the heart controlled the activity of the body by selectively pumping blood to the active parts. Galen, a Greek physician of the third century, performed numerous dissections and discovered seven of the thirteen nerves leading from the brain. He correctly surmised the importance of the brain in controlling behavior, but believed that the nerves he found were a special version of a hydraulic system. He suggested that the blood, which was manufactured in the liver, flowed to the heart, where it was converted into "vital spirits." The vital spirits were then pumped to the brain, where they flowed out through the nerves leading to the muscles and sense organs, resulting in movement and sensation.

The French philosopher René Descartes (1596–1650) represents a transition to "modern" physiological psychology. He adopted mathematics as his basic organizational principle and assumed that the body was a machine which followed mechanical rules. He believed the controlling structure in this machine to be in the brain and explained body movements by the flow of "animal spirits" within the brain to tubes leading to muscles. Muscular movement was accomplished by the balloonlike inflation of the muscles by the animal spirits. Descartes anticipated developments like reflexes and coordinated muscular movements through built-in switching mechanisms within the hydraulic system. He justified his mechanistic view of bodily movements after observing and constructing elaborate moving dolls. (Descartes thus anticipated not only later developments in science but also amusement park technology.)

Although Descartes maintained that the mind and the body operated in separate realms, it was obvious that there had to be some locus from which the mind could control the body. He suggested that the pineal body might be a candidate for the "seat of the soul." The pineal body is a single structure, while most structures in the brain are bilaterally duplicated in each hemisphere. In addition, the pineal body is located in approximately the center of the brain (Figure 1.1), where it could exercise maximum control by manipulating the direction and force of animal spirits to different areas of the brain. By selecting a single tiny structure, Descartes minimized the degree to which the mind (or soul) had to manipulate the physical world.

THE SCIENTIFIC MOVEMENT

A number of writers have explored reasons for the sudden intellectual advances made in Europe during the period of the Renaissance. The invention of the printing press, the development of gunpowder, the discovery of America, each has been suggested as the door that opened new vistas of human intellectual development. All of these landmarks, however, are as much results of the Renaissance as they are causes. People had reoriented their rules for looking at the world. Instead of asking "What are the divine rules that determine events?" the question became "What actually happens when events

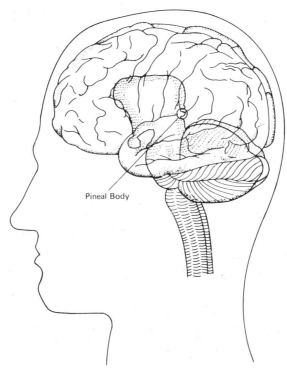

Pineal Body

Figure 1.1 A "ghost view" of the central nervous system showing the location of the pineal body, Descartes' "seat of the soul."

occur?" Instead of trying to dictate how natural phenomena must occur, thinkers began to observe and record how they actually did occur. Rather than be argued on authority, it was found that many questions could be answered by direct observation. The authority became the eyes of the observer—later formalized into the "experimenter."

An early victim of this new approach was the animal spirits explanation for the operation of the body. Experiments indicated that the animal spirits could not be gaseous, because slicing into a muscle did not release bubbles in water, even when the muscle was flexed. It was also noted that muscles could not expand like a balloon on flexion because the volume did not change with flexion.

An alternative principle suggested by Isaac Newton (1642–1727) was that the nerves transmit vibrations along their length, much the way a rope that is snapped sends a wave down its length. This idea is difficult to reconcile with the spongy and flaccid appearance of nerves, but it was compatible with the observed fact that the legs of a frog could be convulsed with mechanical stimulation of the nerve.

Luigi Galvani (1737–1798), an Italian physician, discovered that a frog's legs would twitch when hung by brass hooks on an iron railing if the legs touched the railings. Also working in Italy, Alessandro Volta (1745–1827) showed that contact between two dissimilar metals, such as brass and iron, produces an electric current (the idea behind a battery). Thus was established the possibility that the nerves and muscles work on electrical signals.

The early years of the nineteenth century marked a period of rapid gains in understanding physiology. Charles Bell (1794–1842) in England and François Magendie (1783–1855) in France, working independently, discovered that the nerves could be separated into distinct sensory and motor functions. By severing the dorsal (back) root of the spinal nerves, it was observed that an animal would not move a limb when pricked with a pin. However, the limb could be moved voluntarily by the animal. Thus, the dorsal root must be concerned with sensory messages rather than with movement. Severing of the ventral (front) root eliminated any movement, although the animal would show obvious distress if a painful stimulus was applied to the useless limb. Bell further suggested that since the nerves seemed to serve only one function (sensory nerves conducting toward the brain, motor nerves conducting away from the brain), all nerves are capable of conduction in only one direction.

The discovery that nerves serve a specific function—sensory or motor—led to further probing of nervous system specification. Johannes Müller (1801–1858) formulated his laws of the **specific energy of nerves,** which state that the different senses are served by different nerves. Müller further argued that all nerves probably work on the same principle; that is, all nerves transmit messages using the same mechanism. Thus, the brain does not directly receive colors or sounds, but learns about them indirectly through the activity of the nerves leading from the eyes or the ears.

The law of the specific energy of nerves led neurophysiologists to a new emphasis. The problem became one of tracing the nervous system pathways of the various specialized nerves. Charles Sherrington (1861–1952), an English physiologist, investigated many different reflexes and concluded that there were direct connections between sensory and motor pathways in the nervous system. Sherrington's work on reflexes led him to talk about excitation and inhibition within the nervous system. Excitation suggests that activity of some nerves results in increased activity in the nervous system. Inhibition of a nerve blocks or reduces ongoing activity in the nervous system. The concept of inhibition is extremely important to understanding the integrative action of the nervous system.

The recognition of specialization of nerves in the nervous system led to speculation concerning specialization of areas in the brain. Franz Joseph Gall (1758–1828) and his student Johann Spurzheim (1776–1832) are associated with the pseudoscience called **phrenology.** Basically, phrenologists assume that different parts of the brain serve specific kinds of thought functions. Thus, it is possible to locate the particular areas associated with love, mathematics, logic, anger, and so on. Gall and his followers then argued that the more a specific area is used, the larger that area must become (something like the effect of exercising on muscles). Since the brain is tightly packed in the skull, bumps on the head must reflect the expanded contours of the underlying brain areas. The phrenologists claimed that it was possible to "read" an individual's personality and capacities by measuring the bumps on his head (Figure 1.2). Although Gall was basically correct in assuming localization of function in the brain, the contours of the skull bear little relation to the activities of the brain. Phrenology found little empirical support and lost favor with physiologists, but the idea of localizing functions in the brain remained a positive legacy.

On the basis of systematic studies, Pierre Flourens (1794–1867) noted that certain areas of the brain seemed to be related to certain functions. For example, he pointed out that motor reflexes could be observed when only the spinal cord was intact. Vital functions, such as digestion and breathing, required the lower brain stem. The cerebellum seemed to be involved with motor coordination, and the midbrain areas were necessary for visual and auditory reflexes. To the cortex, Flourens assigned the function of "higher mental processes."

Paul Broca (1824–1880) conducted postmortem examinations on aphasic (without speech) patients and found lesions on the left side of the cortex (Figure 1.3). This "speech area" is still known as **Broca's area,** although Broca went on to label numerically all areas of the cortex. Broca's numerical labels are still employed to specify the geography of the cortex.

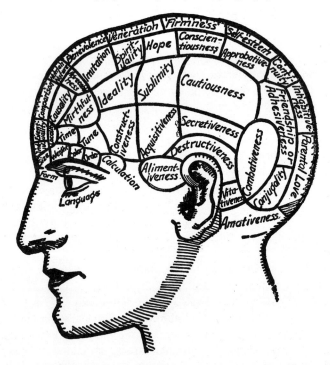

Figure 1.2 A phrenologist's "map" of the bumps on the head labeling the psychological interpretation to be drawn. (Woodward, 1947; via Wenger, Jones, & Jones, 1956, p. 294)

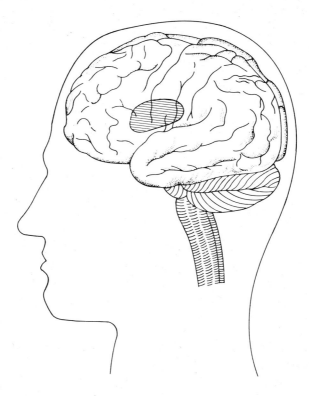

Figure 1.3 Broca's area. The region of the human cortex responsible for the control of speech.

A widely publicized demonstration of the importance of the brain stem was given by a German geneticist, Kolmar van der Goltz (1834–1902), who showed dogs from which the entire cortex had been removed. These animals were presented for display at international congresses, and the remarkable degree of function retained by the dogs led to a reevaluation of the function of the cortex.

The discovery that electricity might be the means by which the nervous system functions allowed the possibility of electrically stimulating parts of the brain. Although stimulation by touching and dropping chemicals on the surface of the brain had generally led to inconclusive findings, Fritsch and Hitzig in 1870 observed that specific movements of the body could be caused by applying an electric current to certain areas of the cortex.

Direct stimulation of the brain with electric currents is now a procedure used by many investigators of brain function. One of the more spectacular demonstrations is the research by Wilder Penfield (1955), who has triggered specific memories by careful electrical stimulation of the cortex of conscious human beings.

The electrical nature of the nervous system meant that it was also theoretically possible to record the ongoing electrical activity of the brain, known as brain waves. As instruments for measuring electrical activity were refined, this theoretical fact became technologically possible. Hans Berger (1929) made the first encephalogram and pioneered its clinical use in identifying abnormalities associated with epilepsy. The alpha feedback devices that give feedback information in sense relaxation training are an extension of Berger's discovery.

MODERN TRENDS

As the twentieth century opened, several general trends were apparent in the development of physiological psychology. Emphasis was on understanding the rules of organization within the nervous system. Thus, the discovery of spinal reflexes and of excitatory and inhibitory connections between nerves, and the location of specific functions in certain brain areas, all led to the increasing understanding of the hereditary circuitry in the brain. This line of investigation is continuing. Today research is being conducted on the highly specialized function of individual nerve cells. At the same time, there has been a branching of interest, with researchers now trying to determine some of the dynamic characteristics of the nervous system. For example, physiological research is attempting to determine the kinds of neurological changes that occur during the learning process as well as what mechanisms account for memory. Some of the earliest speculations on this topic were formulated by the great Russian physiologist Ivan Sechenov (1829–1905), who believed that reflexes could be modified during the life of the organism. In fact, Sechenov thought that all behavior—movements, thoughts, emotions, and so on—represented nothing other than elaborate reflexive activity of the brain.

Sechenov's ideas reached fruition in the work of another Russian, Ivan Pavlov (1849–1936), who discovered, named, and thoroughly researched the conditioned reflex. The conditioned reflex is an example of new neural circuits being created in response to environmental events. Today, research into physiological mechanisms of learning range from conditioned reflexes through human creative thought.

American psychologists have been particularly involved with the neurophysiological correlates of learning. From the esoteric "search for the engram," or the attempt to locate the pathway, circuit, connection, or structure responsible for learning, to efforts to manufacture a "smart pill," attention has centered on the changes that result in "learning." This strong commitment to the nurture side of the nature-nurture controversy is a heritage from early American psychologists, especially John B. Watson (1878–1958). Watson believed that at birth the mind of every individual is a *tabula rasa,* or blank tablet, on which experience will write its indelible message. The work of the Russian physiologists as well as other promising lines of research have considerably eroded this extreme position. At the present time there is a strong

rebirth of interest in the genetic components of behavior. To the neuropsy-
chologist, the genetics of behavior must be mediated by nervous system
mechanisms. Thus, the search has expanded to include material already written on the tablet by the genetic code.

Characteristic of physiological psychology is that technical developments
in other areas of science invariably have an impact on the research into the
nervous system. This is true from the data collection side because the technology provides more and more sophisticated methods for laboratory use.
The use of electrical stimulation of the cortex could not occur until methods
of generating and storing electricity had been discovered. The measurement of
brain waves was not possible until electrical devices were constructed to
measure and record electrical changes. The remarkable development of electronic technology that has taken place over the past twenty years is partly
responsible for the present explosion of information about the nervous
system. Today almost any physiological laboratory is capable of stimulating
and/or measuring the activity of individual nerve cells.

Technological changes also affect the physiological models that are constructed for conceptualizing the operation of the brain. When the limit of
sophistication was understanding how fluids flow through tubes, that was the
model used for explaining how nerves conduct activity from one point to
another. With the discovery of electricity, the nerves were thought of as
transmission wires and the brain as a telephone switchboard. Electromagnetic
fields were later suggested as a possible working model for brain functions by
the Gestalt psychologists. Today, with the development of the computer
and the discovery of holograms, we have contemporary models illustrating
how the brain stores and retrieves information.

In case the reader is left with the impression that localization of brain
functions is completely resolved, the name Karl Lashley must be mentioned.
Lashley (1890–1958) argued against the notion of specific locations for specific functions. In his experiments, he removed parts of the brains of animals
and then observed the kinds of behavior losses that resulted. Lashley concluded that the most important factor was the amount of cortical material
removed, irrespective of where the removal was made. Lashley coined the
terms **mass action** and **equipotentiality** for two principles, respectively:
(1) the brain works as an integrated whole rather than as a series of separate
units; and (2) any part of the brain is as capable of serving a specific function
as any other. Thus, we find that science is confronted with choices, even for
some "established" facts.

On a more pragmatic level, research into the functioning of the human
nervous system is providing exciting and sometimes frightening possibilities
for "mind control." As our knowledge about the operation of the mechanism
increases, so does our capacity to manipulate it.

The use of chemicals to correct or enhance the functioning of the brain
is known as **psychopharmacology.** Today, drugs are commonly prescribed for
psychological states ranging from mild depression through maladaptive

neuroses to debilitating psychoses. Drug therapy is also widely used to control malfunctioning of the brain due to epilepsy. In addition, drugs provide a potential for extending human mental abilities beyond their present natural boundaries. The so-called drug culture has for years argued this feature in the use of marijuana, LSD, and other "mind-expanding" drugs. Commercial drug companies are less likely to advertise their research involving these drugs, but are openly seeking compounds to fill the demand for a "smart pill." On the negative side, the phrase "chemical warfare" once applied only to deadly poisonous compounds, but now encompasses a whole new array of nonfatal compounds that can be used to render a victim mentally incapacitated.

Psychosurgery is another area with great potential for "mind control." Prefrontal lobotomies, which involve cutting connection circuits in the brain, have been employed on mental patients for years. Similar surgery is occasionally employed with certain forms of epilepsy. The discovery of specific control centers in certain portions of the brain means that judicious and selective destruction can radically alter personality characteristics. Although surgical alteration of personality traits has *1984* overtones, the capacity for psychological plastic surgery is entirely possible with the limited knowledge that now exists. Severing the connections between the two hemispheres of the brain has led to some exciting new insights into the brain and behavior. It appears that the two hemispheres have specialized into different modes of thinking. When the two are disconnected from one another, each is allowed to process information independent of the limitations imposed by the other. It may be that our normal thought processes are self-limiting due to the hemispheric intercommunication.

The fact that there are **pleasure centers** in the brain indicates than an individual can be subjected to electronic control. With microminiature electronic circuits, it is possible to implant radio-controlled stimulation units into a human brain. The desired behavior can then literally be turned on or turned off by means of the stimulating transmitter. Once again, this capacity has chilling overtones should the transmitter fall into the hands of a ruthless individual, but the same mechanism has almost limitless potential in the hands of a competent therapist, or even controlled by the individual.

It may not be necessary to go to such surgical extremes to accomplish physiological self-control. **Biofeedback** provides us with information regarding the functioning of specific parts of our own body. If this information is made available to the individual, it is possible to exert control over that specific function. Brain waves, blood pressure, heart rate, digestion, and body temperature are examples of biological functions that have been controlled using biofeedback. At the present time, it seems that if the function can be measured and monitored by the person, then it can be voluntarily manipulated by that person. The relation between certain brain wave patterns and the psychological states achieved in transcendental meditation has already established a brisk market for certain brain wave biofeedback devices.

In many ways, much of present knowledge in physiological psychology will join the list of interesting but superseded facts in the history of the field. The difference is that the advances will occur in years or decades rather than centuries. Many of the "facts" encountered in this text are now being (or have been) modified by newer research data. Although this is frustrating if one is seeking a final answer to a question, it is exciting to be able to watch the process in action.

AUTHOR'S COMMENTS   The advances made in any science are closely related to developments in other areas of human concern. Both ideologies and technology have had an impact on physiological psychology. Developments in electronics have been a major factor in the rapid expansion of knowledge about the nervous system. With the knowledge gained, however, we are rapidly approaching the capacity for "mind control," which has important political and social ramifications.

The single obvious trend in the history of physiological psychology is the increasing specialization of neurological structures. Historically, the nerves went from being viewed as message conductors to one-way conductors to one-message conductors. This trend is continuing for brain structures in general, as will be seen later. Simultaneously developing, however, is the enigmatic countercurrent exemplified by Lashley's work. Although there is definite support for remarkable specialization, the brain is far too dynamic to be merely a collection of single-function structures. The "seat of the soul" is to be found in the interactive, simultaneous activity of many structures scattered throughout the brain.

Basic Vocabulary
and Geography
of the Nervous System

Knowing some of the basic terms and structures in the nervous system will facilitate understanding the structural and functional discussions in later chapters. Simple directions, basic definitions, and landmark structures—all will help locate the important features to be examined in detail later.

DIRECTION TERMINOLOGY

Neuroanatomists use special terms to locate structures in the nervous system (Figure 2.1). For example, in reference to the body of an animal, the terms **rostral** is used to designate direction toward the head of the animal, while **caudal** means toward the tail. In this rubric, the neck is rostral to the shoulders. In describing the development of the nervous system in the growing organism, one may encounter the term **cephalo-caudal,** which means that the development occurs in a general head-to-tail fashion.

When talking about the nerves throughout the body, the usual frame of reference is the brain and spinal cord (the central nervous system). Thus, the term **proximal** means near or toward the central nervous system, while the term **distal** means away from the central nervous system or toward the extremities of the body.

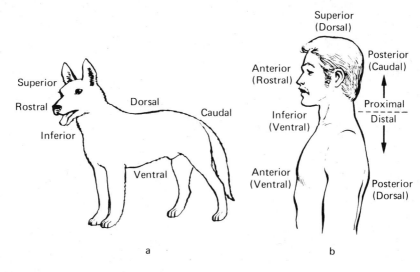

Figure 2.1   Directional terms as applied to the bodies of (a) common vertebrates and (b) primates. (After Milner, 1970, p. 22)

Another directional pair of words is "ventral" and "dorsal." As a general rule, **ventral** means toward the belly of the animal, while **dorsal** means toward the back. In four-legged animals, the latter is synonymous with "above" and "below," but the upright stance of humans has changed the ventral-dorsal plane to a horizontal dimension ("front" and "back").

In most animals, the rostral-caudal organization of the nervous system is linear. That is, the front-to-back orientation of the brain is on the same plane as the animal's spinal cord. In humans, however, the brain sits atop the spinal cord at a right angle to it. Thus, the descriptive terms can be somewhat confusing when transferring from one species to another.

In the human brain (Figure 2.2), "dorsal" means the top portion of the brain (with the head in the normal upright position) and "ventral" means the bottom. Thus, ventral-dorsal can connote different directions depending on location. The belly-to-back dimension is true with reference to the spinal cord and body of animals and humans, and the above-below relationship holds in the brains of all species. The terms **superior** (above) and **inferior** (below) also indicate the vertical location of the structure.

When describing structures in the brain, which is inside the head, it is awkward to use the term "rostral," which means toward the head. Thus, when locating brain structures, the terms "anterior" and "posterior" are used. **Anterior** means toward the front of the brain, and **posterior** means toward the rear, irrespective of species.

The third dimension for brain structures is measured with reference to the distance from the midplane of the brain. Since the brain is bilaterally symmetrical, it is possible to specify the location of corresponding structures in

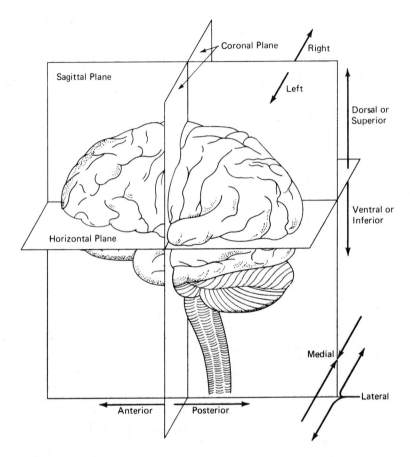

Figure 2.2 Directional terminology as applied to the central nervous system. The three planes indicate the major orientation axes.

both hemispheres with a single measure from the midplane reference point. The term **medial** indicates near or toward the midplane, while **lateral** indicates away from the midplane, or out to the side.

NEUROANATOMY

The nervous system is composed primarily of millions of individual nerve cells, or **neurons.** To oversimplify for the time being, neurons can be described as having two functional components. The **cell body,** including rootlike extensions called **dendrites,** is involved with the ongoing life processes of the cell, as well as with the collection and processing of messages. In other words, the cell bodies seem to be the part of the neuron where information is selected, combined, or modified. The other major component of the neuron is called the

axon, which is a cylindrical extension from the cell body that appears to transmit the processed information to another location (Figure 2.3).

If we look at the basic characteristics necessary to a nervous system (or to a computer, for that matter), we find that there are two fundamental functions—the ability to collect and process information and the ability to transmit information. Although there are varying degrees of neuron specialization in different parts of the nervous system, every neuron exhibits the capacity to accomplish both of these functions. We find that the nervous system is made up of structures that specialize in one or the other of these functions. Instead of being collections of special nerve cells, these structures are concentrated collections of the appropriate component (axon or cell body) of the neurons.

Axons have auxiliary cells that appear to insulate or otherwise assist in the data-transmission process. Since these auxiliary cells are primarily fatty material, they are white in color; axons therefore exhibit a typically white coloration as opposed to the grayer appearance of the unadorned cell bodies. Most people are familiar with the lay term "gray matter" to describe the brain, and it is indeed the gray cell bodies of the nervous system that are involved in the "thinking process." There are two terms for collections of cell bodies. **Ganglia** (singular, "ganglion") are collections of cell bodies clustered into a common area of the body. In the brain and spinal cord, the equivalent of a ganglion is a **nucleus**. (The term "nucleus" is also used to describe a structure found in all living cells, although the context of the term usually avoids confusion.)

The "white matter" of the nervous system consists of bundles of data-transmitting axons that carry information throughout the body. Nerves are bundles of axons that share a common pathway through the body in the

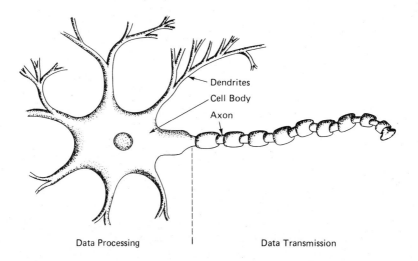

Data Processing   Data Transmission

Figure 2.3   A "typical" neuron, showing its two major structural and functional components. The dendrites are considered specialized extensions of the cell body.

process of transmitting messages from one place to another. Care should be taken to discriminate between the various "nerve" words. A **nerve fiber** is another word for "axon"; a **nerve** is a bundle of axons; a **nerve cell** is an individual neuron; and a **nervous system** is a functional collection of neurons and their connections. When talking about structures within the brain and spinal cord, we encounter the term "tract." A **tract** is a collection of axons that transmit information between various parts in the central nervous system.

Axons conduct in one direction, typically away from the cell body. The major nerves of the body are essentially trunk lines of axons carrying information from the sense organs to and/or from the central nervous system, or the tracts in the spinal cord to and from the brain. In many cases, all of the axons in a nerve or tract conduct in the same direction. A nerve that conducts information from the sense organs toward the central nervous system is called a **sensory nerve,** or more technically, an **afferent nerve.** A nerve that conducts out from the central nervous system to the muscles or glands is a **motor,** or **efferent, nerve.** (A mnemonic aid I have found helpful in remembering these two terms is by the common first letter in the words "afferent" = "approach" and "efferent" = "exit.") If the nerve or tract contains both afferent and efferent nerve fibers, it is a **mixed nerve.**

Whereas neurons talk to one another in an electrochemical language, the stimuli to which the total organism must respond are of much greater variety. Special sensory cells transduce, or convert, light, sound, touch, taste, smell, and so on, into an electrochemical code usable in the nervous system. Psychologists are interested in the wide variety of responses demonstrated by the complete organism. When broken down into its cellular components, we find that "behavior" is either the movement of a muscle or the secretion of a gland (although we are becoming more and more interested in the electrical behavior of the nervous system itself). Sensory cells that interface the outside world and the neurons in the nervous system are referred to as **receptors** or **transducers,** while muscles and glands involved in translating nervous system activity into behavior are called **effectors.**

The **central nervous system (CNS)** can be divided into several easily identifiable structures (Figure 2.4). In the human nervous system, the most obvious structure is the **cerebrum,** or **cortex,** the mass of wrinkled, gray material commonly called the brain. Actually, cortex means "shell," which neatly summarizes the geographic location of the cerebral cortex. The cortex is the outermost layers of the brain. The human cortex represents the culmination of phylogenetic developments in the nervous system (so far, at least). In general, the more rostral the structure in the nervous system, the more complicated the behavioral functions controlled by that structure. The cortex, however, has not had room to continue its forward growth and has begun to fold back and envelop lower brain structures. Since the cortex is the most rostral part of the CNS (if not in geography, at least in terms of nerve pathways and connections), it is considered important to the psychological processes of perceiving and thinking.

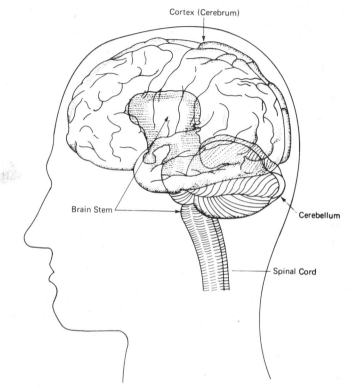

Cortex (Cerebrum)

Brain Stem

Cerebellum

Spinal Cord

Figure 2.4   The central nervous system, locating major components.

Enveloped within the folds of the cortex are a number of structures, connections, tracts, and nuclei, all assigned the general name of **brain stem.** The brain stem acts as an intermediary between the cortex and the outside world. All sensory and motor fibers leading to and from the cortex pass through brain stem structures, and there is building evidence that the brain stem has considerable freedom to modify and adjust input and output. In addition, the brain stem is directly involved with the control of vital processes, such as breathing and heartbeat; motivational factors such as hunger, thirst, rage, and sex; and the wakefulness or alertness of the organism.

Attached to the back of the brain stem, and packed under the cortex, is a relatively large, very complex-appearing structure. The **cerebellum** appears to be involved with coordination of motor patterns of behavior. The cortex may make the executive decision to "walk," but the cerebellum implements the process by insuring that different groups of muscles do not operate out of sequence or otherwise interfere with the walking behavior.

The brain stem connects to the **spinal cord,** which is primarily a trunk line of nerve fibers between the brain and the receptors and effectors of the body. In addition to information transmission, the spinal cord is capable of direct stimulus-response connections. If a certain stimulus occurs, the spinal cord sends the message directly to appropriate efferent nerves as well as to the brain. Thus, a spinal reflex (such as the leg kick when the leg is tapped just below the knee cap) represents one of the simplest behaviors in the nervous system.

AUTHOR'S COMMENTS   The structures of the nervous system were named long before the functions were established. Consequently, most of the structures are labeled according to where they are located and/or what they look like. Occasionally, a functionally related label is found.

There are three important levels in neuroanatomical labeling. The cellular level (individual neurons or parts thereof), the structural level (collections of many neurons), and the systems level (combinations of structures that serve a common functional capacity). The other important discrimination to be made, important at all three neuroanatomical levels, is the difference between cell bodies (data processing) and axons (data transmission).

Psychophysiological Methods

Although physiological psychologists employ many different tools and techniques, there is one fundamental way to establish the relation between the brain and behavior. Assuming that the argument for localization of brain function is correct, then certain structures must be involved in certain behaviors. Similarly, changes in the structure should be associated with corresponding changes in behavior. All psychophysiological methods involve the comparison of differences in the brain with differences in the observed behavior. Sometimes the differences occur naturally, sometimes they are introduced by the researcher, but the correlation of structure and behavior is basic to them all.

PHYLOGENY

Nervous systems differ in a number of ways depending on the age and species of the organism. By observing the behavioral abilities that correspond with the phylogenetic appearance of certain nervous structures, it is possible to draw tentative conclusions concerning what those nervous structures control. For example, the highly developed human cortex is usually cited as the main feature that separates humans from the "lower" animals. Thus, behaviors attributable to humans, such as language and complex thought, are assumed to be cortical functions.

An early method of studying the nervous system involved comparing the characteristics of the nervous systems of a number of different animals with the behavioral characteristics of the same animals. School children learn that the dinosaur had a very small brain and, therefore, did not exhibit the behavioral adaptability of the competing mammalian species. Most people know that humans possess a magnificent cortex, which accounts for their intellectual superiority over less well-endowed animals. Many people also "know" that the convoluted structure of the human brain explains high intelligence. The evidence suggests, however, that degree of intelligence depends upon the number and types of neural connections in the cortex and not the number of convolutions. The apparent relationship between cortical wrinkles and intelligence illustrates a major drawback to the phylogenetic approach; although the correlation is observed, the relationship may be illusory.

As we trace the **phylogenetic scale** from primitive organisms up to and including humans, we find a general progression in development of structures in the nervous system along with a progression in behavioral capabilities (Figure 3.1). In fact, the phylogenetic approach allows us to estimate the evolutionary status of parts of the brain. Terms like "paleocortex" (old brain) and "neocortex" (new brain) reflect the evolutionary aspects of the study of parts of the nervous system.

A major problem with the phylogenetic approach to the study of the brain is that the nervous system is not simply a cumulative collection of building blocks, each serving a specific function. As new structures develop in the evolving nervous system, they take over, supplement, or modify the activities of earlier structures. For example, in humans, removal of the vision portion of the cortex causes blindness. Birds, on the other hand, have no visual cortex, yet obviously have a functioning visual system. (The same may be said about the necessity of a cortex for thinking.) The explanation is that in birds lower brain centers control vision. Humans have these same lower centers, but the newer cortex has taken over so many visual tasks that these primitive centers are no longer capable of handling visual functions by themselves. They are now auxiliary visual structures.

Interest is growing in studying the genetic components of behavior. In the 1920s, Watson succeeded in throwing out the concept of "instincts" to explain behavior. Since then, the emphasis of U.S. scientists has been to study motivation, perception, and learning to explain behavior. European ethologists, meanwhile, have been studying species-specific behaviors such as imprinting, territoriality, and pecking orders. These are relatively complicated behavior sequences that seem to be a part of the genetic heritage of the species.

It appears that behavior may have substantial genetic components. The developing field of behavioral genetics applies the analytical methods of genetics to the study of behavior. Population studies for the frequency of certain behavioral traits, as well as genealogical charts tracing certain traits or abilities, are appearing with increasing frequency. In addition, studies are being conducted that involve selective breeding for a specific behavioral char-

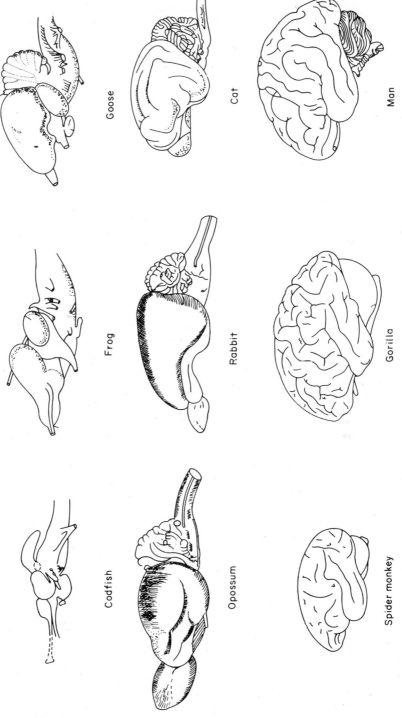

Goose

Cat

Man

Frog

Rabbit

Gorilla

Codfish

Opossum

Spider monkey

Figure 3.1 Brain structures as they appear at various levels of the phylogenetic scale.

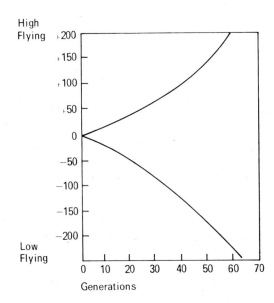

Figure 3.2 Cumulative curves showing flying behavior of successive generations of the fruit fly selectively bred for geotaxis (flying behavior). (Kretch, Crutchfield, & Livson, 1974, p. 21)

acteristic. The fruit fly, for example, can be selectively inbred for "high flying" or "low flying" (Figure 3.2). Selective breeding suggests that this trait follows the same genetic laws that are known to determine structural features like eye color. To the physiologist interested in behavior, there is no difference between the two. Behavior is the result of activity in the structures of the nervous system. Genetic changes in the nervous system will undoubtedly result in behavioral changes.

ONTOGENY

A similar approach to understanding brain functions involves studying the ontogenetic development of the brain and the development of behavior in a single species. It is generally acknowledged that changes can be observed in the growing human brain up to about the fifteenth year (Figure 3.3). These structural changes follow essentially the same pattern for each individual. Similarly, children are able to accomplish certain tasks only after they attain a specific developmental level. Young children lack the coordination for fine motor skills like writing or riding a bike. Jean Piaget has shown that children gain increasing intellectual abilities in a specific sequence as they mature. To the physiological psychologist, this may represent the ontogenetic development of brain structures and/or the "wiring" of connections in the nervous system.

Although a logical method for the study of the nervous system, ontogeny is probably the least useful. For one thing, it relies heavily on the measurement of individual differences. The basic argument says that animals that learn tasks earlier in their life must possess the appropriate neural connections

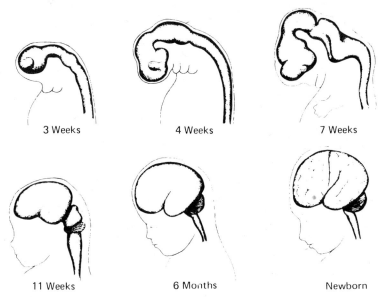

3 Weeks   4 Weeks   7 Weeks

11 Weeks   6 Months   Newborn

Figure 3.3 Brain structures as they appear at various developmental stages in the human. (After Patten, 1953)

earlier than the typical animal in that species. Thus, we must examine the brains of several animals, keeping careful records of the age and behavioral capacities of each individual and compare these with the structures in the brain.

Brain structures, however, are not perfectly correlated with their use, just as blue eyes, brown eyes, and hazel eyes all serve the same function in the process of seeing. Thus, we expect two animals with identical behavioral characteristics to exhibit some normal observable differences in their brain structures. How do we identify the differences associated with function? The answer is that we compare large numbers of individuals until a trend is established. Since such an approach is uneconomical in terms of time, effort, and animals, alternative procedures are usually employed.

Another disadvantage of the ontological approach is that, despite its name, one cannot trace the development of structures and functions in a single individual. In order to examine the brain structures of any animal, the animal must be sacrificed and further ontological development is ended.

Using ontogeny and phylogeny to determine the characteristics of the nervous system is much like observing car performance on a freeway. We may conclude that the larger the car, the faster it goes, or that certain brands or colors seem related to performance, but we could tell much more if we ourselves had a chance to compare the driving characteristics of the different kinds of cars.

The ability to manipulate some of the factors affecting our observations is the real power behind the experimental method. The fact that we can arrange an event to occur when we are ready to observe it and where it will be most effective allows us to make strong deductions about our observations. All of the following methods share the characteristic of being experimental in nature, although the procedure used can also be applied to uncontrolled accidental phenomena, such as disease or injury.

Experimental procedures are also localized in scope. Instead of attempting to look at the entire nervous system, most physiological researchers concentrate on a specific structure within the nervous system and try to ascertain its function and relation to the rest of the system. To do this, one must be able to perform experiments on the target parts of the nervous system with minimum effect on the remainder.

ABLATION

One way to see what a given structure does in a system is to remove or disable that structure and then see what the system can still do, or more directly, what it can no longer do. **Ablation** involves removing some part of the nervous system. Broca identified the speech area of the brain by locating a tumor that had grown on the temporal lobe of a patient who became mute with destruction of the functioning of that area.

A famous example of an accidental ablation is represented by the case of Phinneus Gage, a railroad worker who detonated some dynamite while tamping it with a crowbar. The explosion propelled a piece of the crowbar into Gage's forehead and out the top of his skull, extensively damaging major portions of the frontal lobes of his brain. The first remarkable thing about Gage is that he survived the dynamite and the crowbar. The second is that after recovery, and despite the fact that a considerable portion of brain material had been destroyed, Gage showed a remarkable lack of behavioral symptoms. His language, memory, and logic functions appeared to be unaffected. (Of course, one might question the logic of tamping dynamite with a crowbar in the first place!) What could be observed was that Gage was much less complicated than he had been previously. His anger and happiness were expressed directly and immediately. Rather than concealing or inhibiting the expression of his feelings, Phinneus expressed them in an almost childlike manner.

On the basis of the Gage case and many other bits of evidence, mental hospitals adopted, as a means of treatment, the systematic ablation of the frontal lobes of patients. Instead of a crowbar, a scalpel was used, and instead of directly destroying the frontal lobes, only the connecting pathways leading to and from these lobes were severed. The net effect, however, was the ablation of the frontal lobes from the nervous system (Figure 3.4).

The justification for this rather extreme form of therapy is that patients become more tractable and can be treated by conventional therapeutic means. It is true that, in general, postprefrontal lobotomy patients are more passive and childlike in behavior, although the postoperative symptoms vary widely

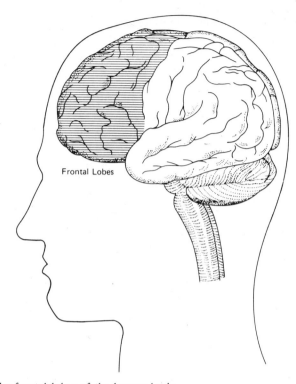

Frontal Lobes

Figure 3.4   The frontal lobes of the human brain.

depending on the patient and the extent of surgery. With the development of effective alternative therapies, prefrontal lobotomies are less frequently done. It is interesting to note, however, that changes in behavior brought about by ablation of a portion of the brain is still considered practical enough to justify its use on thousands of mental patients each year.

For research purposes, and using animal subjects, there are a number of different ways to ablate or lesion specific areas of the brain. Surgical removal of certain structures can be accomplished, although recovery from surgery may be a significant problem. In some cases, portions of the brain can be efficiently removed by inserting a hollow needle into the target area and attaching the needle to a vacuum pump. The prefrontal lobotomy technique effectively removes a structure by severing the connections without disturbing the structure itself. This technique can also be used to eliminate selectively the interaction between two areas without disrupting the connections to other brain structures.

A common ablation technique in research is the use of an electrolytic lesion. If an electric current is passed through the uninsulated tip of a needle inserted into neural tissue, and the current is high enough, the tissue surrounding the tip is burned and destroyed. The advantage of this technique is that the insertion of the needle causes minimal damage to the overlying structures it goes through, and the size of the lesion may be specified by varying the time and level of the lesioning current. Problems with this technique involve the generation of gas bubbles, depositing of metallic ions from the tip of the electrode, and difficulty in controlling the shape of a large lesion due to resistance characteristics of different parts of the brain. Other means of lesioning neural tissue include the use of heat (cautery), cold (cryosurgery), radio waves, X-rays, or even lasers and radioactive isotopes as a means of destroying specific structures in the nervous system.

In some cases, functional ablation can be accomplished without actually destroying the structure or its connections. By subjecting a brain structure to a strong, but not lesion-producing, electric shock, or to certain chemicals, the structure may go into a refractory quiet period and later recover its normal activity. **Electroconvulsive shock,** or electroshock therapy, essentially traumatizes all of the structures in the brain, and the subsequent changes in behavior may reflect the different recovery times for various brain structures. A similar temporary ablation of limited areas of the surface of the cortex can be accomplished by applying chemicals or tapping the exposed brain. When this is done, all measurable brain activity ceases in the vicinity of the insult for a brief (approximately 15 minutes) period of time. This **spreading depression** is probably the explanation for unconsciousness as a result of a blow to the head.

Ablation is an indirect means of determining function. It is something like ripping a part out of a car and then seeing if the car will still run. The organism is no longer completely intact, and that fact alone might account for some of the behavioral changes. Cells have been destroyed, and the resultant healing process could sharply alter the chemical environment of the surviving tissue. Ablation techniques are most powerful if the structure destroyed is the only one involved in a behavior pattern. In most cases, parts of the nervous system are closely interrelated, so that tampering with one structure might upset a delicate balance in a whole network of structures. Sometimes other structures can take over the functions of the destroyed tissue with no observable change in behavior. In other cases, the destruction of a structure results in immediate and obvious changes, but the effect is created by changes in the activity of "untouched" structures.

Because ablation is basically a destructive approach, the resulting observations are made on an abnormal organism. Conclusions from ablation studies should be very tentative. The primary power of the ablation approach is realized when used in conjunction with another technique. This validation across different techniques is generally practiced, but it is particularly important with ablations.

STIMULATION

Galvani's discovery that the nervous system is sensitive to the administration of electric current opened the way for a powerful technique in physiological psychology. Conceptually, the stimulation technique is a simple paradigm.

The experimenter introduces activity into specific parts of the nervous system and then observes the subsequent behavior of the organism. In the earliest work, such as that done by Fritsch and Hitzig, the stimulation was introduced on the motor cortex, and the current resulted in immediate movement of a part of the body. By changing the amount of current, the size of the muscle twitch could be controlled. By moving the electrode to different sites on the brain, different parts of the body could be made to move. In the systematic "mapping" of the body areas, most of the cortex was found to be "silent"; that is, no immediate motor responses could be observed.

Later experiments on the exposed human cortex, with the patient still conscious, revealed that some of the "silent" areas, when stimulated, resulted in the patient's reporting sensory phenomena. Thus, a stimulus to a certain part of the visual cortex may cause the patient to "see" flashes of light. Penfield's stimulation work indicates that other parts of the cortex can initiate or disrupt speech (Figure 3.5). Cortical stimulation may even evoke the recall of past experiences. These experimental phenomena may include complex sequences, such as snatches of conversation or bits of a song, or may involve several senses simultaneously, that is, with the person both hearing

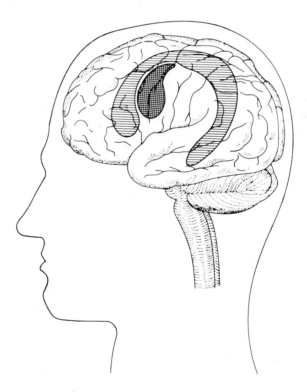

Figure 3.5 Areas within the left cortex where electrical stimulation of the epileptic brain produces vocalization (crosshatched area) and hesitation in speech (lined area).

and seeing the past experience. Penfield also noted that stimulation in yet other areas seemed to evoke emotional responses such as fear or anger.

At the present time, much research involves the stimulation of lower brain structures, which seem to be closely involved with emotional behavior. José Delgado and others have demonstrated that normally wild animals can be made placid, calm animals wildly fearful, tame animals vicious, and so on.

The technology of brain stimulation research has improved to the point where animals are now implanted with stimulating electrodes in conjunction with radio receivers. Thus, the experimenter can remotely introduce the stimulus into a free-ranging animal in its natural habitat. With this device, the experimenter can literally turn on or turn off ongoing behavior.

Another area of concentrated research has resulted from James Olds's discovery that certain areas in the lower brain centers can serve as "pleasure" centers for the animal. Olds has demonstrated that animals will work for the opportunity to receive a "shock" to the brain. In fact, animals may prefer the chance to turn on the stimulus to their own brain over the usual food reward used in psychology experiments. Olds's discovery that there are many areas in the brain which can serve as a reward locus presents a number of exciting research possibilities.

Physiological psychology research involves considerable use of stimulation techniques. The usual method is the use of low-level (so as not to create a lesion) electrical stimulation delivered through an electrode into the desired area. It has been discovered that some chemicals can be injected into brain structures with effects similar to those of electrical stimuli. The unique feature of chemical stimulants is that they may selectively act on certain neural circuits without disturbing others in the same region. Thus, by selecting the stimulating chemical, it may be possible to sort out the functions of intertwined neural circuits.

RECORDING

With the development of transistors and other sophisticated electronic instruments, biological recording techniques have become a powerful tool for the physiological researcher. Basically, a recording apparatus detects the electrical events occurring near an **electrode,** amplifies this signal, and uses the amplified signal to drive some sort of display device such as an oscilloscope or a pen motor. The simplest recording situation utilizes two electrodes. The first electrode is placed in or near the structure in the nervous system that is to be recorded. The second, or reference electrode, is placed in an adjacent, relatively inactive location, and the amplifier strengthens the electrical difference between the two electrodes. By moving the reference electrode nearer the recording electrode, it is possible to narrow the area being effectively recorded. Reducing the size of the electrode also reduces the effective recording area. By altering electrode size and position, a wide range of electrical activity may be recorded. In addition, this simple recording approach can be expanded into a multiple-electrode, multiple-amplifier array. Thus, the activity of several neural structures may be observed simultaneously. The addition of a computer to analyze the recorded information allows the extraction of important information from a formidable pool of activity data.

Berger was the first to record electrical "brain waves" by applying electrodes to the scalp and recording the underlying activity (Figure 3.6). Brain waves (or **electroencephalogram,** or **EEG**) have been utilized in mental hospitals as diagnostic tools for many years. Electroencephalogram electrodes are either small pieces of metal taped to the scalp or pins inserted under the scalp. The recorded electrical activity is the sum total of the activity of millions of nerve cells in the region of the brain nearest the electrode. At the present time, it is unclear how to interpret the electrical activity patterns recorded in the EEG. It may be that the changes reflect the sum of altered activity of individual components. It is more likely, however, that the recorded electrical fields themselves contribute to the total functioning of the system. It is possible to change the activity of individual neurons by placing them in various electrical fields. Thus, the EEG may represent an important component of the functioning of the nervous system.

During the early work with EEG, investigators (and science fiction writers) speculated that if the brain waves could be appropriately decoded, the actual thoughts of the individual could be analyzed and possibly projected onto a screen. In actuality, the EEG is so complex and multifactorial that we will probably never be able to decode the patterns into specific thought categories. The EEG is sensitive to activities and anomalies that involve the entire brain. For example, persons who suffer epileptic attacks have a characteristic EEG pattern of brusts of activity not found in the normal person. Many mental hospitals give an EEG to incoming patients as a routine admission procedure, and occasionally epileptics are diagnosed before the first seizure occurs.

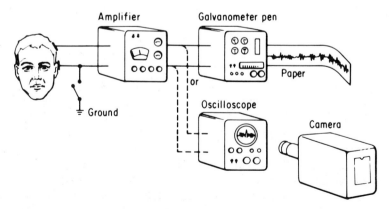

Figure 3.6 Electroencephalogram (EEG) recording apparatus, showing major devices employed. (Thompson, 1975, p. 113)

With the development of on-line computers, which can analyze large volumes of data as they are recorded, EEG is being used in new fields of research. The computer can be programmed to identify significant characteristics from the complex EEG waves and also to reject some of the unimportant information. With this procedure, details become available to the researcher that cannot be seen by looking at the pen recording. There is evidence that measurable EEG changes occur during the learning process and during some emotional states. There is also a possibility that latency of the EEG response over the visual cortex after a light flash may be related to IQ.

Recent research into the characteristics of sleep show the EEG to be a valuable tool in analyzing the stages of sleep a subject is in at different times during the sleeping period. At least four different stages of sleep can be noted by utilizing EEG characteristics combined with recordings of eye movements. The process of recording eye movements (**electrooculogram,** or **EOG**) is basically similar to the EEG recording process, but involves the eye. If two electrodes are placed on opposite sides of the eye, they will detect the electrical activity of the eye lying between them. The eye has a stable electrical field associated with its neural and muscular structures. Thus, if the eye shifts position, the electrical field shifts correspondingly. The EOG electrodes detect the electrical change, which can be electronically amplified and registered on a recording device just as with the EEG.

On a finer level, if the eye is held immovable and the electrodes are placed in or on the eye, it is possible to record the neural activity of the retina as it processes visual information and sends it to the brain. In this case, the **electroretinogram (ERG)** is a recording of EEG-type activity from the nerve cells in the eye.

Other examples of large-scale recordings include the **electromyogram (EMG),** which records the movements of muscles by detecting the electrical changes that occur within the muscle when it contracts. A special use of the electromyogram involves recording the activity changes that occur within the heart muscles, a process resulting in the **electrocardiogram** (abbreviated **EKG** because of the German spelling of the term).

In addition to the placement of the recording electrodes, the size of the electrode determines the field of sensitivity, with large electrodes to record from large regions and small ones to record from small structures. The extreme of this trend is found in the use of microelectrodes with conducting tips on the order of 1 micron in diameter. **Microelectrodes** are made of a metal wire polished to a fine point and then carefully dipped in insulation, or a glass capillary tube is drawn to a fine point and then filled with a conducting liquid. Because of the extremely small conducting area at the tip, microelectrode recording has been available only since the development of modern electronic technology. The field of sensitivity of a microelectrode is so focused that it is possible to record the activity of individual neurons in the intact nervous system. Such **single-unit records** provide valuable data concerning the role of individual neurons in a functional system.

HISTOLOGICAL PROCEDURES

Irrespective of whether stimulation, recording, or ablation is used, the neurophysiological worker must be able to determine exactly where in the brain he is conducting his research. Thus, after making the appropriate manipulations in the nervous system, and after observing the resulting changes in behavior, the researcher must then confirm the identity of the manipulated structure. Many of the tracts and nuclei in the brain are very tiny. In fact, a microscope is the only appropriate instrument for confirmation. In the case of a lesion study, the brain must be examined for the actual brain structures destroyed. In many cases, recording and stimulation studies end by passing a lesioning current through the research electrode, so there is a small lesion at the electrode location. The track of cells torn and displaced by the penetrating electrode can also be used to locate the position of the tip. Sometimes dyes or metallic ions may be deposited at the tip of the electrode to identify the structure.

After the behavioral observations have been made and the necessary electrode-marking procedure has been followed, the experimental animal is sacrificed and the brain is prepared for histological confirmation of the site of the electrode. Brain tissue is relatively soft and flaccid in its natural state and without careful handling is subject to considerable damage. Consequently, brain tissue is usually fixed with a preservative like formaldehyde. The tissue may be soaked in a formalin solution until it is completely saturated. A more common procedure is to perfuse the brain before it is even removed from the skull. The **perfusion** process involves pumping formalin solution through the blood vessels leading to the brain, thus distributing the fixative through the existing plumbing in the animal. Once the brain is saturated with the fixative, it is relatively resistant to damage from normal handling.

After perfusion, the brain is removed from the skull by a process technically known as **extraction.** The process may proceed in a number of ways, but the essential task is to remove the bone and other tissue from around the brain. A variety of bone cutters, crushers, and nibblers are used for dismantling the skull and preserving the underlying brain tissue.

When the brain is available for inspection, there is still a rather large neural mass confronting the researcher. In order to examine the specific structures involved, the brain must be sliced into sections. A **microtome** is an instrument equipped with a cutting blade and an automatic advance device so that the brain being sliced is moved forward a preset distance after each pass of the blade. The slice being taken can be as thin as 1 micron. (If the brain were 1 inch long and 1-micron sections were taken from it, after running it through the microtome, one would end up with 25,340 sections.) Even with 10- or 15-micron sections, the tissue is so thin that it must be carefully handled in order to keep it from tearing, folding, or breaking while being placed on the microscope slide.

After mounting the section on the slide, the slice of brain tissue appears semitransparent with rather indistinct structures ranging from light gray to white. In order to accentuate the structures in the brain, a stain is applied to the section. **Stains** are chemicals that are differentially absorbed by various structures in the brain slice. The usual stains are deposited in nuclei or tracts, which means that the same area of the brain may appear light or dark depending on the stain used.

After locating the site of the tip of the electrode by selecting the section with the maximum lesion or marker, the investigator then refers to a stereotaxic atlas. A **stereotaxic atlas** is a collection of illustrations of brain slices in serial order through the entire brain. Most stereotaxic atlases are **frontal** or **coronal sections,** which are vertical slices from the front to the back of the brain (Figure 3.7). Frontal sections are analogous to the slices in a loaf of bread. Occasionally, one sees a **sagittal section,** which is a vertical slice showing lengthwise views of the brain from one side to the other. The middlemost sagittal section is known as a **midline,** or **parasagittal, section.** Rarely one may see **horizontal sections** of the brain.

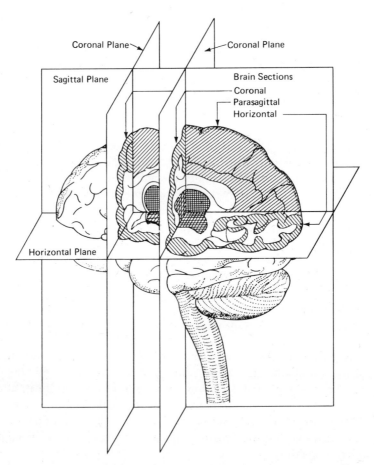

Figure 3.7 The major planes and major cross sections of the central nervous system used to locate interior structures.

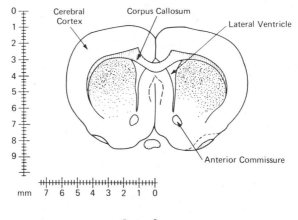

Anterior 1.0 mm

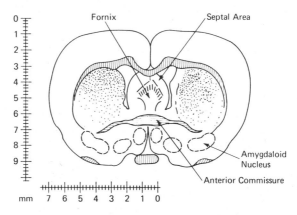

Bregma 0 mm

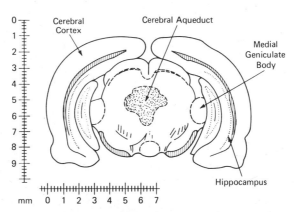

Posterior 5.5 mm

Figure 3.8 Three different coronal sections of the rat brain. Each section is identified by the anterior-posterior distance from a landmark on the skull. (Bregma is the intersection of the frontal and parietal bones.) Examples of brain structures are identified on each section. By the use of an atlas made up of many such sections, the three-dimensional location and extent of any structure can be determined. (After Hart, 1969, pp. 97–102)

By selecting the page in the stereotaxic atlas that matches the microscope slice of interest, the researcher can precisely identify the position of the tip of the electrode. The stereotaxic atlas identifies and labels the structure that is found at that precise location.

The stereotaxic atlas also provides precise three-dimensional information as to the location of that particular point (Figure 3.8). The anterior-posterior location is specified by the page of the atlas that matches the brain section. The ventral-dorsal and lateral-medial locations are also specified by the scale provided in the atlas.

Brain dimensions are remarkably consistent between individuals of the same species. The position of the brain relative to certain external landmarks on the skull is also fairly reliable. The stereotaxic atlas provides location coordinates of the brain structures with reference to these external landmarks. By using the external landmarks and the dimensions supplied by the atlas, the experimenter can determine precisely where to drill a hole in the skull and how far down to insert the electrode to place the tip in a specific brain structure.

Since an error of less than a millimeter may totally miss the target structure, stereotaxic surgery requires precision measurements. For most stereotaxic procedures, a special **stereotaxic headholder** is employed to rigidly clamp the skull in a set position (Figure 3.9). The use of the headholder allows the necessary surgical procedures, especially drilling through the skull, to be accomplished with relative ease and precision. Most stereotaxic instruments

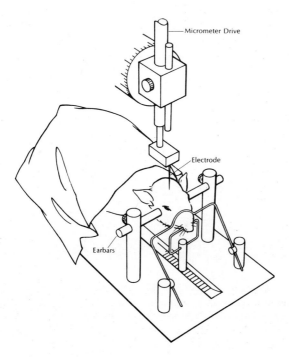

Figure 3.9 A stereotaxic headholder with electrode manipulator. The headholder precisely determines the location and orientation of landmarks on the skull. By using the coordinates supplied by a stereotaxic atlas, the tip of the electrode can be placed in the desired target structure in the brain. (Sheridan, 1976, p. 332)

include an **electrode manipulator,** which allows measured movements of the electrode in the three dimensions supplied by the atlas. Thus, by careful positioning of the skull in the headholder, precise determination of the external landmarks, accurate reading of the measurements in the atlas, and fine adjustment of the electrode manipulator, the researcher has a good chance of placing the tip of the electrode in the target structure. Of course, because there are differences among animals in the size and dimensions of the brain, and because there is room for error in the stereotaxic placement procedure, the location must be histologically confirmed at the end of the research.

AUTHOR'S   The common objective of all psychophysiological methods
COMMENTS   is to establish the relation between neurological structures and behavioral capacities. Two methods—phylogeny and ontogeny—utilize the naturally occurring differences in the CNS of different species or of different-aged individuals of the same species. The other three methods—stimulation, recording, and ablation—primarily involve the artificial manipulation of the structure in some way. There are a number of specific examples of each of these techniques, depending on the particular structure and behavior involved.

A number of sophisticated devices and/or techniques are available to locate and identify a specific structure in the CNS. The stereotaxic apparatus allows the researcher to locate the structure precisely according to reference points outside the skull. Histological procedures are needed to confirm the accuracy of the location after the animal is sacrificed.

Part

II

Basic
Neuroanatomy

As stated earlier, physiological psychology is committed to the idea that we can explain behavior if we can learn about the operation of the nervous system. In order to begin this comparison between structures and functions, it is necessary to take a brief tour of the structures that will be encountered. Chapter 4 on the central nervous system (CNS) identifies the major structures and landmarks found in the system. The student is well advised at this point to spend some time learning the location and general function of the identified structures.

Although "quick and dirty" rules are inevitably wrong when one gets to specific cases, three general rules may help in understanding the organization of the CNS. The first is that the higher the structure in the system, the more complicated is the behavior controlled. By comparing the differences in behavioral capacity at the various levels of the nervous system, it is possible to make some astute guesses regarding the locus of control of a particular function, or vice versa.

A second general organizational principle is that the left side of the brain deals with information and behavior on the right side of the body, and vice versa. The spinal cord and nerves in the body are controlled by a "same-side" principle. The reason for this arrangement is not clear. There are also major amounts of information that are distributed equally to both sides of the nervous system.

The third general rule is that the dorsal half of the nervous system is predominantly sensory, while the ventral half is motor. This rule applies from the cortex through the brain stem to the spinal cord, with the cerebellum providing a highly visible exception.

By using these three generalized rules, it is possible to summarize to a remarkable extent the specific functions of the various CNS components.

The neuronal circuitry within the CNS is so impressive that one often forgets a number of structures that assist the functioning of the CNS. These ancillary structures fall into two general categories: nonneuronal structures within the CNS that assist the functioning of the system; and neural structures outside the CNS that provide a communication network between the CNS and all parts of the body. The peripheral nerves appear to be made up of typical neurons except that they are not as concentrated or protected as those in the CNS. Probably related to this difference is the fact that peripheral neurons have a much greater capacity than CNS neurons to regenerate after injury.

The ancillary structures within the CNS appear to be involved primarily with a support role in the efficient operation of the CNS neuronal circuitry. At the present time, with respect to organization of the CNS, emphasis is on the activity of the neurons. Although the data are only fragmentary, there are hints that the nonneuronal cells may also play an important role in the activity of the CNS.

SUGGESTED READINGS

The human nervous system is a remarkably complex structure. It is complex in the sheer number of cells involved, in the diversity of the different cells, in its organization into functional clusters, in the interconnections among the various functional units, and in the character of the nonneuronal structures which are necessary to maintain efficient operation. The study of structural and functional diversity of the component parts of the nervous system is a field in itself. The following sources describe neurological structures but also provide functional applications and implications.

Bannister, R. *Brain's clinical neurology.* London: Oxford University Press, 1969.
Curtis, B. A., Jacobson, S. & Marcus, E. M. *An introduction to the neurosciences.* Philadelphia: Saunders, 1972.
Gardner, E. *Fundamentals of neurology.* (6th ed.) Philadelphia: Saunders, 1975.
Guyton, A. C. *Function of the human body.* Philadelphia: Saunders, 1974.
Krieg, W. J. S. *Brain mechanisms in diachrome.* (2d ed.) Evanston, Ill.: Brain Books, 1957.
Netter, F. *The Ciba collection of medical illustrations. I. Nervous system.* New York: Ciba, 1968.
Walton, J. *Essentials of neurology.* (2d ed.) London: Pitman Medical Publishing Company, Ltd., 1966.

4

The Central Nervous System

The brain and spinal cord share a number of characteristics and are grouped together as the central nervous system. The CNS is generally regarded as the intermediary-integrator between a stimulus and a response by an organism. Any behavior, ranging from the reflexive jerk of the leg when struck just below the kneecap to the heights of artistic creativity, is somehow related to the cells, structures, and connections within the CNS.

The CNS is an extraordinarily complex collection of neural structures. The sheer numbers of these structures, combined with their novel descriptive labels, are usually sufficient to induce a bad case of shock in the beginning student. In an attempt to lessen this shock, only "major" structures will be described, and a "translation key" will be provided to explain the derivation of a name.

In appearance, the structures of the CNS can be divided into two major categories—white matter and gray matter. This observable difference is convenient as a first estimate of the function of any given CNS structure. Gray matter is associated with the data-processing, decision-making functions in the nervous system. White matter is primarily involved with transmitting information between the processing centers.

EARLY BRAIN DEVELOPMENT

In order to understand the labels, as well as the functions, of the CNS, it is worthwhile to examine the ontogenetic developmental stages in the human brain (Figure 4.1). The development of a line of specialized cells is the earliest identifiable feature in the developing individual. This line of specialized cells begins as a "neural tube," and the tubelike character is still identifiable in the adult human CNS.

As the organism develops, the neural tube develops at one end three distinct swollen areas of accelerated cellular growth. These areas mark the initial growth of the developing brain. Beginning with the endmost bulge, the three portions are the prosencephalon, mesocephalon, and rhombencephalon. The general term "cephalon" comes from the Greek word denoting "head," and these developing structures identify the portions of the cluster of cells that will become the head. The prefixes are similarly logical. "Pro-" in **prosencephalon** means "first" or "foremost" and describes the position of the area on the neural tube. "Meso-" means "middle" and identifies the position of the **mesocephalon.** The **rhombencephalon** is named for its rhomboid shape rather than its position. More common terms for these structures are **forebrain, midbrain,** and **hindbrain** (Table 4.1).

Somewhat later in the development of the nervous system, two addi-

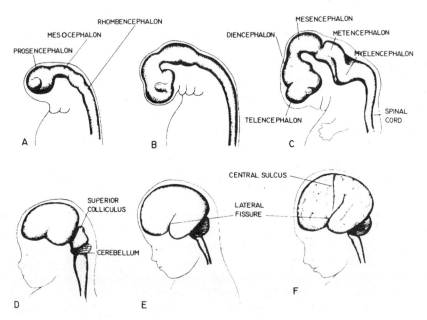

Figure 4.1 The ontogenetic development of the human CNS, showing early and intermediate structures that contribute to the terminology applied to the adult CNS. (After Thompson, 1967, p. 56)

TABLE 4.1   Summary of the Major Structural Terminology Applied to the CNS

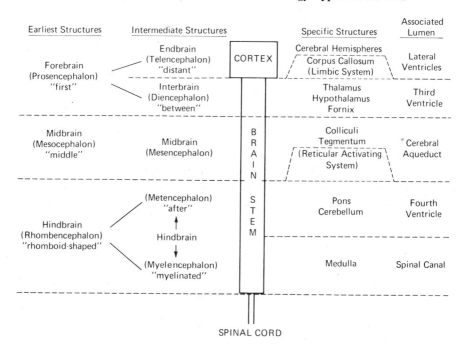

tional swellings may be seen. Thus, we have five units to label. The **telencephalon** is at the very end of the now bumpy neural tube, the label "teleo" meaning "distant." The next lump is labeled the **diencephalon** for its position between other structures. The midbrain is still identified by being in the middle, although the term has been modified from mesocephalon to **mesencephalon.** The hindbrain has been divided into the **metencephalon,** so named because it comes "after" the other structures, and the **myelencephalon,** so called because of its white matter appearance, mostly due to the many neural tracts running between the brain and spinal cord.

THE SPINAL CORD

The spinal cord is the posterior continuation of the brain stem which extends down the hollow tube formed by the vertebrae. Between each vertebra, spinal nerves branch out from the spinal cord and connect to receptors and effectors. The spinal cord serves as a trunkline and distribution structure of nerve tracts between the brain and the rest of the body. The spinal cord also provides connections between the left and right sides of the body and is responsible as well for some primitive reflexive behaviors. For example, an animal with the brain surgically separated from the intact spinal cord is capable of reflexively withdrawing its foot from a painful stimulus, thus the term **spinal reflex.**

THE BRAIN STEM

There is no distinct line of demarcation between the spinal cord and the structures of the brain stem (Figure 4.2). Many spinal cord fibers simply course their way through lower brain stem structures. The **medulla** ("medulla" means "center" or "core") is the first brain stem structure. Externally, the medulla appears to be a slightly enlarged extension of the spinal cord. The enlargement is caused by a number of nuclei interspersed among the ascending and descending tracts. The medulla contains "centers'" for the vital processes of the organism. Life-sustaining activities such as heart rate, breathing rate, blood pressure, food digestion, and nausea will occur in an organism with an intact medulla. In addition to being a way station for neural fibers between the spinal cord and the higher centers, the medulla is also the entry point for most of the cranial nerves.

In describing the functions of the various structures of the CNS, it is

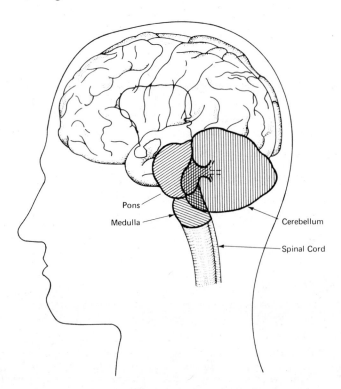

Pons

Medulla

Cerebellum

Spinal Cord

Figure 4.2 Hindbrain structures (and spinal cord) of the human CNS.

easy to slip into a "center-oriented" view of the system. Although it is justifiable to talk about a "heart rate center" in the medulla because stimulation or ablation of these nuclei have a profound effect on the heart rate of the organism, such a label is also illusory. We know, for example, that the heart is capable of maintaining a rhythmic beat when totally isolated from the CNS. The heart rate center in the medulla makes adjustments to this primitive repetitive beat, altering the pulse rate and blood pressure in response to needed circulatory adjustments. Probably even finer adjustments are made to blood circulation by centers yet higher in the CNS. Thus, the heart rate center in the medulla exerts control over the "ryhthmic beat" center in the heart, but is probably in turn affected by a network of other special "centers." For this reason, it is inappropriate to attribute exclusive control to any specific center. With acknowledgment of the technical inaccuracy of the label, we will refer to functional "centers." The label does describe a known function for that structure, and the associated network of tracts and nuclei that share in the control is often not known. Eventually, we will be able to describe the "breathing nervous system" instead of identifying only a few major components.

The **pons** (from the Latin for "bridge") is seen as a pronounced enlargement of the tract structures of the spinal cord and medulla. The primary feature of the pons is that, above this structure, the right side of the CNS predominantly deals with the left side of the body, and vice versa **(contralateral control).** Below the pons, the area of the medulla and spinal cord, the right side of the CNS generally deals with the right side of the body **(ipsilateral control).** The swelling in the area of the pons appears to be primarily due to the effect of the free interchange of millions of axons coursing from one side to the other in the nervous system. Here again, oversimplification may be misleading. Some contralateral systems are found in the spinal cord, and some ipsilateral functions are accomplished in higher centers. A number of the fibers do not cross over at the pons. Generally speaking, however, the CNS is contralateral above the pons and ipsilateral below that structure.

The pons is the connecting point between the cerebellum and the rest of the nervous system. It is also the connecting point for two of the cranial nerves. In addition, the pons contains important nuclei that are involved in the control and coordination of muscular movements as well as sensory motor nuclei for vision and hearing.

The third important structure in the hindbrain is the cerebellum. The cerebellum is relatively large, deeply fissured in appearance, and attached to the dorsal portion of the brain stem. It is divided into two discernible hemispheres and rivals the cerebral hemispheres as the most easily recognized structure in the CNS.

The cerebellum connects to the medulla, pons, and midbrain by three different pairs of nerve fiber stalks. The outer shell of the cerebellum is gray matter with a branching central system of white matter. The cerebellum is mainly involved with coordinating muscular activity, controlling muscle tone and coordinating the activity of different muscle groups involved in tasks like walking. In order to accomplish this coordinating function, the cerebellum utilizes incoming information from the senses regarding the action of the individual muscle groups and information concerning balance and movement from the middle ear receptors. The cerebellum is involved with coordination of the right and left sides of the body, and its connections include and bridge the contralateral and ipsilateral portions of the CNS. In terms of the functional organization of the cerebellar hemispheres, the dorsal third is primarily involved with contralateral body control, and the ventral third is predominately ipsilateral. The middle third exhibits bilateral control—that is, it seems to be equally represented on both sides of the body.

THE MIDBRAIN

The midbrain may be divided into two subareas, the tectum (roof) and the tegmentum (main body) (Figure 4.3). The **tectum** is primarily composed of two pairs of nuclei called the colliculi (Latin for "small hills"), which protrude from its dorsal surface. The **superior colliculi** (higher) are involved with visual reflexes such as blinking, control of pupillary diameter, and adjustment

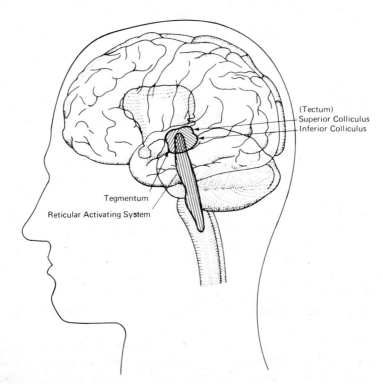

(Tectum)
Superior Colliculus
Inferior Colliculus

Tegmentum

Reticular Activating System

Figure 4.3   Midbrain structures of the human CNS.

of the focus of the lens. The **inferior colliculi** (lower) serve a similar function for auditory reflexes. In humans, this function is probably adjustment of some of the volume-control mechanisms located in the middle ear, although the ability to wiggle one's ears probably also involves inferior collicular activity.

The **tegmentum** is primarily a collection and transmission area for motor messages leading from the higher brain centers down through the spinal cord. Some of the nuclei in the tegmental region appear to be basic "drive centers" (hunger, thirst, sex), although in many ways these represent a continuation of the motivational centers found in the immediately adjacent hypothalamus.

The artificiality of adhering to a strict structure-function organizational plan is illustrated by the difficulty of identifying the unique contributions of the tegmentum. Although the midbrain bulge is definitely seen in the early development of the brain, the modifications that occurred as the adult CNS continued to grow have almost caused this structure to disappear.

A similar example of the structure-function problems is found in the description of the reticular activating system. The **reticular activating system (RAS; also called the reticular formation)** extends through the central portion of the pons, through the midbrain, and into the interbrain. The RAS is a collection of tracts and nuclei which share in the common functional capacity of activating the entire organism. Stimulation of the RAS awakens a sleeping animal and makes an awake animal more alert. Destruction of the reticular structures results in lowered alertness or even an irreversible coma. Although the functional properties of the RAS are relatively well understood, the appropriate structures are not found in a single part of the brain. In addition, the functioning of the RAS shows that lower brain structures may have a profound effect on higher structures. The coma that may result from ablation of the RAS completely debilitates the effective operation of the undamaged remainder of the brain.

THE INTERBRAIN

The interbrain is a region of small, tightly packed areas of white matter and gray matter. One might describe the interbrain as the central switchboard in the complex communication network of the nervous system. The tracts in the interbrain seem to lead to and/or conduct from every structure of the CNS (Figure 4.4).

The dorsal part of the interbrain, the **thalamus,** is the major relay point between the senses and the cortex. All of the senses (except smell) have their major afferent fibers ending in the nuclei in the thalamus. For example, the **lateral geniculate nuclei** (plural because there is one nucleus on each side) receive fibers from the eye and project fibers to the optic areas of the cortex. Similarly, the **medial geniculate nuclei** serve as a relay station for the auditory system. In addition to simply relaying sensory information to higher sensory centers, the thalamic nuclei also distribute the information to other parts

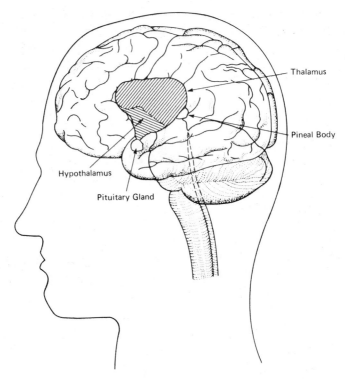

Thalamus

Pineal Body

Hypothalamus

Pituitary Gland

Figure 4.4   Interbrain structures of the human CNS.

of the nervous system. The geniculate nuclei, for example, have branches leading to the appropriate colliculi in the midbrain and also to the RAS.

The nuclei in the thalamus not only distribute incoming sensory information but also accomplish the initial steps of organization and recognition in the sensory system. The higher sensory centers in the cortex are obviously essential to fine discriminations and appreciation of the environment. These centers, however, receive only information that has been preprocessed by the thalamus. Many of the illusions are more the result of thalamic rather than cortical processing. The cortical centers can work only with the information as coded and organized by the thalamus. The **pineal body** is also attached to the thalamus of the interbrain. Although the pineal body (sometimes called a gland) received some attention as Descartes' "seat of the soul," its actual function is still somewhat of a puzzle. Evidence indicates that the pineal body is capable of responding to light. In some species (fish), the pineal is located near the top of the skull and may actually respond to general light levels. It is possible that the pineal is the "internal clock" which manipulates our cycles of activity throughout the day. Probably it is also involved with the reproductive cycles through the hormones it controls.

The ventral portion of the interbrain is appropriately named the **hypothalamus** ("hypo" = "under") (Figure 4.5). If we can simplify the

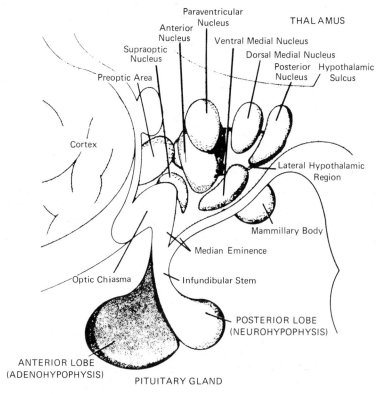

Figure 4.5 The pituitary gland and the nuclei of the hypothalamus. (Curtis, Jacobson, & Marcus, 1972, p. 387)

thalamus into a distribution center for sensory information, we can simplify the hypothalamus as the collection center for response programs. Although movement fibers from the motor areas of the cortex traverse the hypothalamus, this type of response is relatively trivial to the hypothalamus. The nuclei in the hypothalamus appear to be involved with homeostasis, motivation, and emotional states of the organism. Stimulation or ablation of certain nuclei in the hypothalamus produces drastic changes in blood pressure, body temperature, respiration rate, ovulation, and digestion. Other nuclei may be shown to manipulate eating, drinking, and/or sexual behavior. Still other "centers" can produce or cancel rage, fear, passivity, pleasure, or euphoria.

The presence of the multitude of centers in the hypothalamus explain its popularity for neurophysiological research. It appears that a certain center collects relevant information and then either expresses or inhibits the behavior according to the data available. Electrical manipulation of these collection points results in obvious behavioral effects. Thus, the label "center" is applied to the more visible components of the total network of structures contributing data to the decision.

Hanging from the ventral surface of the hypothalamus is the **pituitary**

gland, the "master gland" of the endocrine system. The hypothalamus has nerve fibers extending into the posterior pituitary, but seems to exert a chemical influence on the anterior pituitary through secretory cells in the pituitary stalk. Since it has known centers for emotional behavior and control over the pituitary, it is not surprising to find that the hypothalamus is the coordinating structure for the operation of the autonomic nervous system.

THE ENDBRAIN

By any criterion, the dominant structure in the adult human brain is the cortex. In size, location, number of cells, appearance, and function the cortex is an impressive structure. Thus, the "brain" pictured in most books is dominated by the wrinkled-appearing cortex with the smaller cerebellum tucked under the back portion and a bit of hindbrain protruding out the bottom.

The cortex is a relatively recent phylogenetic development in the CNS. The centers found in the midbrain and interbrain once served as total processing units. As the cortex evolved, this more complicated neural structure assumed and improved on the data analysis. Rather than describing this as a cortical "takeover" of functions, it is more appropriate to say that the various structures have specialized according to their data-processing capacities. It would be inefficient to either maintain or totally abandon lower brain structures whose functions are better accomplished by newly evolved structures. It would be wiser to maintain both structures in a closely intertied system, with each processing aspects of the data for which it is best suited. The relation between the cortex and the brain stem structures is undoubtedly of this cooperative "nervous system" approach.

With the above discussion in mind, the cortex becomes even more impressive, for the part of the cortex that we can see is only the **neocortex.** The neocortex ("neo" = "new") is the most recent phylogenetic addition to the nervous system. The spectacular growth of the neocortex has completely enveloped not only the brain stem structures but also earlier cortical structures. Surrounding the interbrain, but totally covered by neocortex, are cortical structures known as **allocortex** ("old") and **mesocortex** ("middle"; also called paleocortex) (Figure 4.6). There are discernible differences among the various categories of cortex, which justifies the different labels. The major differences are the number of identifiable layers and the complexity of the connections of the constituent neurons.

The more primitive cortical areas, along with their interconnecting tracts, are collectively known as the **limbic system.** Using a single label for this diverse collection of structures is probably more for geographic than functionally descriptive purposes. The fibers for the sense of smell enter the CNS directly through the limbic system, which explains the alternative label "rhinencephalon" ("smell brain"), but the primary sensory area for smell has not yet been located.

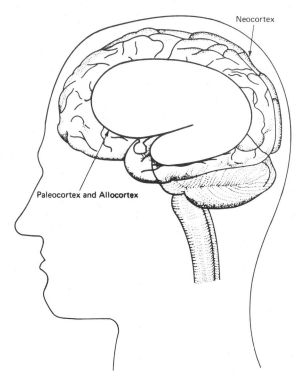

Figure 4.6   Endbrain structures of the human CNS.

Because the limbic system is not yet well understood, considerable contemporary research is concentrated on the structures that make it up. Consequently, the names should be known by the beginning student. The shape of
the structures of the limbic system approximates that of a set of ram's horns,
beginning at the front of the interbrain and curling over the top and out to
each side. The **septal area** and the **amygdala** are joined toward the front and
top of the brain stem. The **hippocampus** and the **cingulate cortex** (or gyrus)
are separated structures curled toward the back and sides.

The limbic system is richly supplied with connections to the neocortex
as well as the underlying brain stem structures (Figure 4.7). It is generally
concluded that the limbic system is involved with motivations and emotions.
There is some evidence to suggest that the limbic system may accomplish
short-term memory. Some social behaviors, such as courtship, mating, and
parental behavior, may also be limbic system functions.

As we ascend the CNS, we find that the structures become both structurally and functionally more complicated. Thus, the "centers" approach of
the brain stem cannot describe the limbic system. The complexity of the
limbic system will undoubtedly dictate corresponding sophistication in research techniques and strategies. We turn now to the most complicated
neural structure of all.

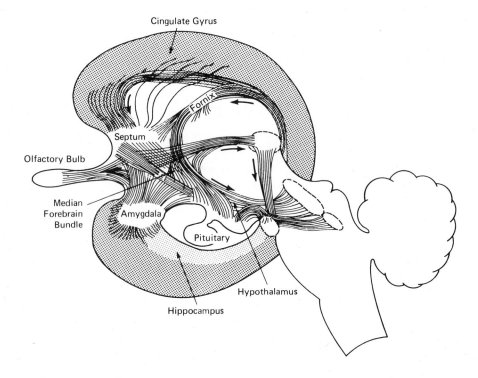

Figure 4.7 Limbic system connections. (Quarton, Melnechuk, & Smith, 1967)

The external appearance of the cortex is of two hemispheres of very wrinkled gray matter. The wrinkles, or convolutions, increase the actual surface area of the cortex by a factor of three. In cross section, the cortex appears to be a uniform layer of gray matter which is folded on itself to form the convolutions. The inside surface of this layer is consistently in contact with a branching arrangement of white matter, so that all areas of the cortex are serviced with communication fibers.

The fissure portion of a convolution is called a **sulcus,** while the hill or ridge between is a **gyrus.** If we were to examine a number of human brains, we would find that the pattern of sulci differ from person to person. Some of the smaller sulci might even be absent. The major ones, however, can be recognized, even though their exact form may not be identical.

Three major sulci are used as landmarks on the human cortex (Figure 4.8). The first, the **longitudinal sulcus,** divides the cortex into the two cerebral hemispheres. Each hemisphere has two major sulci which provide the boundaries for major lobes of the brain. The **central sulcus** extends down from the top of the brain and divides each hemisphere into approximately ⅓ anterior and ⅔ posterior to the sulcus. The **lateral sulcus** extends from the front of the brain and divides each hemisphere into approximately ⅓ ventral and ⅔ dorsal to the sulcus.

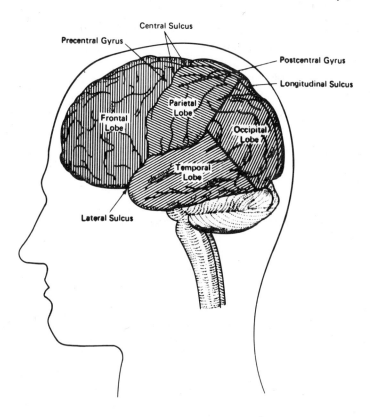

Figure 4.8 The lobes of the cerebral cortex and the major sulci used as landmarks in identifying the lobes.

The regions bounded by the major sulci are called lobes, and there are four identifiable lobes on each hemisphere of the human brain. Thus, the **frontal lobe** is that part of the cortex anterior to the central sulcus. The **temporal lobe** is the mass of cortex folded ventral to the lateral sulcus. The **occipital lobe** is the posterior part of the cortex, and the **parietal lobe** is that region on the top, middle portion of each hemisphere not already claimed by a label. The lobes of the cortex were named after the bones that form the overlying skull.

Since the cortex can be identified in terms of function, the usual way to divide the cortical area is into functional regions. Afferent sensory fibers lead directly to certain areas of the cortex. Since the removal of these cortical areas results in total loss of sensory function, they are called primary sensory areas. The **primary sensory areas** seem to be involved with the direct perception and recognition of the stimulus. From the primary sensory areas a number of association fibers lead to adjacent secondary or association areas for each sense. It is in the sensory association areas that fine discriminations are made, and here recognition and identification are accomplished. Destruction of the association areas does not result in the total loss of sensory function, but does significantly reduce the utility of the sense.

The sensory areas (both primary and association) are found in the posterior three lobes of the cortex. The primary visual area is located at the most posterior portion of the occipital lobe, with the adjacent areas being visual association areas. The sense of hearing has its primary projection area on the temporal lobes, and the sense of touch is found on the parietal lobe along the gyrus posterior to the central sulcus. The primary area for the sense of taste is conveniently located near the area for touch in the tongue.

While the posterior three lobes of the brain are involved with sensory input, recognition, and storage, the frontal lobes seem to be primarily involved with responses. The gyrus just anterior to the central sulcus is the **primary motor area** just across the sulcus from the touch area. Motor association areas are found in nearby regions of the frontal lobe. The rest of the frontal lobe is not easily described in terms of immediately discernible functions. Animals without functioning frontal lobes have difficulty switching to the previously "wrong" reponse in a discrimination-reversal task. Similarly, such animals have trouble keeping track of multiple stimuli, particularly if the stimuli have been used before. Humans with frontal lobe injuries may be observed to "cheat" in working at a task, even though they can recite the rule violated when asked. It is also established that ablation of the frontal lobe lowers the general emotional tone of the organism—the main justification for performing prefrontal lobotomy surgery on certain mental patients.

There is little psychophysiological evidence to support directly the popular notion that the frontal lobes are responsible for human intellect aside from the obvious phylogenetic relation between human behavior and the size of the human frontal lobes. Of course, discrimination-reversal and multiple-stimuli tasks are relatively complex learning tasks. One reason these tasks are difficult is that the animal has to choose from several response programs that have been learned. Rather than being the source of intelligent behavior, the frontal lobes may be able to select from the variety of programs learned and stored elsewhere in the brain. The selection may involve activating the correct response or, more likely, inhibiting the expression of inappropriate responses. Thus, the frontal lobes seem to be primarily concerned with the selection of appropriate behavior (including emotions) rather than with the learning, storage, and expression of the behaviors.

A microscopic examination of the layers of gray matter forming the cortex reveals some interesting features. First, the total thickness of the cortex does not vary appreciably. It ranges from about 1.5 mm in the sulci to 3 mm in the gyri of primates and is a relatively uniform 2 mm in the smooth cortex of the rat. Within this uniform band can be found consistent cellular layers. It is generally stated that the cortex is made up of six layers, although the relative thickness of each layer varies greatly in different regions of the cortex, and sometimes the boundary between adjacent layers is so gradual that it can be seen only because one knows it should be there. There is also some appearance of a columnar arrangement by the cells in the cortex. That is, individual cells are seen to extend through several cortical layers, always at a right angle to the layers. An oversimplified version of the cells found in the cortex would be that there are two types of cortical cells, those that operate entirely within a given layer and those that connect that layer with other layers or other parts of the nervous system.

The fibers leading from the inside surface of the cortex fall into three major categories according to where they connect (Figure 4.9). If the fiber leads to another portion of the cortex in the same hemisphere—if it stays on the same side—it is called an **association fiber.** If the fiber leads to a part of the cortex on the opposite hemisphere, it is called a **commissural fiber.** If the fiber leads to the brain stem, it is called a **projection fiber.**

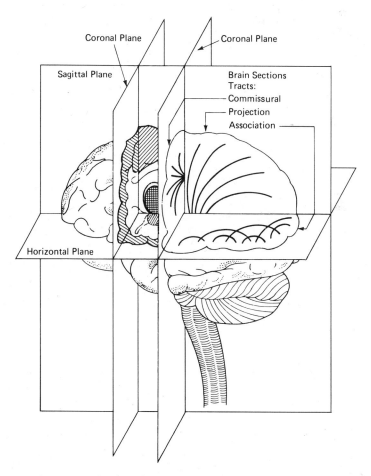

Figure 4.9   The three major types of tracts found in the CNS. Commissural fibers carry information between the left and right hemispheres. Projection fibers carry information between the cortex to the brain stem (and/or the body). Association fibers carry information between cortical regions of the same hemisphere.

In some areas of the CNS, the fibers band together to form prominent tracts. Because of their high visibility, these tracts are often used as landmarks for locating less obvious structures. The commissural fibers leading from one hemisphere to the other form three structures easily recognized in brain frontal sections. The **anterior commissure** and the **posterior commissure** connect the left and right sides of the brain stem, while the **corpus callosum** provides interhemispheric communication for the cortex.

The **fornix** is an easily identified projection tract which connects the hypothalamus in the interbrain to the amygdala in the limbic system. Although the two structures are almost adjacent to one another in the human brain, the fornix follows the evolutionary curl of the ram's horn in the limbic system. This circuitous "detour" means that the fornix appears in a number of brain slices, and its relative position in the slice is a reliable indicator of the locus of that slice. In the posterior portion of the brain, the projection fibers of the **optic tract** also provide a significant landmark.

AUTHOR'S COMMENTS   The important structures of the CNS are listed in the "specific structures" column of Table 4.1. Attempting to describe the CNS in sweeping generalizations does a disservice to its impressive complexity. I have found, however, that there are three basic organizational principles which provide a convenient initial estimate of the function of a structure according to its locus in the CNS. First, the CNS above the pons exerts contralateral control over the body, while below the pons the control is ipsilateral. Second, the dorsal structures in the CNS are usually sensory, or afferent, while the ventral structures are primarily efferent, or motor. Third, there are three general levels of behavior that can be easily identified. The lower brain stem and spinal cord control vegetative functions and reflexes. The limbic system (including the thalamus and hypothalamus) is responsible for more complicated behaviors which might be called motivational, emotional, or instinctive. The cortex is responsible for higher learning and thinking capacities.

Chapter 5

Ancillary Structures

The CNS is uniquely cut off from direct contact with the real world in a number of ways. Encased, enclosed, shock protected, isolated, and able to communicate only through the peculiar electrochemical language of neuronal messages, contact with the real world requires a number of ancillary structures. In this chapter, we will first examine a number of nonneuronal systems that serve to maintain and protect the integrity of the CNS. We will then look at some of the neuronal structures that carry information between the CNS and the receptors and effectors distributed throughout the body.

MENINGES

The CNS is completely encased in a protective package of bone, the brain within the skull and the spinal cord within the column of vertebrae. Between this hard package and its delicate contents are three layers of membranous tissue known as **meninges** (Figure 5.1). The outermost layer, a tough, almost leathery membrane known as the **dura mater** ("dura" = "hard," "mater" = "mother"), apparently serves the function of protecting the brain from contact with rough parts of the surrounding bone. Surgeons and brain researchers must specifically deal with the dura to gain access to the underlying neural tissue, for although it is transparent in appearance, it presents a formidable

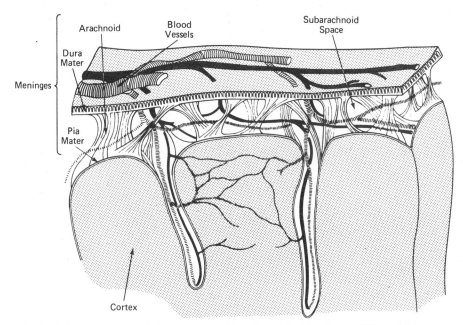

Figure 5.1   The meningeal layers surrounding the CNS. (Gardner, 1975, p. 152)

barrier to some of the delicate electrodes and instruments used in brain research.

Inside the dura is another membrane which is softer and more delicate called the **pia mater** ("pia" = "tender"). One could almost describe the dura as an inner lining of the skull and vertebrae, while the pia is the outer lining of the nervous tissue of the brain and spinal cord.

Enclosed between the dura and pia is a third membrane called the **arachnoid** (from the Greek for "cobweb"). The arachnoid is membranelike in that it provides a thin, inner lining for the dura; however, the arachnoid is also a very spongy structure with a number of fibrous extensions across to the pia. Thus, the nervous tissue is suspended and protected from contact with its bony box. The space between the dura and pia, the **subarachnoid space,** in addition to containing the arachnoid, provides room for blood vessels which have penetrated the dura to distribute themselves over the surface of the brain. The remainder of the subarachnoid space is filled with cerebrospinal fluid, which provides additional hydraulic protection for the suspended CNS.

VENTRICLES

The CNS is not a solid mass of nervous tissue, but actually a hollow tube, with a continuous cavity, the **lumen,** extending throughout its length. This cavity is variously described as a ventricle, aqueduct, or canal, depending on its location and size within the brain and spinal cord (Figure 5.2). In the

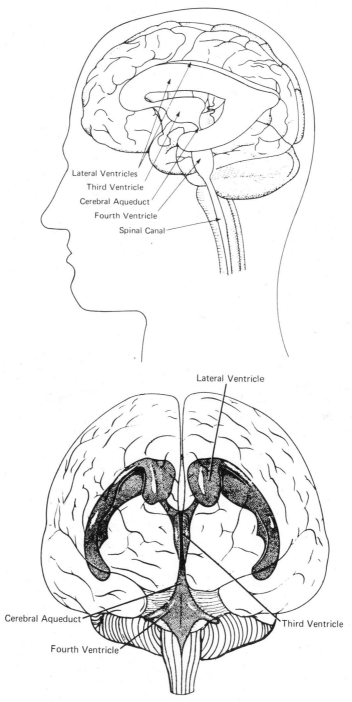

Figure 5.2 The ventricular spaces (lumen) in the middle of the CNS. (Bottom figure, Curtis, Jacobson, & Marcus, 1972, p. 18)

mammalian brain, where the developing cortex has bifurcated into two separate hemispheres, there is a similar branching in the ventricular system. The **lateral ventricles** are the hollow spaces found in each cerebral hemisphere. At the top of the brain stem is the **third ventricle,** with connecting openings to each of the lateral ventricles. The posterior portion of the third ventricle narrows down to a fine tube known as the **cerebral aqueduct,** which leads to the enlarged hollow space at the base of the brain stem called the **fourth ventricle.** The hollow space then narrows once again to become the **spinal canal,** a tube extending the length of the spinal cord. Between the fourth ventricle and the spinal canal is an opening to the subarachnoid space.

The entire ventricular system and subarachnoid space are filled with **cerebrospinal fluid,** a clear fluid quite similar to blood without the red cells. The cerebrospinal fluid is produced in a plexus of capillaries in both lateral ventricles. Apparently some, but not all, of the constituents of the blood migrate through the capillary walls to form the fluid. The fluid then flows down the lumen of the brain and spinal cord and also up around the CNS through the subarachnoid space, where it is absorbed by veins.

BLOOD SUPPLY

The neurons of the CNS are dependent upon an adequate supply of blood for oxygen and nutrients. Some indication of this reliance is seen by the rapid onset of unconsciousness when blood flow to the brain is interrupted. In addition, permanent brain damage will occur if the stoppage is continued mere minutes beyond unconsciousness. Small blood vessels and capillaries permeate the interior of the CNS, extending from larger arteries and veins located on the exterior.

The cortex and spinal cord are supplied by blood vessels which are distributed over the surface within the subarachnoid space. The brain stem structures are supplied by a branching network of large blood vessels which radiate from the ventral surface of the hypothalamus. An unusual occurrence is found in the arterial system supplying the brain stem. The blood vessels form a circle as a center for distribution rather than the usual linear branching pattern. Apparently, this circular distribution system provides needed alternate delivery channels should a blockage occur.

Another unusual feature characterizes the flow of blood to the brain. Researchers have noted that a number of drug compounds which are injected into the bloodstream cannot be found in brain tissue, although the drug has been absorbed by the rest of the body. This phenomenon has been described as the **blood-brain barrier** (Figure 5.3). The blood-brain barrier is apparently a layer of special cells that completely coat the blood vessels in the CNS. Chemicals that flow through the walls of the blood vessels must also traverse this second barrier. These cells seem to be selectively impermeable to compounds that might damage neural tissue.

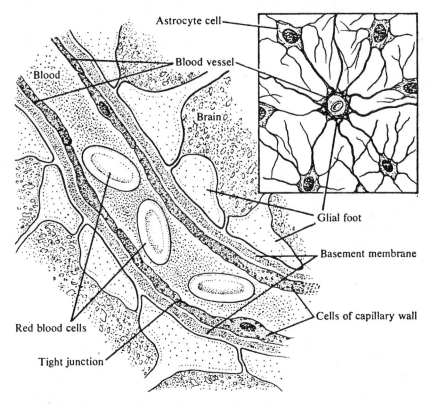

Astrocyte cell

Blood vessel

Blood

Brain

Glial foot

Basement membrane

Cells of capillary wall

Red blood cells

Tight junction

Figure 5.3 The blood-brain barrier. Glial cells line the capillary walls to provide extra protection from selected substances in the bloodstream. (Julien, 1975, p. 17)

GLIAL CELLS

The neurons in the CNS are outnumbered approximately 10 to 1 by a variety of nonneuronal cells known collectively as **neuroglia.** These **glial cells** ("glia" = "glue") are assigned the general task of providing a structural network for the flaccid neurons. The term "glia" now applies to any nonneuronal cell found in the CNS.

The insulating cells which are typically found wrapped around axons are special glial cells called **myelin sheath cells** (Figure 5.4). It is the white coloration of the myelin cells which provides the nerves and tracts with their characteristic coloration. Another glial cell associated with the axon is a fine membranous axonal covering known as **neurilemma.** Neurons with neurilemma have the capacity to regenerate damaged axons, while those lacking neurilemma do not regenerate. For the most part, neurilemma are found on neurons outside the CNS. The cellular components of the blood-brain barrier are also glial cells.

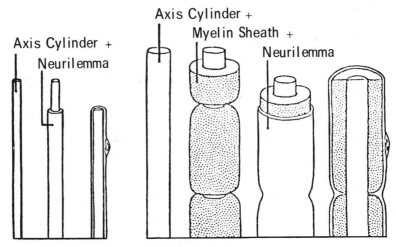

Figure 5.4   Unmyelinated and myelinated axons. Glial cells surround the neuronal axons to assist in their functions. (Gardner, 1963, p. 70)

Electron microscope pictures of neuronal connections usually show a number of glial cells in the adjacent regions. This apparent concentration of glial cells near an information exchange point in the nervous system is probably more than coincidental in the operation of the connection.

Glial cells represent a "silent partner" in the functioning of the nervous system (Figure 5.5). Neurophysiologists concentrate on understanding the activity of the neurons and tend to ignore the relatively quiet glial cells found in the same region. It may be true that the glial cells are simply cells which provide needed support functions for the highly specialized neurons. Possibly, however, the glial cells are integral to the dynamic characteristics of the nervous system. Although the data for understanding the functioning of the nervous system are neuronal activity, the potential involvement of the closely associated glial cells should not be forgotten.

PERIPHERAL NERVOUS SYSTEM

The major structures of interest to the physiological psychologist are to be found in the CNS. Behavior, however, requires interaction with the environment. Since the CNS is completely isolated from the outside environment, there are a number of ancillary nervous structures that serve as an interface between the CNS and the environment. This peripheral system is found coursing throughout the body carrying information from the sensory receptors to the brain, and messages from the brain to the muscles and glands of the body which result in observable behavior.

The peripheral nervous system consists of the afferent and efferent nerves outside the CNS. For reasons of geography, these nerves are grouped into

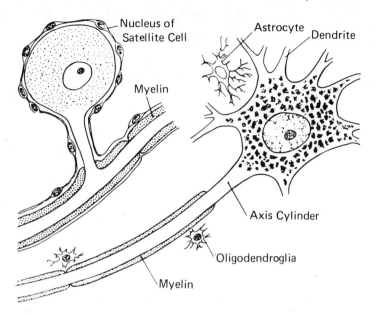

Figure 5.5 Glial cells—nonneuronal cells interspersed among the neurons in the CNS. (Gardner, 1963, p. 70)

three major categories: cranial nerves, peripheral nerves, and spinal nerves (Figure 5.6).

Cranial nerves are the nerves found entering or leaving the CNS through the brain stem—or stated conversely, *not* by way of the spinal cord. The twelve cranial nerves (Figure 5.7) serve the receptors and effectors found in the head. Thus, important sensory functions like sight, hearing, smell, taste, and balance are transmitted through the cranial nerves (Table 5.1). Important motor functions such as eye movement, head orientation, facial expression, and speech are controlled by the efferent fibers in the cranial nerves. Cranial nerves may be afferent, efferent, or mixed. Although there are twelve cranial nerves, each has a bilateral branch; in other words, the cranial nerves enter the CNS in pairs, one on each side. They are numbered according to their point of contact with the CNS, beginning with the most rostral and moving down. Their names usually reflect their function.

The **peripheral nerves** course throughout the body collecting information from the sensory structures and delivering messages to the muscles and glands (Figure 5.8). It is possible to draw a "map" of the body identifying sensory **dermatomes,** or regions of the skin served by each peripheral nerve. If the nerve dealing with one dermatome area is destroyed, the person would have no sense of touch in that region. The boundary layer between adjacent dermatomes is not black and white, so there is an area of overlap at the outer reaches of each dermatome. If a peripheral nerve is for some reason destroyed, the adjacent nerves begin to grow into the anesthetized area, so that sensation

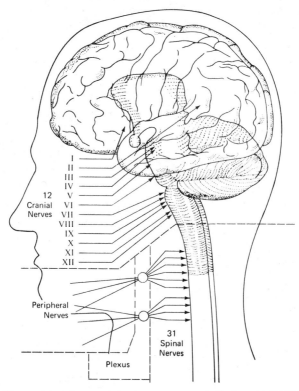

Figure 5.6 The peripheral nervous system components that carry messages between the CNS and the parts of the body.

is gradually reacquired, proceeding from the outer boundaries, and the messages are eventually delivered to the brain through a different, but intact, nerve.

The sensory dermatome illustrates the fact that nerves with a common function—to carry sensory information from one skin area—seem to be grouped together into a common structure in the nervous system. As will be seen subsequently, this structural-functional relationship seems to be a general pattern in nervous system organization. There is a similar set of specific muscle groups served by the efferent neurons found in a given peripheral nerve. Because the muscles are within the body, the motor "map" is not so easy to draw, although the organizational principles remain the same. In addition, there are afferent neurons serving internal receptors in the body which are not shown on the sensory dermatome.

The peripheral neurons connect the receptors and effectors to the neurons in the spinal cord, but the peripheral nerves do not extend the entire distance. Instead, the neurons recombine to enter the spinal cord through the spinal nerves. There are 31 pairs of **spinal nerves** exiting from between the vertebrae of the backbone, with members of each pair leading to

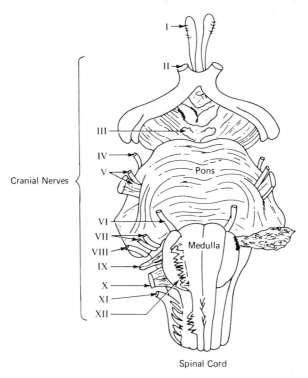

Figure 5.7 A ventral view of the brain stem showing the location of the 12 cranial nerves. (I) Olfactory; (II) optic; (III) oculomotor; (IV) trochlear; (V) trigeminal; (VI) abducens; (VII) facial; (VIII) acoustic; (IX) glossopharyngeal; (X) vagus; (XI) accessory; (XII) hypoglossal. (Gardner, 1975, p. 164)

each side of the body. The spinal nerves are identified by the region of the backbone at which they enter the spinal cord. There are five regions of the backbone: (1) the cervical region with eight spinal nerves; (2) the thorasic region with twelve nerves; (3) the lumbar region with five nerves; (4) the sacral region with five nerves; and (5) the coccyx with one nerve. Within a given region, the nerves are identified by number in cephalo-caudal order.

Each spinal nerve serves successively higher (or lower) sections of the entire body (Figure 5.9). In fact, if a person were sitting down, the spinal dermatomes approximate the rings formed by water at increasing depths of approximately an inch at a time. The dermatomes for each spinal nerve are not exclusive but extend into the adjacent dermatomes above and below. Thus, if a single spinal nerve were destroyed, there would be a one-third loss of function in three adjacent dermatomes, but total anesthesia would not occur in any single area. This overlapping of function occasionally conceals the organization of the system, but also provides a vital safety factor. Total anesthesia will not occur in a spinal nerve dermatome without the destruction of three adjacent spinal nerves.

TABLE 5.1   **Summary of the Cranial Nerves** (Wegner, Jones, & Jones, 1956, p. 42)

Number	Name	Origin	Primary Functions
I	Olfactory	Olfactory bulb	Afferent for smell
II	Optic	Diencephalon	Afferent for vision
III	Oculomotor	Midbrain	Afferent and efferent to all eye muscles except two
IV	Trochlear	Midbrain	Afferent and efferent to one eye muscle
V	Trigeminal	Pons	Afferent from skin and mucous membranes of head and from chewing muscles Efferent to chewing muscles
VI	Abducens	Pons	Afferent and efferent to one eye muscle
VII	Facial	Medulla	Afferent from taste buds of anterior ⅔ of tongue Efferent to muscles of face and salivary glands
VIII	Acoustic	Medulla	Afferent from the inner ear (hearing and balance)
IX	Glossopharyngeal	Medulla	Afferent from throat, rear of tongue, and taste buds of posterior ⅓ of tongue Efferent to throat and one salivary gland
X	Vagus	Medulla	Afferent from throat, viscera, and larynx Efferent to viscera
XI	Accessory	Medulla	Efferent to viscera (via Vagus), throat, larynx, and neck and shoulder muscles
XII	Hypoglossal	Medulla	Afferent and efferent to tongue muscles

The area of recombination between the peripheral and spinal nerves is known as a **plexus.** Four major plexus systems are found in the body (Figure 5.10). In a way, a plexus is a neuronal freeway interchange where the axons rearrange themselves appropriately from one type of nerve to another. Eleven of the twelve thoracic spinal nerves do not extend into a plexus, but extend directly into regions of the torso. Irrespective of whether the information is carried through the peripheral nerve-plexus-spinal nerve or through the spinal nerve route, a single neuron transmits information between the receptors and/or effectors in the body and the spinal cord.

The spinal nerves illustrate a number of structural-functional features (Figure 5.11). Since the spinal nerves also occur in pairs, there is the obvious fact that the neurons exiting from the right side of the spinal cord serve the right side of the body, and vice versa. In addition, each nerve branches into two roots as it approaches the spinal cord. The dorsal root carries sensory information into the spinal cord, and the ventral root carries motor informa-

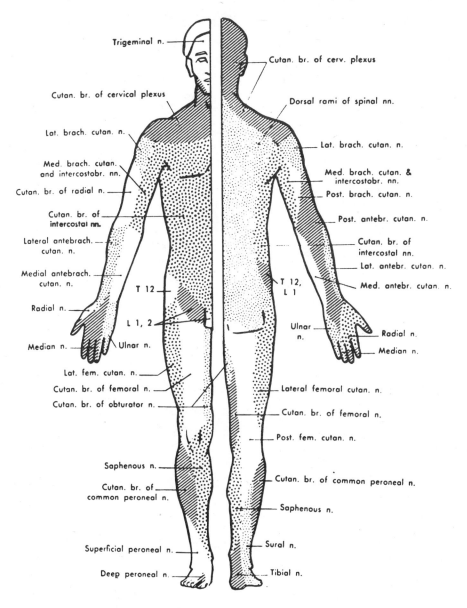

Figure 5.8 Peripheral nerve sensory dermatomes. Different regions of the skin are served by different peripheral nerves. (Gardner, 1963, p. 34)

tion from the spinal cord. Thus, the neurons sort themselves into afferent and efferent functional units as well.

Tucked on each side of the vertebrae of the spinal column is a long string of neural material known as the **spinal ganglia.** These ganglia are comprised of the cell bodies of the neurons supplying the axons of the peripheral

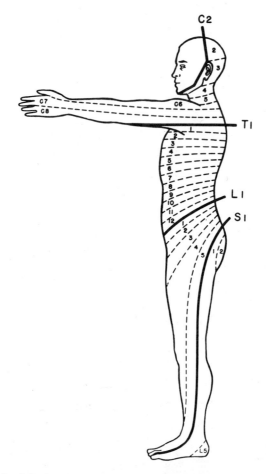

Figure 5.9 Spinal nerve sensory dermatomes. Note that the distribution is different from that of the peripheral dermatomes in Figure 5.8. (Gardner, 1963, p. 36)

and spinal nerves. Generally speaking, the cell bodies of the peripheral nerves are located either in the spinal ganglia or close to the distal organ being served.

The neurons of the peripheral nervous system are the communication lines for activity of the CNS. Any behavior, from a knee jerk reflex to "profound thinking," is accomplished by CNS activity in close harmony with the communication channels to the outside world. Because such behavior is usually considered to be under the control of the individual, this total nervous system is frequently called the voluntary nervous system. Although this function is certainly emphasized by the physiological psychologist, the total nervous system also includes substantial involuntary components. In addition to "unintended" or "unconscious" behaviors, the nervous system includes a complicated homeostatic system to maintain an optimal internal environment for the efficient operation of the body.

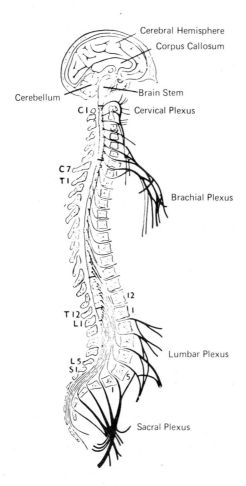

Cerebral Hemisphere

Corpus Callosum

Cerebellum

Brain Stem

C I

Cervical Plexus

C 7

T I

Brachial Plexus

I 2

T 12

L I

Lumbar Plexus

L 5

S I

5

Sacral Plexus

Figure 5.10 Major plexi in the human body. Each plexus is a redistribution center for axons between the spinal and peripheral nerves. (Gardner, 1975, p. 169)

AUTOMATIC SYSTEMS

Two systems with components scattered throughout the body have a direct effect on behavior and show a remarkable degree of internal regulation and coordination. One of these systems, the autonomic nervous system, appears to be primarily neuronal in nature; however, there are also chemical-transmitting agents distributed throughout the bloodstream. The other system, the endocrine glands, seems to be predominantly chemical in nature, but with significant neurological components. The two systems are not exclusive of one another, but share a considerable degree of "cross talk." The combination of the two serves to regulate the internal functions of the body, otherwise known as **homeostasis.**

The **autonomic nervous system** may be described as the "survival" nervous system. In this case, two distinct kinds of "survival" functions are implied. One is to assist the organism to escape or cope with a life-threatening situation. The other is to coordinate, produce, and conserve the bodily resources neces-

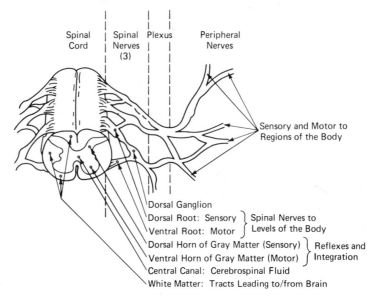

Figure 5.11 The major distributional structures in the nervous system—the spinal cord and the peripheral plexus system.

sary to maintain the organism throughout its normal life span (in the absence of emergency disasters). The autonomic nervous system is divided into two reciprocally active units to meet these two functions.

The **sympathetic nervous system** is the division responsible for emergency survival (Figure 5.12). The effects of sympathetic activity are compatible with a mobilization of the body for a "fight or flight" response. Digestion is stopped, and the blood flowing to the internal organs is redirected to the skeletal muscles, the air passages in the lungs are opened to facilitate oxygen transfer, the heart increases its pumping action, which assists in distributing oxygen as well as other needed substances, and the endocrine system is stimulated to release several chemicals that increase the effectiveness of the entire motor system. Even the erection of the hairs is an autonomic attempt to make us look bigger to help bluff away the source of the threat.

The **parasympathetic nervous system,** on the other hand, appears to concentrate on producing and storing the necessary bodily resources to maximize the longevity of the individual. Digestion of food provides needed nutrients for the body. The bronchi leading to the lungs are constricted and coated with mucous to provide protection from airborne contaminants. The heart rate is slowed to provide adequate circulation of the blood without self-destructing.

The sympathetic and parasympathetic nervous systems combine their seemingly antagonistic functions into a remarkably adaptive survival mechanism. The parasympathetic thrust toward long-run maintenance would be wasted if the organism could not survive an emergency situation. The sympa-

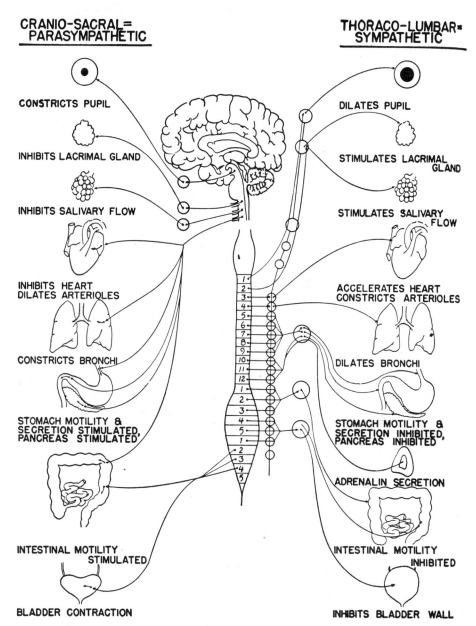

CRANIO-SACRAL= PARASYMPATHETIC

CONSTRICTS PUPIL

INHIBITS LACRIMAL GLAND

INHIBITS SALIVARY FLOW

INHIBITS HEART
DILATES ARTERIOLES

CONSTRICTS BRONCHI

STOMACH MOTILITY &
SECRETION STIMULATED,
PANCREAS STIMULATED

INTESTINAL MOTILITY
STIMULATED

BLADDER CONTRACTION

THORACO-LUMBAR= SYMPATHETIC

DILATES PUPIL

STIMULATES LACRIMAL GLAND

STIMULATES SALIVARY FLOW

ACCELERATES HEART
CONSTRICTS ARTERIOLES

DILATES BRONCHI

STOMACH MOTILITY &
SECRETION INHIBITED,
PANCREAS INHIBITED

ADRENALIN SECRETION

INTESTINAL MOTILITY
INHIBITED

INHIBITS BLADDER WALL

Figure 5.12 The major structural and functional characteristics of the autonomic nervous system. The differences between the sympathetic and parasympathetic systems are seen by comparing the left and right halves of the diagram. (Johnson, DeLanney, Cole, and Brooks, 1961; via Altman, 1966, p. 204)

thetic physiological responses draw freely on the stored materials provided by parasympathetic action. In fact, prolonged activity of the sympathetic nervous system will result in fatigue, shock, or other physical symptoms reflecting the depletion of vital resources to meet the emergency.

In addition to their functional dichotomy, the sympathetic and parasympathetic branches of the automatic nervous system differ in their location in the nervous system. Parasympathetic nerves exit from the spinal cord through the sacral and upper lumbar spinal nerves, while the sympathetic nerves, often leading to the same organ, leave the CNS through the cranial nerves or the coccyx. On examination the neurons serving each system also show a difference. The cell bodies of sympathetic neurons are found close to the spinal cord, forming part of the spinal ganglia. The cell bodies of parasympathetic neurons are distributed throughout the body relatively near the organ being served. Undoubtedly, the difference in neurons reflects the different communication demands of an emergency versus a relaxed situation.

The **endocrine system** consists of a number of secreting organs located throughout the body. Although there is some neurological communication, each endocrine gland primarily responds to chemical levels in the bloodstream. The response of an **endocrine gland** is usually to release a hormone into the bloodstream. Through a complex set of chemical messengers, the endocrine system maintains an effective communication system through the bloodstream. The endocrine system is very complex, since each of the known glands releases several different hormones with different physiological effects (Table 5.2). There are also a number of potential glandular-appearing pockets of tissue scattered throughout the body which are probably also units of the endocrine system.

Endocrine functions are extremely varied. Long-term activity such as manipulation of blood sugar level, metabolism of carbohydrates, manipulation of calcium and potassium levels in the body, and even bodily growth are directly attributable to specific hormones. Several hormones, notably adrenalin, make the muscular system "superefficient" for a short period of crisis. When scared, we really can run faster! Considerable evidence suggests that some of the endocrine cells are also involved in fighting infections or disease. The endocrine system is also involved with the survival of the species through the regulation of the sex hormones, the production of reproductive cells, and the production of milk in the mother.

Although the autonomic nervous system and the endocrine glandular system are usually discussed separately, they obviously must be closely coordinated in at least some of their functions. The most likely site for such coordination may be the ventral surface of the midbrain. Most of the brain centers involved with automatic-type behavior are located in the hypothalamus. Similarly, the pituitary gland, hanging from its stalk attached to the hypothalamus, is called the master gland because pituitary hormones seem to exercise control over the secretions of all the other endocrine glands. It is now established that the posterior pituitary is actually partially neurological in its

TABLE 5.2   Principal Hormones and Their Major Functions (Wenger, Jones, & Jones, 1956, p. 230)

Gland	Hormone	Major Functions
Anterior pituitary	Thyrotrophic (TTH)	Stimulates thyroid secretion
	Adrenocorticotrophic (ACTH)	Stimulates secretion of some hormones of adrenal cortex
	Lactogenic (prolactin)	Stimulates milk secretion by mammary glands
	Luteinizing (LH)	Development of interstitial cells of testis and ovary, and corpus luteum
	Follicle-stimulating (FSH)	Development of spermatogenic tissue in male and follicle in female
	Growth (STH)	Stimulates growth
Posterior pituitary	Oxytocin	Excites nonstriated muscles, especially of uterus; excites mammary glands
	Vasopressin	Produces rise in blood pressure
	Antidiuretic	Prevents loss of water through kidney
Thyroid	Thyroxin	Influences metabolic rate
Parathyroid	Parathormone	Maintains calcium and phosphorous balance in blood
Inlet cells	Insulin	Necessary for utilization of blood sugar
Adrenal cortex	Cortical steroids	Increased carbohydrate metabolism, sodium retention, and potassium loss; some androgenic and estrogenic effects
Adrenal medulla	Epinephrine Nor-epinephrine	Increased sugar output by liver; stimulate most SNS end-organs (differentially)
Ovary	Estrogen	Produces female primary and secondary sex characteristics
	Progresterone	Prepare uterus for implantation of embryo
Testis	Androgen (testosterone)	Sexual arousal; produces primary and secondary sex characteristics

activity. Although psychologists prefer to examine the physiological correlates for behaviors such as "perceiving," "learning," or even "thinking," these behaviors are a luxury afforded the organism only because of the quiet, unconscious operation of automatic systems like the endocrine glands and the autonomic nervous system.

AUTHOR'S COMMENTS   Throughout this text, emphasis is placed on understanding the neuronal circuitry on the CNS. Probably because electronic technology allows relatively direct observation of the electrically active neurons, neurons have acquired a predominant role in the field. There are, however, a number of other communication systems. The bloodstream carries nutrients to the CNS and waste by-products away. In addition, the endocrine system utilizes the blood circulation system to carry its hormones throughout the body. The CNS is known to trigger the release of some of these hormones and, simultaneously, responds to the introduction of other hormones into the bloodstream. Thus, the bloodstream serves as a generalized data-transmission system. The ventricular spaces in the middle of the entire CNS, filled with cerebrospinal fluid which is kept in constant motion by special ciliary cells, is another potentially important facet of the functioning of the CNS.

The glial cells, which are known to provide support, insulation, the blood-brain barrier, and probably energy reserves for the neurons, also exhibit a subtle form of electrical activity. The possible active role glia could serve in nervous system functioning will be mentioned now and again. At the present time, the data are sparse, and the glia still might be primarily "glue."

The autonomic nervous system and the endocrine system are often treated as almost independent entities. Both are peripheral extensions of the "survival of the individual"-"survival of the species" mechanism found in the interbrain-limbic system complex.

III

Basic Neurophysiology

Part III introduces the dynamics of the nervous system. Up to this point, emphasis has been on developing a working vocabulary of the ideas, concepts, facts, and structures that make up the lexicon of physiological psychology. Now we begin to examine how the various components interact to form functional units. Chapters 6 and 7 present the general characteristics of the living cell, with particular reference to the highly specialized cell, the neuron.

Because the neuron is the fundamental unit of the nervous system, it is important to understand its characteristics. Although they differ widely in size and shape, it is generally assumed that all neurons function alike. Thus, the characteristics of the neuron introduced in Chapter 8 establish the limitations and potential of the nervous system. Of particular importance are the electrical characteristics of the postsynaptic potentials and the axon spike. The activity of the axon is a summary statement of the total activity impinging on the neuron. How these data are combined and integrated into a single message is remarkably simple if the basic mechanism is understood.

Chapter 9 deals with the other important concept, that of inhibition. It is relatively easy to see how the activity of a neuron signals information, but it is equally possible that the inactivity of the neuron is just as important. By combining excitation and inhibition, it is possible to devise a neural circuit that will explain almost any behavior.

Once the characteristics of the individual neuron are understood, the focus must be on the connections between neurons. At the present time, knowledge about the synapse is one of the fastest-developing areas in the entire field of physiological psychology. It is becoming clear that the synapse is far from a simple connection between two neurons. The presence of a synapse in a neural pathway inevitably signals a reorganization of the information. The cortex with its acknowledged data-processing ability is a region of synaptic connections. The ability to explain behaviors by using the excitatory and inhibitory activity of the neuron is accomplished through rearranging the synaptic connections.

Chapter 10 provides a brief overview of the effect of drugs on the CNS. This information is included at this point because drugs that affect the nervous system usually do so through the synaptic mechanism. Thus, by examining the effects of drugs, we can learn more about the operation of the synapse.

The material in Part III provides the basic data for understanding the entire nervous system. The structures and functions which are of interest to physiological psychologists are elaborate versions of the characteristics of the neuron and its synaptic connections. The remainder of the text is based on the basic mechanisms discussed here.

SUGGESTED READINGS

The topics introduced in Part III cover a wide range, from the special characterics of subcomponents of the cell to the behavioral consequences of taking various drugs. For this reason, many of the readings cited here are nonoverlapping, that is, none of them is likely to expand on everything discussed in the section. The title usually reflects the area of coverage, although some provide some surprising comprehensive supplementary material.

Black, P. (Ed.) *Drugs and the brain.* Baltimore: The Johns Hopkins Press, 1969.
Eccles, J. C. *Physiology of nerve cells.* Baltimore: The Johns Hopkins Press, 1957.
Eccles, J. C. *The physiology of synapses.* New York: Academic Press, 1964.
Galambos, R. Glial cells. *Neurosciences Research Program Bulletin,* 1964, **2**(6).
Iversen, L. L. & Schmitt, F. O. Synaptic function. *Neurosciences Research Program Bulletin,* 1970, **8**(4).
Jarvik, M. The psychopharmacological revolution. *Psychology Today,* 1967, **1**(1), 51–59.
Julien, R. M. *A primer of drug action.* San Francisco: Freeman, 1975.
Leavitt, F. *Drugs and behavior.* Philadelphia: Saunders, 1974.
Lehninger, A. L. Cell membranes. *Neurosciences Research Program Bulletin,* 1964, **2**(2).
Matheson, D. & Davison, M. (Eds.) *The behavioral effects of drugs.* New York: Holt, Rinehart and Winston, 1972.
Medical Economics Incorporated. *Physicians' desk reference to pharmaceutical specialties and biologicals.* (25th ed.) Oradell, N.J.: Litton Publications, 1971.

Mercer, E. H. *Cells: Their structure and function.* New York: Doubleday, 1962.

Robertson, J. D. The synapse: Morphological and chemical correlates of function. *Neurosciences Research Program Bulletin,* 1965, **3**(4).

Smythies, J. R. The mode of action of psychotomimetic drugs. *Neurosciences Research Program Bulletin,* 1970, **8**(1).

Chapter 6

The Cell

The **cell** is the basic building block of all living matter. Anything that is alive is made up of one or more cells. As life has evolved into multicelled organisms from a one-cell beginning, individual cells have become more specialized to serve specific functions in the organism. Because of this specialization, it is sometimes difficult to recognize the similar features among bone, blood, muscle, gland, and nerve cells. Nonetheless, they all represent specialization of the basic living cell.

"Life" is a word with profound connotations. There is something special about living things that sharply separates them from inanimate objects. Since the cell is the basic unit that reflects this difference, what is unique about a living cell?

CHARACTERISTICS

First, a cell has the ability to harness and transform energy. It can assimilate energy from its environment and convert it for its own activity (Figure 6.1). In plants, the energy source is the sun, and plant cells photosynthesize it to produce chemicals, We of the animal world cannot utilize sunlight directly, but instead consume the chemicals produced by plants for fuel. We then convert the stored chemical energy to a form useful to us. On a cellular level, the final expression of the energy depends on the type of cell.

85

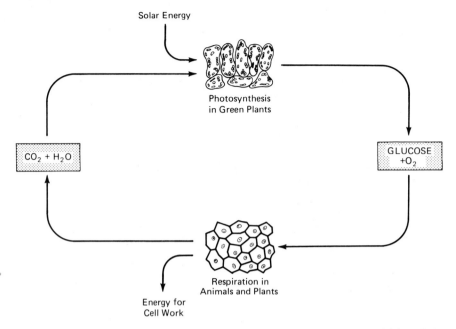

Figure 6.1 Krebs cycle—the basic energy cycle that powers cellular activities. (Lehninger, 1961, p. 65)

A second identifying characteristic of the living cell is its ability to synthesize large molecules. The entire field of organic chemistry is based on the investigation of the unusually complex molecules produced by cells. The early space probes to other planets search for samples of organic compounds on the assumption that only a living cell can produce a complex molecule. Part of the energy conversion from sunlight to chemical reflects the chemical-production capacity in the plant cell. An example of the synthesizing capacity of animal cells is the hormonal output of the endocrine glands.

A third characteristic of the living cell is its ability to reproduce. Cells have the capacity to self-replicate and divide. In a friendly environment, a single cell may reproduce literally thousands of offspring. The remarkably complex adult human organism may be traced to an origin of a single specialized reproductive cell resulting from the union of a sperm cell and an egg cell.

These three special abilities of the living cell can be summarized into a single overriding trait. Cells are able to interact actively with their environment. They utilize raw material available in the environment, they manufacture needed material, and they reproduce to colonize environments that are conducive to the life of the cell. Because environments change, cells must be able to adjust their activity to their environmental conditions. The ability to selectively absorb or reject material from the environment is one such adjustment mechanism.

If we look at each cell in a complex organism, we find an even more complicated example of environmental adjustment. Cells can specialize and colonize together to the mutual advantage of all. Thus, some cells may be especially efficient at movement, but may do so at the sacrifice of manufacturing needed chemicals, while others may have specialized the other way. To oversimplify the process, the glands may produce certain chemicals for the muscles in order for the muscles to be able to move the gland to new supplies of raw materials for chemical production. Most living organisms are a community of tightly interrelated, mutually beneficial, highly specialized cells (Figure 6.2).

This ability of cells to differentiate or specialize their function within the organism increases the adaptive range of the total organism. Much as modern society depends on the specialized skills of experts to solve specific problems to the mutual advantage of all, the community of specialized cells in an organism can successfully cope with a wide variety of environmental challenges. There is a cost in this mode of adaptation, however. The more an individual cell specializes, the more reliant the cell becomes on other cells in the organism to keep it alive. An organism may die because of the failure of a single group of highly differentiated cells.

To the physiological psychologist, an understanding of the specialized individual components of the organism he or she is trying to understand is very helpful. If one accepts the stimulus-response format for describing and

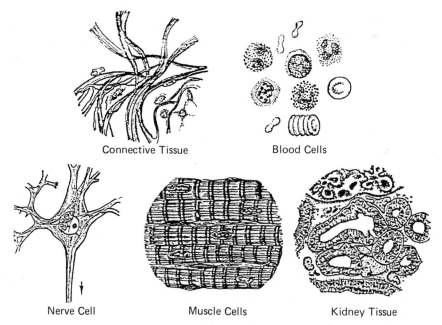

Connective Tissue   Blood Cells

Nerve Cell   Muscle Cells   Kidney Tissue

Figure 6.2 Examples of different types of specialized cells found in the human body. (Guyton, 1974, p. 13)

understanding behavior, there are three major classes of specialized cells that contribute to behavior. Sensory cells detect and encode the stimulus in the environment. Nervous system cells process the sensory information, which is then transmitted to effector cells, which are capable of some kind of response.

Sensory cells have emphasized the ability to harness and transform energy, so that they are extremely sensitive to tiny changes in their environment. We are all aware of the energy requirements of the "five senses," but many other cells have become specialized to monitor other minute environmental fluctuations. Some of these cells are located to sample the external environment of the entire organism. Others are positioned to monitor and adjust the internal state of the organism.

Neurons are cells that have specialized in electrochemical activity. This electrochemical specialization allows the neuron to combine and transmit information within the body. In addition, the glial cells assist the neuronal functions.

To the physiologist, the organism is capable of only two basic response modes, the movement of a muscle and the secretion of a gland. If we are to understand the carefully choreographed response of the millions of cells that make up the psychologist's "response," we ought to understand the variety provided by the specializations among the muscle cells and the gland cells in the body.

Although it is possible to ignore the individual cells that both individually and collectively contribute to the total functioning of the organism, the cell is the basic behavioral unit. Understanding the basic mechanisms in the cell helps us to appreciate the variety and limitations of the myriad of specialized cells in the body.

STRUCTURES

Cells differ so widely that it is misleading to use the term "typical" cell. There are, however, three identifiable shared features that describe a hypothetical typical cell (Figure 6.3). All cells have an outer boundary that circumscribes

Ameba

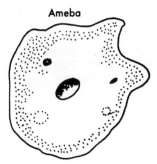

Figure 6.3 A "typical" cell showing some major components. (Leukel, 1972, p. 8)

the "inside" from the "outside" of the cell, a varied collection of materials within the cell, and a large structure found somewhere in the middle of the cell. Each of these features serves specific cellular functions.

The large structure in the middle of the cell is called a nucleus. The cell **nucleus** is the genetic information bank for the functioning of the cell. With recent discoveries concerning the nature of the genetic code, we now know that the chromosomes containing the genes are made up of extraordinarily complex deoxyribonucleic acid (DNA) molecules. Although there are suggestions of extranuclear sources of genetic information, the nucleus is definitely the major source.

The rest of the material inside the cell is called cytoplasm. Generally speaking, **cytoplasm** is an organic "soup" with many substructures floating in it. The cytoplasm is essentially the working material of the cell. Here energy is converted, chemicals are produced, raw material is processed, and waste material is ejected. If we view the cell as analogous to a miniature factory, then the cytoplasm represents all of the production machinery. The nucleus is then the central office from which emerge blueprints and instructions for the operation of the factory.

The building and loading docks of the factory are represented by the **cell membrane,** which is a boundary layer between the cell and its environment. The membrane serves as a protective barrier to the entry of harmful material into the cell. It also must be able to admit substances necessary to the operation of the cell and to release or eject material from the cell. The cell membrane is thus a **semipermeable membrane,** providing a distinct barrier yet allowing free passage depending on the substance. Put another way, the cell membrane provides a sheltered environment for the efficient operation of the internal components.

The three different structures in the cell contribute to different areas of interest in psychology (Figure 6.4). The nucleus provides the genetic information for the activity of the cell. The growing interest in behavioral genetics along with the contemporary emphasis on childhood learning disabilities suggest that the nucleus is an extremely important contributor to behavior. The cytoplasm is the source of movement and/or secretion, the constituents of behavior. It is probable that changes in the cytoplasm reflect the response of the cell to the environment. In other words, learning may be reflected by changes in the cytoplasm. The electrochemical activity of the neurons is almost exclusively due to the special characteristics of the cell membrane.

SUBSTRUCTURES

Knowledge about the mechanisms of cell function is advancing rapidly. The electron microscope and other modern investigative techniques allow us to determine specific details concerning the substructures in the functioning of the cell (Figure 6.5).

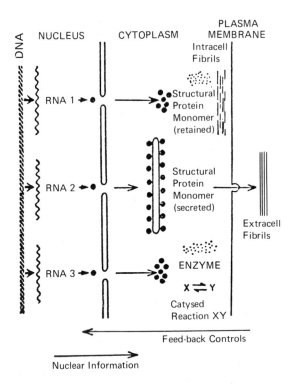

Figure 6.4 The location of various activities within the cell. Genetic information is stored on the DNA molecule in the nucleus. Relevant information is copied by the RNA molecules which carry the information into the cytoplasm where the specified chemical production is accomplished. The chemical products are then either utilized internally by the cell or secreted through the membrane in response to the environment. (Mercer, 1962, p. 44)

In the nucleus of every cell are collections of stringlike structures collectively known as chromatin because of their tendency to absorb stains. The chromatin, or **chromosomes,** are the locus of the genetic information. When a cell undergoes division by the process of mitosis, the number of chromosomes in the nucleus doubles just prior to the cell's division into two parts. Each of the two resulting cells receives a full complement of chromosomes and, consequently, all of the genetic information in the original cell. It is worthwhile to note that all of the genetic information for all of the specialized cells of an entire organism is found in each individual cell. In other words, the genetic information for eye color is in the nucleus of cells for the big toe. Different specialized cells in an organism do not differ in their total chromosomal information, only in the part of the information that is utilized.

Encoding the total genetic information on a molecule presents a problem of mind-boggling proportions. First, the total quantity of information is astounding. Second, the accuracy of the coding mechanism must be nearly absolute, since misinformation usually is fatal to the cell, and sometimes to the entire organism. Similarly, the replication of the information for reproductive offspring allows little room for error. In humans, we know that the genetic information is distributed among 23 pairs of chromosomes (total = 46). The chromosomes differ in size, which undoubtedly reflects differences in total genetic information. The smallest genetic unit is the **gene,** or the code for

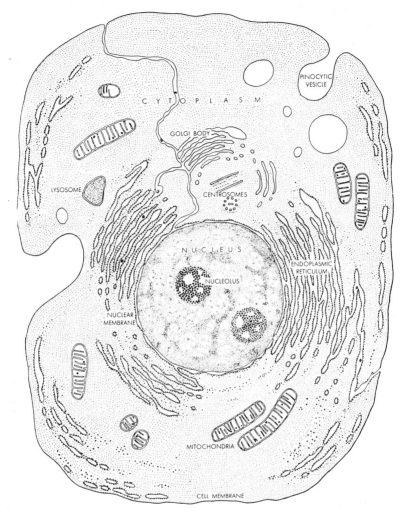

Figure 6.5 An elaborate diagram of the "typical" cell showing component substructures in detail. (Brachet, 1961, p. 55)

a single trait. Genes may uniquely determine a trait or may combine with the information from other genes to establish a trait. In either case, the genes are not located along the chromosomes in any known pattern. Thus, control of closely associated traits is scattered among many different chromosomes.

Since the chromosomes appear in pairs, there are actually two genes for any trait. There is some evidence to suggest that the cell somehow selects the information from one gene or the other, but not both. Thus, the difference between dominant traits—those likely to be expressed—and recessive traits —those not likely to be expressed—is a function of this selective system. We will deal with some of the behavioral ramifications of the genetic mechanism later.

We now know that the chromosomes are actually long double strands of **deoxyribonucleic acid (DNA).** The two strands are connected by complementary bonds, so that each strand is a mirror image of the other (Figure 6.6). The sequence of bonds is the key to the genetic code, and the mirror-image feature of the double strand provides the necessary precise replication mechanism.

DNA is found only in the nucleus of the cell, although the genetic information must be transmitted to all portions of the cell. A closely related chemical called **ribonucleic acid (RNA)** appears to transcribe the relevant portions of the DNA molecule and distribute the information throughout the cell. Thus, RNA is found throughout the cell, while DNA is restricted to the nucleus.

A **nucleolus** is a distinct spherical structure within the nucleus. At the present time, the nucleolus appears to be primarily involved in the manufacture of RNA molecules. RNA represents an interesting substance to the physiological psychologist. Since RNA replicates only selected portions of the

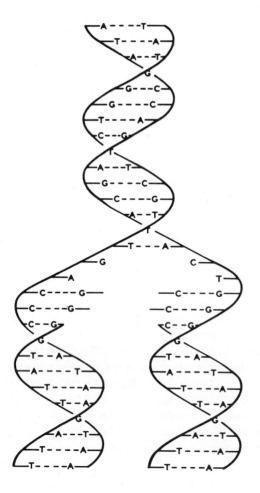

Figure 6.6 A simplified version of the double helix DNA molecule. The complementary pairs of the four-letter "alphabet" allow precise encoding and replication of genetic information. (A) Adenine, (G) guanine, (C) cytosine, and (T) thymine. (Sutton, 1962; via Altman, 1966, p. 28)

genetic information on the DNA molecule, RNA reflects some adjustment to the special demands on the cell. RNA changes have been observed in neurons during the learning process. Thus, it is possible that DNA represents the genetic code, while RNA somehow can encode environmental information.

The cytoplasm, or the production portion of the cell, also has sub-structures that can be identified. Most important are the **mitochondria,** which extract and produce energy for the operation of the cell. The usable energy source for cellular activity is the **adenosine triphosphate (ATP)** molecule, which yields energy when one of the three phosphate groups are detached to form **adenosine diphosphate (ADP).** ATP is essentially a freshly charged storage battery, while ADP is a discharged battery. The major function of the mitochondria is to extract the energy from organic fuels by "burning." The oxidation process yields energy, which is used to reattach a third group to the discharged ADP molecule. In order to accomplish this oxidation process, the mitochondria require a constant supply of fuel and oxygen, and must also be able to get rid of combustion by-products. The ATP is then used as an energy source by other structures in the cytoplasm.

Lysomes are structures in the cytoplasm only slightly smaller than the mitochondria. It appears that the **lysomes** are involved in breaking down large molecules into their component building-block units. To this extent the lysomes represent a digesting organ for the conversion of organic fuels into usable molecules. Some of this material undoubtedly is then further processed by the mitochondria in ATP production. Other material serves as raw material for other production activities of the cell. The lysome represents an encapsulated concentration of material that, if released, will result in the destruction of the cell through digestion. This rather grim prospect suggests another possible function of the lysome: it may be a part of the cell's defense system to destroy unwanted substances which invade the cell.

Scattered throughout the cytoplasm are many tiny structures called ribosomes. **Ribosomes** appear to be the site of protein synthesis. The RNA which copied the information on the DNA in the nucleus provides a "blue-print" for constructing the complex protein molecule. Other prominent structures in the cytoplasm, the **Golgi bodies,** appear to take the manufactured proteins and combine them with carbohydrates to form a number of cellular secretions. From saliva, through mucous, to resilent cartilage and even tooth enamel, the Golgi apparatus appears to produce a variety of important secretions. We have far from exhausted the structures located in the cytoplasm. Others provide the mechanism for movement, for separating the reproducing cells into two segments, and for many other important cellular functions.

The final major component, the cell membrane (Figure 6.7), is a complex structure which totally surrounds the nucleus and cytoplasm. Made up of a double layer of lipid molecules, the cell membrane shows a number of unique qualities. It can selectively admit or block the movement of certain molecules into or out of the cell. Thus, there is often an unequal concentration of chemicals across the membrane. In terms of the cell, the membrane can selectively

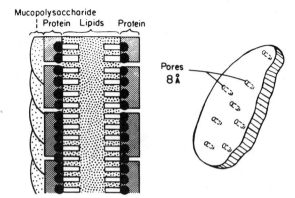

Figure 6.7 A model of the molecular organization of the semipermeable cell membrane. (Guyton, 1974, p. 16)

retain or reject specific compounds from the interior of the cell. This selectivity is so efficient that the membrane can allow the flow of very large molecules without increased leakage of smaller molecules. In addition to this remarkably selective passive semipermeability, the membrane also contains a mechanism for active transport of molecules. This "sodium pump" uses some of the cell's energy supply system to actively move molecules through the membrane opposite to their normal flow. This combination of selective permeability and active transport is very important to understanding the operation of neurons. The membrane is not a uniform structure surrounding the cytoplasm, but has a number of specialized regions over its surface. These differentiated regions, like the endoplasmic reticulum and the vacuoles, appear to be special regions for interactions with the surrounding environment.

We find then that even the generalized cell is a remarkably complicated structure with a number of highly specialized substructures. Most of the cells in the human body have evolved far beyond this generalized prototype and have acquired highly unique and specialized functions. We will concentrate on the features that contribute to the operation of the nervous system, but knowing the basic design of any cell will help in understanding the highly specialized ones.

AUTHOR'S   The cell, in its various specialized forms, is the basic unit
COMMENTS   for all of the functions of the human body. The emphasis in this text is on the cells peculiar to the CNS, but it is worthwhile to know the generalized capacities of any cell.

The cell is made up of many subcomponents, but for general reference, it can be divided into three functional structures. The nucleus provides the genetic information which establishes the "living" characteristics of the cell. Removal of the nucleus disrupts the functioning of the cell, even though the other necessary components are still present. The major volume of the cell is made up of cytoplasm, the "working fluid" in the cell. Cytoplasm is actually composed of many substructures, each accomplishing one facet of the total cellular activity. The membrane of the cell establishes the boundary between the cell and the "outside world." The cell membrane is simultaneously a barrier and the means of commerce between the interior and exterior of the cell. As more is learned about the neuron, the transport of material into and out of the cell becomes an extremely important area of concern to physiological psychologists. Instead of each cell existing as an independent unit, there is considerable chemical exchange between cells as a result of the ability of the membrane to selectively absorb or secrete specific chemical substances.

Of the many substructures found in the cytoplasm, the mitochondria are the most distinctive. The mitochondria are basic energy-conversion units for all cellular work. A concentration of mitochondria in the cell indicates that significant cellular activity is occurring in the immediate vicinity.

The Neuron

A neuron is a single cell specialized to receive, process, and/or transmit information within the body. The neuron accomplishes these functions by allowing ions, or electrically charged molecules, to flow through the membrane, resulting in an electrical event. Although describing a "typical" neuron is almost as misleading as describing a "typical" cell (Figure 7.1), neurons have a number of characteristic qualities. A conventional neuron is bipolar in nature, specialized to gather information at one end and to transmit data at the other. Neuron length ranges from less than 20 microns to over a meter. The transmitting portion of the neuron also ranges from 1 or 2 microns to 50 microns in diameter. The data-gathering structure of the neuron may collect information from a single source or branch out to monitor the activity of literally thousands of cells. As should be expected from their varied size and shape, neurons exhibit a wide latitude in their functional characteristics.

STRUCTURES

The data-collection characteristics of the neuron membrane appear to have become specialized in branching, rootlike extensions called dendrites. The dendrites branch out from the cell body to make contact with a large number—possibly thousands—of other neurons. The information from these cells is collected and combined in the membrane of the dendrites and cell body.

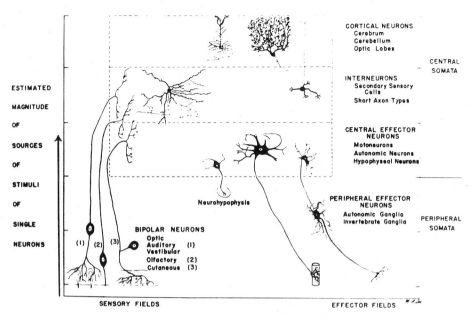

Figure 7.1 Examples of the variety of neurons found in different locations in the nervous system. (Bodian, 1952, p. 3)

The cell body, or **soma,** of a neuron is the portion containing the nucleus of the cell. The cell body region, which usually includes a considerable portion of the cytoplasm, is necessary for the continued life and functioning of the cell. If a neuron is cut, the portion that is severed from the nucleus will die. The intact soma of a mutilated cell will usually survive and in some cases regenerate the missing portion. The soma combines the information from the dendrites in addition to receiving information directly from other neurons.

Since the activity of the neuron may be measured as an electrical event, the collection and combining process is accomplished in a single representative electrical potential. Extending from the cell body is a large, trunk-like extension known as the axon (Figure 7.2). The axon takes the summarized electrical signal and transmits the information along its length. In most cases, the information on the axon is then transferred to the dendrite of another neuron, and the process is repeated along another element of the neural pathway. Because information is gathered by the dendrites and soma and transmitted outward along the axon, a neuron is a polarized system. That is, a neuron conducts in a specific direction.

At the end of the axon, the neuron swells into a bulblike structure known as the **axon bouton.** The bouton is the mechanism for transmitting the neuronal activity to another cell. Two successive cells in a neuronal pathway are not in actual physical contact, but are separated by a narrow gap known as the **synapse.** When electrical activity arrives along the axon, the bouton releases certain chemicals into the synaptic cleft. These chemicals precipitate elec-

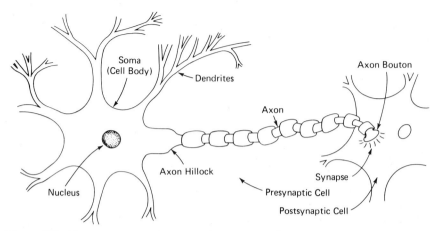

Figure 7.2   The neuron as a component in a nerve pathway.

trical activity in the dendrites of the receiving cell. The synapse is also polarized in that the bouton releases synaptic chemicals and the dendrite (or soma) receives them. For this reason, the **presynaptic cell** refers to the transmitting bouton, while the **postsynaptic cell** refers to the receiving dendrite.

DENDRITIC ACTIVITY

In order to understand the electrical activity of a neuron, we must look at the structure and environment of the neuron. Basically, the neuron is a bag of "salt water soup" immersed in a different "salt water soup." The fact that different salt solutions are found inside and outside the cell signals a corresponding difference in ionic concentration (Figure 7.3). The neuron membrane maintains a higher concentration of negatively charged ions inside the cell and a higher concentration of positively charged ions outside. Thus, the **electrical standing potential** of the inside of the neuron is about 70 millivolts (mV) more negative than the outside. To accomplish this standing potential, the membrane keeps sodium (Na^+) and chlorine (Cl^-) outside and potassium (K^+) and negative organic ions inside. Even though the membrane is selectively permeable to ionic flow, eventually, enough ions leak through the membrane to equalize the electrical state across the membrane. The **"sodium pump"** somehow actively transports sodium ions to the outside of the cell and potassium ions to the inside. There are undoubtedly similar "pumps" for other ions, but we will describe only the sodium-potassium mechanism. The sodium pump consumes cellular energy, so that the standing potential of the neuron cannot be maintained if the flow of blood to the cell is disrupted. The standing potential gradually falls from —70mV toward zero. If blood flow is reestablished, the —70mV potential is slowly reattained be-

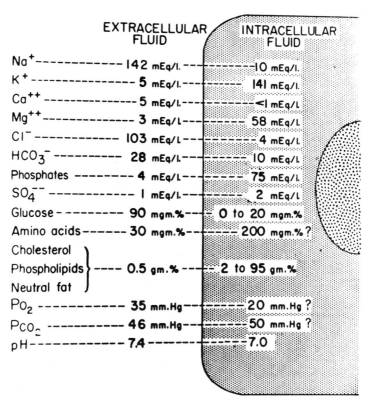

Figure 7.3 Concentrations of various chemicals found in the intracellular and extracellular fluids. (Guyton, 1974, p. 43)

cause the sodium pump is reactivated. Depending upon the neuron being measured, a standing potential may range from —60 to —90mV.

The selective permeability of the membrane to sodium and potassium ions is the key to understanding the electrical activity of the neuron. When the neuron is at rest, there is a high concentration of sodium ions outside the cell and a high concentration of potassium ions inside. Both kinds of ions carry a positive electrical charge, which contributes to the —70mV resting potential. If the membrane allows the sodium ions to flow inward, the electrical potential swings toward the positive. If, on the other hand, the membrane allows the potassium to flow outward, the electrical imbalance is increased.

The electrical activity of the cell is the result of the inward and/or outward flow of these positive ions. Since the flow is the result of the standing ionic imbalance, the resting cell is actually in a "charged" state. Any relaxation of the membrane to ionic flow will result in electrical activity. The direction of ionic flow determines the direction of the electrical change; the amount of ionic flow determines the magnitude of the change.

If our "typical" neuron is undisturbed and supplied with adequate oxygen and nutrition, the —70mV standing (or resting) potential is maintained over the entire membrane surface. Stimulation of a point on the dendrite can cause a localized flow of ions with an accompanying localized disturbance in membrane potential. Since the stimulus is usually caused by the axon or bouton of a preceding neuron across the synapse, this localized distrubance is known as a **postsynaptic potential.** If sodium (Na^+) ions flow into the neuron at the point of stimulation, the ionic imbalance is decreased, the electrical potential across the membrane moves toward zero, and the cell is **depolarized.** Thus, we may monitor the activity of the cell by measuring the electrical changes that accompany ionic flow. Depending on the magnitude of the synaptic stimulation, the postsynaptic potential may be a small or large shift from the standing potential. In either case, the flow of ions through the membrane causes a spreading wave of depolarization from the point of stimulation. The postsynaptic potential thus spreads like the ripples on a pool from the disturbance of a pebble (Figure 7.4) dropped on the surface, with the spreading wave of depolarization becoming weaker with increasing distance.

After the stimulus causing the postsynaptic potential disturbance ceases, the membrane and sodium pump reestablish the equilibrium of the standing potential. There is a period of time when the depolarization of the postsynaptic potential may be detected after the stimulus has ceased. To reiterate the pond-pebble analogy, the water is disturbed where the pebble struck the surface of the water for some time after the initial splash. The fact that the postsynaptic potential is distributed over both time and space is necessary for the data-processing functions of the neuron.

The soma membrane exhibits a similar response to synaptic stimulation, except that the postsynaptic potential is typically **hyperpolarized** instead of depolarized. Hyperpolarization is accomplished by the membrane becoming

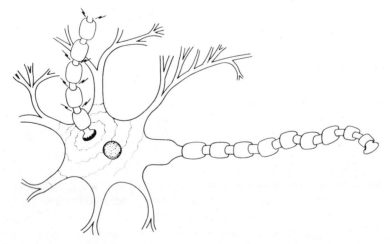

Figure 7.4 Neuronal electrical activity. Activity conducted down the axon of the presynaptic cell is transmitted across the synapse where the postsynaptic potential spreads outward from the point of stimulation along the membrane surface.

more permeable to potassium (K+) ions which flow out of the neuron. Thus, the cell loses positively charged ions, and the electrical potential becomes more negative. The hyperpolarized potential shows the same characteristics as the depolarized potential in the slow geographic spread and the slow temporal return to the normal standing potential (Figure 7.5).

If two closely spaced regions of the cell are depolarized, a point on the membrane between the two sites will reflect the combined effects of the two postsynaptic potentials. Similarly, two areas of hyperpolarization show an additive character between them. If a region is simultaneously subjected to a depolarizing and hyperpolarizing effect, the membrane potential at the intermediate point will reflect the polarity and relative strength of the two. Because the postsynaptic potential spreads across the surface of the membrane, and the disturbance lasts after the stimulus is gone, the potential at any point on an active neuron depends on the history of activity at that and adjacent points on the membrane.

AXONAL ACTIVITY

The point at which the axon joins the cell body is called the **axon hillock.** The axon hillock is also the site of a profound change in the electrical response of the neuron to stimulation. The cell body and dendrites show their slow (1 meter/second, lasting 5 milliseconds or more) depolarization and hyperpolarization. The axon shows a brief (1 millisecond or less), rapidly conducted (up to 100 meters/second) depolarization of approximately 110mV. The axon hillock translates the activity of the soma into the activity of the axon.

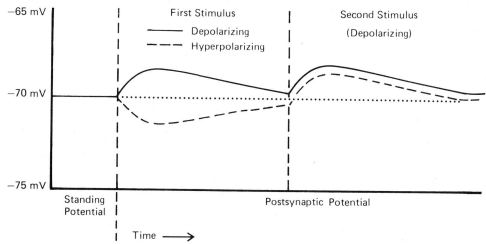

Figure 7.5 The temporal characteristics of a postsynaptic potential. An induced shift in either direction from the −70mV standing potential is followed by a slow return to the normal standing potential.

If we artificially stimulate the axon by changing its −70mV standing potential with a small plus or minus electrical signal, the axon exhibits a response quite similar to that of the postsynaptic potentials of the cell body. That is, there is a brief period of spreading activity with a gradual return to the normal standing potential. Because this localized activity is a prelude to the characteristic transmitting activity of the axon, these potentials on the axon and axon hillock are known as **generator potentials.** If the generator depolarizes the axon more than +15mV (creating a potential of −55mV or less), the axon response is quite different from that of the cell body (Figure 7.6). First, the depolarizing flow of sodium (Na+) ions becomes uncontrolled through the cell membrane. It seems as though there is a total collapse of the axon membrane to sodium ions, and the inrushing flood of positively charged ions drives the potential of the cell from its −55mV trigger potential to +40mV! Within 0.5 milliseconds the membrane suddenly becomes transparent to the outward flow of potassium (K+) ions, returning the potential of the axon to approximately −70mV. The membrane is then reestablished, and the sodium pump begins evacuating the axon of excess sodium and recapturing the lost potassium. Because of its magnitude (110mV) and rapidity (1 millisecond), this event looks on an electrical recording like a spike, which is the origin of the term. Because the **axon spike** is caused by the collapse of the normal standing potential, each spike is total and equal. Thus, the axon fires in an "all-or-none" fashion once the trigger point is reached.

Since the fluid inside and outside the axon is electrically conductive, the

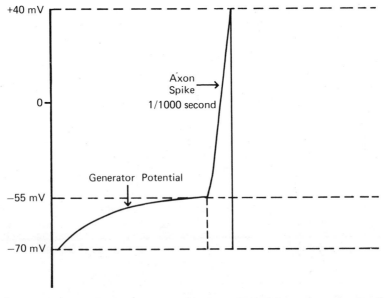

Figure 7.6 The initiation of an axon "spike." A depolarizing generator potential, if strong enough to move the axon to −55mV, precipitates the "all-or-none" nearly instantaneous axon spike.

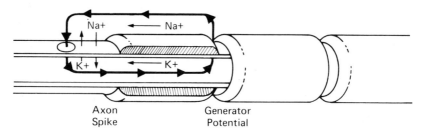

Figure 7.7   The flow of electricity (heavy arrows) and the movement of sodium (Na+) and potassium (K+) ions during an axon spike.

total depolarization at the locus of an axon spike will evacuate adjacent regions of ions. Thus, the initial inward flood of sodium ions will drain sodium ions from the surrounding area. Removal of these positive (Na+) ions from the outside of the cell decreases, or depolarizes, the membrane at this point. If the depolarization reaches the −55mV trigger potential, that portion of the axon membrane undergoes the sequence causing a spike potential. The "collapse" of the axon membrane thus precipitates a collapse in adjacent regions of the membrane, which causes membrane collapse further along the axon. The axon spike is initially triggered in the axon hillock by the electrical activity of the soma. The spike, once triggered, proceeds down the axon in the self-propagating manner described.

As the wave of depolarization advances along the axonal membrane, the membrane sequentially collapses to sodium, then potassium, and then re-establishes itself (Figure 7.7). Within 1 millisecond the membrane recovers and is capable of going through another spike sequence. One might think of the axon as a length of dynamite fuse. As a match is applied to one end, only localized warmth occurs until the flashpoint of the powder in the fuse is reached. If ignition occurs, the burning powder ignites powder further along the fuse until the flame reaches the end. If it were possible to make a fuse that regenerated the burned powder so that more than one touch of a match could be transmitted, the analogy would be complete. Such a regenerating fuse would be able to conduct several advancing waves of flame simultaneously along its length. Similarly, the axon allows multiple spikes to be transmitted along its length. Since the axon spike is "all or none," it is important to note that the speed of conduction is not related to the intensity of the original stimulus. The dynamite fuse burns equally well whether ignited by a match or a blowtorch.

Although the speed of conduction is constant for any given neuron, different neurons conduct at different speeds. The speed of conduction is related to the presence of supplementary, nonneuronal cells associated with the axon. Myelin sheath cells are small cells (Schwann cells), primarily composed of a fatty material, which wind themselves tightly around a segment of the axon. The function of the myelin sheath appears to be to provide an insulation cover for the axon membrane. The myelin sheath cells are spaced along the length of the axon much like beads on a string. The cells are separated by a gap (called **nodes of Ranvier**), leaving the axon membrane periodically uncovered. The axon spike appears to skip from one node to the next along the length of the axon. This **saltatory conduction** is accomplished by the ionic flow through the axon membrane at each node. Axons vary in diameter and in the characteristics of the myelin sheath. Large, heavily myelinated axons can conduct at a rate of up to 100 meters/second, while smaller, unmyelinated fibers may accomplish only 20 meters/second.

The myelin sheath, combined with the interspaced nodes, provides more than electrical insulation for the axon. The energy demands of the axon spike would be extreme if applied to the total area of the axon membrane. The myelin provides an impermeable region over much of the surface of the axon. The nodes apparently allow sufficient area for the necessary interchange through the membrane to allow efficient functioning of the cell.

As is the case with the axons with which they associate, myelin cells vary greatly. The myelin is different in the brain, spinal cord, and periphery. Myelin also differs for different species. Even the "unmyelinated" cells have some insulation. Instead of cells wrapped tightly around each axon, un-myelinated axons have Schwann cells tightly packed in the spaces between the axons (Figure 7.8).

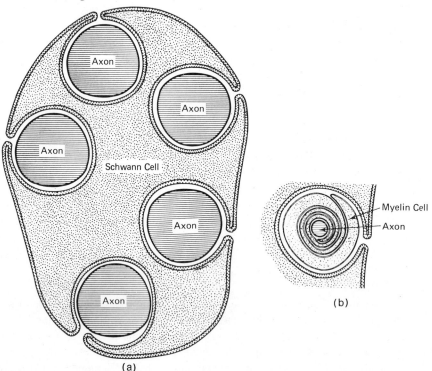

(a)

(b)

Figure 7.8 Unmyelinated (a) and myelinated (b) axons shown in cross section with associated glial cells. (After Gardner, 1963, pp. 74–75)

To back up and look at the entire active neuron, we find that the dendrites are depolarized by synaptic activity which spreads along the membrane surface. If the depolarization spreads to the axon hillock and results in a potential less than −55mV, an axon spike is triggered. Hyperpolarization of the soma counteracts the tendency of the axon hillock to spike; thus, hyperpolarization decreases axon activity. Once a spike is triggered in the axon, it travels the entire length of the axon. The size and speed of each axon spike are constant for any given neuron. The arrival of the electrical axon spike at the axon bouton triggers the release of transmitter chemicals into the synaptic cleft.

AUTHOR'S   The characteristics of the neuron determine the potential
COMMENTS   mechanisms of any nervous system. Although deceptively simple in terms of the range of activity available to them, neurons, when combined into a nervous system, are the mechanisms for all behavior.

The important action of the neuron appears to be the electrical activity observed at the cell membrane. The neuron establishes and maintains an electrical standing potential across the membrane. This potential is the result of selective permeability of the membrane, combined with the active transport accomplished by the "sodium pump." The sodium pump appears to establish the equilibrium electrical potential across the membrane and is a major energy consumer.

Changes away from this equilibrium standing potential seem to be caused by changes induced in the permeability of the membrane to certain electrically charged ions. Such electrical disturbances take two forms: the slow, spreading, fading, gradated activity on the cell body and dendrites; or the precipitious, rapid, total collapse and recovery on the axon. Both electrical events are based on changes in the neuronal standing potential.

The difference in activity is significant in terms of the functions of the two regions of the neuron. The cell body (and dendrites) collect, combine, and summarize the information impinging on the cell. The axon encodes and transmits the summarized message to other neurons. It is these activities that combine to account for all behavior.

Excitation
and Inhibition

The neuron collects information from many sources and integrates this data into a single representative message to be transmitted along the neural pathway. A common procedure to measure the characteristics of the summary message is to record the electrical spike activity of the axon (single-unit record). Thus, we can measure directly the effective activity of a neuron by recording the sequence of spikes generated on the axon. The recording and interpretation of axonal spikes in the intact, active nervous system provide valuable information about the functional characteristics of the neuron.

The "all-or-none" nature of the axon spike presents an interesting coding problem to the neuron. Obviously, it would be advantageous to be able to discriminate between an intense stimulus and a mild one. Single-unit recording of axonal activity shows that a mild stimulus results in the generation of a few axon spikes per second, while an intense stimulus creates a rapid generation of spikes (Figure 8.1). Thus, intensity information is coded on the axon into frequency of spike occurrence. An examination of the characteristics of the soma and axon reveals how this code occurs.

Recall that the postsynaptic potential on the soma and dendrites has two characteristics. First, the localized disturbance in the membrane potential spreads slowly across the surrounding membrane. Second, the membrane requires time to reestablish the −70mV resting potential if a postsynaptic potential occurred. Since the localized disturbance can, and does, spread as far as

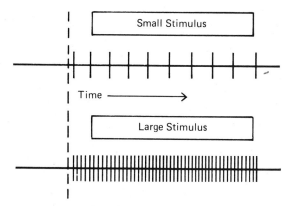

Figure 8.1   The axonal code for intensity. The "all-or-none" axon spikes encode gradated information into frequency (spikes/unit time).

the axon hillock, it constitutes the generator potential that precedes the axon spike. If the disturbance depolarizes the membrane, the axon hillock is moved closer to its —55mV trigger point and a spike is more likely to occur. Thus, a depolarizing potential "excites" the axon. Conversely, a hyperpolarizing potential "inhibits" or makes an axon spike less likely.

SUMMATION

Since we are more interested in the generation of an axon spike, we will examine the **excitatory postsynaptic potential (EPSP)** first. With the possible exception of a few very tiny neurons, a single EPSP is incapable of generating a spike at the axon hillock. A major consideration is that most EPSP's occur in the dendrites of the neuron, which is a considerable distance from the axon hillock. By the time the EPSP has spread to the axon hillock, it is too small to trigger a spike. To depolarize the axon hillock to the necessary —55mV trigger level, the neuron must accumulate a number of depolarizing dendritic events. Individual EPSP's are added together to precipitate a spike. This feature of additivity (also called **summation**) is accomplished by the fact that each excitatory synapse depolarizes the membrane whether it is active or at rest. If the membrane is resting at —70mV, then the depolarization (say +10mV) occurs from that level. If, however, the membrane is already partially depolarized, then the +10mV shift occurs from that point. To follow this simplified example, one synaptic event would depolarize the membrane to —60mV, not enough to trigger a spike. Two such synaptic events occurring simultaneously close to one another would result in a combined depolarization of +20mV, which would trigger a spike. Summation occurs in two different ways, either by two neighboring presynaptic neurons firing at about the same time or by a single presynaptic neuron firing in rapid succession. Although the mechanism is essentially the same, the combination of activity from two different locations is known as **spatial summation,** while the combination produced by the same unit firing in rapid succession is known as **temporal summation.** Both types of summation can combine to integrate simultaneously over time and distance.

The fact that summation appears to be necessary to trigger a spike in the postsynaptic cell provides a potentially useful function for the nervous system. Single-unit recordings of axonal activity indicate that an axon occasionally fires without a known stimulus. The postsynaptic neuron essentially ignores such individual events and responds with a spike only if the message is repeated or confirmed by another cell.

Because the spread of the postsynaptic potential becomes weaker over distance, there is another mechanism of selection operating on the neuron membrane. An EPSP generated relatively near the axon hillock will have a greater chance of generating a spike than an EPSP generated on the distal end of a dendrite. Thus, synaptic junctions differ in their ability to trigger spike activity as a result of location (Figure 8.2). Synapses on the tips of the dendrites may need to combine the depolarization of literally hundreds of events to trigger a spike at the axon hillock. Synaptic functions are also morphologically different, so the possibility exists that some synaptic junctions may be more effective than others in generating a postsynaptic potential. These are undoubtedly only the simpler mechanisms for giving some synapses higher postsynaptic priority.

The synapses that result in an **inhibitory postsynaptic potential (IPSP)** are located on the soma, much closer to the hillock than the dendritic location of EPSP's. It appears that the cell is organized so that the ability to block or inhibit axonal activity is a very important function. The spatial and

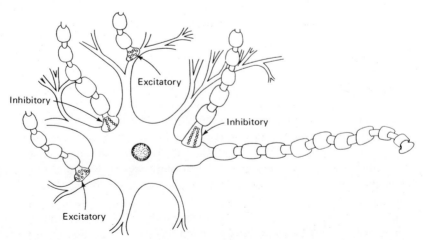

Figure 8.2 Excitatory and inhibitory synapses differ in appearance and location on the postsynaptic neuron.

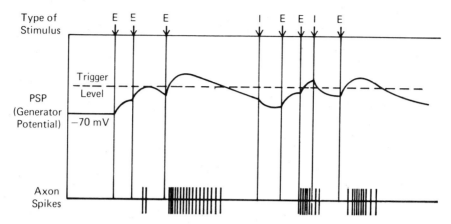

Figure 8.3 A comparison of the postsynaptic potential with axonal spike occurrence. Spike frequency is directly related to membrane depolarization, which is determined by the pattern of stimulation arriving on the cell.

temporal summation properties of the hyperpolarizing IPSP appear to be similar to the depolarizing EPSP. If the axon hillock is hyperpolarized to a potential greater than −70mV, more of an EPSP is needed to trigger a spike.

AXONAL CODING

The axonal equivalent of an IPSP is the reduction or absence of axon spikes. When the soma is hyperpolarized, the axon hillock is shifted electrically further away from the −55mV trigger point. When the IPSP ceases, the axon hillock returns to its more sensitive level (Figure 8.3). Although the mechanism is not completely understood, a neuron that has been inhibited usually responds with a brief burst of axon spikes when the inhibiting stimulus is terminated.

A burst of axonal activity signals one of two possible events: the introduction of an EPSP or the termination of an IPSP. Stated conversely, the sudden cessation of axonal activity may signal the introduction of an IPSP or the termination of an EPSP. If we translate this information in terms of a stimulus, we find that two important dimensions of the stimulus are when it starts and when it stops. We also find that activity of the axon indicates a signal, but so does a "burst of quiet."

If we could picture the electrical behavior of the neuron membrane over the entire cell, it would appear something like this. Waves of depolarization would be generated at active synaptic sites on the dendrites. Each wave would be seen spreading along the membrane surface for 20 to 30 milliseconds until it had faded away. Two or more waves would combine their effects to generate stronger waves, which would last longer and spread further. If the wave action were strong enough by the time it has reached the axon hillock, axon spikes would be seen flashing and skipping down the axon. Simultaneously, we would see another type of wave action on the soma which muffles or absorbs this activity. One might think of IPSP's as "oil on troubled water."

So far, we have been concentrating on the initial occurrence of an axon spike. Since the spike is essentially completed in 1 millisecond, what then happens? If the axon hillock were still depolarized below the —55mV trigger potential, another spike is generated. This sequence will repeat itself until the axon hillock is no longer depolarized below the trigger level. Thus, any EPSP strong enough to keep the hillock depolarized for a length of time will result in a train of spikes being generated in the axon. The greater the depolarization, the longer the spike train and the faster the rate of spike activity.

The axon spike is the result of the sequential collapse of resistance to sodium (Na$^+$) and potassium (K$^+$) ions, which accounts for the rapid change from —55mV to +40mV back to —70mV (Figure 8.4). In addition, the spike is followed by a wave of after-effects which lasts from 80 to 1000 milliseconds. These after-effects appear to be the activity of the sodium pump moving sodium ions (Na$^+$) outside of the cell and potassium (K$^+$) ions inside. Immediately after the axon spike, the membrane is hyperpolarized, and later it swings slightly depolarized before the normal standing potential is reestablished. As we now know, hyperpolarization or depolarization makes the axon spike harder or easier to generate. Thus, duration of these after-potentials creates a change in the receptivity of the cell known as **refractory periods** (Figure 8.5).

During the time of the actual spike occurrence, the axon at that point is not responsive to stimulation of any kind. This **absolute refractory period**

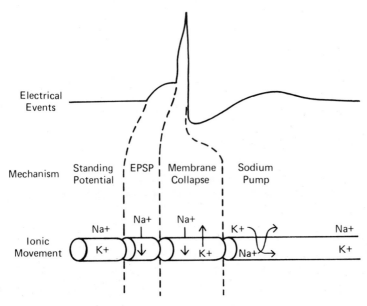

Figure 8.4 A comparison of electrical and chemical events in the active axon. The electrical axon spike directly reflects the movement of electrically charged ions through the axonal membrane.

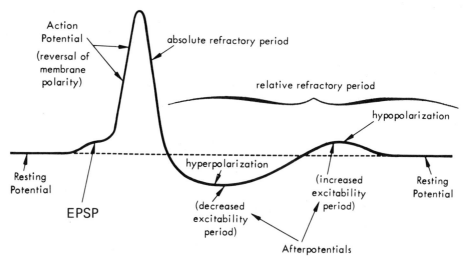

Figure 8.5   The electrical events associated with the axon spike. The afterpotentials directly affect the responsiveness of the cell to a second stimulus. (After Altman, 1966, p. 193)

lasts for the duration of the spike (about 1 millisecond). The **relative refractory period** varies from cell to cell, but always involves an initial period of hyperpolarization followed by depolarization. The sequence of sensitivity surrounding an axon spike is as follows: increased sensitivity (generator potential), total insensitivity (absolute refractory period), relative insensitivity, supernormal sensitivity, and subnormal sensitivity. Thus, the state of depolarization or hyperpolarization of the axon hillock also depends on the recent spike activity of the axon as well as on the activity coming by way of the soma.

The refractory period accomplishes two important functions for the neuron. First, it reduces the membrane surface involved in propagating a spike. Second, it probably preserves the integrity of the spike moving down the axon. Recall that the occurrence of a spike at one node precipitates a spike at the next node on the axon. Since this is basically an electrical event, the mechanism should work in both directions. What keeps the spike at any node from triggering the node that caused it to fire? Apparently, the "sending" node is still hyperpolarized by the refractory activity (and therefore inhibited) during the firing of the second node. By the time the first node has returned to normal sensitivity, the spike has moved beyond the second node. In this way, the refractory period keeps the axon from suffering paroxysms of spikes leaping back and forth between nodes.

The relative refractory period is also involved in the frequency coding characteristics of the axon spikes. Assume that the generator potential barely fires the axon spike. The axon will not be triggered again until it reaches the depolarization stage of its refractory period. A stronger depolarizing stimulus will cause the axon to fire before it is out of its relative inhibitory stage. An extremely strong depolarization will cause the axon hillock to fire as soon as it is out of the absolute refractory period. In this manner, the stronger the stimulus, the faster the generation of the next spike. Since the latter part of the relative refractory period involves a moderate depolarization, the axon hillock is actually supersensitive to signals that follow the preceding spike by the appropriate delay.

OTHER INFLUENCES

So far we have examined only the changes in neuronal activity that result from synaptic activity on the soma and dendrites. Neurons and their interconnecting synapses constitute a delicately balanced system, and there are a number of other factors that might cause a change in neuronal activity.

Although it is not thought of as inhibition in the usual sense, neurons exhibit a type of inhibition to overstimulation. Since the activity of the neuron requires energy expenditure, neurons cannot maintain prolonged periods of high activity. This version of neuronal fatigue provides a self-limiting mechanism in the operation of the cell.

The activity of neurons is also affected by oxygen deficits and surpluses, certain vitamin imbalances, and a number of drugs which change the ionic balance across the membrane. Although not technically part of the normal excitation and inhibition in the nervous system, such disturbances in the normal operation of the cell can result in obvious behavioral changes. A comatose state, drowsiness, restlessness, and irritation are some examples.

The synaptic mechanism includes a number of carefully balanced chemical components which affect the transmission of information between neurons. Any change in this balance can either enhance or decrease information flow in the neural network. The synapses are especially subject to drugs. Chapter 9 outlines some of the possible neuronal sites for the action of a variety of drugs.

Neurons are known to interact outside the synaptic mechanism. The axons bundled together into a common nerve generate electrical fields which are known to affect the sensitivity of neighboring axons. Thus, parallel fibers indirectly affect each other, although not in the usual sense of sharing a common neural pathway. Perhaps this is the mechanism for **irradiation.** If a strong, constant stimulus were presented, the nervous system would undergo a type of recruitment where an increasing number of sensory fibers show a response. The irradiation in the sensory system then causes a corresponding increase in the association and motor areas.

The glial cells surrounding the neurons are also candidates for involvement in excitation and inhibition in the nervous system. Some glial cells show slow, relatively long-lasting electrical changes which could serve as biasing fields to adjust the sensitivity of the neuron. It is possible to electrically "hold" a neuron at a higher than normal or lower than normal standing potential.

This would, of course, change the responsiveness of the cell. Another possibility is some sort of direct chemical interchange between neurons and glial cells. As knowledge progresses, we may find that we cannot think of an individual neuron, but that the true "unit" is some combination of neuronal and glial cells.

NERVE CIRCUITRY

At the present time, however, research is concentrating on neuronal circuitry. We will be primarily concerned with understanding the "wiring diagrams" among the neurons in the CNS. The simple neuronal characteristics described so far allow us to begin some initial sketches for the mechanisms behind known behavioral phenomena.

A simple excitatory circuit of neurons will account for direct stimulus-response type behavior like the spinal reflex. The receptor and responding muscle need to be connected only by a chain of neurons, all "wired together" by excitatory synapses (Figure 8.6).

The spinal reflex involves not only the twitch of a single muscle but also the simultaneous relaxation of the opposing muscle. In order for a person to withdraw a hand from a stimulus, the muscles that extend the hand to the stimulus must be relaxed. A division in the neural circuit could provide an excitatory branch stimulating the withdrawing muscles while simultaneously the other branch inhibits the extending muscles.

The spinal reflex can occasionally be dangerous to the organism. For example, we may need to handle a very hot object in spite of the resulting damage to our hands. An object hot enough to cause burns will activate the "drop it" reflex. An inhibitory synapse near the axon hillock of one of the neurons in the spinal reflex circuit could prevent this "wired-in" behavior. Thus, if we were handling nitroglycerine or Mother's favorite china, we might restrict the damage to our burned hands. Examination of the neural circuitry involved in spinal reflexes shows that there are inhibitory neurons leading from the cortex which lead to the soma of cells in the circuit (Figure 8.7).

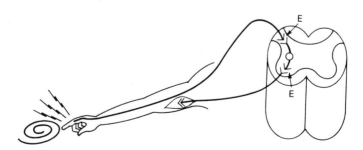

Figure 8.6 A simple reflex. The pain receptors in the finger are directly connected to the withdrawal muscles by means of two excitatory synapses in the spinal cord.

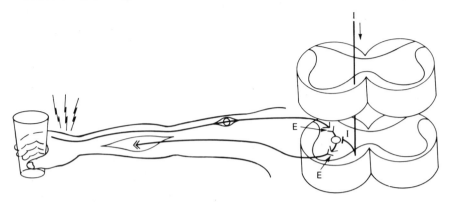

Figure 8.7 An inhibited reflex. Inhibitory information from the brain blocks the transmission of information along the reflexive pathway.

   The fact that it is possible to override reflexive behavior by inhibiting its expression illustrates once again the importance of inhibition in the functioning of the nervous system. The primitive areas of the brain stem have many centers that control specific features of behavior. Higher (and less primitive) centers control more complicated behaviors partially by coordinating and orchestrating the timing of the lower behavioral components. We usually consider "thinking" to be the generation of appropriate behavior, but it might also be described as the ability to inhibit inappropriate behavior. The mark of the "civilized man" is the ability to avoid "acting without thinking" or "losing one's head" in a crisis.

   If we look at connections between nuerons, we find another indicator of the importance of inhibition in the system. Frequently a long axon does not synapse directly onto a neuron, but instead transmits to a tiny neuron that connects to the target neuron (Figure 8.8). These tiny interneurons serve

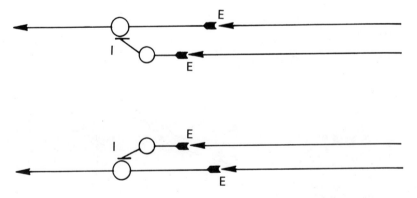

Figure 8.8 Two neuronal pathways with an inhibitory component. Frequently the inhibitory cells appear as small "special" cells which convert excitatory information to inhibitory.

two functions. First, such an interneuron is almost always inhibitory on the postsynaptic membrane. Second, such interneurons usually have synaptic branches which intercommunicate several other neural circuits.

So far we have an organism capable of a number of simple, prewired reflex-type behaviors, but we are rather hard pressed to account for more long-term adaptive behaviors like "learning." Neuronal activity does not provide much time for learning to occur. The axon spike lasts only 1 millisecond. Even the "slow" potential changes of the postsynaptic potential last for about 50 milliseconds. The simplest reinforcement theories require a scale of several seconds. How can we store activity for the necessary length of time? A clever answer to this problem is provided in the reverberatory circuit. A **reverberatory circuit** is a pathway of neurons that forms a closed loop (Figure 8.9). That is, the activity is passed from one neuron to the next in a circle. Activity can be maintained on such a reverberatory circuit indefinitely, or until an inhibitory signal stops it. Reverberatory circuits keep the activity in the system long enough for learning mechanisms to operate. "Learning" probably represents some more permanent changes in the neuronal circuit.

AUTHOR'S COMMENTS   The waves of electrical activity spreading across the membrane of the soma and dendrites are added together wherever they coincide. This additivity occurs over both space and time. The capacity to use spatial and/or temporal summation to form a single representative message at the axon hillock is the information-collection portion of the neuron.

If the membrane were depolarized sufficiently at the axon hillock, an axon spike would be triggered which travels the length of the axon. If the membrane were still sufficiently depolarized after the first spike occurrence, a

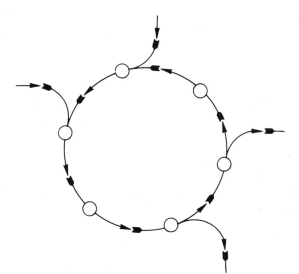

Figure 8.9   A schematic diagram of a hypothetical reverberatory circuit. This mechanism allows activity to be "recycled" for periods of time beyond the capacity of the individual neuron.

train of spikes would be generated until the membrane moves back past the trigger level. Thus, spike activity reflects the magnitude of the generator potential.

If the electrical activity is in the hyperpolarizing direction, the axon is less likely to trigger a spike. The inhibition, or blocking, of neuronal activity is probably as important to the overall functioning of the nervous system as the excitatory process.

Chapter 9

The Synapse

The "point of contact" between the axon bouton and the soma or dendrite of the succeeding neuron is actually a gap. This gap, known as the synapse, or **synaptic cleft,** is the area of communication between two neurons. The synaptic mechanism exhibits a number of interesting characteristics. First, the synapse is polarized so that activity is conducted only from the pre-synaptic membrane of the axon bouton to the postsynaptic membrane of the soma or dendrite. Second, the synaptic mechanism results in a delay of approximately 50 milliseconds, which can be used to estimate the number of synapses between two points in a neural pathway. A third characteristic is that the postsynaptic membrane cannot be electrically stimulated. The synapse seems to be an electrical insulator, not a conductor. The fourth characteristic is that transmission across the synapse can be radically modified by introducing a wide variety of chemicals into the synaptic region.

The above combination of characteristics argues against electrical transmission across the gap between the neurons. It appears that electrical interaction is not the primary mode of neural communication. At the same time, electrical communication cannot be totally dismissed. The electrical activity of neighboring cells can affect the characteristics of a neuron. We have already discussed axons recruiting other axons in the same nerve. In addition, we can subtly change the standing potential of a neuron by changing the electrical field surrounding it. An electroencephalogram (EEG) is a measurement of electrical fields created by activity in the brain, which means that individual neurons are exposed to electrical field interaction of this type. In addition, the **ephapse,** or **electrical synapse,** has been observed in primitive nervous systems, so it is difficult categorically to rule out its existence in more complex nervous systems.

SYNAPTIC MECHANISM

In order to understand the synaptic mechanism, we should create a new "neural unit" (Figure 9.1). The synapse involves a close interrelation between the axon bouton of the "sending cell," the chemicals found in the region of the synaptic gap, and the membrane of the "receiving cell." Because of the polarity of the synapse, the term **presynaptic membrane** indicates the membrane of the sending cell and **postsynaptic membrane** that of the receiving cell.

It is well established that the transmitting agent in the synapse is a chemical (Figure 9.2). Electron microscope pictures of the axon bouton show a number of tiny bubbles or packets of transmitter chemicals clustered near the presynaptic membrane. The arrival of an axon spike at the terminal bouton triggers the release of a specific amount of the transmitter chemical. The transmitter is ejected into the synaptic gap and drifts across to the postsynaptic membrane where it is absorbed. The absorption of the chemical trig-

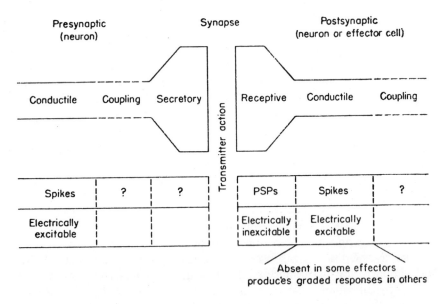

Figure 9.1   The synapse considered as a unit between the presynaptic and postsynaptic neurons. Axonal spikes, synaptic chemical activity, and postsynaptic potentials all must encode and transmit information along neuronal pathways. (Grundfest, 1967, p. 355)

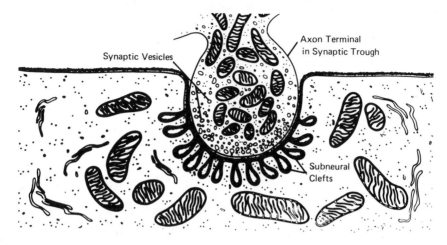

Figure 9.2   A motor endplate. The synapse between the motor nerve and a muscle cell. (After R. Couteau. From Bloom & Fawcett, 1968)

gers a change in the ionic balance across the membrane, which is observed as the electrical postsynaptic potential.

The packets, or **synaptic vesicles,** in the axon bouton appear to be precisely measured amounts of freshly produced transmitter chemicals. There is some evidence that the bouton is the final stage of a long assembly line beginning with the raw material in the soma and extending the length of the axon to final packaging in the bouton. Packaging the transmitter chemical into packets accomplishes two purposes. It "premeasures" the amount of transmitter released, and the membrane of the packet also protects the transmitter molecules from destruction by other chemicals found in the cytoplasm of the bouton.

The synaptic vesicles are produced in the interior of the bouton and are transported to the presynaptic membrane (Figure 9.3). The arrival of the axon spike somehow "breaks" the two adjacent membranes, so that the contents of the vesicles are ejected into the synaptic gap. Evidence suggests that there is a "one spike, one vesicle" correspondence in this release mechanism.

The postsynaptic membrane appears to have special receptor sites which respond to the transmitter chemical. The arrival of the chemical appears to change the permeability of the postsynaptic membrane to either sodium or chlorine ions. Thus, the transmitter creates a postsynaptic potential that either depolarizes or hyperpolarizes the membrane, causing an EPSP or an IPSP. The postsynaptic potential is detectable 0.8 milliseconds after release of the transmitter chemical. The 50-millisecond synaptic delay is due to the time it takes for the generator potential to reach the trigger voltage in the axon hillock.

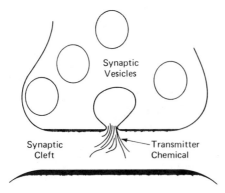

Figure 9.3 Synaptic activity. A packet of transmitter chemical (synaptic vesicle) is secreted into the synaptic cleft.

Whether a postsynaptic neuron is excited or inhibited by synaptic activity seems to be related to the characteristics of the receptor sites in the postsynaptic membrane. The same transmitter chemical may produce an IPSP or EPSP in the postsynaptic cell. In general, synapses on the dendrites of a neuron are excitatory, while synapses on the cell body, or soma, are inhibitory (Figure 9.4). The electron microscope suggests that there may be two distinct categories of synaptic structures corresponding to this important functional difference.

TRANSMITTER CHEMICALS

Although the synaptic mechanism appears to be standard, different neuronal circuits utilize different chemicals. Such complex names as acetylcholine **(ACh),** norepinephrine **(NE),** epinephrine **(E),** 3,4 dihydroxyphenylalanine

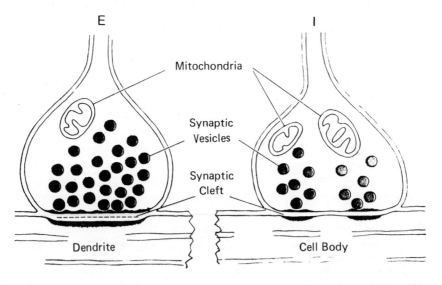

Figure 9.4 Diagram of excitatory and inhibitory synapses. (Eccles, 1965, p. 58)

(dopa), 3,4 dihydroxyphenylethylamine **(dopamine),** serotonin (5-hydroxy-tryptamine, **5-HT**), and gamma amino butyric acid **(GABA)** are among the known transmitter chemicals, and there are undoubtedly others yet to be discovered.

The profusion of known transmitter chemicals makes it difficult to sort out their functions in ways other than simply learning their names. Most of these chemicals are also produced and released into the bloodstream by non-neuronal cells. E and NE, for example, are produced in large quantities by the adrenal glands and released as a part of the sympathetic nervous system activity. Obviously, flooding a neural pathway with free "transmitter" would alter the activity of that system!

The fact that there are different neuronal circuits in the CNS that operate by means of different transmitter chemicals provides two important insights to the functioning of the total system. First, two different neuronal systems may be closely interwoven with a minimum of "cross talk." Second, the administration of drugs may markedly affect the chemical balance of certain systems, with little or no effect on others.

Cholinergic fibers (those activated by ACh) are primarily associated with fast-conducting motor fibers involved with muscular control. Cholinergic fibers are also found throughout the CNS and parasympathetic nervous system (Table 9.1). Adrenergic fibers (NE, E, dopa, dopamine) are associated with the sympathetic nervous system. GABA may be involved with inhibitory activity in the CNS. 5-HT is known to affect the mood of the individual.

The electron microscope reveals that some synapses have a rather elaborate molecular structure associated with the synaptic space. The surface of the presynaptic membrane in some cases is organized into a geometrical matrix which may serve as both an organizer and guide for the release of synaptic vesicles. In addition, there is some evidence for some structural development occurring in the synaptic cleft itself. Any structures that bind the presynaptic membrane to the postsynaptic membrane obviously can improve the efficiency of transmission across the synapse.

DRUG EXPERIMENTS

Most of the drugs that affect the nervous system interfere in some way with the synaptic transmission mechanisms. The cholinergic synaptic mechanism was the first identified and the most thoroughly studied, which explains why it is used as the model for the other systems. Two specific drugs that interact with the cholinergic mechanism provide additional insight into the mechanism.

Curare is a poison South American natives place on the tips of their blowgun darts. The action of curare is to block the postsynaptic receptor sites for the muscles. The efferent nerves continue to transmit and release ACh toward the muscles, but the curare plugs the receptor sites so that there is no

TABLE 9.1   Usual Responses of Organs to Autonomic Impulses (Gardner, 1975, p. 345)

Organ	*Cholinergic*	*Adrenergic*
Eye	Stimulates ciliary muscle and sphincter pupillae—pupillary constriction to light and during accommodation	Pupillary dilation—stimulates dilator pupillae and possibly radial fibers of ciliary muscle
Lung and trachea	Stimulates secretory cells and smooth muscle—serous and mucous secretions, narrowing of bronchioles	Inhibits smooth muscle—relaxation of bronchioles
Lacrimal, nasal, palatine, and salivary glands	Stimulates secretory cells—serous (watery) secretions	Either no important effect, or else a thick, mucous secretion
Gastrointestinal system	Stimulates secretory cells and smooth muscle—digestive secretions, peristalsis, evacuation. Inhibits sphincters	Inhibits peristalsis—stimulates sphincters
Liver and pancreas	Stimulates pancreatic cells, including beta islet cells	Probably no important effect on liver; stimulates alpha cells of pancreatic islets
Suprarenal medulla	Secretion of epinephrine and norepinephrine	
Urinary bladder	Stimulates smooth muscle (detrusor)—emptying of bladder	Questionable effect on emptying. May activate internal sphincter during ejaculation
Uterus Genitalia	Uncertain and variable Erection	Uncertain and variable Ejaculation
Sweat glands	Secretion	No significant effect except in palms
Arrectores pilorum	No effect	Erection of hair—stimulation of smooth muscle

Heart
  S-A node
  Atria
  A-V node
  Ventricles
	
	Decrease in heart rate
	Decrease in contractility
	Decrease in conduction
	——
		
		Increase in heart rate
		Increase in contractility
		Increase in conduction
		Increase in contractility

Blood vessels
  Coronary
 	
  Skin
  Muscle
 	
  Viscera
	
	?
	
	?
	?
	
	?
		
		Constriction (α receptor); dilatation (β receptor)
		Constriction
		Constriction (α receptor); dilatation (β receptor)
		Constriction; dilatation in liver

muscular postsynaptic response. The poisoned animal actually dies from a muscular inability to respond to the nervous system signals. The usual cause of death is a consequent inability to breathe. Fortunately for the native hunters, curare is destroyed by the digestion process, so meat from the poisoned animal is safe to eat. Modern surgery occasionally uses a muscle relaxant derived from curare, in conjunction with an artificial breathing apparatus, of course.

Strychnine, another neurotoxic poison, acts on another part of the synaptic mechanism. Although there appears to be a "one spike, one packet" rule for transmitter release, each vesicle contains many hundreds of molecules. Some of these molecules do not locate a receptor site and are consequently found floating in the synaptic space. Such molecules represent a real danger to the synaptic transmission system, since an increasing concentration of transmitter means that the postsynaptic cell will approach a state of random chemical stimulation if these molecules drift into receptor sites. To prevent this possibility, a chemical called **cholinesterase** neutralizes the ACh molecules in the synaptic gap so that a dangerous concentration does not occur. Strychnine reduces the concentration of cholinesterase.

A strychnine-poisoned organism consequently builds up a dangerous concentration of ACh in the synaptic gap. Each additional nerve spike floods the synapse with more transmitter. Eventually, the postsynaptic cell is literally flooded with stimulation, and the neuron response begins to be random instead of a response to real signals. This "runaway response" releases even more ACh further down the neural pathway. Eventually, the entire nervous system is so saturated with ACh that each of the cells is random firing. The behavioral indication of this neural "runaway" is seen as a convulsion. One of the systems affected by a full convulsion is again the breathing muscles.

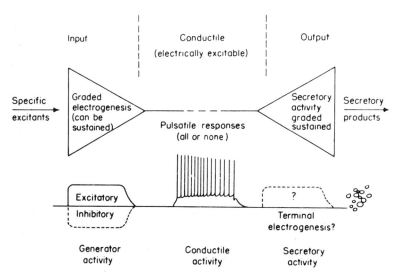

Figure 9.5 A stylized neuron summarizing the encoding and transmission mechanisms. (Grundfest, 1967, p. 354)

124   Basic Neurophysiology

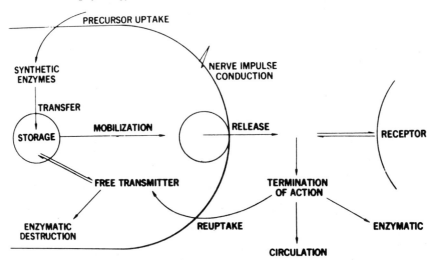

Figure 9.6 A summary of the chemical events that occur at the synapse. (Kopin, 1970, p. 27)

The "telephone wires" of the nervous system, namely the axons, transmit in the form of the "all-or-none" spikes. A rapid train of spikes results in a heavy concentration of transmitter in the synaptic gap, with a prolonged and pronounced postsynaptic potential (Figure 9.5). The train of neural pulses is thus converted into intensity information for processing. The difference between this concentration of transmitter and that caused by curare is that only a few circuits are involved.

The action of curare and strychnine illustrate only two chemicals that alter the nature of the cholinergic synapse. Any chemical that affects the production, packaging, release, movement, or absorption of the transmitter chemical will alter the transmission across the synapse (Figure 9.6). The synaptic region contains many chemicals that adjust the concentration of transmitter chemical before, during, or after it has crossed the synaptic gap. As with strychnine, the effect on the synapse was actually due to the change caused in one of these supplementary chemicals. Thus, there are many different ways the synapse can be altered.

The complexity of the synaptic mechanism probably reflects the importance of neural connections in understanding the functioning of nervous systems. Although the individual neuron is the basic building block in any nervous system, the system becomes interesting when we begin to discover how the building blocks are connected.

AUTHOR'S COMMENTS   The synaptic mechanism is a complicated one. Transmitter chemicals are manufactured, packaged, released, neutralized, absorbed, and recycled. To assist in this process, several other chemicals are found in the presynaptic bouton, the synaptic space, and the postsynaptic cytoplasm. Chemicals are being circulated in both directions in the synaptic region and are also being transported in the interior of the neuron. The electrical information on the neuron is converted to a chemical medium, which is then reconverted into an electrical event on the postsynaptic membrane. The synapses in the nervous pathway are detectable in that they slow down the speed of transmission on the pathway.

Chemical synapses have certain advantages. A synapse is polarized so that information is transmitted in one direction. Different transmitter chemicals mean that different pathways can be intermixed without "cross talk." The gap between the neurons represents a point of external access to the neural pathways. The release of adrenalin in states of high emotion could have a direct effect on the transmission along adrenergic pathways.

Although the synapse may reduce the speed of information conduction along the pathway, the presence of a synapse signals data are being processed. Inevitably, the neural information is reorganized as a part of the synaptic process. The synapse is the site most frequently implicated in the mechanisms that might account for "learning."

Chapter

10

Drug Effects

A wide variety of drugs have behavioral consequences. From pain suppression through mood changing to mind alerting, the magic of neuropharmacology has a considerable impact on our lives. All indications point to the conclusion that what we have seen is only the initial phase of a growing capacity to alter behavior chemically. Records of mental hospitals show an impressive reversal in the number of hospitalized patients since the introduction of the first psychopharmaceutical compounds (Figure 10.1). For times of stress (or for some individuals, any time), we can take a pill to go to sleep, wake up, keep alert, calm down, and so on. Then there is, of course, the growing number of "mind-expanding" drugs which may provide an introduction to psychological spheres not available by any other means.

Most of the drugs that affect the nervous system do so through some impact on the synaptic mechanism (Table 10.1). Since we are in the process of learning about the synaptic mechanism itself, new knowledge about drug effects is inevitable. Conversely, the discovery of new drugs often leads to new insights about the synapse. Most drugs are used because of their known effects on the individual long before the actual mechanism of that action is understood. As we compare the chemical similarities and differences with the psychological effects of the various drugs, we can extract some common mechanisms. By seeing how certain types of chemicals affect behavior, we gain knowledge about the chemical processes involved in the operation of the nervous system.

The multiplicity of different transmitter chemicals means that there are many different synaptic circuits, each with its own unique responses to drugs (Figure 10.2). Two drugs may have similar effects in one system but sharply different ones in another system. Since all of these are interconnected in the nervous system, it is difficult to extract the components leading to the total effect of the drug.

Usually, however, drugs that exert a similar psychological effect seem to involve the same general physiological mechanisms. The following discussion samples some common categories for psychological drugs along with a brief summary of their known locus of action in the nervous system.

CNS DEPRESSANTS

The delicate chemical balance found in the synapse probably maintains an optimal state for transmitting information. Most of the psychologically significant drugs disrupt this balance, resulting in a less efficient operation of the synaptic mechanism. Many different compounds seem to share the general effect of progressively disabling the normal functioning of the CNS. Although individual drugs within this category may differ in terms of route of administration (Table 10.2), potency, or length of action time, the general action and resulting effects may be best described as a depression of the normal functioning of the CNS.

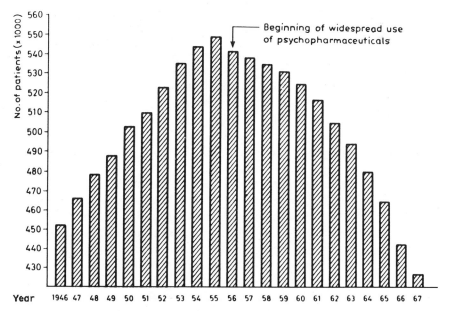

Figure 10.1 Number of resident patients in state and local government mental hospitals in the United States, 1946–1967, based on United States Public Health Service figures. (Efron, 1968, p. 2)

The entire CNS is not equally subject to depressing effects of these drugs. With increasing drug dosage, a progressive loss of functioning may be observed. The sequence of behavioral effects reflects a hierarchical organization of behavioral control. The sequence may be best approximated by comparison with a behavioral phylogenetic scale. "Higher" patterns of behavior disappear with relatively small doses of the drug, while more "primitive" functions are more resistant. Eventually, a lethal dose of any of the CNS depressants is possible if the dosage is sufficient to disrupt the life-sustaining activities of the CNS. Death is usually caused by the debilitation of the breathing centers in the medulla.

In addition to the behavioral effects, corresponding impact on EEG patterns are observed. With the administration of a CNS depressant, the EEG pattern moves from a typical waking pattern to the slower-wave activity typical of a sleep state. The alleviation of pain, distress, and numbness of the extremeties are other indicators of the loss of neural efficiency.

The CNS depressants are often considered to be quite distinct because of their different behavioral applications. Less potent drugs are commonly employed for their milder effects, while more potent compounds may have only medical applications. For the most part, however, the CNS depressants all follow the same general pattern. This fact is particularly important in the case of individuals who may inadvertently consume two different drugs while unaware of their common additive effect. An overdose of a CNS depressant can be accomplished through the cumulative debilitation of "safe" levels of two or more CNS depressants.

Among the drugs known for their milder CNS effects are the sedatives, tranquilizers, and alcohol. These compounds are used primarily for their relaxing and disinhibiting psychological effects. Alcohol (technically **ethyl alcohol**) is so widely used for its social and individual effects that it is not usually classified as a drug. Another alcohol, **chloral hydrate,** is utilized as a "truth serum" because it disinhibits the tendency to respond to direct questions. A variety of sedatives and relaxants are used intermittently and/or constantly by individuals whose tolerance for stress is being exceeded. Sleeping pills are an obvious example of low-level CNS depressant compounds.

At the present time, tranquilizers are the most prescribed class of prescription drugs. Although the tranquilizers technically fall under the CNS depressant category, their widespread usage and knowledge of their unique impact on the CNS warrants their more extensive treatment in a subsequent section.

Drugs that disable the CNS to the point of sleep are known as **hypnotics,** while those that result in a sleep state so deep as to alleviate normal responsiveness to pain are **anesthetics.** The **neurotoxic poisons** obviously go beyond anesthesia. The difference between a general anesthetic, which acts on the entire nervous system, and a local anesthetic, which incapacitates only a specific region, is primarily in the mode and locus of administration.

TABLE 10.1   Actions of Drugs on Synaptic and Neuroeffector Transmission (Koelle, 1968, pp. 643–644)

Mechanism of Action	System	Drugs	Effect
1. Interference with synthesis of transmitter	Cholinergic Adrenergic	Hemicholinium α-Methyl-p-tyrosine	Depletion of ACh Depletion of norepinephrine
2. Metabolic transformation by same pathway as precursor of transmitter	Adrenergic	α-Methyldopa (Aldomet)	Displacement of norepinephrine by false transmitter (α-methylnorepinephrine)
3. Blockade of transport system of axonal membrane	Adrenergic	Imipramine, amitriptyline	Accumulation of norepinephrine at extracellular sites
4. Blockade of transport system of storage granule membrane	Adrenergic	Reserpine	Destruction of norepinephrine by mitochondrial MAO, and depletion from adrenergic terminals
5. Displacement of transmitter from axonal terminal	Cholinergic Adrenergic (rapid, brief) Adrenergic (slow, prolonged)	Carbachol Ephedrine, tyramine Guanethidine	Cholinomimetic Sympathomimetic Depletion of norepinephrine from adrenergic terminal
6. Prevention of release of transmitter	Cholinergic Adrenergic	Botulinus toxin Bretylium	Anticholinergic Antiadrenergic

7. Mimicry of transmitter at postsynaptic receptor	Cholinergic
	  Muscarinic
	  Nicotinic
	Adrenergic
	  Alpha
	  Beta
		
		Methacholine
		Nicotine
		
		Phenylephrine
		Isoproterenol
			
			Cholinomimetic
			Cholinomimetic
			
			Sympathomimetic
			Sympathomimetic

8. Blockade of endogenous transmitter at postsynaptic receptor	Cholinergic
	  Muscarinic
	  Nicotinic
	
	Adrenergic
	  Alpha
	  Beta
		
		Atropine
		d-Tubocurarine, hexamethonium
		
		Phenoxybenzamine
		Propranolol
			
			Cholinergic blockade
			Cholinergic blockade
			
			α-Adrenergic blockade
			β-Adrenergic blockade

9. Inhibition of enzymatic breakdown of transmitter	Cholinergic Adrenergic	Anticholinesterase agents (physostigmine, disopropylphosphorofluoridate [DFP]) MAO inhibitors (pargyline, nialamide, tranylcypromine)	Cholinomimetic Accumulation of norepinephrine at certain sites; potentiation of tyramine

THE CLINICAL APPLICATION

PSYCHOTROPIC DRUGS AND THEIR EFFECTS

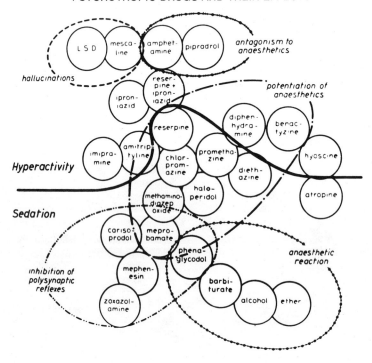

AUTONOMIC EFFECTS

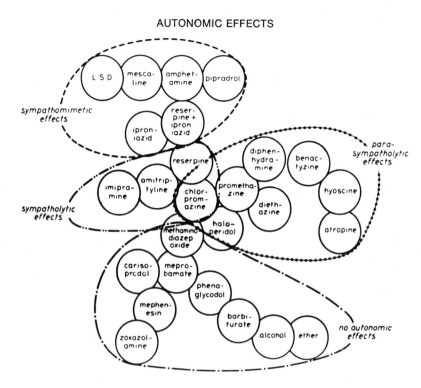

Figure 10.2   A diagram of some drugs arranged according to their overlapping effects and/or usage. (Longo, 1972, pp. 4–5)

The **barbiturates,** all of which share a common chemical nucleus but differ in attached compounds, occupy the entire range of CNS depressant effects. One of the unfortunate by-products of the barbiturates is that prolonged usage results in a physical dependence. The addiction process is apparently the result of compensatory adaptation by the nervous system to function in spite of the barbiturate chemical. This results in a decreasing effectiveness of a given dosage, and the possibility of a dangerous imbalance in the synaptic chemicals when the barbiturates are discontinued. A real danger from the sudden withdrawal of barbiturates is death from convulsions created by the overcompensation of the nervous system. Even the "non-barbiturate" sedatives should be used with caution, because they are still CNS depressants of considerable potency. The nonbarbiturate label is largely a chemical technicality in that the central chemical ring is different. The difference is so slight, however, that it is questionable whether its sedative action is any different in terms of the action on the nervous system.

The final major class of CNS depressants includes opium and the **opiate derivatives.** Like the barbiturates, the opiates share a chemical similarity, with

TABLE 10.2   Routes of Drug Administration (Leavitt, 1974, pp. 24–25)

Route	Advantages	Disadvantages
Oral	Convenience	May cause emesis; some drugs are destroyed by digestive enzymes; food in stomach retards absorption, but some drugs are irritating when taken on empty stomach; some drugs are metabolized by the liver before they pass into the systemic circulation; patient must be awake and cooperative
Injection	Often the only route which provides complete absorption, it is generally more rapid and predictable, thus dose can be selected with greater accuracy	Pain; difficulty of self-administration; need for aseptic technique to minimize danger of infection; greater likelihood of systemic reaction
a. Intravenous	Greatest precision in obtaining particular blood concentration; effects are immediate; only route for certain irritating substances; dose does not have to be given all at once, but can be adjusted to response of patient	Unfavorable reactions are more likely to occur than with other routes; more skill is required; once a drug is injected, there is no retreat (with other routes, absorption can be slowed or stopped); if injection is too rapid, patient may suffer "speed shock"
b. Intramuscular	Some irritating substances can be given by this route; muscle forms a depot for some drugs such as penicillin, so permits continuous action over many days	
c. Subcutaneous (under the skin)	Absorption rate is slow and even, so sustained effects can be achieved; some hormones can be implanted under the skin, and will slowly be absorbed over months	Drugs must be nonirritating to tissues
d. Intraperitoneal (into the peritoneal cavity)	Very convenient for small laboratory animals	Very painful to humans
e. Intrathecal (into the spinal subarachnoid space)	Rapid local effects on central nervous system; by-passes blood-brain barrier	Possibility of damage to spinal nerves

TABLE 10.2   (Continued)

Route	Advantages	Disadvantages
Inhalation	Inhaled gases and volatile drugs gain rapid access to the circulation; used when there is lung disease and drug is meant to act on lungs	Difficult to regulate dose; may produce irritation of pulmonary endothelium
Implanted cannulae	Important in behavioral research; hollow needles are permanently implanted in specific parts of the brain; drugs are administered in liquid or crystalline form, producing very localized effects. See Grossman for description.	

slight differences which account for differences in their specific effects. The opiates are also likely to result in a physical dependency with prolonged usage.

TRANQUILIZING DRUGS

The hallucinogenic drugs are usually cited as prime examples of our "drug culture." If one looks at the data, the tranquilizers deserve both the title and reputation. Tranquilizers are the most prescribed, most used, and most abused class of drugs. As noted earlier, tranquilizers may be any of the drugs that result in a relatively mild state of depressed CNS functioning. Because of their unique psychological effects, two drug families are categorized as tranquilizers.

The first major class of tranquilizers includes the **myorelaxant drugs.** Myorelaxant drugs, such as meprobamate, better known as Miltown or Equanil, decrease the tension in the skeletal muscle system by decreasing the synaptic efficiency of the efferent motor neurons. To be an effective tranquilizer, of course, the synaptic action should not be totally stopped, as is possible with a paralytic drug like curare. The myorelaxant drugs decrease muscle tone and muscle responsiveness, which leads to substantially reduced sensory feedback indicating tension. Apparently, a major component of tension is the sensory feedback from muscles which are tensed to respond. The muscle tension leads to phychological tension, which keeps the muscles tense, and so on. This destructive feedback loop can be broken by decreasing the efficiency of the motor neurons. An equivalent nondrug treatment of nervous tension is the training of deep-muscle relaxation techniques.

Most myorelaxants affect the activity of structures in the CNS. Tranquilizers typically reduce the activity of the reticular formation. The reduction in activity might be due only to the lowering of muscle input signals to the RAS, but the drugs probably include some direct CNS effects. RAS activity is directly related to the state of alertness in the organism, so the drug mechanism for a possible tranquilizing effect is obvious. RAS activity level is also known to affect muscle tension, so establishing the "primary affect" will require additional data. The myorelaxants increase resistance of the cortex to epileptic-type seizure activity. This could be due only to the lowered activity of the RAS, but probably indicates direct effects on the neural circuits in the cortex.

A class of tranquilizers known as the **benzodiazepines** (but better known under the brand name Valium and Librium) seem to share the general characteristics of the myorelaxants, but with more pronounced effects on the RAS and other CNS structures. The benzodiazepines are undoubtedly the most prescribed tranquilizers at the present time. Because of the anticonvulsant effects, the benzodiazepines are used to alleviate the symptoms of epilepsy. They also find clinical application in counteracting the adverse effects of overdose of a variety of nervous system stimulants.

STIMULANTS

Like the CNS depressants, stimulants are a wide variety of drugs that have a general effect on the CNS. Instead of decreasing the synaptic efficiency, the stimulants seem to change the synaptic mechanism so that it overresponds. Strychnine is technically a stimulant to the cholinergic nerves because it removes the inhibiting effect of cholinesterase. Strychnine is best known for its neurotoxic poison effects, but in sublethal doses strychnine may be employed to improve the efficiency of the cholinergic nervous systems.

Caffeine is the stimulant most commonly used. For some people, that "morning cup of coffee" seems absolutely necessary to prepare the system to meet the new day. Coffee drinking alone accounts for the annual consumption of 15 million pounds of caffeine in the United States. A contributor to the quick energy release of a candy bar is the caffeine contained in chocolate.

Caffeine is a general stimulant to cellular activity, with the effect somewhat concentrated on nerve cells. Thus, caffeine increases the general activity level of the CNS. The nervous system appears to show the same sequential sensitivity to stimulants as it does to depressants. Low doses of caffeine result in mental alertness and increased efficiency. Higher doses result in the hyperresponsiveness and motor tremor known as "coffee nerves." Even higher concentrations may result in breathing complications, since the brain stem is affected.

Nicotine is another widely used stimulant which appears to affect the entire CNS. Like caffeine, higher doses of nicotine can result in hyperresponsiveness or even convulsions. Usually, however, dosage level obtained through smoking is acceptable in terms of CNS effects. The use of general

CNS stimulants like caffeine and nicotine may result in a period of depression when use is suddenly discontinued. This, in part, accounts for the difficult time some individuals have when they attempt to "kick the habit."

Technically speaking, all of the drugs discussed in the remainder of this chapter qualify under the general rubric "stimulants." Since their mode of action and behavioral applications are fairly distinct, they will be treated in separate categories.

ANTIDEPRESSANT DRUGS

The level of interneural nonadrenalin (NE) and serotonin (5-HT) is intimately involved with the mood of the individual (Figure 10.3). Drugs that increase the amount of these two chemicals generally move the individual toward the euphoria end of the mood scale, while depletion results in depression. NE and E are catecholamines, while 5-HT is an indoleamine. This direct relation between mood and amine level has led to the **amine theory of mood.** There are several ways that the level of transmitter amines can be enhanced (Figure 10.4).

The **tricyclic antidepressants,** so named because of the presence of three rings in their molecular structure, appear to block the reabsorption of the transmitter amines by the presynaptic bouton. Apparently, transmitter molecules floating in the synaptic space can be reabsorbed and reused by the presynaptic bouton. Tricyclic antidepressants stop this reabsorption, leaving

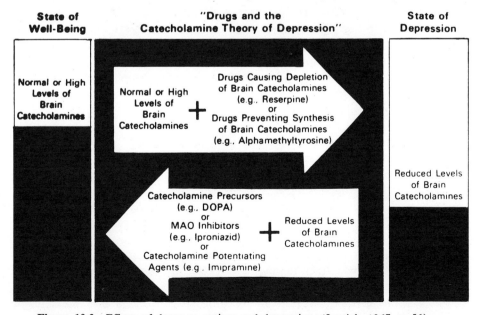

Figure 10.3 Effects of drugs on amines and depression. (Jarvick, 1967, p. 56)

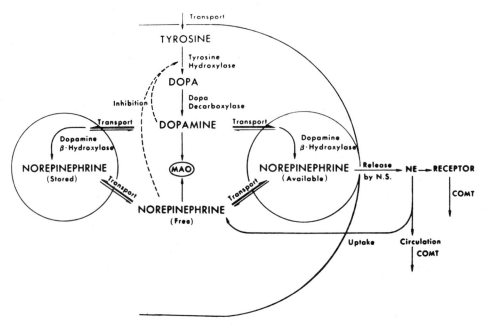

Figure 10.4 The adrenergic synapse. The chemicals named are those naturally occurring in the synaptic mechanism. Drugs can be administered to alter the synapse at many points in this process. (Kopin, 1970, p. 29)

a higher concentration of the transmitter in the synaptic space. As is the case with cholinergic neurons and strychnine, increase in synaptic transmitter concentration tends to increase the synaptic activity of the cells.

Another way to increase the NE and 5-HT in the synaptic space would be to increase the amine productivity of the presynaptic bouton. We observed previously that the membrane of the synaptic vesicles protected the transmitter chemical from destruction by enzymes found in the cytoplasm of the bouton. In adrenergic systems, one of these enzymes is called monoamine oxydase (MAO). When MAO encounters a molecule of NE or 5-HT, it neutralizes it by oxidizing the molecule. This apparently prevents the build-up of a dangerous concentration of free transmitter molecules inside the bouton.

The ability of the presynaptic bouton to reabsorb and repackage transmitter molecules provides an efficient mechanism for recycling these chemicals. It is also much simpler for the cell to produce needed packets or vesicles. The chemical destruction by MAO undoubtedly reduces the speed of vesicle production. In the case of some types of depression, this limiting action by MAO results in an inadequate supply of transmitter amines for the normal operation of the neurons. The family of drugs known as **MAO inhibitors** all provide their antidepressant effect by interfering with the normal function of MAO. Apparently, the increased concentration of transmitter in the bouton increases the amount of transmitter released into the synaptic space, which moves the individual toward euphoria or away from depression.

The MAO mechanism in the bouton illustrates the complexity of the synaptic machinery. Apparently, MAO is part of a carefully balanced system to prevent overproduction of the transmitter chemicals. In the normal state, this mechanism must keep the bouton within relatively narrow bounds with regard to transmitter concentration. Catechol-o-methyl transferase (COMT) is a control chemical found in the synaptic cleft which serves a cholinesterase-like function on the adrenergic system. In addition, COMT neutralizes the transmitter chemical after it is absorbed into the postsynaptic membrane. We find that the entire synapse is a carefully balanced homeostatic chemical system. There is evidence to indicate that the psychotic condition known as manic-depression may represent unusual fluctuations in the ability of this sytem to control amine levels. If the homeostatic mechanism cannot maintain the optimal level, the resultant excess or deficiency may be expressed as a psychotic pattern of behavior.

The use of electroshock therapy in the treatment of depression involves the same synaptic mechanism. Although there undoubtedly are other physiological effects, the massive electrical insult to the CNS triggers a measurable increase in the turnover of NE. This helps to account for the positive effects of electroshock on depressed psychotic patients.

The "pleasure centers" in the brain are also related to the amine theory of mood. The pleasure centers in the median forebrain bundle of the hypothalamus are composed of many adrenergic or serotoninergic fibers. Electrical stimulation of these neurons will increase the transmitter amine level. The pleasure effect would be the result of the higher amine level caused by the activity of these specific neurons.

One of the earliest drug treatments for manic patients was the injection of **lithium,** an element closely related to sodium and potassium. The introduction of lithium to the nervous system increases neuronal absorption of NE and 5-HT while simultaneuosly reducing the rate of release of the two transmitter chemicals during neuronal activity. Both of these effects result in lower anime levels, which would alleviate manic symptoms. Drugs that reduce the amount of NE and/or 5-HT in the synaptic space are known to reduce manic behavior or to create a depressive state.

ANTIPSYCHOTIC DRUGS

Some of the drugs already discussed have obvious antipsychotic behavioral applications. The ability to manipulate transmitter amine levels allows treatment of most of the manic-depressive psychoses. The powerful tranquilizers can alleviate the overpowering fears and suspicions which debilitate other phychotic patients.

In addition, there are a number of powerful drugs that are potentially effective in treating more complicated psychotic symptoms. Schizophrenia, although a difficult psychosis to cleanly diagnose, may respond to drug therapy.

Rauwolfia serpentina is an East Indian shrub, the roots of which have been used for centuries in the preparation of potions to treat madness. **Reserpine** is the active ingredient extracted from *Rauwolfia* and presently being administered to schizophrenic patients. Reserpine is known to block the storage of transmitter amines into vesicles in the bouton, and the unpackaged amines are then oxidized by the MAO in the bouton. The consequent lowering of transmitter amines would account for the calming effect produced by reserpine. Reserpine, however, is more than a simple CNS depressant. It appears to lower selectively some parts of the nervous system while enhancing the action of other parts.

Another major class of antipsychotic drugs comes from the phenothiazine family, of which chlorpromazine is the best example. The **phenothiazines** are tricyclic molecules and demonstrate a corresponding stimulating effect on the adrenergic systems. In addition to affecting adrenergic systems, chlorpromazine is anticholinergic, antihistaminic, and antiserotonic! With this combination, it is difficult to speculate as to the specific mechanism that attenuates the psychotic behavior.

An interesting observation is that most of the antipsychotic drugs bring on the symptoms of Parkinson's disease. Parkinson's disease is marked by muscular tension, tremors, and hyperreflexivity. The patient has difficulty overcoming the muscle tension to accomplish movement, and then the movement is usually too fast and too much. Thus, the therapist must choose carefully between the psychological impairment of prescribing too little of a drug versus the physiological impairment of prescribing too much. In psychotic patients that naturally develop Parkinson's disease, psychotic symptoms are often attenuated.

Parkinson's disease is a progressive deterioration of a special motor pathway system known as the extrapyramidal system. The extrapyramidal system branches away from the major motor tract, which goes through the pyramidal portion of the brain stem, and connects to the muscle by a different route. It is interesting to speculate on this interrelation between psychotic symptoms and the special motor control provided by the extrapyramidal system. Prolonged use of the antipsychotic drugs may cause permanent chemical lesions in the extrapyramidal system.

HALLUCINOGENIC DRUGS

Everyone knows about the existence of hallucinogenic drugs and has probably formed an opinion as to their appropriate place in society. Interest in these drugs on the part of scientists has somewhat waned, since the possibility of a chemically induced psychosis has not led to a better understanding of those that occur naturally. There is still a considerable interest in the "conscious-ness-expanding" potential of this type of drug or the possibility of enhancing creative mental activity.

In general, the hallucinogenic drugs fall into three classes. The first class seems to block the action of the cholinergic fibers, especially in the parasympathetic nervous system. The anticholinergic drugs include **atropine, scopalamine,** and the naturally occurring substance **belladonna.** Anticholiner-gic drugs are used to counteract the physical symptoms of Parkinson's dis-ease, but at the psychological cost of possible hallucination. Anticholinergic drugs generally cause a dulling of the senses, a withdrawn and anxious emo-tional tone, and a confused state as an after-effect. The general pattern is a diminution of the action of the cholinergic fibers in the nervous system. A possible mechanism for the hallucinatory effect might be a reduction in the inhibitory functions of the sensory circuits.

The other two classes of hallucinogenic drugs appear to act in a quite different manner. These drugs, **LSD, mescaline, psylocybine,** and related com-pounds, seem to enhance the activity of the adrenergic and/or serotoninergic neurons. Thus, a part of the "high" of these drugs appears to be related to the increased activity of the parasympathetic nervous system. As may be noted from discussion of other mood-changing compounds, norepinephrine and serotonin seem important to the psychological state of the individual.

The action of this class of hallucinogens is closely related to the remark-able chemical similarity between the molecular shape of the drug molecule and the transmitter molecules NE and 5-HT. LSD is very similar to serotonin, while mescaline is quite close to norepinephrine. It appears that the similarity to the transmitter substance increases the activity of the corresponding neurons. It has been hypothesized that the hallucinogenic drug might directly stimulate the receptor site of the postsynaptic molecule, which then makes the drug an artificial transmitter chemical.

A more recent speculation is that the drug molecule "fools" the cor-responding oxidizing compound in the synaptic cleft. The "eraser molecule" captures the drug molecule because of the chemical similarity, but cannot oxidize it and cannot release it. This effectively reduces the concentration of the eraser molecules in the synapse, which increases the effective concentration of the real transmitter. Thus, the hallucinogenic effects are probably due to the enhanced activity caused by the increased concentration of the real synaptic transmitter. This latter mechanism would explain why LSD produces pro-longed hallucinatory effects, although the free chemical is detectable in the brain for only a brief period after administration. It may also explain the profound psychological effects resulting from minute LSD doses.

It is possible that the hallucinatory drugs actually act on different seg-ments of a common mechanism if we assume that the cholinergic system is precisely balanced by the activity of the adrenergic and/or serotonergic systems. Hallucinatory states may be the result when this balance is tipped to favor the adrenergic and/or serotonergic systems.

AUTHOR'S The chemical nature of the synapse apparently allows rela-
COMMENTS tively free access to nervous system action by drugs circulating in the bloodstream. Some of the psychologically important drugs alter
the activity of the individual neurons, but most may be shown to have their
effect through some part of the synaptic mechanism. With five known synaptic
transmitter chemicals (and others yet to be discovered), the variety of potential response sites to a specific drug is impressive. In addition, the role of
the blood-brain barrier in selectively admitting or rejecting drugs from the
CNS allows a wide latitude in responsiveness to drugs.

One of the better established drug effects is that manipulation of the
amine neurotransmitters (NE and 5-HT) directly affect the mood of the
individual. The various ways amine level can be manipulated by different drugs
illustrates the generality of the amine theory of mood as well as the complexity of the synaptic mechanism.

Many of the drugs prescribed for their psychological effect are used
because they do something. This extremely pragmatic justification has led us
into our own peculiar form of "drug culture," but knowledge is gradually
being developed to account for the drug action. As drug effects provide more
information regarding the synaptic mechanism, the dangers of indiscriminate
drug use become more apparent. The complexity and self-adjusting nature
of the synaptic mechanism provide many points for chemical damage, possibly permanent. The potential for such neurological damage is not restricted
to the so-called illegal drugs but also applies to prescription drugs administered
to alleviate psychological symptoms.

IV

Neural Connections

Now that the individual components of the nervous system have been introduced, we need to put them together in some coherent fashion. The complexity of the human CNS makes it difficult to attempt this task with the total system. A number of different lines of research choose different ways to parcel the nervous system into units that are easier to comprehend. Some researchers concentrate on simple organisms with very simple nervous systems. Others focus on specific subunits of the more complex nervous system. Fortunately, the data are not in disagreement as a result of the different research strategies. It appears that there are organizational principles which are common to nervous systems in general. Although specific details vary greatly, the basic operation and interaction of the neurons and synapses seem to follow a consistent pattern. The organization of these elements into nervous systems also appears to follow general rules.

The visual system provides one model for establishing general principles. A well-defined, easily controlled stimulus, combined with the ability to record the evoked potentials in the nervous system, provides a powerful tool in decoding the neuronal information-processing system. By careful analysis of the changes that are introduced at each synaptic junction in the visual pathway, it is possible to deduce some of the connections that account for the observed activity.

The sensory cells, or transducers, which respond to the external stimulus and translate the message into the electrochemical currency of the nervous system are the first step in the encoding process. Sensory cells select which stimuli will be detected by their sensitivity characteristics. The size and/or intensity of a stimulus is encoded according to basic principles common to most transducers.

The first synaptic junction in the sensory pathway reorganizes the information into a different code. Some sensory neurons can and do accurately transmit the characteristics of a steady-state stimulus; however, the majority show a pronounced response to the stimulus onset or offset with relatively rapid adaptation to a steady stimulus. Thus, the sensory system selects the moving or changing aspects of the stimulus at the sacrifice of a totally accurate presentation of unchanging aspects of the environment.

The sensory pathways for olfaction are not completely understood and may provide an exception, but all sensory systems appear to have important nuclei in the thalamic portion of the brain stem along with significant interaction with the reticular formation. These lower brain centers are the evolutionary inheritance of earlier nervous systems that did not have higher cortical nervous system structures. In the mammalian system, these lower sensory nuclei seem to have specialized to process specific dimensions of the incoming stimulus. The information branching into the RAS appears to be mainly stimulus cues that pose a potential survival threat to the organism. Thus, intense stimuli, movement, and certain other "attention-grabbing" stimuli appear to have priority channels to the RAS and consequent high-attention value for immediate processing in finer detail by the cortical sensory regions.

The thalamic sensory nuclei appear to have evolved into "primitive" sensory information centers. Much of the activity observed in these centers appears to be involved with locating the source of the stimulus rather than with analyzing the characteristics of the stimulus itself. Thus, the thalamic nuclei are typically involved with mediating the orientation or movement of the sense organ to focus more effectively on the stimulus.

The cortical sensory regions appear to be involved with analyzing the actual stimulus dimensions. The primary sensory area typically responds to basic stimulus characteristics. The adjacent association regions, which get their information from the primary cortical region, seem to provide more complicated levels of analysis, for example, recognition. As research continues in tracing this increasingly complex code, it appears that regions of the cortex not previously thought to provide sensory functions will respond to sensory stimulation at an extraordinarily complex level. Thus, the sensory system consists of a sort of information pyramid. Each synapse signals increasing complexity in terms of the sophistication of the information encoded.

The fact that the information is radically reorganized at each level in the sensory pathway means that the sensory system does not operate on a simple point-to-point transmission mechanism. That is, the organization of the visual cortex is not an electrical mosaic corresponding to the "picture" being seen by the eye. The sensory systems appear to be organized along a "feature" scheme. As more research is conducted, this coding scheme will be more accurately described. In the meantime, some of the logical ramifications of a "feature-detector" system alter our theories of how the entire nervous system works.

SUGGESTED READINGS

Because of the contribution to understanding general neural functioning, many of the "professional references" cited for Part I of this text include extensive material regarding sensory coding and/or neural connections. The references listed below focus on sensory research, especially the feature detector characteristics in sensory systems.

Barlow, H. B. & Hill, R. M. Selective sensitivity to direction of movement in ganglion cells of the rabbit retina. *Science,* 1963, **139**.

Beidler, L. M. & Reichardt, W. E. Sensory transduction. *Neurosciences Research Program Bulletin,* 1970, **8**(5).

Bekesy, G. von. *Sensory inhibition.* Princeton, N.J.: Princeton University Press, 1967.

Hammes, G. G., Molinott, P. B. & Bloom, F. E. Receptor biophysics and biochemistry. *Neurosciences Research Program Bulletin,* 1973, **11**(3).

Hubel, D. H. The visual cortex of the brain. *Scientific American,* 1963, **209**(5), 54–62.

Hubel, D. H. & Wiesel, T. N. Receptive fields, binocular interaction and functional architecture in the cat's visual cortex. *Journal of Physiology,* 1962, **160**(1).

Kuffler, S. W. Discharge patterns and functional organization of mammalian retina. *Journal of Neurophysiology,* 1953, **16**.

Kuffler, S. W. Excitation and inhibition in single nerve cells. In *The Harvey Lecture Series* 54. New York: Academic Press, 1960.

Lettvin, J. Y., Maturna, H. R., McCullock, W. S. & Pitts, W. H. What the frog's eye tells the frog's brain. *Proceedings of the Institute of Radio Engineers,* 1959, **47**.

Chapter

11

Transducers

In the study of physiological systems, transducers provide the communication link between the CNS and the outside world. The term **transducers** is an engineering term applied to any device that converts one form of energy into another. The typical home high fidelity system, for example, converts the electrical or mechanical information stored on a tape or record into electrical information, which is amplified and then converted into air movement, resulting in sound. The phonographic cartridge is a transducer that converts motion created by the passing groove of the record into an electrical message. The pick-up head on a tape deck generates the necessary electrical signal on the basis of magnetic fields recorded on the tape. If a microphone were connected to the amplifier, the physical movement of air molecules would be converted into the necessary electrical information. Even the loudspeaker is an example of a transducer, since it converts electrical energy into air motion. Almost any electrical appliance transduces electrical energy into heat, light, or motion. The film in a camera transduces light into chemical changes. A thermometer transduces temperature changes into motion. Guns, TV sets, meters, automatic control devices, all are examples of transducers.

Although the muscles and glands qualify as transducers because they convert neural messages into movement or chemical changes, the term "biological transducer" is usually applied to the receptors or sensory cells of the body. We often find that the receptors are categorized into the "five

145

basic senses": sight, hearing, taste, smell, and touch. These five functional categories certainly are important in detecting events outside the organism, but this scheme provides some significant problems. There are a number of transducers hidden inside the body which monitor a variety of internal states and functions. Thus, the "outside world" to the CNS is not the outer skin of the body but actually includes the body itself.

TYPES OF TRANSDUCERS

Transducers are usually classified according to the type of energy they transduce. Biological transducers must convert information into the electrochemical activity employed by the neurons. In terms of input information, we find that there are four basic types of biological transducers: those that respond to radiant energy, to mechanical motion, to chemical changes, and to electrical fields. The **radioreceptors** are necessary for vision. The radiant energy spectrum includes more than visible light, however, and all of the temperature sensors fall within the radioreceptor category. The skin transducers which give us the impression of hot or cold, as well as some extremely finely tuned internal receptors which monitor and maintain mammalian body temperature, are examples. **Mechanical receptors** involve the detection of air movement for the sense of hearing as well as vibration and pressure on the surface of the skin. There are also mechanicotransducers in the muscles to indicate position and tension, pressure detectors for the efficient functioning of digestive organs and the circulatory system, and the motion and position information provided by the vestibular senses that tell us if we are motionless, moving, turning, or upside down. **Chemotransducers** are the probable mechanism for the sense of taste and smell. Internally, transducers that monitor the chemical concentration of a wide variety of substances such as oxygen, nutrients, hormones, proteins, amines, and salts are found throughout the body. Sites for these vital chemical homeostatic sensors are necessary in the digestive organisms, bloodstream, and many areas of the CNS. **Electrotransducers** are known in several nonhuman species, particularly fish. Technically, the electrical responsiveness of neurons qualifies them as electrotransducers.

BIOLOGICAL TRANSDUCERS

Sensory cells appear to fall into two morphological categories (Figure 11.1). Some transducers seem to be specially modified dendrites of a neuron. A depolarization is produced on the dendrite with the introduction of the stimulus. This receptor potential then behaves in the same way as a postsynaptic potential in terms of the generation of a spike on the afferent axon.

The other major class of transducer cells seems to require a close interrelation between a highly specialized transducer cell and an associated neuron.

Although the connection between the transducer and the associated neuron appears to be similar to a synapse, physiological recordings indicate that the transducer cell does not generate a spike. Electrical activity of the receptor cell results in the generation of spike activity in the associated neuron. Some two-cell transducer systems apparently employ a hyperpolarizing receptor potential to initiate spike activity rather than the normal depolarizing potential. The two-cell transducer system appears to follow the same coding schemes as the single-cell transducers. Close examination of the specialized transducer cell shows that they are specially evolved ciliary cells. **Ciliary cells** (hair cells) are primarily found in the ventricular spaces of the CNS. These cells are capable of movement of the hairlike extensions which seem to keep the cerebrospinal fluid in motion within the ventricles. In the ontogenetic develop-

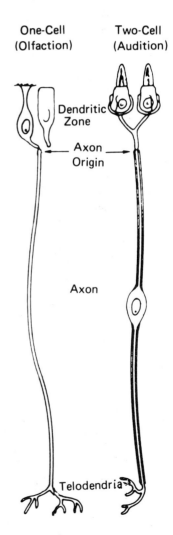

Figure 11.1 Two types of transducers. One-cell transducers seem to be specialized neurons with highly modified dendrites. Two-cell transducers seem to involve an especially evolved transducer cell closely associated with a neuron. Both systems convert external energy into the axon spike frequency code. (Bodian, 1962, pp. 323–326)

ment of the nervous system, some of these ciliary cells became specialized receptor cells. The receptor cells in the ear are called hair cells, which identifies the similarity rather clearly. The hairlike extension of the olfactory transducers is similarly obvious. The outer segments of the rods and cones in the eye, which are full of a visual pigment, do not appear very hairlike. There is, however, a marked constriction between the inner and outer segments of the cell. One can interpret this constriction as the beginning of the hair, which has then puffed up with the photosensitive chemicals necessary for the transduction of light.

STIMULUS DIMENSIONS

The development of the capacity to place a microelectrode in or near the axon to record spike activity allows us to monitor the coding characteristics of a sensory system. If we place a microelectrode near a sensory neuron, and then stimulate that neuron by introducing the appropriate external stimulus to its transducer, the resulting neuronal activity is known as an **evoked potential.** By systematically changing the characteristics of the stimulus and simultaneously "wiretapping" the resulting evoked potentials, we gain considerable insight into the organization of neurons in sensory systems.

A good transducer provides an accurate translation of the characteristics of one form of energy when it converts it into another. We can specify four basic dimensions that are common to all forms of energy. The four ways can be summarized in the following questions: What is it? How strong is it? How big is it? How long did it last?

The question "What is it?" corresponds to the engineering dimension of **quality** (Figure 11.2). There is a qualitative difference among light, sound, and smell. Quality is coded in the nervous system according to the type of transducer activated. The difference between vision and hearing is a matter

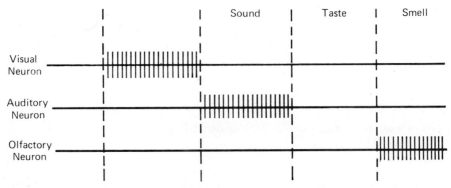

Figure 11.2 Neuronal coding of quality. The nervous system identifies the kind of stimulus that is occurring by which neurons are active.

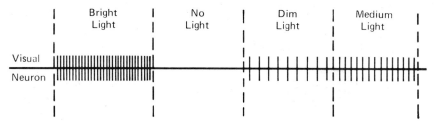

Figure 11.3 Neuronal coding of quantity. The amount or intensity of the stimulus is reflected in the frequency of the axon spikes.

of which nerves are active. The neuronal activity is identical in the optic and auditory neurons. The early doctrine of the "specific energy of nerves," which states that nerves respond only to a certain type of energy, is due entirely to the specialized transducer which generates the neural activity. Direct electrical stimulation of the optic nerve or the optic areas of the brain results in "light flashes" or other visual phenomena. Some types of blindness are the result of permanent damage to the radiotransducers (rods and cones) of the eye. Research is being conducted to use a manufactured transducer like a TV camera to provide electrical signals which can be fed directly to the primary visual area of the brain. The result would be a pattern of neural activity which would be "seen" by the blind patient. The answer to the question "What is it?" is "Which neurons are active?"

The second question—"How strong is it?"—is the equivalent of the engineering dimension of **quantity.** A stimulus can be either weak or strong, whether it is a light, sound, or touch. We have seen that the operation of the neuron encodes the strength of the postsynaptic potential into a frequency code of axonal spikes. Thus, the more intense the input stimulus, the faster the spike rate of the stimulated axons (Figure 11.3). The neurological equivalent of "How strong is it?" is "How fast is the neuron firing?"

"How big is it?" is the equivalent of the engineering dimension of **extent.** Extent at first appears to overlap with quantity, but it is a separate characteristic. Extent is the visual difference between a 12- and a 25-inch TV set when viewed from the same distance. The quantity of each visual stimulus can be independently manipulated by adjusting the brightness of either set. For the sense of touch, extent is the major difference between lying on a featherbed versus on a bed of nails. The total pressure is the same (your weight), but the extent (distribution) of that stimulus makes a considerable difference! The CNS sees the extent dimension in terms of the total number of neurons involved in transmitting the stimulus (Figure 11.4). "How big is it?" becomes a question of "How many neurons are active?"

The last dimension is **duration,** or "How long did it last?" Duration describes the temporal characteristics of the stimulus. Sensory neurons demonstrate a distinct change in axonal spike rate when a stimulus is introduced or removed (Figure 11.5). Sometimes the change is a burst of spike activity,

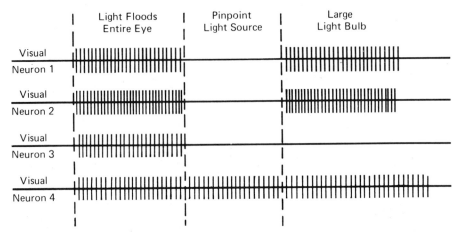

Figure 11.4   Neuronal coding of extent. The size of the stimulus (as opposed to the intensity) is reflected by the number of neurons simultaneously active.

sometimes it is the abrupt cessation of axon spikes. Sensory neurons are often described according to the type of response they show to stimulus onset and offset. The CNS encodes duration by transducing when the stimulus appeared and when it disappeared.

SENSITIVITY

We are willing to pay a considerable amount of money for the advantages of a high fidelity stereo system over a cheap record player. Both devices accomplish the necessary transduction task, except one does its job much more accurately. The low-priced record player is not as sensitive to tiny changes in the stimulus, and consequently, it does not have the tonal quality we enjoy from a more sensitive system. For obvious reasons, sensitivity is also an important characteristic of a good biological transducer system.

Engineers measure sensitivity in a number of different ways. Here we begin to gain an appreciation of the biological transducers in the body. Al-

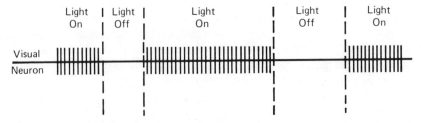

Figure 11.5   Neuronal coding of duration. Sensory neurons register the onset (or offset) of the stimulus by a sudden increase (or drop) in activity.

though manufactured transducers are capable of matching, or even exceeding, the performance of biological transducers along any single dimension of sensitivity, few manufactured devices show the broad combination demonstrated by the typical biological devices. Comparing input and output characteristics of a transducer is the way an engineer measures sensitivity. The equivalent in psychology is known as psychophysics. As the name implies, **psychophysics** compares the physical traits of the stimulus with the psychological trait of how the stimulus is perceived. Although it is possible to measure the input-output characteristics of an individual biological transducer by using the microelectrode techniques, most transducers operate as a component of a sensory system. Psychophysics usually studies the characteristics of the entire transducer system.

The **absolute threshold** is a measure of the lowest level of energy necessary for the transducer system to operate. Psychophysical studies indicate that there is an absolute threshold for the operation of each of the senses. There is a light too dim for us to see, sounds too soft to hear, and so on. When we examine the performance of the individual transducer within the system, however, the performance of the biological transducer is spectacular. If we provide a stimulus that is optimal for the transducer, it is almost impossible to escape detection.

Transducers also have an upper limit, or **terminal threshold,** of operation. If the stimulus becomes too strong, the transducer can no longer encode an increase. This upper limit may occur in one of two ways. The transducer may be responding at its maximum rate, and any further increases are impossible; or, the gigantic energy onslaught begins to destroy the transducer itself. Like most delicate instruments, the extremely sensitive biological transducers can be destroyed by overstimulation. The auxiliary structures in the sense organs are often designed to provide special protection for the transducers and to extend the range of stimulus intensities that can be tolerated. An obvious example is the contraction of the pupil of the eye to reduce the total light intensity under bright viewing conditions.

The difference between the absolute threshold and the terminal threshold represents the range of stimulus intensity that the transducer can operate (Figure 11.6). This **dynamic range** of biological transducers is their truly remarkable characteristic. The combination of extreme sensitivity combined with a tolerance for effective operation under intense stimulus conditions is rarely found in man-made systems. The sense of touch has a mere 1000 to 1 ratio for a dynamic range, while the auditory system can function effectively over a 10 million to 1 ratio!

An important contributor to the extensive dynamic range of the senses is the basic coding characteristic of the transducers. Doubling the intensity of the stimulus does not double the rate of spikes in an evoked potential. Between evoked potential records and psychological studies, it is well established that the transducers code the stimulus intensity on a logarithmic scale. A logarithm is the exponent of the numeral 10. Thus, the number 100 has a

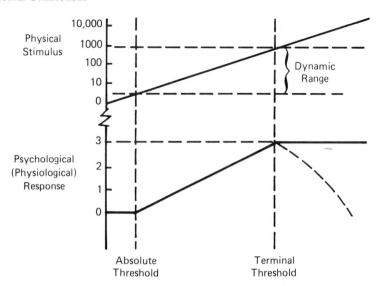

Figure 11.6 Typical psychophysical characteristics of a sensory system. The system fails to detect extremely low stimulus levels and begins to break down under too intense bombardment. Between these two extremes, the axon frequency follows the logarithmic value of the physical stimulus intensity (note the values on the physical stimulus scale).

logarithm of 2 because it is 10^2, and 1000 is expressed in logarithm 3 because 1000 is 10^3. To return to the sensory neuron, if the spike rate is twice as fast for one stimulus, the stimulus is ten times as strong. A spike triple indicates a thousandfold stimulus difference, and so forth.

Such an exponential coding mechanism has obvious advantages for a system requiring a broad dynamic range. A difference in stimulus intensity of 1 million to 1 would entail a 6 to 1 change in spike frequency. This exponential relationship appears to be the general characteristic of the transducers themselves. Electrophysiological recordings of the activity of the transducers show a logarithmic relationship between stimulus intensity and transducer activity.

In addition to an exponential coding mechanism, there is the possibility that different transducers serving the same sense have different sensitivity ranges. Thus, it may be that a "sensitive" transducer responds to very low signal levels, and another "insensitive" cell picks up the chores at higher intensities. This mechanism is known to exist in the moth auditory system, and would extend the effective range considerably, given adequate protection for the "sensitive" cells from damage.

There is yet another dimension of sensitivity to a transducer. Within its dynamic range, how accurately does it maintain a "high fidelity" correspondence between the input stimulus and the output activity? Distortion can enter into the performance of some transducers in certain parts of their operating range.

The exponential coding mechanism seems to be reliable over most of the dynamic range of the typical biological transducers. The psychophysical term for this measure of sensitivity is the "differential threshold." The **differential threshold** is the minimum change in energy that can be detected by the sensory system. Another term for this is the **just noticeable difference (JND).** As would be expected from an exponential coding system, JND's increase exponentially with the intensity of stimulation. Weber first noticed this relationship and summarized it in the fraction $\Delta I/I$. In other words, the minimum detectable change is some constant fraction of the stimulus intensity. If $\Delta I/I$ for weights was 1/10, then we would be able to detect which of two paper cups was heavier if one contained 9 pennies and the other 10. If the cups were filled with 100 pennies, we could not detect the difference contributed by 1 penny, but would need a minimum difference of 10 pennies. The constant ratio between JND and stimulus magnitude is a convenient estimate of the sensitivity of the system to changes. The smaller the value of the fraction, the more sensitive the transducer. The Weber fraction is the easiest to understand but the least accurate psychophysical function to describe stimulus magnitude. Fechner's logarithmic rule is a more accurate description. The best psychophysical function over the greatest part of the dynamic range is Steven's power law, which measures the stimulus and the perceptual value on a logarithmic scale.

Another notable characteristic of at least some transducers is the rapid replacement process associated with the cells. Estimates are that the taste transducer cells have a very short lifespan. Experiments in the rat indicate that these cells are replaced every ten days on the average. The receptor portions of the photo transducers in the eye are also constantly being replaced. Thus, sensory systems seem to operate with structures that are in a constant state of flux.

Neurophysiologists are actively investigating sensory cells. The exact transducer mechanism that results in a receptor potential is not known in most cases. Consequently, the discussion of each of the types of transducers must be incomplete and fragmentary. Nevertheless, we will examine some tentative possibilities for the transducer action as well as some of the operating characteristics for each type of transducer.

RADIOTRANSDUCERS

The human eye receives light information by means of rods and cones, so named because of the shape of the transducer segment (Figure 11.7). The phototransduction mechanism in the rods and cones of the eye is relatively well understood. The outer segments of the receptor cells contain photopigments which are bleached by light and regenerated in the dark. The completely bleached pigment is colorless, and the totally regenerated pigment is purple. The bleaching process occurs in four distinct steps, and each step creates an electrical change (the receptor potential) due to the chemical

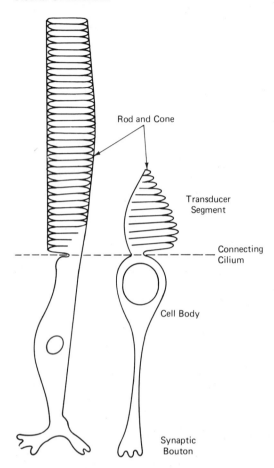

Rod and Cone

Transducer
Segment

Connecting
Cilium

Cell Body

Synaptic
Bouton

Figure 11.7 Radiotransducers, the rods and cones in the human eye. Light-sensitive photopigments located in the laminations of the outer segments generate electrical activity, which is synaptically transmitted along the optic pathway.

process of bleaching. The dark-adapted eye contains primarily regenerated pigment molecules. In higher light levels, a higher proportion of the pigment is bleached. If the light is constant, equilibrium is established between the rate of bleaching from the light and the regeneration by the cell. Increasing or decreasing the light level creates a corresponding increase or decrease in the bleach rate, accompanied by an electrical generator potential.

The combination of rods and cones in the human eye provides a unique combination of transduction properties. The rods are very sensitive to low light levels, while the cones work at higher intensities and add color information. The absolute threshold for an individual rod may be a single quantum of light. Apparently, the nervous system needs to combine the information from approximately seven quanta of light to reach the absolute threshold for color vision.

The absolute threshold for the eye is 0.00001 millilamberts. Since absolute thresholds are on such a miniscule scale, it may help to translate these intuitively difficult numbers onto a scale that we are capable of experiencing or imagining. A common measure of light energy involves a standard candle (which is one candlepower of light energy). The dark-adapted human eye is capable of seeing a standard candle three miles away! Since a candle gives off heat as well as light, the visual receptors are not utilizing all of the energy radiating from the candle.

Beginning with the absolute threshold as a baseline, we find that the dynamic range of the human eye functions efficiently over a range of 10 billion to 1! The usual result of too intense light stimulation is heat destruction of the cells because the intense light includes radiation from the infrared region of the spectrum. Thus, the transducers work to the point where they begin to cook.

The eye is not the only locus of radiotransducers. The pineal body, for example, will generate an electrical response to a light stimulus. There is some evidence to indicate that animals which show seasonal changes in behavior do so in response to the length of daylight, and that this changing light factor is not detected by means of the visual system. The pineal body may serve this function, at least in species where light can penetrate the skull and other surrounding tissue. Heat is also a portion of the electromagnetic spectrum, so the warm and cold receptors in the skin are also examples of biological radiotransducers. The sensors that adjust and maintain the precise mammalian body temperature of 98.6 degrees F must accomplish extreme precision with a corresponding reduced dynamic range.

MECHANICOTRANSDUCERS

Mechanicotransducers indicate pressure, strain, and/or movement from many locations on the surface and interior of the body. The sound transduction in the ear is an example of a quite sophisticated mechanicotransducer system (Figure 11.8). The known mechanicotransducers are often very different in appearance, but the suspected mechanism seems to be the same. Motion in the transducer site causes a change in the permeability of the cell membrane. Investigators now suspect that the depolarizing receptor potential is generated on specific transducer sites on the membrane. The actual mechanism is not yet established, although the physical deformation of "holes," or "gates," in the membrane could account for the flow of ions.

The known lower threshold for hearing involves a movement of the eardrum of 10^{-11} cm. If we were to expand the eardrum so that it was 6000 miles in diameter, approximately the diameter of the earth, the threshold motion in the middle of this gigantic membrane would be less than 1/10 of a millimeter! This minimum detectable movement on the normal-size eardrum is approximately 1/10 the diameter of the hydrogen atom.

Sound is not measured in quantal packets like light, so it is difficult to establish an absolute minimum. The extraordinary sensitivity of the hair cells to vibration (0.0002 dynes/cm^2) definitely approaches a practical limit. Under optimal perceptual conditions (in a totally soundproof, sound-ab-

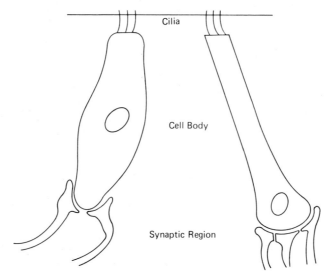

Cilia

Cell Body

Synaptic Region

Figure 11.8 Mechanical transducers, human hair cells in the cochlea. Sound waves stretch or compress the cilia in the hair cells, resulting in an electrical event.

sorbent room with no other source of sound), a person is capable of "hearing" the impact of air molecules striking the eardrum due to Brownian motion! This sound (sort of a soft hissing sound) is interrupted approximately once a second by a louder hissing sound. The latter is the noise created by the blood coursing through the capillaries servicing the hearing apparatus. Once again, we find that the transducers are about as sensitive as they can possibly be.

The dynamic range for the sense of hearing extends to about 10 million times the absolute threshold. At this value, physical damage is incurred, and sound becomes felt and not heard. The ears cannot operate for sustained periods at the upper end of their dynamic range, which accounts for the need for ear protectors in environments with sustained or repeated high-noise levels.

CHEMOTRANSDUCERS

The chemotransducers monitor the level of chemical concentration for a number of substances inside the body as well as provide the basis for the chemical senses of taste and smell (Figure 11.9). The best available theory concerning the transduction process involves a chemical "lock and key" hypothesis. That is, there is something about the shape of the activating molecule that matches or fits a particularly shaped receptor site in the transducer membrane. When an appropriately shaped molecule exactly fits the receptor site, a receptor potential is generated through the depolarization of the membrane. The lock and key hypothesis has the advantage of explaining how similarly shaped molecules need not occupy the same receptor site,

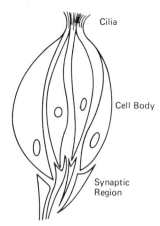

Cilia

Cell Body

Synaptic
Region

Figure 11.9   Chemotransducers, a human taste bud.
Molecules contacting the special cilia generate an
electrical event.

much as similarly shaped keys need not necessarily operate the same lock. The
chemical lock and key hypothesis is analogous to the action of the transmitter
chemical on the postsynaptic membrane, except that chemical compounds
from the external environment cause a depolarization of the membrane.

The absolute threshold of selected chemoreceptors in both taste and
smell has been shown to be a single molecule. If the chemical substance is
one to which the transducer is especially sensitive, the absolute threshold
appears to be the minimum possible stimulus. Of course, if there are no receptor sites for a particular substance, then we may be unaware of the existence of the substance in any concentration. In the case of the sense of smell,
humans are relatively sensitive to the odor of the vanillin molecule. The minimum concentration is 4.5 million molecules per cubic centimeter of air, which
translates to 1 out of 6 trillion air molecules. If we were to expand the size
of air molecules to the size of ping-pong balls, and made the vanillin molecule
a small light bulb, we would be able to tell which of two 500-yard cubes filled
with ping-pong balls contained a single light bulb. Stated another way, we
would be able to detect 44 light bulbs in a cubic mile of ping-pong balls at a
single sniff. The dynamic range for the sense of taste is a relatively low
100,000 to 1, with the sense of smell probably about the same. The upper limit
of the chemotransducers seems to be when the chemical concentration is so
great that the receptor sites are saturated.

ELECTRORECEPTORS

Electroreceptors are primarily found in fish and have not been identified in
humans. There is, of course, the electrical sensitivity of the neurons, but this
is not usually considered a transduction process. Some of the painful effects
of electrical shock stimulation undoubtedly involve the direct stimulation of
the neurons.

The sensory cells in some fish have a specific sensitivity to electrical fields. These receptor cells are often associated with an electrical-generation capacity in the fish. These two capacities allow the fish to use a sort of electrical "radar" to perceive the surrounding area in murky waters. Other fish have the electrotransducers without any known mode of generating a field. These fish apparently utilize externally created fields. The electrotransducers appear to be highly specialized versions of the neuron and are responsive to extremely small electromagnetic fields. Some of these electrically sensitive fish could detect the current from a flashlight battery if it were connected to the ends of a 300-mile-long pond.

AUTHOR'S COMMENTS   The CNS is composed of neurons and neural activity. The sensory information processed by the CNS differs primarily in locus of the activity. Biological transducers detect external stimuli and translate the dimensions of the stimulus into the electrochemical currency of the nervous system. Different transducers are specialized to detect different types of energy.

When the stimulus is appropriate to a biological transducer, the engineering operating characteristics of the device are impressive. Transducers are typically about as sensitive to extremely low stimulus levels as is physically possible. These same transducers will tolerate abusively high stimulus levels without self-destructing. Between the extremes of this upper and lower operating limit, the transducer typically provides an accurate encoding of the changes in the incoming stimulus.

The "outside world" of the CNS is filtered by means of the characteristics of its transducers. The transducers represent the first in an elaborate information-encoding sequence which culminates in the "perceptual" activity of the neocortex.

Chapter 12

Sensory Inhibition

The transducer is primarily an input device for the sensory system. The spatial senses (vision, hearing, touch) are all provided with a complex neuronal network for transmitting the transduced information to the brain. This network "codes" the information for transmission along the afferent nerves. Neurophysiological research indicates that the information is not kept separate for each receptor cell. Most afferent neurons transmit sensory information collected from the transducers. In the process, some information is lost, while other information becomes emphasized. Understanding this process of data selection and integration provides valuable clues concerning the operation of the nervous system in general. First, a study of data being transmitted to the brain allows us to establish the data utilized by the CNS and to deduce its functional characteristics. Second, the neuronal connections found in the peripheral sensory systems represent a less complicated nervous system which reflects fundamental principles in the more complex CNS. Third, a sensory system is relatively accessible for study. Most sensory systems are less elaborately protected than the CNS. Another aspect of accessibility is that one can experimentally manipulate the activity of the sensory system through evoked potentials.

Of all the primary senses, the sense of sight is most important to humans. Much information is taken in through the ears, nose, mouth, and skin, but the eyes are generally considered to be paramount. In addition, light can be controlled more easily and precisely than other stimulus media. Consequently, most sensory research has been conducted on the visual sense.

"ON"-"OFF" CELLS

Early models of the sensory neural code were based on a purely excitatory model. The sensory neuron becomes active when the transducer is stimulated and is quiet during periods of nonstimulation. Such cells are known as **"on" cells,** since they become active while the light is on (Figure 12.1).

Further research showed that some visual neurons, however, tend to become inactive when the light is turned on, but respond to light turned off with a burst of spike activity. Such cells are known as **"off" cells** (for the obvious reason), but their operating characteristics require that we go beyond a simple excitatory model for sensory neuronal activity.

An unstimulated neuron typically shows a low rate of spontaneous spike activity. Thus, an "on" cell actually goes from a low level of activity to some higher level when the stimulus occurs. A neuron that is inhibited responds with a burst of spike activity when the inhibition is removed.

The "off" cells apparently represent the activity of inhibitory processes in the sensory system. If the activity of the transducer inhibits the afferent neuron, then when the stimulus is turned off, the cell will respond with a burst of activity when released from the transducer inhibition. This "off" burst of spike activity is probably more elaborate than a simple "rebound" or "spike debt" phenomenon, since the strength of the "off" response is related to the intensity of the light change rather than to the duration of the stimulus. Thus, the inhibitory processes are not merely a "clamp" on excitatory activity, but appear to be actively involved in encoding stimulus characteristics.

In the mammalian eye, if the afferent neuron is directly connected to the transducer, the synapse seems to be excitatory, and the afferent neuron is an "on" cell. If, on the other hand, the cell is indirectly connected to the transducer, the intermediary cell seems to provide an inhibitory synapse that

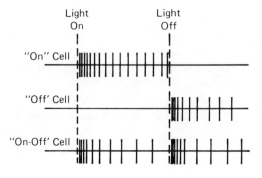

Figure 12.1 The response of "on-off" cells to a light stimulus. Such cells respond with a burst of activity to light onset and/or offset. Notice that the spike rate is not constant even though the stimulus is.

converts the neuron to an "off" cell. Some neurons can be found with both an "on" and an "off" burst of activity **("on-off" cells).** These cells are assumed to be connected to the transducers with both direct (excitatory) and indirect (inhibitory) connections, the excitatory function accounting for the "on" discharge and the inhibitory connections causing the "off."

The "off" response of some sensory cells has important implications for a model of neural circuitry. Obviously, a purely excitatory model is inadequate. In addition, however, "off" cells indicate that the visual system is concerned with the disappearance of light as well as with its onset. "Off" cells would also be responsive to the appearance of a dark object, so both types of cells report a new event in the visual environment. Similarly, the "silence" of an "on" cell would signal a dark stimulus. Thus, the visual system seems to include two complementary (or opposite) coding schemes.

The common denominator of the "on-off" cells is that they are responsive to changes in the visual environment. Another type of inhibition actually supresses the response of either type of cell to a prolonged constant stimulus which further emphasizes change.

ADAPTATION

When we first enter a movie theater from daylight, we can see the picture projected on the screen but can barely, if at all, make out the aisle and seats in the darkened theater. With great difficulty, we grope our way to a seat. After remaining in the darkened theater a few minutes, we find that we can see the interior of the theater quite clearly, and we can watch the blind struggles of newcomers as they enter. Our eyes have **adapted,** or adjusted, to the darkened condition, so that they can now function at the lower light levels. "On-off" cells show spike activity similar to an adaptation mechanism. If we stimulate the eye by turning on a light and leaving it on, an "on" cell responds with a burst of activity at the onset of the stimulus. The rate of firing decreases over time, however, and if the light is left on long enough, the cell eventually returns to its spontaneous firing rate. Adaptation occurs in individual neurons in the visual system. Thus, the "on-off" cells report a change in light level (on or off), but are relatively insensitive to prolonged ambient light levels. Adaptation can be demonstrated to occur at several levels in the sensory system, including the transducers. It seems to be a general characteristic to adjust to the ambient stimulation level.

Adaptation is another type of inhibitory process. Some adaptation is the result of internal changes in the transducer cells, for example, the bleaching of the photopigments in the rods and cones of the eye. The attenuation of spike activity in sensory neurons seems to occur faster than the changes in the transducer sensitivity. In other words, a major component of sensory adaptation seems to be a function of neuronal circuitry. Adaptation, whether transducer or neuronal, provides an important function in the sensory system. The system is essentially readjusting to the new stimulus level. Both the "on" and the "off" cells approach their resting state of activity. This means that the system is becoming maximally responsive to any change from this new level. The introduction of a new light or a dark change will cause a burst of activity in the "on" or the "off" cells, respectively. Thus, the organism is "tuned" into the environment in a way that provides maximum opportunity to respond to new events.

RECEPTIVE FIELDS

The discovery of "on-off" cells was made by recording from neurons in the visual system and flooding the entire eye with the light stimulus. The hypothesized neuronal network to explain the "on-off" cells suggests some interesting possibilities with a more restricted stimulus. If we reduce the stimulus to a small spot of light, we might observe varying behavior from an afferent neuron, depending on how that neuron was connected to the stimulated receptors.

In the case of the "on" cell, stimulation of any of the receptors that made a direct connection with the neuron from which we were recording would result in an "on"-type response (Figure 12.2). If the stimulus fell on receptors not connected to the neuron, there would not be a response to the stimulus. It should then be possible to measure the **receptive field** for that cell. A receptive field may be considered a map of the transducers that feed information into a certain neuron. In the case of the eye, the receptive field is that region of the retina that, when stimulated, results in an evoked potential from the recorded structure. Receptive fields can be similarly located on certain regions of the skin for specific "touch" neurons.

If the neuron is an "on-off" cell, and if the excitatory and inhibitory information comes from different groups of receptors, it is possible to establish an "on" region and an "off" region within the receptive field (Figure 12.3).

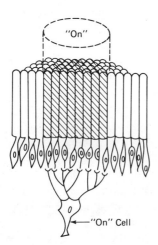

Figure 12.2 A hypothetical synaptic network for an "on" cell. The activity of the photoreceptors within a limited region converge on a single neuron. The population of transducers which synapse on the cell determines its receptive field.

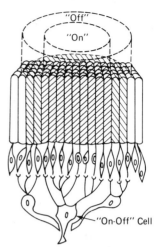

Figure 12.3 An "on-off" cell ("on" center). The same excitatory synapses as the "on" cell (Figure 12.2) with additional inhibitory cells carrying the activity of surrounding photoreceptors. The total receptive field is established by the population of transducers which excite or inhibit the "on-off" cell.

Usually, there is a central region that yields an "on" response and a peripheral region of "off" activity; such cells are called **"on-center" cells.** It is not too difficult to imagine that the neuron is directly connected to the receptors in the "on" region, and that the information from the peripheral regions of the field comes through the inhibitory intermediary neurons. It should be noted that there are also **"off-center" cells** in the visual system. It is not impossible to imagine an area of indirect connections surrounded by direct connections, but the mechanism for "on-off" fields probably is more complicated than it would first appear.

Most discussions of visual fields imply that the "on" and "off" fields are circular and concentric, like the rings around a bulls'-eye. The receptive field for any visual neuron is usually neither of these. In addition, visual receptive fields have been shown to change with the intensity of the stimulus light. For any given brightness, a visual field may be established, but there are different visual fields for different levels of brightness. Changeable receptive fields substantially complicate the problem of explaining the coding mechanisms of the sensory nervous system. With this acknowledgment of complications, we will consider visual fields as though they were essentially circular and approximately concentric. Such an approach makes it much easier to speculate on the possible mechanisms.

Manipulating the size of the light stimulus on an "on-center" receptive field creates a peculiar reversal in neuronal activity. If the stimulus spot is very small and falls entirely within the "on" area of the receptive field, the cell will show "on" activity. Increasing the extent of the stimulus increases the vigor of the "on" response so long as the stimulus falls only within the "on" region. If we continue to expand the extent of the stimulus, the cell will eventually exhibit a decrease in its response. As the stimulus infringes on the surrounding "off" region, the strength of the "on" response is less because of the subtractive effect of the inhibitory processes.

The idea that a cell reporting "on" in a certain region will reduce its activity by stimulation of a neighboring region has important ramifications in understanding certain perceptual phenomena. **Lateral inhibition** describes the connections and process that lead to the reduced neuronal activity. Lateral inhibition is easiest explained by recording from a different kind of eye.

Insects and some sea animals (such as the horseshoe crab) have a compound eye. Instead of a single lens that focuses the light on an array of receptors like humans have, horseshoe crabs have a large number of narrow-angle, individual eyes, each with its own lens and its own sensory cells. Adjacent "eyes" in this multifaceted system respond to unique but overlapping segments of the visual world. The individual eyes in the compound eye are called ommatidia, and each ommatidium can be individually stimulated and recorded from. Observing the evoked potential of neighboring ommatidia to a constant-brightness light stimulus yields the following data (Figure 12.4). If cell A alone is stimulated, there is a strong "on" response from cell A and nothing from cell B. Stimulation of B alone is similarly predictable. Simultaneous stimulation results in the expected "on" response from each cell, but

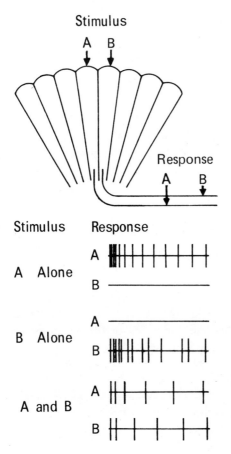

Figure 12.4 Lateral inhibition in the compound eye. Stimulus A and Stimulus B fall only on eye segment A and B, respectively. The activity of a neighboring cell inhibits (reduces spike frequency) the response of the transducer cell.

the intensity of the response is sharply reduced. In other words, the activity of the neighboring cell somehow inhibits the activity of a given cell. Adjacent cells must be interconnected in some inhibitory network (lateral inhibition).

The compound eye in the horseshoe crab and the complex retinal connections in the mammalian visual system result in a similar phenomenon. The information about the visual world is coded by the cellular response to a central excitatory field surrounded by an inhibitory field. If the stimulus is restricted to the excitatory region, the cell gives a clear and distinct "on" response. If the stimulus is of such extent to also stimulate the surrounding inhibitory region, the cellular response is much less distinct.

The net effect of the lateral inhibition mechanism is that the visual neurons not only code the brightness characteristics of a stimulus but simultaneously respond to the stimulus characteristics of the surrounding area. A small spot of light will result in a greater evoked potential than the same spot of light encircled by other lights. By adjusting the stimulus parameters carefully, a given cell will give a greater response to a dim spot of light than to a brighter light flooding the whole eye.

The perceptual result of lateral inhibition is that visual discontinuities are enhanced, while uniform fields are deemphasized. The **border contrast** effect illustrates this characteristic of lateral inhibition. If we carefully observe our perception of a visual display that fills the left half with a solid white stimulus and the right half with a uniform black, we will find that the white and black surfaces appear to be uniform except at the border where the two meet. The brightness appears accentuated on each side of the border.

If we systematically analyze the activity of the cells reporting this array, we find why the border appears enhanced. Cells with a receptive field totally in the white region of the display are active, but simultaneously inhibited by the similar surrounding activity. Cells near the black border, on the other hand, have a significant part of their inhibitory field that is not being stimulated. Thus, these cells show a "brighter" response to the white stimulus.

Cells with receptive fields totally in the black region of the display are relatively inactive because of the low stimulus level. Cells near the white border are rendered even less active by the inhibitory effect of their stimulated neighbors. Since brightness is coded in terms of cellular activity, the regions near the border appear "super white" or "super black."

Another example of border contrast may be observed when you are sitting in a bathtub of hot water or a swimming pool of cold water. Admittedly, all of the affected skin area reports "hot" or "cold," but the message comes through most distinctly at the ring around the skin formed by the surface of the water. The thermal border between the air and the hot or cold water is definitely enhanced!

Lateral inhibition also results in the accentuation of small points or narrow lines. In some cases, a poorly defined stimulus may be sharpened by the lateral inhibition mechanism so that the stimulus is easily perceived. This function is probably necessary for the perception of pitch in the ear. It appears likely that some form of lateral inhibition occurs in all sensory systems.

AUTHOR'S   The visual system appears to accentuate the role of discon-
COMMENTS   tinuity or change in transmitting the information to the
brain. The accentuation is accomplished by means of different inhibitory
processes that are a part of the afferent neural circuitry. "On-off" cells respond to temporal changes in the visual environment. To assist in this process,
adaptation readjusts the system to be maximally responsive to any change in a
steady stimulus.

Lateral inhibition, on the other hand, accentuates spatial discontinuities.
The lateral inhibition mechanism sharpens indistinct images, accentuates fine
details, and emphasizes the contrast at borders. All of these tend to heighten
the ability to perceive and evaluate objects in the visual field.

Each of these known phenomena causes the neurons in the visual pathway to deviate from a code which only reports the stimulus characteristics.
The visual system appears to sacrifice encoding absolute stimulus characteristics to report relative information. The lateral inhibition mechanism
introduces an important nervous system device. In addition to the "vertical"
pathways transmitting information from the transducers to the CNS, these
pathways are interconnected by "horizontal" cells. The resultant network
provides opportunities for elaborate exchange of information at each succeeding level. Such a "vertical-horizontal" latticework appears in many higher
nervous system structures.

13

Feature Detectors

Adaptation and border contrast show that the perceptual system emphasizes certain features from the total stimulus display. Visual research in many species indicates that visual information is coded into a number of highly specific "features." Cells with special feature-transmission characteristics are found at all levels between the transducers and the brain. Lateral inhibition creates the border contrast phenomenon, causing us to "misperceive" shades of gray because of the surrounding field. We usually tend to "blame" the cortex for this misperception. Since lateral inhibition occurs before the message leaves the eye, the misperception is an inherent part of the information received by the brain. Many perceptual phenomena may be attributed to the coding characteristics of the sensory pathway. To put it another way, significant data processing occurs before the cortex receives information.

An "on-center" cell is especially tuned to report a very specific feature, namely, a light that exactly fills its excitatory field. A light with lesser extent will not stimulate all of the excitatory transducers. A light of any greater extent will introduce inhibitory activity, which will decrease the total activity of the cell. Thus, we could describe an "on-center" cell as being especially suited for reporting a "light patch" of a certain size. Similarly, an "off-center" cell may be called a "black patch" detector because of the characteristics of the stimulus that stimulates a maximal response from this cell.

Pioneer work in recording from such specific feature detectors consisted of recording evoked potentials while bombarding the eye with a variety of visual stimuli until a maximum response was obtained from the cell. One of the first such experiments revealed that cells in the frog's eye would respond only to a horizontal border that was darker below and lighter above. Other cells were activated by a concave line moving in the direction of concavity, and still others responded only to a small, dark, moving spot. This is not an exhaustive list of the special visual cells in the frog's eye, but it exemplifies the variety of feature detectors discovered.

The "small, dark, moving spot" detector probably accounts for a basic characteristic of frog behavior. Anyone who has captured and/or kept frogs knows that frogs eat live flies but ignore dead ones. Many a youngster has learned the valuable skill of capturing or stunning flies without killing them to meet the finicky appetite of a pet frog. Others have learned to dangle a dead fly on a string in order to fool their pet into eating. It would seem that the small, dark moving spot detector may actually be a "fly," or "bug," detector in the normal frog perceptual world. Since this **bug detector** would not be activated by a nonmoving stimulus, dead flies do not meet the stimulus conditions to be seen! It turns out that the frog is not averse to dead flies at all if he could only see them! The string ruse merely introduces the necessary movement. Another way to stimulate the bug detector is to keep the fly suspended and unmoving, but slowly shift the background scene. For example, place the frog in a circular container, suspend the fly inside, and slowly rotate the container. The frog will shift with the moving background scene, and the stationary fly will appear to be moving in the opposite direction. Thus, the movement need not be the stimulus itself; shifting the eye (or the whole frog) can cause the stimulus to move across the receptors, and the cell will respond.

The frog's visual system may actually be so primitive that stationary objects actually disappear because the information is not coded and transmitted to the brain. We higher animals, of course, can perceive stationary objects. Stop and recall, however, how difficult it is to see a deer that is "frozen" until it flicks an ear or otherwise provides a movement cue. Put another way, if we want someone to notice us, we do not stand still! Waving and jumping up and down introduces an important "feature" to our visual display in terms of our noticeability.

In the frog, the survival value of a bug detector is obvious, and there is a certain elegance in finding this important environmental feature being especially coded early in the sensory process. The horizontal border (dark below and light above) detector similarly serves a potentially valuable function for a wild frog who needs to keep track of the surface of a pond. The moving convex shape detector has been suggested as necessary to keep track of hungry large-mouth bass. Since the detector exists, it probably has some functional significance in the frog's visual world.

Visual feature detectors are a rich source of research data on the visual system. The following examples are a sample of the known feature detectors in frogs, rabbits, cats, and monkeys. Some of the neurons are in the eye, others are found in the visual cortex, and still others are located at all intermediary points along the visual pathway. Certain feature detectors differ in their location with different species. The necessary neuronal connections are probably similar, irrespective of their precise location.

STRAIGHT-LINE DETECTORS

Some axons in the visual system show a burst of spike activity to a specific straight line. The line must fall on a certain portion of the retina and must be oriented so that it is at a precise angle. A line of the correct orientation but not falling on the precise location of the retina causes no response. A line in the right location but oriented incorrectly causes only a minimal response. A line in the right place and at the right angle causes an obvious response!

In most cases, a feature detector is stimulated in a manner similar to the "on-off" detectors. In the case of the **"straight-line" detector,** the line is actually a bar of light that is turned on and off. The straight-line detector responds to this stimulus with an "on"-type response.

It is relatively simple to devise a neuronal circuit to account for the straight-line detectors (Figure 13.1). If the neuron were simply connected to a straight row of photoreceptors by means of excitatory synapses, it would respond with a maximum response to the stimulus that simultaneously activates that group of transducers. This is the probable mechanism, except the straight-line detector cells are technically connected to a specific row of "on-center" cells. Thus, the bar of light stimulates a row of transducers that are in the "on" region of a specific group of "on-center" cells which all impinge on the straight-line detector with excitatory synapses. Photostimulation of the appropriate population of transducers activates all of the "on-center" cells, which creates a deluge of excitatory synaptic activity on the straight-line detector. Stated simply, it is a straight-line detector because it is wired that way.

MOVEMENT DETECTORS

By assuming a slightly different response characteristic for the cell, we can use the same circuitry to explain the occurrence of another feature detector. Some visual neurons respond to movement to the right or left (or up and down). Such a **"movement" detector** can be explained by hypothesizing that the cell combines or integrates the activity of all of the "on" cell's activity (Figure 13.2). In other words, as long as any of the "on" cells are active, the movement detector is active. Since the "on" cells are known to demonstrate adaptation if the stimulus motion is stopped, the intermediary "on" cell ceases firing, and the movement cell is not stimulated. The bug detector in the frog's eye is similarly explained, except the intermediary "on" cells are

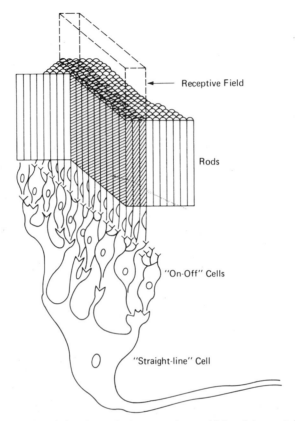

Figure 13.1 A scheme for the retinal connections which might explain a straight-line detector. Notice that the "straight-line" cell summarizes the information from certain "on-off" cells, which in turn summarize the activity of the phototransducers, which are positioned to respond to a straight-line stimulus.

not restricted to a straight line. Since the frog's bug detector is responsive to a black spot, this cell must be connected to "off-center" neurons in the frog's retina.

DIRECTION DETECTORS

Most movement detectors are more selective than the bug detector. Movement detectors are typically highly selective to movement in a certain direction. Thus, the cell may respond for movement from left to right, yet be completely quiet when the stimulus moves in the opposite direction. Once again, we will hypothesize that the **"direction" detector** is connected to a straight row of "on" cells (Figure 13.3). In order to restrict the response to a stimulus moving from left to right, it is necessary to hypothesize a directional form of

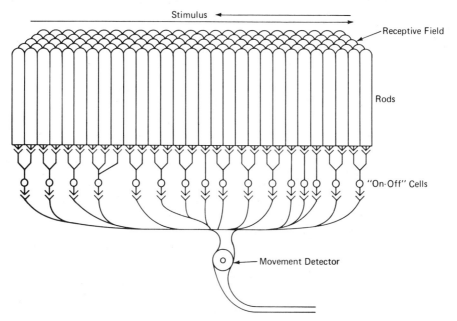

Figure 13.2 A movement detector. Hypothetical (and stylized) synaptic connections for a cell which would respond to movement to the left or to the right.

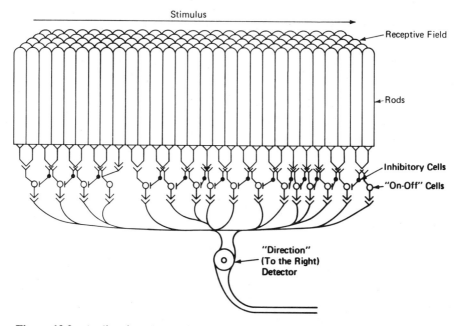

Figure 13.3 A direction detector. Adding the small black inhibitory cells between adjacent retinal regions converts a movement detector to a directionally sensitive visual cell.

lateral inhibition. If the activity of each "on" cell inhibits the transmission (but not the activity) of the adjacent "on" cell to its left, the directional sensitivity is explained. A stimulus progressing from left to right will sequentially activate the row of "on" cells, with a resulting chain of excitatory synaptic events depolarizing the direction detector. The inhibitory connections will be inhibiting activity that has already occurred. Movement of the stimulus from right to left will create a wave of inhibitory activity which blocks the transmission ability of each cell just before it becomes active. The effect of this circuitry is that each "on" cell is stimulated by the transducer activity, but the activity is not transmitted because of the directional inhibitory connections.

Since the "on" cells adapt, we can perform an interesting experiment on a direction detector. We can introduce a stimulus, move it in the "non-preferred" direction but stop it in the middle, and then start it again. If the movement is stopped long enough, the "on" cell will adapt, meaning that the inhibition of the transmission of the neighbor(s) to the left is also stopped. Then when the movement is resumed, the direction detector should become active until the inhibitory wave is reestablished. This is what happens. Direction detectors are capable of responding to movement in the "wrong" direction, but only for a brief period. Movement in the "right" direction will continue for the entire length of the receptive field.

Direction and movement detectors respond with a spike rate directly related to the velocity of the stimulus. This is completely compatible with the hypothesized neural mechanism. The faster the movement of the stimulus, the more the synaptic activity on the movement detector, and the greater the depolarization which leads to a high spike rate. In terms of the stimulus dimensions, quality is the direction of the movement, and quantity is the speed that it is moving.

Direction detectors also respond to a stimulus that is moved diagonally across its receptive field (Figure 13.4). If the movement includes some of the "preferred" direction, the cell responds with a lower level of activity. Analysis shows that the direction detectors respond to the movement component of the preferred dimension. To the technically minded, this means that the direction detectors can respond to their own Cartesian vector coordinate of any movement. If this feature were fully utilized, four basic direction detectors (up, down, right, left) could code all visual movement. Instead, there are an infinite number of directions represented by direction detectors. Redundancy (or overlapping of functions) is frequently found in the components in a nervous system.

COMPLEX FEATURES

"On-off" cells are found in the retina of the eye, only one synapse away from the phototransducers. Straight-line, movement, and direction detectors are found after the second synapse in the pathways leading to the visual cortex.

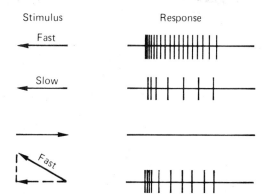

Figure 13.4 Response characteristics of a direction detector. The
cell responds to any component of
the motion which lies in its "preferred plane." Thus, in the bottom
example, the cell responds to the
slower horizontal component of the
diagonal stimulus.

Recording in the visual cortex shows what occurs after yet another synaptic
junction in the pathway. Cortical cells can be found in the cat that respond
only to straight lines in a certain orientation and moving in a certain direction!
A line at the wrong angle or moving in the wrong direction or in the wrong
part of the visual field will not cause the cell to fire. The neuronal circuitry
to explain such a cortical cell is a combination of those already observed
(Figure 13.5). Straight-line detectors with receptor fields in a row on the
retina are synaptically connected to a directionally sensitive cortical cell. Because there is at least one more level of complexity that has been observed,
these moving straight-line detectors have been labeled **simple cortical cells.**

The **complex cortical cells** exhibit most of the same characteristics as the
simple cortical cells except that the length of the stimulus lines is also critical.
A line that is too short or too long causes a diminution in the magnitude of the

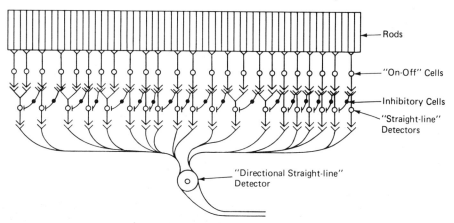

Figure 13.5 A scheme for a simple cortical visual cell which responds to a straight
line, moved in a specific direction. Notice that the final cell is found in the cortex (at
least in some animals). All of the schematic diagrams indicate steps along the visual
pathway without necessary reference to their CNS location. The location may be different
with different species.

neuronal response. Apparently, the complex cortical cells have a surrounding inhibitory area which makes them maximally sensitive to a line of a specific length. The neuronal circuitry needed to explain the behavior of complex cortical cells involves excitatory connections with simple cortical cells combined with inhibitory connections with adjacent cells. Complex cortical cells are much more "precise" in the nature of their necessary stimulus than the more general simple cortical cells.

As stated previously, most movement detectors respond with activity directly related to the speed of the motion. Others, however, seem to respond selectively to slow movement. The faster the movement, the less the response; thus, there are also "slow" detectors. Recent research has indicated that there are feature detectors which respond to certain straight-line intersections. These "angle" detectors, when combined with the straight-line detectors, would provide all of the stimulus elements needed to perceive the outline of most objects in our visual world. In each case, we can hypothesize a neuronal circuit with combinations of excitatory and inhibitory cellular connections which account for the cell's response.

A feature-detector mechanism is probably involved with depth perception. Some cortical cells respond only to a common visual stimulus presented to specific regions of both eyes. These **"binocular disparity"** detectors would provide immediate three-dimensional (distance) information.

It is difficult to anticipate the upper limit for the specific intent of feature detectors. From the primary visual areas on the cortex, information is sent to the association visual areas. In monkeys, visual information is then transmitted to the inferotemporal region of the cortex. Inferotemporal cells have been demonstrated to respond only to the appearance of a monkey hand, the shadow of a hemostat, or a bottle brush. Since this cortical region seems to be involved with the recognition of visual stimuli, recognition may consist of the activity of an extraordinarily complex cell.

Other research has located a cell that responds whenever a new visual stimulus appears. Such a **"novelty" detector** has obvious survival value, but defies structural description. There is the distinct possibility that we have a separate cell for distinguishing friends from strangers.

Feature detectors probably exist in the other senses. Experiments in monkeys have shown auditory cells that respond only to the sound of a monkey's cry.

FUNCTIONAL APPLICATIONS

The present emphasis on straight lines is largely an artifact of the stimulus displays presently utilized in visual research. Even at this relatively naive level, however, we can draw a number of conclusions about the functional organization of the nervous system. In the eye of the rabbit, for example, the receptive fields for direction detectors are concentrated in a band across the middle of the animal's field of vision (Figure 13.6). Most of these direction detectors have a predominately horizontal orientation. From the rabbit's point of view, the direction detectors are concentrated in a band along the horizon and specialized to report movement along that band. Since the rabbit is a land-dwelling animal, most land predators (coyotes, humans) will appear within this band of motion sensitivity. Thus, the rabbit has a concentration of movement detectors located where the perception of such motion is likely to contribute most to its survival. After detecting a predator, if the rabbit resorts to full flight, the horizontal motion detectors then provide vital information concerning the location of trees, rocks, and shrubs which are whizzing through the visual world of the fleeing rabbit. The motion detectors that monitor the sky portion of the rabbit's visual world are not concentrated in the horizontal plane. Although not as heavily concentrated, the motion detectors here seem to be oriented in all directions. This arrangement of movement detectors is more suited for detecting aerial predators such as hawks.

The highly functional concentration of feature detectors where they will be most useful to the survival of the organism is logical but enigmatic. How do they become so concentrated? Experiments with rearing kittens in restricted visual environments indicate that kittens reared in a world of vertical stripes lose most of their horizontal straight-line detectors. Litter mates reared in a world of horizontal stripes lose most of their vertical detectors. There is little doubt that the unused neuronal circuits atrophy with disuse. It is not yet clear whether additional circuits are established to focus on the

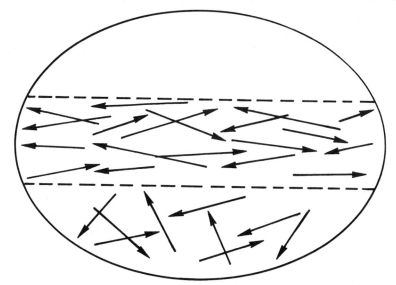

Figure 13.6 A rabbit's eye view of the moving world. A concentration of horizontally oriented direction detectors is found in the portion of the visual field which normally sees the horizon. The upper portion of the visual field contains more randomly oriented detectors, while there are essentially no direction detectors "looking" downward.

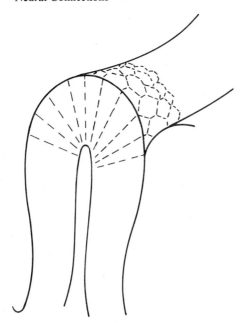

Figure 13.7 A cross section of a cortical gyrus sketching the possible columnar organization suggested by the cortical location of common direction detectors.

features that are encountered. In either case, the visual system does develop a preponderance of neurons appropriate to the environment experienced.

Simple and complex cortical cells provide a hint of a columnar organization in the cortex (Figure 13.7). Although there is no obvious anatomical indications of the difference between adjacent columns, the activity of the various cortical cells indicates that functional columns exist. If the recording electrode penetrates the gyrus perpendicular to the surface, and then moves directly down a column, all of the cortical cells are responsive to a line oriented in the same direction. If we record from cells in the same column, we need not rotate the line to stimulate the detector, although we will have to move the location of the line, or the direction of movement. If the electrode penetrates the gyrus at an angle, so that it traverses several columns in succession, it is necessary to readjust the angular orientation of the line as new cortical columns are encountered.

We know that the feature detectors become active when a specific stimulus is presented to the eye. We assume that the activity of this cell signals the occurrence of that stimulus. It then follows that if we were to stimulate a feature cell artificially, the associated feature would be perceived by the organism. If we were to stimulate electrically the axon of a straight-line detector, the visual system would report the occurrence of a straight line. Such an experiment has obvious logistic limitations, since it requires human subjects to report the feature that occurs. There may be an example of a naturally occurring stimulation condition in certain humans.

Individuals who suffer from migraine headaches often report a concomitant visual phenomenon known as fortification illusion (Figure 13.8). The sufferer experiences a spreading wave of jagged straight-line segments followed

Figure 13.8 A "fortification illusion" sketched by an individual with migraine headaches.

by a wave of visual insensitivity. The term "fortification" applies to the similarity of the visual appearance to maps of military fortifications.

Migraine headaches are known to be associated with a change in the blood flow to cranial arteries. Such a circulatory disruption can create a wave of spreading depression on the visual cortex. The spreading wave of activity may artificially stimulate the cortical feature cells, creating the perception of straight lines. The following wave of neuronal depression is associated with the visually insensitive area that follows the appearance of the fortification for several minutes. Some migraine headaches are accompanied by an analogous touch phenomenon, which probably indicates a similiar effect in the bodily sense area on the parietal lobe. Motor effects and short-term disability are also known to occur if the migraine affects the motor area of the frontal lobes.

The existence of movement detectors provides an explanation for a common perceptual phenomenon. It has been known for a number of years that two lights flashing alternately at a certain rate are invariably perceived as a single light moving back and forth between the two light sources. This perception of motion when it is not there is known as the **phi phenomenon.**

The phi phenomenon is the basis of moving pictures, television, some neon signs, many theater marquees, and some automobile turn signals. In each case, the illusion of movement is created by the carefully timed sequence of lights in slightly different locations. The circuitry that explains motion detectors codes movement and sequential position in exactly the same way.

Recall that the motion detector was connected to a straight row of "on" cells. A stimulus that generated activity in any of these cells created a wave of excitatory activity in the motion detector. Now, instead of moving the light across the visual field of the "on" cells, arrange an array of lights, each one of which will stimulate a different "on" cell. Sequentially flashing, each light will create a wave of excitatory synaptic activity on the motion-detecting cell. Since the cell responds only to the neuronal activity of the "on" cells, it receives exactly the same information from a moving light or a carefully timed sequence of separate flashing lights. Thus, the phi phenomenon is a direct function of the feature-detection organization in the visual system.

AUTHOR'S Feature detectors are a logical and pragmatic extension of
COMMENTS the lateral inhibition mechanism. The visual system appears
to emphasize those dimensions of the environment that have crucial importance to the organism. The discovery of a bug detector in the frog elegantly
illustrates the utility of a feature-encoding mechanism. The discovery of a
"monkey paw" cell in the cortex of a monkey indicates that the feature-
extraction process may be extended to much more complicated applications
in higher animals.

Feature-detector research is by no means complete. It is inevitable that
other feature cells will be discovered. Thus, changes in the explanations for
the encoding and decoding of information in the visual system will be in a
state of flux for some time. Motion and direction information is known to be
of use in controlling reflexive eye movements, which explains why these
feature dimensions "attract our attention."

Chapter

14

Sensory Organization

Feature detectors are an important component of a sensory system. A list of individual feature detectors provides useful data about the process of perception as well as the operation of functional synaptic connections. A sensory system is more than a collection of independent features. Perception involves the simultaneous integration of the information from every facet of the system. Although the discovery of new components will undoubtedly alter interpretations, it is possible to outline some tentative sensory organizational principles.

SPECIALIZATION IN THE SENSORY FIELD

The horizontal movement detectors in the rabbit are especially concentrated in that portion of the rabbit's visual field where horizontal movement is most likely to occur, and where such information is most valuable for the animal's survival. Feature detectors are not distributed uniformly throughout the visual field, but are distributed according to their contribution to the visual process. Most of the detectors that were discussed occur in the periphery of the visual field. In other words, feature detectors code the visual world that we perceive out of the "corner of our eye." The center of our field of vision is possibly organized along different lines. There is evidence to indicate that the central

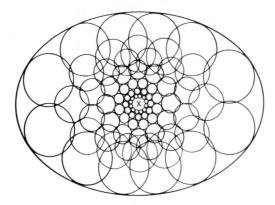

Figure 14.1 Distribution and size of typical receptive fields. The extreme periphery is marked by very large (and relatively poor acuity) receptive fields. As the distance from the fovea (X) decreases, the size of the field decreases, and accuracy increases.

part of our vision may have receptor fields only one transducer in extent. As a general rule, as we move farther out into the periphery, the receptive fields of visual neurons become larger and larger (Figure 14.1). The receptive fields in the extreme periphery may include thousands of transducers. The visual acuity of a cell with a perceptual field of thousands of transducers cannot be very good. Thus, the extreme periphery ought to be a blur of not very precise visual information.

This, in fact, is the case. Cells with their receptive field in the periphery provide only crude information to the total visual impression. The extremely precise visual information that we call 20/20 vision is available only in about 1 degree of the center of our total visual field. This visual angle fills approximately the diameter of a dime held at arm's length. As we move outward from this tiny area of precise visual information, the message becomes more and more "fuzzy." Examination of the relation between the areas of the retina and the corresponding areas on the visual cortex shows that approximately 50 percent of the visual cortex is activated by the 1 degree center of the visual field. By moving the eyes, we can "scan" the visual scene with this extremely precise visual system. The feature detectors in the periphery inform the visual system where important features are located. By using this area of precise visual information to sample the important features of the total visual world, we collect enough information to see it all "clearly."

A list of visual characteristics that would be important to the survival of the individual would include a number of the characteristics of the feature detectors. Stationary objects are less likely to pose survival problems than moving objects. Predators need to locate their prey, and the prey needs to be alert to approaching predators. Motion detectors alert us to one of the most important survival features in our environment. The sudden appearance or disappearance of an object would similarly warrant immediate scrutiny. The "on-off" cells alert us to such occurrences. In visually examining an object, the maximum information is found in the contours, borders, edges, corners, and so on. Thus, the feature detectors indicate the location of such high-information features for the rapid and efficient use of the narrow field of accurate vision.

Advertisers have known for years that motion will "catch the eye." Rotating signs, flashing lights, bright colors with highly contrasting borders, all attract attention by stimulating feature detectors that increase the likelihood the eyes will scan that feature. In some cases, a feature is nearly impossible to ignore. Movement invariably causes a "glance" in that direction. Usually, we make a quick evaluation of the source of the movement without conscious awareness of the process. Occasionally, such stimuli are so compelling that they become an annoying distraction, and we have to take measures to protect ourselves from our own feature detectors.

The gradual increase in receptive field size toward the periphery is another mechanism for focusing the high-acuity visual region. The detectors in the extreme periphery simply transmit that there is "something out there." As the eyes move in that direction, the stimulus is moved into increasingly selective visual fields. More precise information is being coded while the eyes are in motion. The decreasing size of the visual fields toward the center allows us to "steer" the eyes with increasing accuracy to look precisely at the stimulus.

A somewhat analogous situation is noted in the sense of touch. Different areas of the skin are relatively sensitive or insensitive to fine differences in touch information (Table 14.1). When we wish to process fine tactile information about an object, we usually use the fingertips, an area where the touch perceptual fields are very precise. Babies gain touch information by means of an even more sensitive area. The lips have tactile fields even smaller than the fingertips.

Growing evidence suggests that much of the eye movement is controlled by circuits associated with peripheral feature detectors. In primitive animals lacking a cortex, visual processing is accomplished in a region called the optic tectum. In the human CNS, this tectal area still exists in the form of the superior colliculi, but the fine visual processing is found in the occipital lobes of the cortex. In fact, removal of the cortical primary visual area results in blindness; the human tectum is no longer capable of the visual processing necessary for vision. The superior colliculi are still connected to the eyes by a branch of the main visual pathway. Evoked potential recordings in this branch suggest that the axons which branch toward the colliculi are predominately

TABLE 14.1   Accuracy of Localization of Pressures for Various Bodily Regions
(Wenger, Jones, & Jones, 1956)

Region	Error (cm)
Forehead	0.63
Lip	0.10
Chin	0.54
Forearm (volar)	0.85
Back of hand	0.65
Palm	0.43
Fingertip (volar)	0.10
Thigh	1.60

movement detectors. The human colliculi control the oculomotor reflexes, which means that these structures are responsible for the automatic glance toward a source of movement. The tectum is still intimately involved in the processing of visual information. The cortex has taken over the fine sensory processing, but the tectum provides vital preliminary work!

Feature detectors suggest that the synapses do much more than simply transfer the message to another neuron in the pathway. The postsynaptic cell integrates the total incoming information from many presynaptic cells into a single output message. The data-integration process is cumulative at each synaptic junction in the visual pathway. The transduced visual information is converted into "on-off" messages one synapse away from the transducer. At the second synapse, straight-line and directional movement is coded. It takes another synaptic combination of straight-line detectors to explain, for example, simple cortical cells. Each synapse in the visual pathway is reason to suspect the occurrence of a new and more complicated feature detector. The "lower" features are not always lost but are often also transmitted to the optic cortex. The optic pathway is essentially cumulative, retaining the "simpler" information codes but adding more "feature" channels with each synapse.

CONVERGENCE

The complex feature detectors in the visual system require a remarkably sophisticated set of neuronal synaptic connections (Figure 14.2). A straight-line detector, for example, must be connected to a certain group of "on-off" cells which lie in a straight row across some part of the visual field. Each of these "on-off" cells must be connected to a specific population of transducer cells, all located in a restricted region of the retina. If the retina is stimulated with precisely the "right" straight line, all of the transducers become active. The activity of several transducers converge on each "on-off" cell, and the "on" cells, in turn, converge on a single straight-line detector. This straight-line detector is undoubtedly one of a number of similar cells that converge on another cell further down the line to specify a more complex feature.

Convergence is, of course, the logical product of a neuron with its ability to combine multiple postsynaptic potentials into a single axonal message. There is a certain elegance in the discovery that the neuronal summation capability is apparently utilized in such a straightforward manner.

DIVERGENCE

If the nervous system were strictly a convergent system, then we would find millions of transducers converging on thousands of "on-off" cells, which would converge on hundreds of straight-line detectors, which would converge on tens of simple cortical cells, which would possibly culminate in "the" single

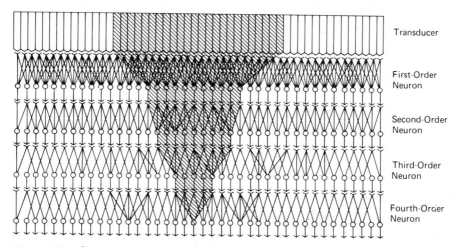

Figure 14.2 Convergence. The probable "wiring diagram" for feature detectors. The activity of many transducers converges through several intermediary levels to a single cell.

paramount visual feature. This, of course, is not the case. The visual information is continually rearranged into new stimulus features, and there is an increasing number of different dimensions being extracted and transmitted as the synaptic distance from the transducers increases.

The information from a single transducer is shared by the mechanisms of many feature detectors (Figure 14.3). A straight-line detector does not have exclusive rights to the information from all of "its" transducers. Other straight-line detectors function in the same visual region. Some of these detectors have receptive fields that cross one another. The transducer located at the intersection undoubtedly contributes to the activity of either straight-line

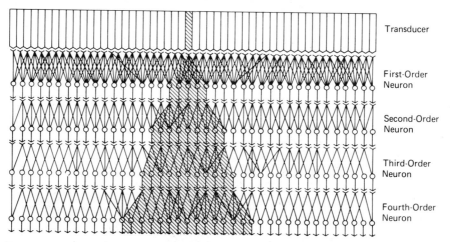

Figure 14.3 Divergence. The activity of a single transducer contributes to the information arriving at many higher-order cells.

detector. Thus, many straight-line detectors share the information from the transducer located at an intersection. This example is oversimplified, since there are intervening "on-off" cells involved in the mechanism. Therefore, the information from a single transducer must be distributed to all of the "on-off" cells with a receptor field encompassing that transducer. This information is then combined and redistributed to all of the feature detectors that utilize these "on-off" cells as a source of information. Simultaneous with the convergence of information from many transducers to a single feature detector, information from a single transducer is **diverging** to be a component in the activity of many feature detectors.

The optic pathway is a complicated network of neuronal connections. Visual information is being redistributed and processed in complex ways that make it difficult to imagine how the visual cortex can "see" anything but a confusing array of straight lines, motions, and other coded features. A single point of light, which stimulates only a few receptors, may cause activity that spreads everywhere, so that the cortex would seem to have no chance to locate the original source. At this juncture, it would seem far simpler and more logical to design a simple point-to-point transmission system. That is, information from a transducer is carried by a single axon to the cortex where the visual array is reconstructed in an unambiguous manner. The combination of convergence and divergence does not sacrifice the basic information and has significant advantages over a point-to-point system.

PARALLEL CONDUCTION

Precise location information appears to be irretrievably lost in the ambiguous receptive field of an "on-off" cell. Whereas the transducer was telling us "It's right here!" we find that the "on-off" cell is saying "It's somewhere in this area." A number of "on-off" cells are simultaneously stimulated by the transducer, although each of them reports for different (but overlapping) receptive fields. If all of these cells shout "I see it!" at the same time, the brain can conclude that the stimulus lies in the region of overlap of the active receptive fields. The location of the stimulus is approximately indicated by several cells, but the exact location can be precisely determined as the area where they all agree (Figure 14.4).

It is possible to hypothesize a location detector in the brain that responds only when this unique combination of "on-off" cells is active. In its simplest form, the activity of a single transducer is transmitted to the brain by means of several "on" cells, where the information reconverges on a single location detector. This system is known as **parallel conduction,** since the same message is divided among several transmission channels.

Parallel conduction has an important advantage over a point-to-point system (Figure 14.5). If one transmission channel is destroyed, the information is still transmitted. If a channel is lost in a point-to-point system, there

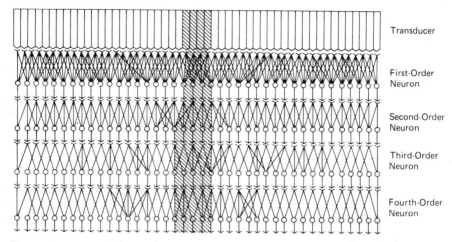

Figure 14.4 Parallel conduction. The combination of convergence and divergence results in information being transmitted along several parallel pathways. (The "rule" used for activation is that at least two synapses must be active to trigger each neuron.)

will be a "hole" in the picture where the information is missing. If the message is distributed among ten parallel transmission lines, the loss of one line means that the information is still transmitted along the remaining nine lines. Since the neurons are subject to damage and/or replacement, parallel conduction allows the system to use alternate routes. Even the loss of 50 percent of the transmission lines allows a considerable amount of information to be transmitted, and by adjusting the threshold of the receiver cell, one might be able to "reconstruct" a reasonable facsimile of the total message. If the re-

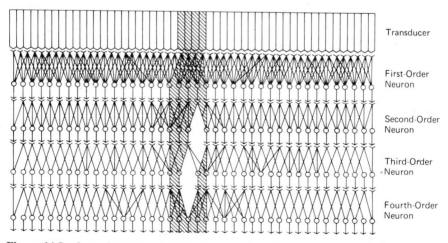

Figure 14.5 One advantage of parallel conduction. The loss of a second-order and a third-order neuron does not disrupt the information flow. The same fourth-order neurons respond to the stimulus despite disruption of some of the pathways.

ceptive fields of two "on-center" cells overlapped in a tiny area, simultaneous activity of these two cells would accurately locate the stimulus. Thus, two channels can be quite precise, and additional channels only confirm or increase the precision of the message.

Enhanced precision is another advantage of a parallel conduction system. Each channel provides an independent estimate of the characteristics of the message carried. There are data suggesting that individual neurons may deviate from a precise logarithmic code of stimulus intensity. If each cell approximates a logarithmic code, then a statistical average from all channels can be more accurate than any single channel is capable of transmitting.

It was mentioned earlier that neurons occasionally show a burst of activity without an obvious stimulus as the cause. This extraneous "noise" has been a nuisance to scientists taking single-unit recordings and a puzzle to understanding the operation of the nervous system. From the point of view of a receiving cell, extraneous activity of this kind may not be such a problem. Assuming a ten-channel parallel system, we find that the receiving cell obviously reports when all ten channels are active. It probably reports when a large proportion of the channels agree there is a signal, which would compensate for any faulty channels. This same cell will probably "ignore" a burst of activity from only one channel if the other nine are all quiet. The cell can "decide" whether it is a real "signal" or simply "noise" on the basis of agreement among the channels. The neuronal mechanism for this "decision" is easily explained in the spatial-summation capacity of the neuron.

A PHILOSOPHICAL DIGRESSION

The discovery of feature detectors has revolutionized our understanding of the nervous system. Feature detectors are not figments of our theoretical imagination; you can stimulate the eye of the animal with the appropriate straight line and observe the response of the straight-line detector. Different lines, those in a different part of the visual field, those oriented at a different angle, and so on, are coded by other straight-line detectors. Although the system lacks the immediate simplicity of the point-to-point system, it has some real advantages, and there is empirical proof of its operation.

Unfortunately, this "one special cell for each feature" leads to a logical impasse. The total number of different straight lines to be coded approaches infinity! There are not enough cells in the entire nervous system to handle all of the possible straight lines we may visually encounter.

There are several possible compensatory schemes to avoid this logical predicament. Each straight-line detector may process a class of highly similar straight lines. Detectors are concentrated in the most efficient visual regions and only sparsely distributed in lower-priority regions. Either of these would reduce the numerical demand on the nervous system, but the number of straight-line detectors is still formidable. Straight-line detectors code a single stimulus dimension. The known dimensions of movement, direction, and angles accentuate the numerical demands. We have not yet considered the problem of color vision coding, and there are undoubtedly other specific features yet to be discovered. In summary, the nervous system cannot afford the luxury of spending a visual neuron completely on a single specific feature.

The neuron must encode more than a single dimension. Consider the parallel conduction channels and the ability of such a system to reject "noise." If an individual cell in the network becomes active, the mechanism rejects that activity unless it is corroborated by similar activity of other channels. Perhaps that activity of the single cell is not merely random "noise." The activity may represent the encoding of another dimension. A cell may be capable of encoding two different visual features. If one of these features is a straight line, then the cell will respond with a burst of activity when the appropriate straight-line stimulus occurs. This activity will coincide with the activity of other straight-line channels. If the other feature of this cell is "moving black spot," when the cell responds, it will coincide with the rest of the moving black spot detectors, but will be a straight-line maverick. If it responds to a straight line, the situation is reversed. The cell is capable of "specializing" in several different features. The nervous system determines which feature is being transmitted by the combination of cells active at any given time.

By allowing each cell to encode multiple dimensions, combined with the parallel channel transmission system, we have substantially changed the amount of information that can be encoded in the system. Rather than being limited to the number of individual cells, we are now talking about the total number of synaptic junctions that may be formed. With approximately a million neurons in the optic nerve, the number of transmission combinations is theoretically adequate to the task. In terms of cellular combinations, the number of potential cellular connections in the brain exceeds the number of atoms in the universe!

AUTHOR'S COMMENTS   Feature detectors are well-established components in the visual system. The implications of a feature-encoding sensory system have several ramifications to understanding the operation of the nervous system. First, a simple "point-to-point" TV analogy is inappropriate. Second, extracting certain "important" features implies that there are certain "unimportant" features that are probably ignored. Third, the occurrence of the feature detectors is functionally determined, with detectors concentrated in regions of the visual field where those features are most likely to occur. Fourth, feature information is distributed among the visual structures in the CNS. "Primitive" information is channeled to the brain stem structures, while "precision" information is sent to the cortex. Fifth, the feature detectors must be components of a sophisticated interconnected system. Lateral inhibition, convergence, divergence, and parallel conduction all could combine to form a remarkably adaptive sensory system that uses feature detectors as basic units.

V

Sensory Systems

The neurological processing of sensory information appears to follow common basic principles, but each sensory system has evolved unique characteristics oriented toward the requirements of its own stimulus realm. The transducers that have evolved to detect the variety of stimuli may be characterized as being as sensitive as is physically possible. This extreme sensitivity provides both a significant strength and weakness in the sensory system. Because the transducer cells have an impressive dynamic range, they are also subject to damage from abusive stimulus levels. These destructive levels are frequently encountered in the normal environment. To assist in controlling the stimulus impinging on the transducers, the sensory systems typically include elaborate auxiliary structures. These complicated structures provide two important stimulus-controlling functions: (1) when the stimulus is very weak, the structures help to focus or aim the sensory organ so that the stimulus is delivered most efficiently to the transducers; and (2) if the stimulus is of higher intensity, the structure provides a number of protective functions to attenuate the stimulus to tolerable levels.

Assuming that the stimulus is delivered effectively to the transducers, we find that each sensory system has special characteristics according to the transducer response in converting the stimulus characteristics for transmission in the nervous system. In addition, the sensory pathways are more than simple telegraph wires in the system.

The elaborate nervous system associated with each sensory system begins at the first synaptic junction in the sensory pathway. In addition to the manipulation of the stimulus by the auxiliary sensory organ and the signal adjustments due to the transducer characteristics, signal strength is also adjusted within the neuronal network. The incoming information is also sorted into features, which means that certain stimulus dimensions are given higher priorities, and other dimensions are essentially ignored. Each synapse and/or nucleus in the pathway represents a new level of data-information extraction in the sensory pathway.

If examined one component at a time, the individual parts of any sensory system may be simply described in terms of a specific contribution to the sensory experience. Such analysis is misleading, however, because the components are closely interrelated with other components in the total system. For example, the auxiliary organ often introduces distortion into the incoming signal. The data extraction by the neural network often compensates for the distortion. For each of the sensory systems, perceptual phenomena have been selected unique to that system. In most cases, the phenomena illustrate, or are explained, by the known characteristics of the structures and organization of the system.

SUGGESTED READINGS

Michael, C. R. Receptive fields of single optic nerve fibers in a mammal with an all-cone retina. *Journal of Neurophysiology,* 1968, **31**(2).

Michael, C. R. Retinal processing of visual images. *Scientific American,* May 1969, **220**(5), 104–114.

Perkel, D. H. & Bullock, T. H. Neural coding. *Neurosciences Research Program Bulletin,* 1968, **6**(3).

Spinelli, D. H. Visual receptive fields in the cat's retina: Complications. *Science,* 1966, **132**.

Vallecallu, E. & Svaetichin, G. The retina as a model for the functional organization of the nervous system. R. Jung & H. Kornhuber. (Eds.) *The visual system: Neurophysiology and psychophysics.* Berlin: Springer-Verlag, 1961.

Wagner, H. G., MacNichol, E. F., Jr. & Wolbarsht, M. L. The response properties of single ganglion cells in the goldfish retina. *Journal of General Physiology,* 1960, **43**.

Wagner, H. G., MacNichol, E. F., Jr. & Wolbarsht, M. L. Functional basis for "on"-center and "off"-center receptive fields in the retina. *Journal of the Optical Society of America,* 1963, **53**.

Wagner, H. G. & Wolbarsht, M. L. Studies on the functional organization of the vertebrate retina. *American Journal of Opthomology,* 1958, **46**.

Chapter 15

Vision

The most thoroughly studied of all of the sensory systems is the visual system (Figure 15.1). Ease of stimulus control, relatively easy access to the receptors and associated neuronal structures, and the importance of visual cues in the human environment—all conspire to make vision the most important sensory system to physiologists.

STRUCTURES OF THE EYE

The human eye is a spherical, fluid-filled semielastic body located in a bony orbit in the skull. There are a number of structures outside the eye itself that protect and/or assist the eye in its function. The bones of the eyebrow and cheek surround and protect the eye from major assault by external objects. The softer, movable eyelids provide protection from smaller objects, as well as supply a frequent wiping action to maintain the eye in a moistened condition. Three pairs of muscles rotate the eye within the socket. Tear ducts secrete a bathing and protective fluid which washes away foreign particles that land "in the eye."

The human eye is often compared to a camera. Both are basically a light-proof, darkened chamber with a small window in front. Light rays are admitted through the window and focused to form an image at the back of the

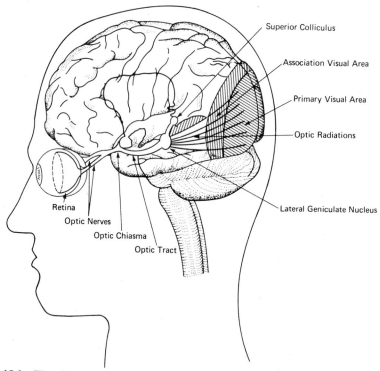

Figure 15.1   The visual system.

chamber. The photosensitive materials (film chemicals or transducers) are located at the back of the chamber.

The eye is basically a ball of three layers of semielastic material surrounding a fluid (Figure 15.2). The shape of the eye is maintained by the internal pressure of the fluid, much like an inflated ball. The outermost layer of the eye is called the sclera, or sclerotic coat. The **sclera,** an extension of the dura mater surrounding the CNS, is the tough exterior of the "ball." Most of the sclera is white in color, so that it reflects away unwanted light. In the front of the eye, the sclera is a transparent structure known as the **cornea.** The sclera and cornea are the main structural members of the eye.

Lining the interior of the sclera is a second layer known as the choroid coat. The **choroid coat** provides blood vessels to maintain the cells of the sclera as well as neuronal tissue in the interior of the eye. The choroid is also the source of the clear fluids filling the interior of the eye. The dark color of the choroid absorbs stray light in the interior of the eye.

Lining the interior of the posterior half of the eye is the retina. The **retina** is a layer of phototransducers and associated nervous system that accomplish the initial steps in the visual process. The retina will be discussed in considerable detail later in this chapter.

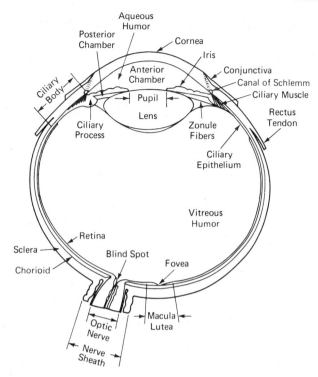

Figure 15.2   The major structures in the eye. (Walls, 1963, p. 7)

If we look at the eye in terms of the light pathway, the first structure we encounter is the cornea. The cornea is the most important single structure in focusing the incoming light rays to form a coherent image on the retina. The cornea must be transparent in order to accomplish its light-transmission function, so the normal network of blood vessels is absent from corneal cells. This is one reason why corneal transplant surgery can be accomplished without the normal foreign tissue rejection by the antibody systems. Anyone who has sustained a scratched cornea knows that this structure is endowed with pain receptors. Astigmatism is an optical irregularity of the cornea. Scar tissue, diseases, and vitamin deficiencies can all create an accumulation of opaque material in the cornea which reduces the optical properties of the structure.

Immediately behind the cornea is the fluid-filled **anterior chamber.** Contrary to what one might expect, the **posterior chamber** is not the huge space in the middle of the eye, but a small space between the lens and the iris. The anterior and posterior chambers are filled with **aqueous humor** (watery fluid). The fluids in the eye are being constantly generated from the blood vessels in the choroid. The aqueous humor in the anterior chamber is allowed to drain from the eye through special canals at the boundary between the sclera and the cornea. If these canals in some way malfunction, pressure is built up inside the eye. Glaucoma is the neurological damage incurred by the cells in the retina as a result of excess internal pressure.

The iris of the eye is the next structure encountered along the light path. The **iris** is a specialized structure evolved from the choroid coat and is seen as the colored portion of the eye. The blue or brown eye pigment in the iris absorbs light. The iris can be adjusted to control the amount of light entering the eye through the **pupil,** the black spot in the middle of the iris. The iris is a muscular structure with a set of radiating muscles which can expand or dilate the pupil and an encircling set of sphincter muscles which can close the pupil much as one can pull the strings on a purse. Automatic circuits connected to the retina expand or contract the diameter of the pupil to adjust to different light levels. This pupillary reflex of decreasing pupil diameter with the introduction of light is one of the last reflexes to disappear before the death of an individual. The pupillary response to light is one of the faster-adapting mechanisms in the eye. It is interesting to note that the diameter of the pupils is not only responsive to light level but also indicates the emotional state of the individual. The autonomic nervous system appears to be involved in adjusting the iris to more than merely brightness.

Suspended behind the iris is the lens of the eye. Light that is allowed to enter the pupil is then subjected to a final focusing adjustment by the lens. The **lens** is a structure of transparent, although slightly yellowish, semi-crystalline cells packed together in successive layers something like an onion. The yellow color provides a filter to absorb damaging levels of ultraviolet light before it reaches the retina. Although we usually think of the lens as the primary light-focusing structure, it actually provides only fine adjustment for the major focusing done by the cornea. The lens is somewhat elastic and can be flattened or thickened. Focus is accomplished by either the suspensory ligaments stretching the lens thin or by ciliary muscles counteracting the ligaments and allowing the lens to assume a thicker shape. The lens is automatically adjusted to provide the clearest image on the retina. The image focused on the retina is inverted; that is, objects in the right portion of the visual field are projected on the left retina of both eyes, high objects project on the bottom of the retina, and so on.

Visible light includes a range of wavelengths which we perceive as colors. Different wavelengths focus at different distances through the same lens. Certain "op art" displays take advantage of the fact that the lens cannot focus all colors simultaneously. A painting of intense blue and red swirls presents the eye with a sharp disparity in the appropriate focal length. Such pictures appear to "vibrate" as the lens is rapidly shifted back and forth attempting alternately to focus the two colors.

After traversing the lens, the light is then transmitted through the large middle portion of the eye filled with **vitreous humor** (glassy fluid). The vitreous humor is quite similar to the aqueous humor except that the material is slightly jellylike. The vitreous humor provides some structural support for the eye even if there is a loss of fluid pressure in the eye.

THE RETINA

The final structure in the light pathway of the eye is the neural tissue making up the retina. If we peer through the pupil of an eye with the aid of an opthalmoscope, we can look at the neural tissue directly. Thus, the phrase "the eye is the window of the brain" takes on double meaning. Doctors use this observation opportunity to determine several conditions in the CNS.

The healthy retina presents a relatively uniform, pinkish appearance when observed through the pupil. Three outstanding features are immediately noticed. First, the middle of the pinkish field contains a yellowish area. This "yellow spot," known as the **macula lutea,** marks the position of the **fovea.** The fovea is located in the middle of the field of vision and accomplishes a highly specialized, ultrafine focus vision as distinguished from the surrounding peripheral area. The second noticeable feature is a network of blood vessels coursing across the front of the retina. The neurological tissue in the retina is so thick that cells at the vitreal surface (toward the vitreous humor) are not supplied from the choroid coat. The third feature is the point at which all of these blood vessels enter the eye. Since the blood vessels penetrate the retina at this point, there is no room for transducer cells. Thus, each eye has an area with no transducers, known as the **blind spot.** In addition to providing a point of entry for the blood vessels, the blind spot also provides a point of egress for the axons of the neurons in the retina. Thus, immediately behind the blind spot on the retina is the optic nerve leading to the brain.

The retina is a complicated neural network with distinct layers relating to concentrations of transducers, cell bodies, synaptic regions, axonal areas, and so on (Figure 15.3). These layers can be summarized into three func-

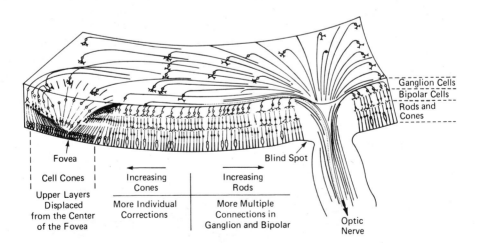

Figure 15.3 The retina, showing the fovea and blind spot. Notice that the retina is inverted; that is, the photoreceptor layer is the furthest from the light source. (Polly, Apple, & Bizzel, 1975, p. 344)

tional levels. Basically, the retina consists of a layer of phototransducers with two distinct layers of associated neurons. Notice that the layer of receptor cells is the last layer in the light path! The reason the transducers are located behind all of the neural tissue appears to lie in the ontogenetic development of the eye. The rods and cones appear to have evolved from the ciliary lining of the ventricles. The eye begins as a hollow, stalklike extension from the CNS. Eventually, the hollow neural material collapses back on itself, with the ciliary cells destined to become transducers trapped in the middle. This ontogenetic sequence also explains why the retina can become detached relatively easily from the back of the eye.

Beginning at the back of the retina with the transducer cells, we find that the human eye contains both rods and cones. Named according to their anatomical shape, rods and cones serve separate visual functions. The **rods** are very sensitive in low levels of light but provide "black-white" vision. In the human eye, the rods are found in the periphery of the eye but not in the fovea (Figure 15.4). For this reason, the peripheral regions of the eye are more sensitive to low levels of light illumination. A simple experiment will illustrate this distribution. On a clear night, start looking at progressively smaller stars. Eventually, you will find a star that disappears when you look directly at it but is distinctly "there" each time you look away. This intensity is below the threshold of the foveal cones but is successfully detected by the peripheral rods.

The **cones,** on the other hand, are especially suited for higher illumination levels and provide us with the additional feature of color vision. Since humans are predominately diurnal (daytime) creatures, the center of our field of vision (fovea) is devoted to higher light-level environments.

The difference between the rods and cones is now known to be a difference in the characteristics of the outer segments that accomplish the transduction operation. Both types of transducer cells store a photopigment in horizontal laminations in the outer segment. The rods store **rhodopsin** in indi-

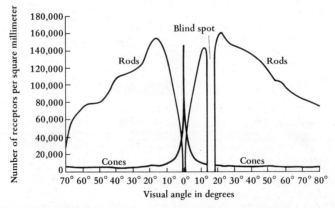

Figure 15.4 Density distributions of rods and cone receptors across the retinal surface. (Pirenne, 1967, p. 35)

vidual discs, while the cones store three types of **iodopsin** in continuous laminations. Slight differences in the absorption characteristics of the three types
of iodopsin account for the ability to discriminate between different colors.

The basic mechanism seems to be that the visual pigments absorb light,
causing a chemical change that creates an electrical event, which can be
recorded as the electrical receptor potential. The color of the photopigment
molecule bleaches with absorption of light. Bleached pigment appears clear,
which means that it does not absorb additional light. Thus, the pigment itself
provides an automatic adaptation device. Under high light intensities, many
pigment molecules are bleached and cannot absorb the excess light. Under
low levels (which means low bleach-rate conditions), the metabolic activity
of the receptor regenerates the bleached molecules so there are more un-
bleached molecules available to absorb the available light. The amount of
"sensitive" pigment is adjusted to match the sensitivity requirements of the
viewing condition.

The temporary blindness that occurs upon entering a darkened theater
from bright levels of light represents the time necessary for the pigment to
regenerate. The dark-adaptation curve shows a distinct discontinuity concomitant with the differential sensitivity of rods and cones (Figure 15.5).
The cones adapt first, followed by the more sensitive rods. The break in the
adaptation-sensitivity curve represents the switch from day vision to night
vision. Because of the two types of vision, it is possible to circumvent part
of the dark-adaptation process. Rhodopsin does not absorb light in the far
red end of the spectrum, while cones are sensitive to this spectral region. If we
were to wear deep red goggles while waiting to enter a theater, the rhodopsin
could not be bleached, and we would have very efficient night vision if we
took off the goggles in the darkened theater. Most animal species have specialized their visual capacity for day (cones) or night (rods). Nocturnal animals normally shun the "blinding light" of day, so it is difficult to observe
their normal behavior. By placing them in a deep red illuminated environment,
our cones can observe their activity easily, although their rods are reporting
a "night condition."

The next layer in the retina consists of bipolar cells. **Bipolar cells** vary
in the number of receptors that they collect information from, but the bipolar
cells generally gather information from several receptors and pass on the
summarized information in the visual pathway. Generally speaking, the "on-
off" cells are found in the bipolar layer of the retina. Bipolar cells gather,
summarize, and transmit information in the visual pathway. In addition, there
are a large number of cells that integrate information between neighboring
bipolar cells. Horizontal cells provide interconnections between transducer-
bipolar synaptic areas.

The bipolar cells synaptically connect with the **ganglion cells,** which form
the third layer of cells in the retina. The ganglion cells appear to connect with
a large number of bipolar cells. Since straight-line and movement detectors
have been recorded in the ganglion cell layer, it appears that the ganglion

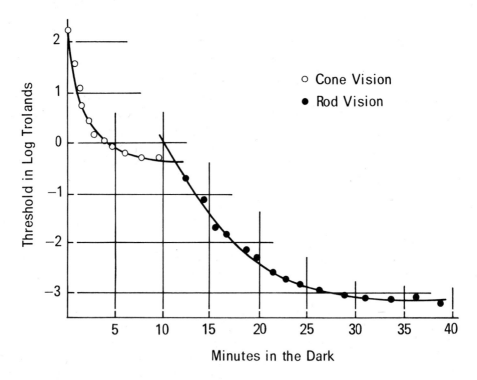

Figure 15.5 Dark-adaptation curve. The initial adaptation is due to the adjustment made by the cones, and the sudden subsequent drop represents the slower adaptation of the more sensitive rods. (Hect, Haig, & Chase, 1937, p. 837)

cells follow the proposed connections for the feature detectors discussed previously. In the synaptic region between the bipolar and ganglion cells, there are also found a number of cells that interconnect horizontally to transmit information between adjacent synaptic areas. The axons from the ganglion cells course across the front surface of the retina to the blind spot to make up the axons of the optic nerve.

It would seem optically inefficient to pack the cell bodies of the neurons making up the optic nerve in front of the receptor cells. The fovea, or center of our field of vision, does not have such optical obstruction. The layers of the retina in front of the fovea are pushed to one side so that the center of the fovea is exposed transducers. Because the overlying retinal layers are pushed aside, the fovea is also called the **visual pit,** a term describing the retinal depression. The displaced neural network away from the visual pathway allows precise image formation on the receptors. The small region of foveal vision is scanned across the visual field to provide precise visual information throughout.

In addition to the neuronal constituents of the retina, two additional features deserve mention (Figure 15.6). The layers of the retina are bounded on the vitreal side and between the outer segments and cell bodies of the

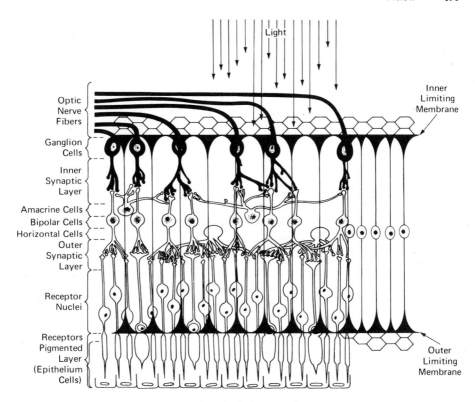

Figure 15.6 Schematic diagram of the cellular and synaptic layers found in the human retina (periphery). (From Dowling & Boycott, 1966, p. 85)

rods and cones by the **inner and outer limiting membranes.** Each membrane appears to be a continuous structure sharply delimiting a retinal layer. Both membranes are actually a mosaic of tuliped extensions of cells extending between the two membranes. In other words, the two "different" membranes are actually formed by parts of the same cells. Here is another enigmatic example of the presence of glial cells in an important neural structure.

We have been preoccupied with transmitting the light to the transducers, and the transduced neural information to the brain. What happens to the light that is not used by the rods and cones? The light-adapted eye contains a visual pigment that is thoroughly bleached and will absorb little light. The light that is not absorbed by the pigment in the rods and cones progresses to the last layer of the retina, known as the **pigment epithelium.** The pigment epithelial cells contain a dark pigment that absorbs the excess light. The pigment epithelium presents some remarkable light-controlling capacities. Originating as ciliary cells on the "other side" of the chamber that produced the rods and cones, the epithelial cells produce their own unique piqment molecules to control excess light without the transducer properties of the visual pigments.

In humans, the pigment epithelium is primarily an absorbing medium.

In many nocturnal animals, the epithelium is a reflective surface. If light is not absorbed by a rod on the first trip through the retina, the light is reflected back for a second try. Under very low light conditions, this effectively "doubles" the light source. The "eye shine" of deer or cats when caught by automobile headlights represents the light that has entered the eye, gone through the retina twice, and escaped the eye again.

VISUAL PATHWAYS

Visual information traverses two synaptic exchanges in the retina. The axons from the ganglion cells extend across the vitreal surface of the retina to the blind spot, where they form the optic nerve. Estimates are that there are approximately a million axons in each optic nerve. The optic nerves from each eye converge together at the **optic chiasma** and then separate again to form the optic tracts. These ganglion cell fibers finally terminate in the lateral geniculate nuclei (in the thalamus), where the third synaptic exchange occurs. The information is then carried to the primary visual areas of the occipital lobes of the cortex by means of the **optic radiations** (Figure 15.1).

A small proportion of the fibers in the optic tract branch away from the main visual pathways to carry information to the superior colliculus and other structures in the tectal regions of the midbrain. In lower animals (without an optic cortex) the optic tectum provides the visual functions. In higher animals the colliculi seem to be involved with reflexive eye movements. Many of the fibers leading to the colliculi are from peripheral movement detectors. Visual information is also transmitted to the RAS, and oculomotor control is known to include the cerebellum; thus, the visual pathways in the brain stem are extensive and complicated.

Approximately 50 percent of the optic cortex is devoted to foveal information and the other 50 percent to the remaining 95 percent of the peripheral retina. The fovea is equally represented on the two hemispheres of the occipital lobes, and the information is about equally represented from each eye.

The peripheral field is divided in a unique manner. If the visual field were divided into a right half and a left half, we would approximate the division between the visual lobes. The left hemisphere processes the visual information coming from the right visual field from both eyes, and the right hemisphere deals with the left field. This division provides a type of contralateral control. One way to observe this contralateral relationship is to record EEG activity from the occipital region while moving a stimulus from right to left in the visual field of the subject. A wave of EEG activity will be noted moving from left to right across the back of the head.

If we examine the visual pathways, it becomes obvious that the only place where the information from both eyes can be concentrated on one side or the other is at the optic chiasma (Figure 15.7). Each optic nerve carries 100

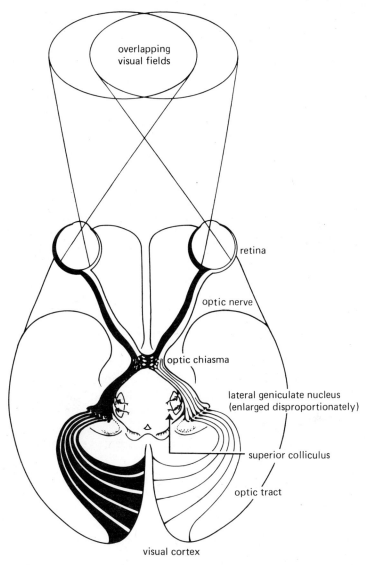

Figure 15.7 Schematic diagram of the visual pathways. Information from each side of the visual field is transmitted to the contralateral visual cortex. (Haber & Fried, 1975, p. 44)

percent of the information from one eye, and each optic tract carries 50 percent of the information from each eye. Thus, half of the axons from each eye cross over to the contralateral side in the optic chiasma. The 50 percent crossing over come from the nasal (toward the nose) retinal area from each eye. Since the nasal half of the retina transduces the image from the outside half of the visual field, each hemisphere receives information from the contralateral visual field. To put it another way, the fibers from the right portion of the retina stay toward the right side all the way back to the right occipital lobe. Because of the inverted image on the retina, this means that the information from the left visual field follows this pathway. All of the visual structures posterior to the optic chiasma process the contralateral field. The degree of cross-over at the chiasma is directly related to the location of the eyes in the head. Animals with eyes located on the side of the head have almost totally independent visual fields from each eye, and almost all of the fibers from each eye cross over to the contralateral side in the chiasma. In different animal species, the location of the eyes moves toward the front of the head, the amount of visual field overlap increases, and the proportion of fibers remaining in the ipsilateral optic tract increases. If the visual fields overlap, there is an advantage to comparing the information concerning the same stimulus source. By redistributing the fibers at the chiasma, cells with receptive fields in the same visual area arrive in a common cortical region.

Binocular vision is an important feature of the human visual system. The eyes are located in the front of the head where there is almost total overlap of the visual fields of each eye. Important distance cues are found in **convergence** (the extent to which we have to "cross" our eyes to focus on an object on the fovea of each eye) and **retinal disparity** (the different locations of the image on the two retinas due to distance). Retinal disparity can be observed by looking at the far corner of a room and then alternately winking the eyes. Objects at an intermediate distance can be seen to be shifting back and forth depending on which eye is open. This shifting represents the retinal disparity between the two eyes due to the approximately 2½ inch separation between the eyes. Recent research into visual feature detectors suggests that there are "retinal disparity" detectors in the visual cortex. These cells respond if the same stimulus is presented to both eyes, but only if the stimulus is a certain distance away.

It appears that the lateral geniculate bodies consist of six identifiable layers arranged somewhat like the layers of an onion. It is possible to record the activity from each of these layers of tightly packed cell bodies. These recordings indicate that successive layers are alternately contralateral or ipsilateral in terms of the eye that must be stimulated to activate the cells. Only the cortex combines overlapping information from the two eyes.

COLOR VISION

Color vision, and the associated condition of color blindness, have presented a fascinating problem to the physiological psychologist. About a century ago, two competing theories were proposed for the color vision mechanism, and data were found to support both of them. The **trichromatic theory** claimed that there are basically three different cones: those that responded to red, green, and blue (Figure 15.8). All of the colors in the spectrum are mixtures of these three primary colors. The colored pictures seen in photographs and television are actually such a three-colored mixture.

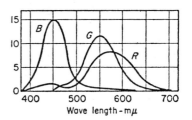

Figure 15.8 Spectral absorption curves hypothesized for a trichromatic color system. 400 mu is
the purple end of the spectrum, while 700 mu
is the deep-red end. The three systems respond
differentially to the different colors in the spectrum. (S. Hect, 1930, p. 241)

The **opponent process color vision theory,** on the other hand, argued
that there are four primary colors, with red-green and yellow-blue serving as
two opponent pairs (Figure 15.9). Intermediary colors are a combination of
these two basic mechanisms. Negative afterimages (seeing a green image
after staring at a red object) are the opponent rebound from stimulating the
color mechanism in one direction. Color blindness usually occurs in one of the
opponent pairs.

In the late 1950s, single-unit recording in the lateral geniculate nucleus
of the monkey revealed that the outer two layers contained color feature
detectors that responded maximally to red, green, or blue stimulation. The
third and fourth layers showed an excitation response to one of the opposition colors, with inhibition occurring in response to the opposing color! Both
theoretical systems were used to encode color information. Further research
is revealing the neural mechanisms for the color vision phenomenon.

The cones contain three different visual pigments, each of which is sensitive to different regions of the spectrum. Thus, there are three types of cones
that respond differently to red, green, or blue light. The cones are not "pure"
responders; that is, the "red" cone responds at a lower level to yellow, green,
or even blue (Figure 15.10). It is a "red" cone because of its maximum response. In order to sharpen the difference in response rate between two color
receptors, there are neurons that are excited by "red" cone activity and
inhibited by "green" cone activity. Such a neuron would respond with an
"on" response to a red stimulus and an "off" response to a green stimulus.
The neural network extracts sharpened color information from the transducers
by utilizing inhibitory connections. Just as the feature detectors discussed
in previous chapters extract and emphasize lines, angles, and borders, color
vision involves a process of feature detector-type connections.

It is possible to account for negative afterimages—the appearance of
a green color after staring at a red object and then shifting to a colorless

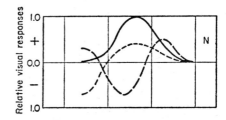

Figure 15.9 Spectral absorption curves
hypothesized for an opposition color system. The solid line represents the achromatic (noncolor) response curve. (Hurvich
& Jameson, 1957, p. 397)

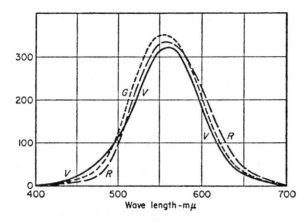

Figure 15.10 Spectral absorption curves for a three-color system. Opposition responses could be obtained from neurons excited or inhibited by the activity of two of these. The red-green system would compare the response of curves "R" and "G," and the blue-yellow system would compare the response curves of "V" and "R." (S. Hect, 1930, p. 248)

surface—as the adaptation of these opponent feature detectors. Thus, the neuron adapts to the constant red and then responds with a burst of "green" activity. Color blindness is caused by the absence of one of the three color pigments. Since color blindness is known to be a genetic trait, it is probably caused by the inability to produce the appropriate amino acid, which then leads to the inability to produce the appropriate pigment. If the "red" cones actually produce a "green" pigment, then the "red-green" neurons will have no difference to detect. Such an individual will be red-green color blind. Red-green color blindness can also occur if the green receptors are genetically miscoded to produce a red pigment. Either situation will result in an inability to code a difference, although there is a subtle difference as to the type of color error produced according to which pigment is miscoded. The rarer blue-yellow blind person has matching pigments in his or her blue-yellow system. The totally color blind person has only a single cone pigment, so no difference occurs in any of the color feature systems.

In addition to color blindness, some people have a color weakness in that they do not show normal sensitivity when discriminating between similar hues. It now appears that these individuals have an anomalous pigment that falls somewhere between the normal color vision pigments. Since the color feature detectors are working from a different basis for comparison, their activity is similarly shifted, resulting in abnormal color perception in some parts of the spectrum.

FEATURELESS PERCEPTION

Earlier in this chapter, the eye was compared to a camera. Yet the eye is not a high-quality camera. The lens is not color corrected, which means that some colors will be out of focus. Even if the lens were more optically precise, the muscles that manipulate the lens have a natural tremor, so that the lens is always quivering slightly. The gelatinous material making up the vitreous humor is not the clearest optical medium, so the image is further degraded. The rods and cones of the eye face the wrong way and are hidden behind two distinct layers of neural networks, not to mention a maze of blood vessels. One of the conditions a doctor looks for when examining the eye is the degree of distortion in the blood vessels. The extent of the distortion provides an estimate of the patient's blood pressure history. When subjected to high pressures, either chronic (high blood pressure) or acute (physical effort or sudden emotion), the blood vessels sometimes rupture. The released blood cells are ejected into the fluid just in front of the retina, causing even more interference in the light path. Eventually, the blood cells flow toward the canals in the front of the eye and are evacuated. This cleansing process is relatively slow, and most of us have a number of blood cells in front of the retina, especially in times of stress. These cells are the little "blobs" or "chains" seen floating through our visual world. If the cells are in front of the fovea, they cast a shadow on the cones, and we see them. **Floaters** show a maddening tendency to elude direct inspection. If we see one off to one side and try to look at it, it keeps drifting just ahead of our gaze. Since the floater is inside the eye, it will move with the movement of the eye, thereby maintaining its relative position in our visual field. Similarly, floaters are dffi-cult to look away from. The floating movement is due to the fact that the fluid on the eye is not rigidly attached to the eye, and thus some movement is detected.

In addition to inefficient optics, interfering structures, and an internal dust storm of blood cells, the eye is subject to constant movement. The external muscles of the eye cannot hold the eye steadily on target. Fine recording shows that there are several different component twitches and drifting move-ments in the eye when it is being held steady. If we want a better picture with a camera, we can put it on a tripod to hold it steady, but the eye is in constant movement.

Instead of being a disadvantage, the involuntary movement of the eye is useful and probably necessary to the highly efficient functioning of the visual system. Recall that adaptation is a common trait of the visual system. The "on-off" cells at the bipolar layer show obvious and rapid adaptation. Since most (if not all) of the feature detectors rely on the "on-off" cells for informa-tion, they too adapt relatively quickly. We can directly observe the adaptation process by making a ping-pong ball **Ganzfeld** and placing it over our eyes. If the ball contains no seams or brand name, the eye is now confronted with a visual display devoid of features. There are no lines, edges, borders, and so on. By changing the light transluminating the Ganzfeld, we can stimulate the "on-off" detectors, and by placing a colored filter in the light path, we can obtain a clear perception of color. If we maintain a constant colored illumination, the color fades to a gray relatively quickly. Even a white light seems to fade in intensity until it is a sort of nondescript perception of "not light and yet not dark" known as "neural gray." It seems that the "on-off" detectors must be stimulated in order for vision to function.

Under normal viewing conditions, the visual world is full of features.

The constant twitching, jerking, and drifting of the eyes moves the image of these features across the retina. Thus, the "on-off" cells are in constant activity even though there is no movement in the perceptual scene. The Ganzfeld deprives the eye of any features to sweep back and forth across, and total adaptation can occur.

This is also why we are not aware of the shadows of the blood vessels on the front of the retina. The shadow is there, but it falls on the same population of rods. The blood vessels are translucent enough to allow some light to pass through. Imagine a case where a person looked first from a white sheet of paper to a black sheet. The rods and cones would report an "off" response since the light striking the retina became darker. The receptors behind the blood vessels would report exactly the same thing. The light going through the blood vessels would reduce sharply in exactly the same fashion. Since the "on-off" cells adapt to constant stimulation, the fact that these cells are partially shadowed will be adapted to. In experiments with images stabilized on the retina, the image disappears in less than a second.

If the muscles of the eye were precise enough not to twitch and drift, the outside visual world would disappear within a second of when we stopped our eyes to look at something (moving objects excepted, of course). Thus, the "involuntary" eye movements keep the "on-off" cells in a constant state of activity. Instead of being a disadvantage, the eye movements are necessary to maintain the image!

AUTHOR'S COMMENTS   In many ways the eye is an impressive optical instrument. Many of its structures are quite efficient at delivering a quality image to be transduced by the rods and cones. In other ways, however, one cannot help but notice some apparent "optical errors." Optical aberrations and interference would seem to negate the good design features.

Most of these "errors" occur in the peripheral region of the retina. The fovea is positioned and designed to receive a relatively "clean" image. Although the analogy is tempting, the eye is simply not intended to be a high-quality camera. Most of the formidable expense of a good camera is created by the necessity of producing an apparatus capable of delivering a good image to all portions of the film plate. The visual system, however, needs only a high-quality image in the 1 degree of visual angle occupied by the fovea. The remainder of the retina essentially tells the visual system where to aim this narrow region of precise vision.

Many of the "optical errors" may be more appropriately described as an optical design strategy that meets various demands of the system in different regions. The periphery does not require precise optical focus, so why provide it? Because of the computerlike data extraction being accomplished by the feature detectors in the visual pathway, some of the "optical errors" may represent an image improvement for feature detection. When the entire system is considered, the visual capacities are very impressive.

16

Hearing

After vision, hearing is probably the next most important sensory system to humans (Figure 16.1). Together with a spoken language, the sense of hearing provides a major communication channel between individuals. Radios and telephones are both examples of communication instruments that are exclusively auditory. In addition, millions of dollars are spent each year on high fidelity sound equipment and records or tapes. Yet as modern technology makes possible increasingly sophisticated audio instruments, it also generates higher and higher noise levels which are destructive to the hearing mechanisms. Thus, we are at a technological crossroads where the sense of hearing can be more appreciated than ever before, yet the same sensory system is subjected to serious abuse.

THE EAR

The ear comprises all of the apparatus that receives and transduces sound energy and transmits the resulting neural activity to the brain. As is the case with the visual neural structures, the division between the ear and the CNS is largely a geographic rather than a functional labeling scheme. Significant neurological data processing occurs in the ear and auditory pathways.

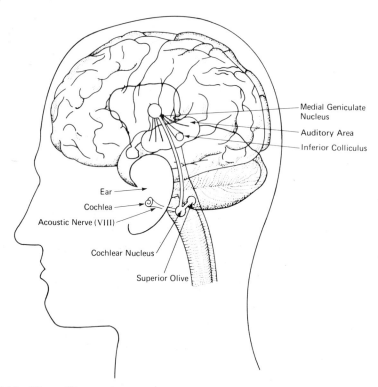

Figure 16.1 The auditory system.

The ear can be divided into three separate geographic units (Figure 16.2). The **outer ear** consists of the structures we can conveniently see without violating the integrity of the organism. The **middle ear** consists of structures normally hidden from us, which are active in the sound-transmission process but are not intimately involved with the transduction process. The **inner ear** consists of the mechanisms directly involved with the transduction of sound into neural information. By some evolutionary sequence, the inner ear also provides the transducer organs for two different bodily senses. The inner ear, technically called the **labyrinth,** is divided into the **cochlea** (involved with hearing) and the **vestibular organ** (involved with balance and motion). Since both senses involve mechanicotransduction, the combination is not as unlikely as it first appears.

The outer ear in some animals consists of only an eardrum. The **eardrum,** or **tympanic membrane,** is a membrane, under moderate tension, that responds to sound vibrations transmitted through the air. The vibratory response of the eardrum is in turn transmitted by the middle ear structures to the transducers of the inner ear. The eardrum provides a protected environment for the delicate auditory structures behind it. Essentially, the eardrum is a barrier to foreign material yet is transparent to sound vibrations.

Insects have auditory "eardrums" in the membranes between hard seg-

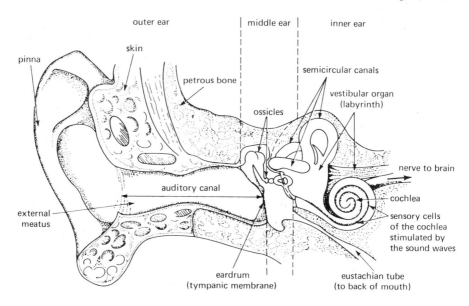

Figure 16.2   The ear and vestibular system. (Davis, 1953, via Milner, 1970, p. 220)

ments of their body. Frogs have large eardrums on each side of the head. Most animals, however, have a more elaborate external hearing apparatus. In the human ear, the eardrum lies approximately an inch inward from the surface of the head. Thus, the eardrum is protected by the bony shell of the skull. The tube leading from the outside surface to the eardrum is known as the **auditory canal.** The length and cross section of the auditory canal form a resonating tube which enhances the loudness of certain pitched sounds. The resonant frequency of the human ear enhances the normal frequencies of the human voice.

At the outer end of the auditory canal is the **external meatus,** which is the "ear" in everyday jargon. The megaphone shape of the meatus provides a medium of sound concentration by channeling the sound onto the auditory canal. The shape of the meatus ensures that sounds coming from in front will be more easily conducted into the auditory canal than sounds from behind. High-pitched sounds coming from behind are attenuated, or weakened, by the meatus. The relative intensity of high-frequency sounds provides a cue for locating the front to rear source of a sound. Animals with a highly mobile external meatus can precisely locate a sound source by "aiming" the receiving apparatus, much the way we can fixate our eyes. Those of us who can accomplish the stunt of wiggling our ears probably demonstrate a vestigial example of this auditory aiming apparatus.

The middle ear in the human auditory system consists of three tiny bones called **ossicles.** These three bones (malleus, incus, and stapes; or hammer, anvil, and stirrup, depending on the language) form a chain of vibratory segments between the eardrum and the cochlea. The cochlea is filled with a fluid, which is a more efficient sound-conducting medium than air, but more force is required to move a fluid. The ossicles of the middle ear convert the amplitude of the vibrations on the eardrum to power the movement of fluid in the cochlea. The vibration produced by air movement on the eardrum is relatively large but relatively weak. The conversion action of the ossicles in the cochlea is small but powerful. It is analogous to our attempting to lift a car. Most of us cannot directly lift a car, but if we use a 20-foot board as a lever, we can accomplish the feat. By moving the long end of the board, we can exert tremendous lifting power at the short end. The ossicles accomplish a similar mechanical conversion in the middle ear.

Under stimulus conditions of very low sound levels, this mechanical transmission system must be as efficient as possible to deliver all of the vibrations to the transducers. If the sound vibrations are very large, however, preservation of all of the stimulus is not necessary and is even potentially destructive. The three ossicles in the middle ear are hinged together by ligaments with muscular components. Under extremely low sound levels, the hinges are pulled tight to preserve all movement. Under high noise levels, the muscles relax and allow the ossicles to slip past one another. In this way, the destructive levels of sound are attenuated by wasting some of the motion into slippage between the ossicles. This is one reason why we perceive a loud sound that we do not expect as louder than a sound of the same level that we anticipate.

The middle ear includes a hollow chamber containing the ossicles. In order for the eardrum to vibrate freely to the external air movement, there must be an air space behind the eardrum. If the pressure in this air space is too disparate from the outside, the eardrum will bulge inward or outward, making it less responsive to sounds. Unequal pressure explains the change in hearing sensitivity when ascending or descending in an airplane. The external air pressure changes too fast for the pressure in the middle ear chamber to be compensated. It is possible to manipulate directly the inner ear pressure by holding the nose and blowing or inhaling to force the desired change. The **Eustachian tube** connects the middle ear to the back of the throat. The interaction of the jaw muscles and the Eustachian tube creates a situation where the ears are affected by jaw movement. Thus, chewing gum or yawning "massages" the Eustachian tube, which facilitates air pressure compensation, and the ear may be temporarily rendered less sensitive. Thus, we may have an automatic device that protects our ears from the sounds of our own voice (and possibly our own popcorn eating).

THE COCHLEA

The auditory portion of the inner ear lies in the cochlea, a hollow, bony structure coiled much like a snail shell and embedded deep in the skull. The cochlea contains the transducer mechanism and is totally filled with fluid (Figure 16.3). The stirrup, one of the ossicles, connects to the small mem-

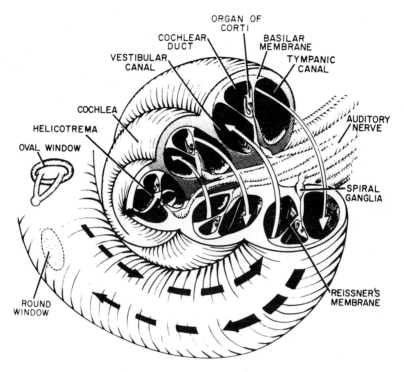

Figure 16.3   The cochlea. (Curtis, Jacobson, & Marcus, 1972, p. 374)

branous **oval window.** Since fluids are incompressible, and the walls of the cochlea are rigid, these vibrations would be totally lost except that there is a second membranous window in the wall of the cochlea called the **round window.** The fluid displacement at the oval window is transmitted to the round window, allowing the intervening fluid to move in response to the sound vibrations. The movement of the fluid, in turn, creates movement in membranes located between the round and oval windows.

It is easier to understand the functioning of the cochlea if we conceptually uncoil it into a long cone. If we lay the cone on its side and place a membrane across the interior of it to divide its length into an upper chamber and a lower chamber, we have the essential configuration of the cochlea. The movement of the stirrup attached to the oval window moves the fluid in the upper chamber, displacing the intervening membrane to move the fluid in the lower chamber, which in turn is allowed by the movement at the round window. The movement of the membrane is by mechanicotransducers placed along the length of the membrane. The membrane does not completely isolate the two chambers at the tip of the cone. This gap, the **helicotrema,** allows fluid to flow between the upper and lower chambers. In case of extreme fluid movement by the sound vibrations, excess fluid pressure can "leak" around the membrane through the helicotrema.

The upper chamber is actually composed of two parts, with the lower division, or middle chamber, bounded above by a very thin membrane known as **Reissner's membrane.** Attached to the basilar membrane is a complicated structure known as the **organ of Corti** (Figure 16.4). It is in the organ of Corti that sound transduction is actually accomplished. The transducers are **hair cells** embedded in a matrix of supportive cells on the **basilar membrane.** The hair cells are divided into two distinct populations according to their location in the organ of Corti. The inner hair cells are virtually attached to the bony shelf of the cochlear shell and are not likely to be moved by vibrations of the basilar membrane. The more populous outer hair cells (a ratio of about 6 to 1) are located in the middle of the basilar membrane, where they are most likely to experience the vibratory stimulus. All of the hair cells have their hairlike extension embedded in the overlying **tectorial membrane.** Up and down movement of the basilar membrane stretches or compresses the hair cells. The geometry of the basilar membrane and the tectorial membrane is such that the relative movement is a powerful back and forth shearing action between the two. The hair cells in the organ of Corti are angled so they will be more sensitive to this lateral movement. When one considers the loss of amplitude from the eardrum to the oval window, and then distributes this reduced motion along the length of the basilar membrane, it appears that the hair cells in the ear must detect an extraordinarily tiny stimulus, even by transducer standards.

The actual mechanism is more complicated than just described. The cochlea in cross section is more than a simple membrane and two chambers. The "membrane" described in the previous paragraph is more accurately the entire triangular-shaped chamber enclosing the complicated hearing mecha-

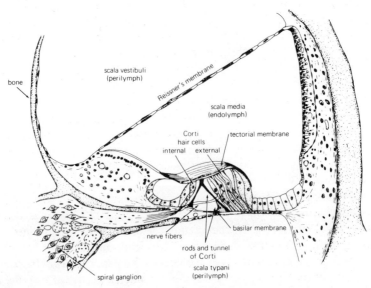

Figure 16.4 The organ of Corti. A cross section of the second turn in the cochlea of a guinea pig. (Davis, 1953, via Milner, 1970, p. 234)

nism. The two chambers above and below this middle region are filled with a fluid called **perilymph.** The fluid within the triangular chamber is a slightly different fluid called **endolymph.** Since the transducer cells are completely bathed in the endolymph of the middle chamber, there is reason to believe that this fluid is suited for the efficient functioning of the cells. This notion is supported by the fact that the hair cells in the associated vestibular apparatus are bathed in endolymph by means of a connecting canal from the cochlear middle chamber. Recording of the electrical states inside the cochlea reveals that the endolymphatic chamber is electrically more negative than the surrounding perilymphatic medium. Perhaps this electrical differential contributes to the transducer activity.

To reconstruct what we have systematically dismantled, the movement of the basilar membrane creates a powerful "shear" force on the inner and outer hair cells by the relative movement of the tectorial membrane. The organ of Corti, which was described in cross section, extends the entire length of the cochlea (except for the helicotrema) and contains approximately 28,000 hair cells. This entire structure is coiled about three and one half times, so the chambers, membranes, and organ of Corti are all spiral shaped. Sound vibrations transmitted to the fluid in the upper chamber spiral along the upper chamber, creating movement in the lower chamber, which is relieved by the round window. There is a tendency to refer to the basilar membrane as the transducing body. When the term is used in this somewhat loose manner, the reference is actually to the entire middle chamber in the cochlea.

THE AUDITORY PATHWAY

Each auditory nerve contains approximately 30,000 neurons which enter the center portion of the cochlear tube and have their dendrites located near the hair cells in the organ of Corti. The cell bodies are located just outside the cochlea, forming a structure called the **spiral ganglion,** so named because the neurons follow the spiral shape of the cochlea. The auditory pathway consists of the cochlear nucleus, the superior olive, the inferior colliculus, the medical geniculate nucleus, and the primary auditory cortex (Figure 16.5). There are considerable contralateral interconnections at the superior olive. In addition, several pathways branch from the main auditory pathway to carry information to the RAS and the cerebellum. These branch pathways apparently involve information important to alertness and motor reflexes. The primary auditory cortex is located in the temporal lobes, immediately below the central fissure.

Electrical recording of the activity in the auditory nervous system reveals a number of interesting features. If an electrode is placed inside the cochlea, it is possible to record the electrical response to an impinging sound. The electrical response will accurately follow a sound up to 20,000 cycles per second (the upper range of human hearing). Since neurons are limited to

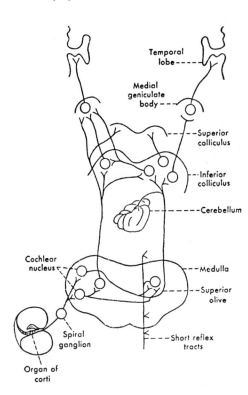

Figure 16.5 Schematic diagram of auditory pathways. (Davis, 1953, via Wenger, Jones, & Jones, 1956, p. 161)

approximately 1000 spikes per second, this cochlear response is amazing. The electrical response is so accurate that the cochlear can be used as a microphone in an amplified sound system, and the reconstructed sound coming from the speaker is recognizable. The **cochlear microphonic** gets its name from its functional similarity to a conventional microphone.

It is generally accepted that the cochlear microphonic is the combined transducer activity of the hair cells in the organ of Corti. It could possibly be related to the electrical difference between the two fluids across Reissner's membrane. In either case, the frequency response inside the cochlea is an example of the transduction of sound energy into an electrical signal.

Biological records from neurons progressively further away from the cochlea show that the high-frequency response is rapidly lost. The auditory nerve and cochlear nucleus show an upper frequency limit of about 3000 Hertz (Hz), or cycles per second. The lateral lemniscus, the pathway between the cochlear nucleus and the inferior colliculus, is limited to about 1000 Hz. By the time we get to the temporal auditory cortex, the neurons seem to follow only up to 100 Hz.

Estimates are that each auditory nerve cell establishes synaptic communication with 75 to 100 cells in the cochlear nucleus. About twice as many fibers leave the cochlear nucleus as enter it, so there must be a great deal of information overlap, as in the visual pathways. Since information is transmitted to the contralateral side in the medulla, the structures in the auditory pathway share information from both ears.

Apparently, sound frequency is a "feature" in the auditory system. Distinct regions of the auditory cortex respond to high-, middle-, or low-pitched sounds. Similar recording along the auditory pathway suggests that cells responding to a specific frequency range are found clustered together. As we record higher and higher in the auditory pathways, we find that the cells progressively respond to narrower frequency bands. The auditory cortical cells, however, respond to a wider frequency range. Apparently, the frequency "feature" is analyzed in lower centers, while the cortical areas respond to complex sound analysis (such as speech patterns). This organizational scheme is analogous to the known feature detectors in the visual system.

AUDITORY PHENOMENA

The mechanism by which auditory neurons are "tuned" to a certain frequency range has been located in the cochlea. The basilar membrane is set into vibration by the in and out motion at the oval window. The inward displacement of the oval window "travels" along the length of the basilar membrane (Figure 16.6). The oval window is then pulled out by the sound action. This opposing action tends to dampen or stop the wave traveling along the basilar membrane. The slower the frequency of the sound, the farther the wave travels along the membrane before it is dampened. The effect on the basilar membrane of a train of waves at a certain frequency is to produce a "standing wave" or bulge on the basilar membrane which remains relatively stationary as long as the sound continues. The point of maximum displacement of this standing wave depends on the frequency of the impinging sound. High-frequency sounds create a standing wave fairly close to the base of the cochlea. Intermediate sounds are located at about the midpoint, and very low tones are at the far end of the membrane, near the helicotrema.

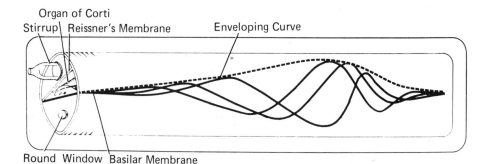

Figure 16.6 The place theory of pitch perception. The cochlea has been uncoiled and simplified to show how the point of maximum vibration moves along the length of the basilar membrane to different pitch tones. (Curtis, Jacobson, & Marcus, 1972, p. 324)

This **"place theory"** probably explains how most of our pitch perception occurs. The electrical activity that takes place in the cochlea of the guinea pig in response to various sounds shows that the receptor potential moves along the spiral length of the cochlea in the manner described. The neurons receiving information from the various points on the cochlea retain their topographic relationship during synaptic transmission along the auditory pathway. The primary auditory cortex can be mapped according to areas that respond to high-, medium-, or low-frequency sounds.

Careful investigation of the basilar membrane shows that the standing wave produced by a pure tone extends over a considerable length of the membrane. How then can auditory nerve cells respond to a precise tone? The answer appears to be by lateral inhibition. The neurons responding to the point of maximum vibration inhibit the transmission of the less active cells on each side. Lateral inhibition may be operating at each synaptic junction along the auditory pathway, for the cells become more precise in the frequency with each synaptic interchange approaching the cortex. With the appropriate lateral inhibition connections, a vibration along a considerable length of the basilar membrane would be perceived as a single "point" where the stimulus was maximum. Large-scale models that vibrate like the basilar membrane have been laid on the skin of the arm. It appears that the skin processes the vibrating stimulus with a similar lateral inhibition mechanism. Even though the membrane can be shown to be vibrating along a two- to three-inch region, the subject can point to an exact spot on the arm where the vibrations are felt. A shift in this total vibratory region is perceived as a distinct shift in the "point." Although the total vibration is 95 percent overlapping, the lateral inhibition in the skin receptor mechanism can immediately report the small shift.

Recording in the auditory nerve shows that the place-coding mechanism is not the only frequency-coding mechanism. The auditory nerve will "follow" a tone up to approximately 3000 Hz with matching 3000 Hz electrical activity. Thus, according to the **frequency theory,** the auditory nerve also transmits the pitch by behaving like a telephone wire and electrically matching the stimulus frequency. The total electrical response of all of the neurons in the auditory nerve allows the nerve to "follow" a frequency three times faster than the maximum firing rate of the individual neurons. The voltage of the auditory nerve response drops to about half between 800 and 1000 Hz. As the frequency of the sound increases, the neurons fire in exact correspondence until the refractory period of each neuron will not allow the neuron to recycle in time. At this point, the neuron skips the next peak, but successfully responds to firing to every other sound peak. The auditory nerve can then transmit a 1400 Hz electrical signal by having half of its neurons fire at 700 Hz for alternate wave peaks and the other half for the intervening peaks, also at 700 Hz. Thus, the total nerve can transmit the higher frequency by using the individual neurons in alternating volleys. At about 2000 Hz the amplitude again drops by about one third. The neurons are now following every third peak—the limit they can recycle and follow. At about 3000 Hz the tone frequency is no longer discernible. The undamaged human ear can respond within the range of 20 to 20,000 Hz. The "volley" transmission system appears to work from 20 to 3000 Hz, and the cochlear place mechanism works from about 1000 to 20,000 Hz. The area of overlap, 1000 to 3000 Hz, is a region of important sounds to the human. For example, the human voice is largely contained within this frequency range. In this relatively narrow but extremely important range, the auditory system utilizes two parallel frequency-coding mechanisms.

As individuals become older, particularly men, the upper frequency limit is gradually lost (Figure 16.7). The average adult male is insensitive to tones higher than 16,000 Hz. This may reflect accumulated damage to the hair cells or age changes in the hearing apparatus.

If an individual is subjected to an extremely loud, pure tone, deafness may occur for that specific tone. Such tonal gaps probably reflect the destructive results of extreme distortion of the organ of Corti at the point where the standing wave is greatest. The outer "hairlike" extensions of the transducer cells can be ripped out of the tectorial membrane by the overwhelming shearing forces that are generated, and the disconnected transducers are consequently no longer sensitive to sounds. Tonal gaps as a result of cochlear damage present a vexing problem to the design of efficient hearing aids. Most hearing aids are designed to amplify sounds equally across the auditory spectrum. Thus, the amplification by the hearing aid overstimulates the intact hair cells in undamaged regions in order to provide sufficient stimulation for the damaged cells.

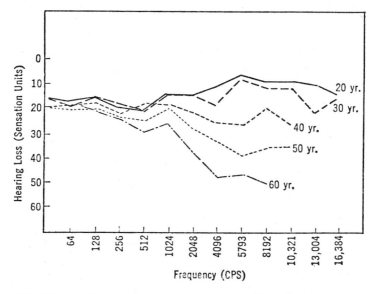

Figure 16.7   Hearing loss as related to age in human males. (Bunch, 1929, p. 634)

TABLE 16.1 Approximate Loudness of Different Sounds as Measured on the Decibel Loudness Scale (Christman, 1971, p. 232)

Level in Decibels

140	
	50 hp siren at a distance of 100 feet
	Jet fighter taking off—80 feet from tail
130	
	Boiler shop
Damaging	Air hammer—at position of operator

120	Rock and roll band
	Jet aircraft at 500 feet overhead
	Trumpet automobile horn at 3 feet
110	
Damaging if prolonged	Crosscut saw at operator's position

100	Inside subway car
90	Train whistle at 500 feet
80	Inside automobile in city
70	Downtown city street
	Average traffic
60	
	Restaurant
50	Business office
	Classroom
40	Inside church
	Hospital room
30	Quiet bedroom
	Recording studio
20	
10	Threshold of hearing—young men

Titanus, or ringing in the ears, is apparently the result of spontaneous activity in the hair cells of the cochlea. Such activity may be a symptom of ongoing neurological disease or damage. The ringing in the ears after exposure to loud sounds may well be the spontaneous firing of cells that have been or are close to being damaged.

Unfortunately, there is a cumulative effect of prolonged exposure to sound levels that would not be damaging if experienced briefly (Table 16.1). Thus, we may note a ringing in the ears after being exposed to a "non-destructive" but prolonged sound.

High fidelity sound systems present some novel situations to the person aware of the characteristics of the auditory system. The intact, undamaged cochlea is limited to 20,000 Hz. Sound-response curves illustrating the superiority of a particular amplifier and/or speaker system usually emphasize the "extended range" of the advertised product. In most cases, this extended range is in a frequency range beyond human hearing capacity! The advantage gained by the extended range is in the enhanced "sharpness" and quality of the sound waves within the range of normal hearing.

Probably more important to the hearing apparatus is the power utilized in a typical high fidelity system. Hi-fi buffs who insist on using full volume could be subjecting themselves to damaging levels of sound. As the hearing deteriorates, the individual can compensate by purchasing more power.

AUTHOR'S   ·   The elaborate apparatus which constitutes the outer, mid-
COMMENTS   dle, and inner ear provides a sophisticated stimulus-controlling device to optimize the signal to be transduced into the nervous system. Because of the place-dependent response of the basilar membrane to different tones, much of pitch perception is determined by these "external structures" that channel the incoming signal so that only a limited population of hair cells is stimulated. There is little doubt that the precise location of the point of maximum displacement on the basilar membrane is established by the lateral inhibition mechanism in the auditory neural pathway. The features that are encoded in the auditory system are not as well established as those in the visual system; however, it is assumed that a similar data-extraction mechanism operates in the auditory system.

17

The Chemical Senses: Taste and Smell

The senses of taste and smell involve the detection of molecular substances from the outside world. Whereas the eyes and ears sample stimuli from the environment, light and sound constitute an indirect currency with the originating object. The chemical senses, on the other hand, involve direct contact with molecules from the outside world. The senses of taste and smell are closely associated. The most obvious example is the loss of important taste qualities when the sense of smell is incapacitated. There is reason to suspect that each of these senses is a specialized version of a general chemical-detection system.

Most mucous membranes are provided with free nerve endings that provide pain information in response to certain chemicals. Substances such as ammonia, onion, and chlorine are detected not only by their characteristic qualities of taste or odor, but nonspecific information about their immediate presence is directly reported by free nerve endings in the eye. Although employing such tricks as not breathing through the nose while slicing an onion may reduce the discomfort, a considerable part of the "crying" response is related to vapor contact with the eye as well as with the nose. Certain spices directly stimulate free nerve endings in the mouth rather than the classic taste receptors. The common chemical sense seems to be an extremely primitive system for detecting and avoiding harmful substances. The transducers appear to be free nerve endings of neurons rather than sophisticated transducer cells, and the response appears to be primarily one of pain rather than a more subtle sensory quality.

TASTE

The receptors for taste are located on the surface of the tongue, larynx, pharynx, and other regions in the mouth (Figure 17.1). In children, taste buds are known to occur on the inner surface of the cheeks, but these disappear with adulthood. The receptors are clustered together into taste "buds," so named because of their flower bud-like appearance. The cell bodies of the receptor cells form the main body of the bud, with each cell contributing a single hairlike process to the cluster at the tip of the bud. These hairlike extensions are known as **microvilli** and are probably the actual site where taste transduction occurs.

The typical taste bud is embedded in surrounding tissue, with only the protruding microvilli coming into contact with substances taken into the mouth. Since a taste receptor must give the organism early warning of hazardous substances taken into the mouth, it should be able to function efficiently

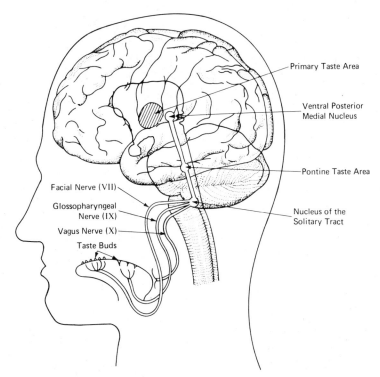

Figure 17.1 The gustatory system.

when exposed to a wide variety of compounds. The taste buds are able to respond accurately to high concentrations of solutions that are destructive or fatal to other living cells. Although the tongue is sensitive to the taste of the substance, poisons (0.1M sodium cyanide) can be left on the surface of the rat tongue for a period of time that would be fatally absorbed by the animal if applied to the cheek.

Even though taste buds show a remarkable resistance to chemical damage, the average lifespan of an individual transducer cell in the bud is approximately ten days. New cells are constantly generated from the surrounding epithelial cells, which then form the outside layers of the bud. The individual cells migrate slowly toward the center of the bud, where they die. The short lifespan of the individual cells is probably related to the chemically destructive environment to which they are subjected. The resulting constant turnover state of the cells making up an individual taste bud provides some interesting data-processing problems between the transducers and the nervous system. Destruction of the nerve servicing a taste bud stops the mechanism that produces new transducer cells. Thus, the taste bud deprived of neural connections slowly disappears. When the neurons regenerate their dendritic processes, transducer cells are again produced, and the taste bud reappears. Taste preference changes from sweet to bitter as an individual grows older, perhaps reflecting a change in the population of taste cells produced.

Taste buds differ in supportive structure in different regions of the mouth. The anterior two thirds of the tongue is covered with raised **papillae,** which are seen as small red dots on the surface of the tongue. Each papilla has a number of associated taste buds, the microvilli of which are directly exposed to solutions of the tongue. Two other types of papillae are recessed at the bottom of deep grooves in the posterior third of the tongue. Solutions must be "worked" down into these grooves in order to come into contact with the taste buds. It appears that the movements of the tongue itself accomplish this transport function.

Because of their far greater accessibility, most of the research on the taste buds involves those found in the raised papillae on the anterior surface of the tongue. It is relatively easy to record from the neuron servicing an individual papilla and also fairly simple to stimulate the same papilla with known solutions. Since the taste buds are morphologically indiscriminable (and also in a constant state of cellular flux), the observed data may be appropriately generalizable to all taste cells. The distribution of different taste sensitivities on the surface of the tongue (Figure 17.2), as well as different nervous pathways for the types of papillae, argue for caution in making generalizations.

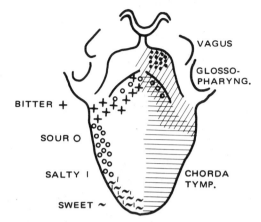

Figure 17.2 Distribution of sensitivities on the tongue to various taste stimuli. The regions of the tongue served by the three cranial nerves involved with taste are also indicated. (Schneider, 1964)

GUSTATORY PATHWAYS

Both myelinated and unmyelinated fibers transmit information from each taste bud. The neuronal dendrites extend up toward the base of the bud where several are enveloped by taste cells in the bud. Each transducer cell envelops several neuronal cells, and vice versa.

Neurons from the raised taste buds in the anterior two thirds of the tongue conduct information to the medulla through cranial nerve VII (Figure 17.3). Information from one type of recessed bud in the posterior third of the tongue enters the CNS through cranial nerve IX. The remaining taste receptors in the mouth and throat transmit information through cranial nerve X. The taste pathways converge on the **nucleus of the solitary tract** in the medulla and synapse in the pontine taste area. The pathway then extends into the **ventral posterior medial** nucleus of the thalamus. Some gustatory fibers remain ipsilateral, while others cross over to the contralateral side before arriving at the thalamus. From the thalamus, the taste information projects to the lower

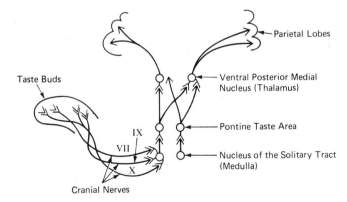

Figure 17.3 Schematic diagram of the taste pathways.

portion of the parietal lobes of the cortex. The primary cortical area for taste is located at the bottom of the central fissure near the sites for touch reception in or near the mouth and slightly posterior to the areas controlling mouth and tongue movements. Thus, the "taste" areas are a part of a community of mouth-related cortical areas.

TASTE PHENOMENA

The four primary dimensions of taste are sweet, sour, bitter, and salty.

Careful measurement shows that different regions of the tongue are sensitive to certain taste stimuli. A relatively neutral taste stimulus, like a clean silver spoon, will elicit the different tastes by touching various parts of the tongue. Since all areas of the tongue respond to all four primary taste stimuli, it appears that there is a difference in sensitivity to different componds rather than a distribution of primary receptors.

The stimulus for salty and sour substances appears related to the ionic constituents that contact the receptors. Positively charged ions like Na^+ or K^+ are the usual stimuli for a salty taste. Thus, common table salt (sodium chloride) tastes salty because of the sodium ion. Sour is the gustatory response to the H^+ ion found in acids. Acidic substances such as lemon juice are typically sour in taste.

Sweet and bitter compounds are typically composed of relatively large molecules. Sweet appears to involve two types of molecular substances. Artificial sweeteners, such as saccharin or cyclamates, are actually heavy metal salts. Apparently, the larger molecular size results in the sweet taste. It is also possible that all salts can potentially stimulate the sweet receptors, since most salts taste sweet in very low concentrations. The other molecular substance to stimulate a sweet taste is represented by the relatively simple organic compounds. Sugars and a wide variety of other natural sweet compounds are usually the products of living matter. The more complicated organic compounds are associated with a bitter taste. A typically bitter response is stimulated by the alkaloids (caffeine, nicotine, strychnine, and so on). Since a bitter taste usually results in rejection of the compound by the mouth, there exists an automatic device to protect the body from the usual toxic effects of alkaloid compounds.

It is well established that each taste bud will respond to more than one taste quality, and usually will respond to all taste stimuli. All taste buds have a unique taste "profile," with some showing higher sensitivity to certain taste stimuli than others. The distribution on the tongue of buds with a common high sensitivity for a particular taste dimension apparently explains the "silver spoon" taste changes. It should be emphasized, however, that no two taste buds have been found to have identical taste profiles.

The response characteristics of a taste bud are not the total response of primary taste cells making up the bud. Microelectrode recordings of individual taste cells indicate that each cell has its own response profile to a spectrum of taste qualities (Figure 17.4). This multidimensional system is maintained in the entire gustatory nervous system. The thalamic taste neurons show a narrower range of activity in their response profile, but still respond to several taste qualities. A few cells in the primary cortical area have been found to respond to more than one primary taste, but none has responded to all four. Apparently, the narrowing of the response profile is due to neural lateral inhibition, but the mechanism remains multidimensional.

A multiplex coding system would account for a number of puzzling taste phenomena. The salt and sour tastes appear to be mutually inhibitory. Applying salt to a (sour) grapefruit simultaneously attenuates both taste qualities. A subliminal concentration of a sweet solution on one side of the tongue increases sensitivity to a sour substance applied on the other side. The familiar change in the taste of certain foods if taken after certain other foods is an additional example. A meal prepared by—or for—a connoisseur is a carefully choreographed sequence of taste experiences. Much of the experience is in the blending of tastes and aftertastes.

Neurons in the taste pathway may connect to more than one taste bud. This creates the unique situation where stimulation of one taste bud may cause a measurable response in an unstimulated neighboring bud. Obviously, such interconnections add yet another complicating factor in understanding the taste mechanism.

MULTIMODAL RECEPTORS

In addition to "pure" taste buds, there are receptors on the tongue that respond to other stimulus dimensions not normally associated with taste. Rats and frogs have receptors apparently tuned to respond to distilled water, normally

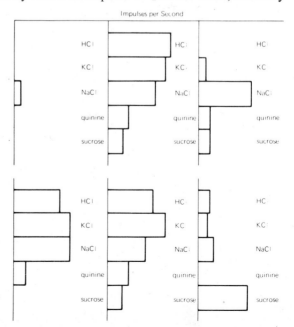

Figure 17.4 Response profiles of six different chorda-tympani neural fibers to five different chemicals applied to the tongue of the rat. (Pfaffman, via Milner, 1970, p. 136)

considered a tastelsss substance. Taste buds respond to warmth and/or cool-ness, and there are also touch receptors found on the tongue.

Warm foods may actually taste different when cold. The touch informa-tion from the release of entrapped bubbles in carbonated beverages is an important component in the appreciation of the drink. Rats may be "re-warded" with a stream of cool air, which they will "lick" as though it was water. Thus, we find that the sense of taste goes beyond a simple chemical sense.

THE TRANSDUCER MECHANISM

The microvillus of the taste cell is assumed to have chemically specific receptor sites which result in a receptor potential when the site is occupied by the appropriate chemical. Theories vary as to whether the receptor site is a physi-cal "hole" that can be occupied only by molecules of a specified shape or some kind of protein or enzyme-binding mechanism at the surface. This hypothesized mechanism is analogous to that involving the postsynaptic membrane of the neuron. Instead of being activated by a transmitter chemical, certain chemicals of external origin result in cellular activity.

The specialized receptor site explains why compounds highly similar in chemical makeup may differ widely in taste. The analogy is that of the "lock and key" mechanism mentioned in Chapter 11. Two keys that are quite similar may not necessarily operate a particular lock. In most cases two very similarly shaped but different-tasting molecules differ in that one has an obvious taste while the other is without taste. Just as the "wrong" key will not open the lock, the "wrong-shaped" molecule will not activate the receptor. If the receptor site is general enough, a number of different molecules in a common class may "fit" the same taste quality.

The lock and key hypothesis also explains why similarly tasting sub-stances usually have a common chemical trait (such as were described for the four primary tastes). At the same time, the mechanism is capable of handling the occasional exception where the molecule "ought to fit" but does not.

The simplest form of this lock and key mechanism would have one re-ceptor type for each of the primary taste sensations. Since all taste cells have been shown to respond to all four tastes, each microvillus probably contains all types of receptor sites. Differential sensitivity can be explained by position-ing different numbers of each type of receptor on any given cell.

If this simple four-site mechanism is true, there must be some critical difference in the dimensions of the site. Individual taste cells respond differ-ently to two different salt compounds. For example, one cell may respond with more activity to a sodium salt than to a potassium salt, while a neighboring transducer may "prefer" potassium. Such differences create problems for a four-site taste mechanism, but hypothesizing an individual site for each taste molecule would seem necessary to explain all of the different response profiles. This solution seems to create more problems than it solves!

Whether the mechanism is a specific site or a generalized site with crucial dimensional characteristics, the phenomenon of "taste blindness" is compatible with the lock and key theory. Phenylthiocarbimide (PTC) is a compound that is distinctly bitter tasting to about 70 percent of the people, while the remainder find it without any remarkable taste feature. The ability to be a taster or nontaster follows Mendelian inheritance patterns and, apparently, is related to the genetic design of the "lock" for the bitter receptor site. It is interesting to note that PTC nontasters are not inferior to tasters in sensitivity to other bitter-tasting compounds.

Whatever the action of the receptor site, the general assumption is that transduction occurs because of the chemical characteristics of the stimulus. Chemical reactions are known to speed up with temperature. Thus, low-temperature compounds will be slower to react chemically with the transducers. In hard water areas, people may utilize this taste-deadening feature by keeping a jar of water in the refrigerator.

If the process were exclusively chemical, the taste sensations should be enhanced with warm and/or hot substances because of the increasing rate of the chemical reaction. In fact, taste sensitivity remains constant or even decreases with increasing temperature above normal body temperature. The warm and cold receptors mixed into the sense of taste may account for the change. In any case, more than a simple chemical process is involved.

SMELL

Millions of dollars are spent to manipulate our olfactory experience. The aerosol spray can industry seems bent on misleading our olfactory sense. We can buy personal deodorants to counteract odors from parts of our body, pet deodorants to make our pets more socially acceptable, and space deodorants to conceal the odors in our home. After successfully neutralizing unwanted odors, we can then inject our environment with another compound designed to delight the sense of smell. Perfumes (or after shave lotions), artificial food flavorings (which are primarily odor cues), or our choice of spice, floral, or forest scents for the room all illustrate our penchant for olfactory camouflage. It is even possible to purchase the smell of a "new car" in a package much less expensive than previously available.

The sense of smell is of crucial importance to the survival of the species. Mating behavior in lower species is extremely dependent on the sense of smell. The olfactory sex attractant in the female moth which can attract male moths more than half a mile down wind is a compelling example. In lower mammalian species, destruction of the olfactory bulb often results in an inability of males to mate successfully with receptive females. Phylogenetically speaking, the chemical sense of smell was developed before either vision or hearing.

In spite of its importance, less is known about the sense of smell than any other sense. Even though we do not usually attribute unusual sensitivity to the human olfactory system, the absolute threshold to some compounds is surprising. At the same time, the olfactory sense is remarkably fast adapting, so that we can become insensitive to high concentrations in a short period of time. These two characteristics make it almost impossible to present the individual with adequate and reproducible stimulus conditions. The researcher is constantly caught between adaptation and contamination.

The location and neurological network associated with the sense of smell also make data collection awkward for the physiologist (Figure 17.5). The transducer cells are located in a network of bone and sinuses, and even the receptor cells are embedded in a bony structure. To make matters worse, the afferent nerve fibers are very short and very fine, making penetration of individual neurons by microelectrodes almost impossible. In addition, the neural pathways in the olfactory bulbs are extremely diffuse, which means that there are no obvious olfactory pathways but a complex network of olfactory structures. Smell is the only primary sense that does not have a major nuclear

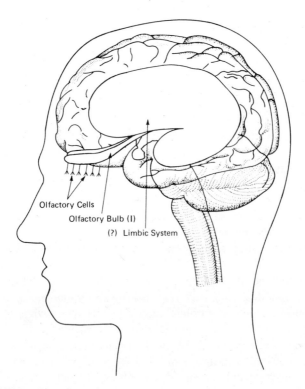

Figure 17.5   The olfactory system.

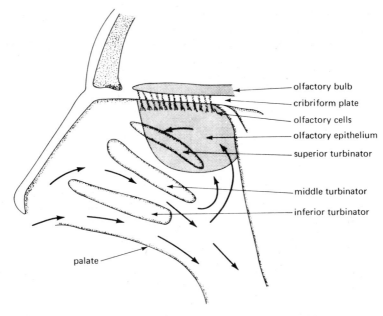

Figure 17.6   Cross section of the nose. (Adey, 1959, via Milner, 1970, p. 139)

synaptic junction in the thalamus. Smell is also the only primary sense that does not have a primary cortical area, although the frontal lobes show olfactory activity. In summary, the olfactory system, though a primitive sense, is one of the most complicated for research activities.

OLFACTORY STRUCTURES

The 60 million olfactory cells are located in the olfactory epithelium lining the top and back of the nasal chambers (Figure 17.6). Each olfactory cell has a number of hairlike processes called cilia protruding into the nasal chamber. It is assumed that these cilia are the locus of transducer action. The cilia are bathed in mucous, so molecules that are effective stimuli for the sense of smell must be aeromatic (airborne) and then soluble in mucous.

Under normal breathing conditions, only about 5 percent of the air breathed through the nasal chamber comes into contact with the olfactory epithelium. Most of the air is conducted through passages lower in the chamber which have no known sensory cells. Much of the particulant matter (odors and dust) is caught in the mucous in these chambers. Breathing through the mouth, of course, bypasses the olfactory epithelium totally.

Thus, we find that the sense of smell samples only a small percentage of the airborne environment under normal circumstances. There are, however, ways to increase the airborne substances coming into contact with the olfactory epithelium. Sniffing increases the total air flow through the nasal chambers, but more important, the partitions within the nasal chamber are such that sniffing creates additional turbulence in the area of the sensory cells. In addition to this voluntary air-volume control, the autonomic nervous system can change blood flow to the tissue lining the nasal chamber. The vasodilation causes the tissue to swell, thereby reducing the size of the air passages, while vasoconstriction can increase the amount of air entering the nose.

OLFACTORY PATHWAYS

The olfactory epithelium consists of three types of cells (Figure 17.7). **Basal cells** appear to attach the epithelium to the bony **cribriform plate** which forms the top of the nasal chamber. The **olfactory receptor cells** are distributed throughout the epithelium with their cilia extending out from the surface of the epithelium and their unmyelinated axons reaching back toward the basal cells and eventually through the cribriform plate. The receptor cells are packed between a number of supportive cells known as **sustentacular cells.** Since the sustentacular cells lack axons, they are assigned the task of holding the receptor cells to the basal cells. The surface end of these "supportive" glial cells contains tiny hairlike microvilli. Thus, the surface of the olfactory epithelium presents a "fuzzy" surface of longer ciliary processes of the receptor cells against a background field of microvilli of the interstitched glial cells. It is estimated that the total surface area presented by the ciliary processes alone easily exceeds the total surface skin area of the body.

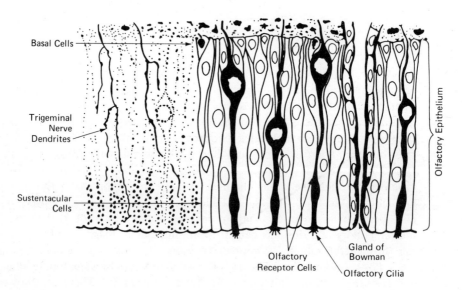

Figure 17.7 The olfactory epithelium. (Rusmussen, 1943, via Christman, 1971, p. 331)

The unmyelinated axons from the receptor cells join with the axons from other cells to form bundles of nerves. These bundles extend through approximately twenty perforations in the bony cribriform plate dividing the nasal chamber from the cranial cavity holding the CNS. The twenty olfactory nerves then enter the olfactory bulbs, or cranial nerve I. The axons of the receptor cells synaptically connect with two types of cells in the olfactory bulb. The tufted cells extend to the amygdaloid cortex located inside the temporal lobe. The rest of the pathways of the olfactory system are so diffuse that they can be best described as speculative and/or complicated (Figure 17.8).

Recordings of the activity of the primary olfactory fibers in the frog indicate that the typical sensory cell maintains an irregular level of ongoing activity. Olfactory stimulation results in an excitatory increase or inhibitory decrease in this activity level. The receptors seem to be similar to the taste buds in that there is usually a response of some kind to any olfactory stimulus. The response profile appears to differ with each cell. Thus, it is possible to find one cell that is excited by two different odors, while another cell shows opposing activity to the same two stimuli. This opposing characteristic seems to be unrelated to the "similarity" of the odor stimuli. As long as the odors are discriminable, it is possible to find a sensory cell with opposing electrical responses. Thus, the brain must decode a complex pattern of excitation and inhibition which is unique to each odor. While it is possible to hypothesize neural interconnections that could result in specific olfactory "features," it is not presently known where (or if) such mechanisms are to be found.

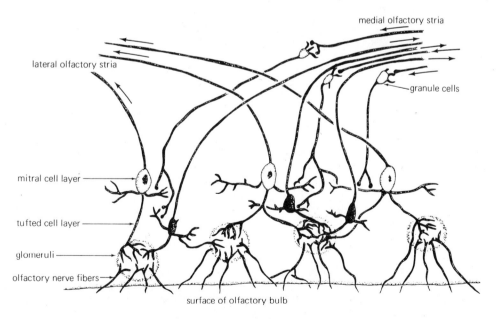

Figure 17.8 Schematic diagram of olfactory bulb connections. (Milner, 1970, p. 141)

THE TRANSDUCER MECHANISMS

The lock and key hypothesis discussed for the taste cells is the most promising theory for the sense of smell. At the present time, seven primary olfactory receptor sites have been suggested, corresponding to the smells: camphoraceous, pungent, ethereal, floral, pepperminty, musky, and putrid (Figure 17.9). Molecules that elicit each dimensional response fit into an appropriate receptor site according to its three-dimensional molecular shape. This stereochemical theory has successfully predicted the odor of some artificial substances. Since the receptor cells respond to all substances, each receptor cell must have a full compliment of all seven of the primary receptor sites.

The similarity between the senses of taste and smell, including the mechanism of transduction, also poses a perplexing problem. The hypthesized transducer mechanisms are assumed to be located on the microvilli of the taste cells or the ciliary processes of the olfactory cells. The electrical receptor potential occurs within approximately 20 milliseconds of stimulus arrival. The distance between the hairlike outermost extensions of the receptor cell makes a passive electronic spread, such as the postsynaptic potential on the neuron, impossible within this time period. Thus, there must be some special generator

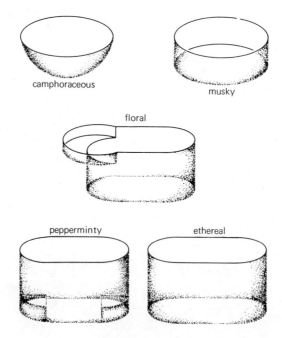

Figure 17.9 The suggested shapes for five of the receptors for a stereochemical (lock and key) theory of odor perception. Molecules with a positive charge have a pungent odor, and negatively charged molecules yield putrid regardless of shape. (Amoore, 1964, via Milner, 1970, p. 142)

mechanism at the base of the hairlike site. Obviously, much is left to be learned about the chemical transducers.

AUTHOR'S   The chemical senses are the means by which the organism
COMMENTS   "samples" external substances directly. In the most primitive case, the free nerve endings provide direct pain information generated by some chemical substances. In the more refined chemical senses of taste and smell, strong evidence suggests that there are certain "primary" dimensions of the stimulus. These are usually related to the characteristics of the molecule providing the stimulus and are frequently described by a lock and key analogy.

The primary taste or smell qualities lead to assuming primary receptor transducer cells. Evoked potential recording indicates that each transducer cell responds to many (if not all) of the primary stimulus cues. Two transducer cells are distinguished by the specific profile generated for each by equal exposure to various primary substances. Such multiple sensitivity is relatively easy to resolve in the context of the sensory networks already hypothesized for other modalities.

18

The Bodily Senses

The previous chapters have been concerned with "external" senses. That is, the stimuli have originated outside the organism. Sight, hearing, taste, and smell all give important information concerning the world surrounding the organism. The systems loosely collected together in this chapter are primarily concerned with the characteristics of the organism itself. It should be recalled that to the CNS anything outside the dura mater (or the skull and vertebrae of the backbone) constitutes the outside world. The neuronal activity of the afferent nerve reporting a stomach ache is using the same information-transmission system that the eyes use to observe a star millions of miles away.

THE SKIN SENSES

The skin is a highly complex organ in its own right (Figure 18.1). Providing an outer barrier for the delicate complex of cells making up the organism, the skin is also an active participant in several bodily functions. Temperature regulation is accomplished through adjusting blood flow near the surface, as well as through the familiar "sweating" response which provides evaporative cooling. A certain degree of respiratory exchange is also accomplished across this "sensory" organ, and the skin is capable of producing certain hormones, primarily in response to sunlight.

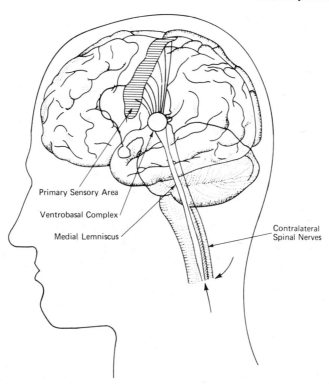

Primary Sensory Area

Ventrobasal Complex

Medial Lemniscus

Contralateral
Spinal Nerves

Figure 18.1   The cutaneous (skin senses) system.

The skin is divided into two major layers, the dermis and the epidermis (Figure 18.2). The dermis is a layer of sweat glands, hair follicles, blood vessels, smooth muscles, and receptors that make up the organ components of the skin. The epidermis is an overlying protective layer of skin cells enervated only by free nerve endings. The epidermis does not have blood vessels. The outermost layer of the epidermis is actually dead skin cells that form a protective layer between the living cells of the skin and the surrounding hostile environment. These dead cells are abraded or sloughed away to be constantly replenished from the living cells of the epidermis.

The primary stimuli for the skin are generally established as being touch, warmth, cold, and pain. By carefully touching a small area of the skin with each primary stimulus, it is possible to "map" the receptive areas of the skin. The skin is insensitive to certain primary stimuli in certain areas. Thus, an area of the skin may respond to the touch of a warm, pointed rod but not to the temperature. Other regions may be sensitive to warmth (something like experiencing the warmth from the sun) but not to touch. If we were to map a square inch of the skin with one hundred squares, and then systematically stimulate each square with the four primary stimuli, we would find that some squares would be insensitive to all of the stimuli, others would respond to one or two, and a few would respond to all four.

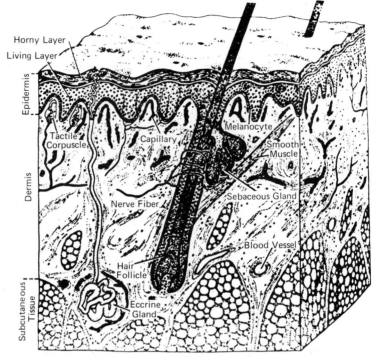

Horny Layer
Living Layer
Epidermis
Tactile Corpuscle
Capillary
Melanocyte
Smooth Muscle
Dermis
Nerve Fiber
Sebaceous Gland
Blood Vessel
Hair Follicle
Subcutaneous Tissue
Eccrine Gland

Figure 18.2   A cross section of the human skin including many sensory transducer cells. (Montagna, 1965)

Since there are a number of "sensory-appearing" cells in the skin, it seems likely that each specialized receptor is the transducer for a primary sensory quality (Figure 18.3). The most frequent sensory cells are the **free nerve endings,** essentially dendritic branches of neurons that seem to have acquired primitive transducer capacities. The remainder of the sensory cells lie deeper in the dermal layer of the skin and appear to be free nerve endings encapsulated in special auxiliary structures. Careful mapping of the skin response with subsequent histological confirmation of the underlying sensory cell type shows no reliable relationship. Although there is evidence suggesting specific structures for certain sensory qualities, there are inevitably exceptions that prevent an absolute conclusion. The highly specialized auxiliary structures must contribute to the skin sensory apparatus, but their precise function is unclear. One suggestion is that the encapsulating structures primarily provide protection for the sensitive free nerve endings. The cells may be so delicate and the stimulatory abuse on the skin so great that the transducers would be damaged if left unprotected.

Some evidence to support this protective supposition derives from a sub-cutaneous sensory cell which has been carefully investigated. The **Pacinian corpuscle** is an onionlike encapsulation of a free nerve ending that reports

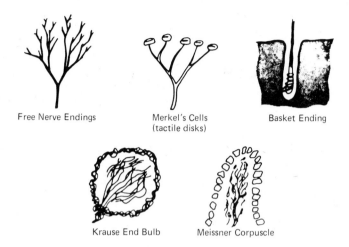

Free Nerve Endings

Merkel's Cells (tactile disks)

Basket Ending

Krause End Bulb

Meissner Corpuscle

Figure 18.3 Some representative skin transducer cells. (Christman, 1971, p. 350)

"deep pressure" (Figure 18.4). The corpuscle responds to a deforming pressure of as little as 0.0001 inch. After careful peeling away of the successive layers of the "onion," there is no diminution in receptor sensitivity. The bare nerve ending appears to be the transducer site. Only free nerve endings are found in hairy skin, but obviously, hairy areas are sensitive to the full range of tactile sensations. Hairless skin areas (like the inside of the hand), which exhibit the full variety of encapsulations, are regions of maximum exposure to abusive levels of stimulation.

The sensitivity of the skin differs with the area of the body. For example, the entire trunk region contains fewer sensitive spots per unit area than any other portion of the body. The surface of the hands and feet is relatively high in concentration of sensory "spots," as is the face, with the lip area the most sensitive of all.

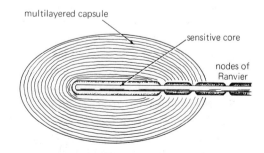

multilayered capsule

sensitive core

nodes of Ranvier

Figure 18.4 Cross section of a Pacinian corpuscle. (Milner, 1970, p. 127)

THE SOMESTHETIC PATHWAYS

Fibers from the transducer cells in the skin extend to the spinal cord. The route taken depends on the area of the skin where the transduction occurs. Each axon follows its course through the appropriate peripheral nerves, plexus, and spinal nerves according to the dermatome maps of the skin. The afferent cell bodies are grouped in the spinal ganglia on each side of the spinal cord, so the conducting fibers of the somesthetic system are preganglionic (before the cell body).

The fibers leading to the spinal cord are of two major types: large, myelinated fibers that carry touch information and smaller, unmyelinated fibers that carry temperature and pain messages. The two types of fibers are mixed together in the peripheral nervous system, but separate at the synaptic connections in the spinal cord. Two different somesthetic nervous systems are identified in the spinal cord.

The heavily myelinated fibers feed into the **lemniscal system** (Figure 18.5). Although there are several different parallel pathways in the spinal cord, all of the pathways cross over to the contralateral side and converge to form the medial lemniscus through the midbrain, ending in the ventrobasal complex of the thalamus. From here the information is transmitted directly to the primary cortical somesthetic area. The primary somesthetic area is along the posterior gyrus of the central sulcus (Figure 18.6). The foot (and tail) regions of the body are located on the top region of the gyrus, and higher regions of the body are noted as we progress down the gyrus. The most ventral area serves the touch functions of the mouth and tongue (near the area for taste).

The unmyelinated fibers synapse with afferent nerves in the spinal cord that make up the extralemniscal system. The **extralemniscal system** is an extremely diffuse network of pathways that seem to be marked by *not* being found in the medial lemniscus (Figure 18.7). Branches of the extralemniscal system are known to lead into the reticular activating system, the cerebellum, and several distinct nuclei in the thalamus. Extralemniscal system activity results in activity in many regions of the cortex.

NEURONAL ACTIVITY

Recording the evoked activity of first-order somesthetic neurons demonstrates a number of characteristics of nervous system organization. The receptive fields of the sensory neurons vary with their location on the skin. In general, the fields are larger for the torso and become smaller toward the extremities. Some of the somesthetic receptive fields are not contiguous, so the receptive field may consist of several tiny "islands." As a general rule, the larger the diameter of the fiber, the smaller the receptive field, and vice versa.

The touch neurons in the somesthetic system respond to different intensi-

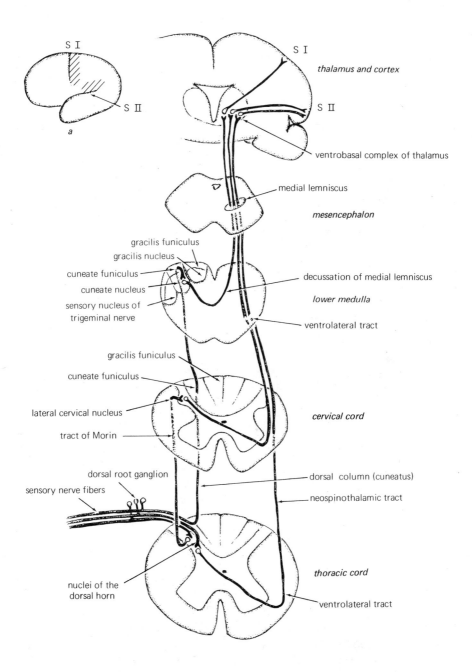

Figure 18.5 Schematic diagram of the lemniscal pathways. (Milner, 1970, p. 150)

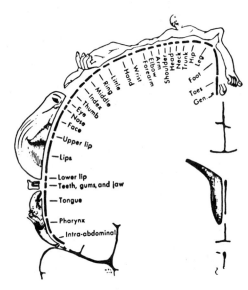

Figure 18.6 Sensory homunculus. A coronal section of the human cortex through the primary sensory area, with an adjacent pictorial display of the body part involved when that point on the cortex is artificially stimulated. The line segments and labels provide a more precise summary of the homunculus. (Penfield & Rassmussen, 1950, via Wenger, Jones, & Jones, 1956, p. 297)

ties of stimulation. Some respond to the slightest contact with the skin, while others respond only to pressures that deform deeper dermal regions. There is evidence to separate these two types of touch into separate categories, since they provide distinctly different subjective qualities of touch. Touch neurons also differ in the range of stimulus intensity to which they are sensitive. Thus, the neurons may be divided into "small," "medium," and "large" stimulus units.

Many touch receptors are exclusively responsive to touch. They are normally quiescent—they exhibit no background activity—show rapid adaptation to a sustained stimulus, and appear unaffected by temperature. Other touch receptors appear to be combination touch-temperature units. Here the background activity of the cells is a reflection of the temperature. The cells change their activity when a touch stimulus is applied. The touch response occurs only within a relatively narrow band of temperatures, although different cells respond within different temperature bands. These cells show only a slight adaptation to steady stimuli of either touch or temperature.

The precise receptive fields of the peripheral first-order neurons seem to be completely lost in the diverging and converging circuitry within the spinal cord. Many units in the thalamus may have a receptive field that incorporates one half of the body area. Such cells may be ipsilateral or contralateral in the locus of their receptive field, but also involve less obvious organizational patterns. Some may respond to stimulation of only a single limb, others to stimulation on the head and not the body, and still others only to stimulation above or below the waist.

Thus, we find that the higher-order neurons have gigantic receptive fields. In addition, many of these cells respond to more than one stimulus quality, and each stimulus has its own receptive field! This general hierarchy may be analogous to the visual and auditory systems. The peripheral portions

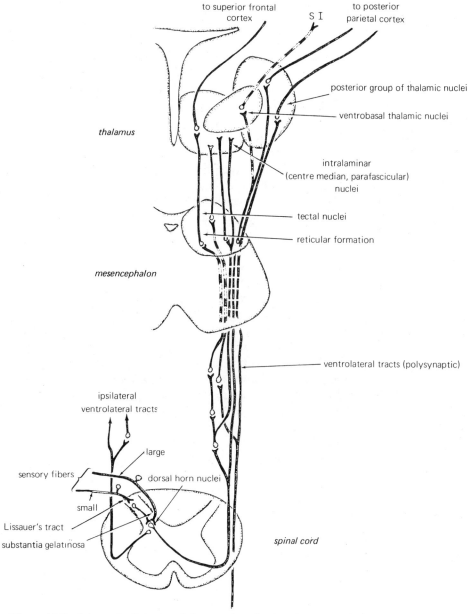

Figure 18.7 Schematic diagram of the extralemniscal pathways. (Milner, 1970, p. 151)

of the sensory system extract stimulus location information, while the cortex is specialized to extract specific stimulus features regardless of location. Somesthetic cortical cells located in the same "column" of the cortex appear to share a common somesthetic "feature," either in terms of the type of stimulus or the area of the receptive field.

THE KINESTHETIC AND VISCERAL SENSES

In addition to the enormous number of receptor cells located in the skin, sensory transducers are located in most of the internal structures of the body. All of the viscera have stretch receptors that monitor fullness of the digestive organs. The muscles have stretch receptors that monitor the degree of strain or tension of the muscle (Figure 18.8). The tendons have similar "strain gauges" to indicate position and tension. By means of these internal sensory devices we are able to know the position of our limbs without looking at them. Accurate and coordinated muscular control relies on a constant feedback of information regarding the progress of the individual components.

The internal senses seem to share a number of characteristics with the skin senses. Many of the specialized sensory encapsulations found in the deeper layers of the skin are the same as those found in internal structures. The pathways appear to be similar and, in many cases, shared. Even the restricted sensory field is retained, although evolutionary modifications have moved the position of many internal structures, so that the organization is not as easily mapped as for the skin dermatomes.

The preceding section on the skin senses treated the sensory activity of the skin as a passive, receiving structure. This, in fact, is not the way the sense of touch is usually employed. The sense of touch provides us with an active, exploring interaction with the world. Observe a child in a toy store to see how compelling the sense of touch is in learning about the environment. Even adults in a grocery store must manipulate many of the items before making a purchase decision. The weight of an object is measured by the muscle tension and tendon stretch created when the object is hefted. In order to enhance the discrimination, we often gently toss the object up and down to bring more sensory units into play. The hardness of an object is judged by a carefully balanced interplay between the object's surface yield as measured by

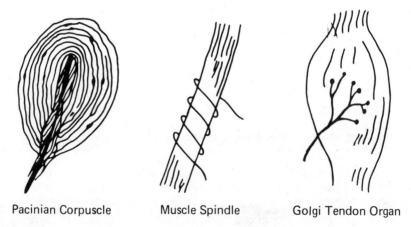

Pacinian Corpuscle   Muscle Spindle   Golgi Tendon Organ

Figure 18.8   Subcutaneous transducer cells. (Christman, 1971, p. 366)

the skin senses and the amount of probing pressure applied with the muscles. The sense of touch is enriched tremendously by being able to move the fingers over the surface of the object. Texture (hard, smooth, rough, and so on) involves gauging the panoply of touch sensations being swept past the sensors in the moving fingertip.

It would seem appropriate to abandon the geographically based separation of the skin and internal sensory systems and lump them together into a meaningful, unified functional unit. Such a complex interplay of sensory information from throughout the entire body is called the **haptic sense.**

THE VESTIBULAR APPARATUS

Chapter 16, it will be recalled, stated that the inner ear is divided into two sections. The cochlear portion is involved with the transduction of sounds, and the vestibular portion is concerned with motion and position (Figure 18.9). The **vestibular apparatus** resembles the cochlea in that it is a hollow, bony structure filled with perilymph and containing a membranous inner chamber with receptor cells bathed in endolymph. The chambers and fluids are physically contiguous with the counterparts in the cochlea. Technically speaking, the vestibular apparatus is phylogenetically older than the cochlea,

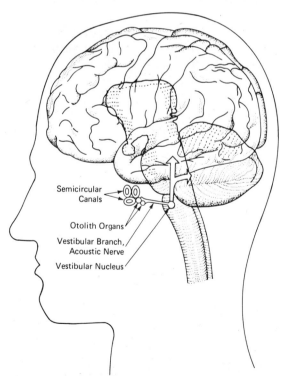

Semicircular
Canals

Otolith Organs

Vestibular Branch,
Acoustic Nerve

Vestibular Nucleus

Figure 18.9 The vestibular system.

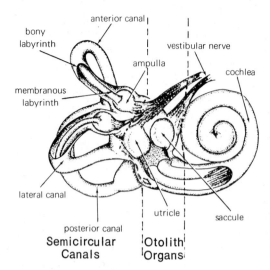

anterior canal

bony
labyrinth

vestibular nerve

ampulla

cochlea

membranous
labyrinth

lateral canal

utricle

saccule

posterior canal

Semicircular
Canals

Otolith
Organs

Figure 18.10   The vestibular apparatus.   (Geldard, 1953, via Milner, 1970, p. 210)

although it is difficult at this point to determine which is borrowing what from the other.

The vestibular apparatus can be divided into two sections (Figure 18.10). The **semicircular canals** are specialized to detect angular acceleration caused by rotation (or cessation of rotation) of the head. The **otolith organs** are gravity detectors and indicate position relative to this cue. The transducers for both functions are found in the **vestibular epithelium** lining each section. Structurally, the vestibular epithelium resembles the olfactory epithelium in that it is a matrix of transducer hair cells held in place by interstitched supportive glial cells. The vestibular epithelium lines the interior surface of the bony vestibular apparatus, although there is a narrow cushioning space filled with perilymph separating the two. The hair cells are oriented so that their ciliary hairs extend into the endolymph-filled space bounded by the membrane. The sensory cells are concentrated in relatively small regions of the total membrane surface.

THE OTOLITH ORGANS

The otolith organs are two relatively large, bulbous chambers attached to the cochlea. In most marine animals, there are three otolithic chambers, but in land animals one seems to have been converted to detecting sound vibrations. The two otolithic chambers have their patch of sensory hair cells oriented in different positions within the chamber. In the **utricle**, the sensory patch is located on the floor of the chamber, while in the **saccule**, it is vertically oriented on the "inside wall." The cilia of the sensory hair cells are embedded in a gelatinous structure which overrides the entire sensory patch (Figure 18.11). Embedded in the outer surface of this structure are calcium carbonate secretions known as otoliths, after which the structures are named. The

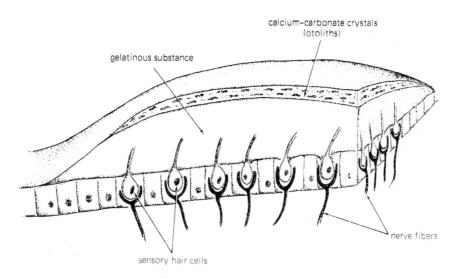

Figure 18.11 The transducer portion of an otolithic organ (utricle or saccule). (Goddard, 1953, via Milner, 1970, p. 210)

gelatinous nature of the overriding structure allows it to shift from side to side. This lateral movement creates a shear force on the cilia of the hair cells which is transduced into sensory information. The otoliths apparently provide needed additional mass on the outside surface of the structure to emphasize the shifting action.

For example, the structure attached to the hair cells of the vertically oriented sensory patch in the saccule is displaced downward by the pull of gravity. If a person were to lie down, the gravitational pull would be toward the rear, and the sensory cells in the utricle would also be stimulated. Apparently, the sensory cells in the vestibular apparatus respond only to shear force and not to compression or stretching. In this characteristic the sensory cells are like the hair cells in the cochlea.

If we are in an automobile or airplane that is accelerating, the otolithic structure will be shifted in the direction opposite to the line of acceleration. Thus, the otolithic organs respond to changes in momentum, either from speeding up or slowing down. At a constant velocity, the otolithic structure returns to its "zero position," so no vestibular perception of motion is noted in an airplane flying straight and level. Acceleration, deceleration, air pockets, and side winds will all create a shift in the otolithic structure with the resulting impression of movement. Pilots who fly "by the seat of their pants" are actually utilizing the otolithic organs as the primary source of information.

Modern high-performance aircraft exceed the capacity of the otolithic organs. One difficult task for a jet pilot is to learn to trust his aircraft instrument dials rather than this own vestibular senses, particularly when confirmatory visual information is lacking. For example, modern jet aircraft can accelerate for several seconds. If this occurs in level flight, the otolithic structure is displaced slightly toward the rear of the pilot's head. This shift indicates that "down" has shifted to the rear. In other words, one feels as though the aircraft is climbing. The pilot who succumbs to this cue tries to lower the nose of the aircraft to get back to "level." Taking this course of action, however, puts the plane into a dive, which causes it to accelerate, and once again one feels as if the plane is climbing! Unless reason, vision, or some other response interferes with the process, the pliot pays a high price for a "natural" response.

THE SEMICIRCULAR CANALS

The semicircular canals are three bony tubes that loop outward from the utricle. One lies essentially in the horizontal plane, while the other two are oriented vertically. The two vertical canals form a right angle oriented toward the outer ear. Thus, the three canals are positioned in roughly orthogonal planes of a three-dimensional space. The semicircular canals are sensitive to angular rotations of the head.

To better understand the characteristics of the horizontally oriented canal, imagine that the head is turned rapidly from left to right. The fluid in the canal will remain relatively stationary. Just as rotating a glass of water containing an ice cube results in relatively little motion of the ice cube, rotating the canel in the plane of the loop results in little motion of the endolymph.

The hair cells protruding into the endolymph are bent by the apparent "flow" resulting in a sensory response to the rotation of the head. At one end of its loop each semicircular canal has a bulge called the **ampulla** (Figure 18.10), in which the rotation receptor cells are located. The hair cells, with their associated support cells, form a ridge across one side of the chamber. The cilia of the receptor cells are embedded in a gelatinous cupola that forms a "gate" across the ampulla chamber (Figure 18.12). Fluid motion through the ampulla causes the cupola to "bend" or "swing" in the direction of the fluid flow. The attached sensory hair cells are connected at the "hinge" of the gate, so substantial shearing forces are generated against the cilia of the transducer cells.

Because of the right angle orientation of the three semicircular canals, any rotational motion of the head (and body) is resolved into a three-dimensional component signal. Only occasionally is the rotational motion exclusively confined to a single canal. As in the otolithic organ, the sensory cells in the semicircular canals do not respond to constant velocity rotation. Thus, we would adapt to the rotation of a constantly moving merry-go-round. The fluid inside the canals acquires the momentum of the moving container, and the cupola returns to its neutral position. When the rotation stops, the fluid momentum causes a reverse flow, and the deceleration is detected.

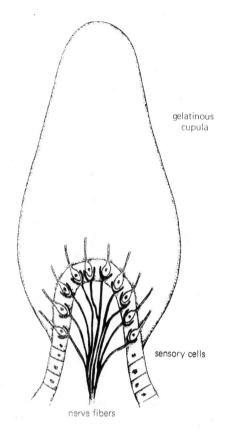

gelatinous
cupula

sensory cells

nerve fibers

Figure 18.12 Section of a christa, the transducer organ in the semicircular canals. (Milner, 1970, p. 211)

THE VESTIBULAR PATHWAYS

The hair cells in the vestibular apparatus have no apparent axon. Instead, the hair cell body is totally enveloped in a flask-shaped network of dendritic branches from an auditory bipolar cell. The axons from these bipolar cells are bundled together to form the **vestibular nucleus** located in the medulla. Different portions of the vestibular nucleus can be identified as serving either the semicircular canals or the otolithic organs.

From the vestibular nucleus, the branches are many and varied (Figure 18.13). Efferent fibers are seen joining motor tracts in the spinal cord, and other vestibular fibers enter the cerebellum. The major tract ascends to the oculomotor nuclei in the thalamus. Since the vestibular sense is intimately involved with balance and body movement as well as with head and eye motion, the functional significance of these tracts seems logical and appropriate.

The close connection between the oculomotor nucleus and the vestibular nucleus is highly adaptive. The eyes, located in the head, are confronted with an interesting geometric problem. How is it possible to "track" or fixate

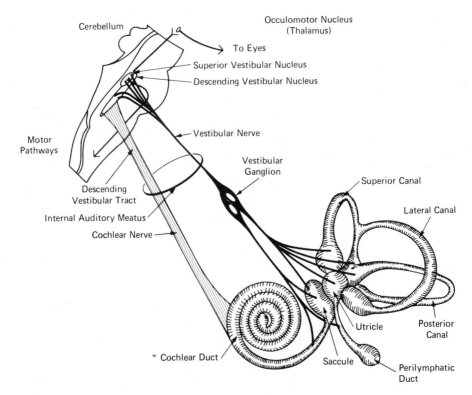

Figure 18.13 Schematic diagram of the vestibular pathways. (House & Pansky, 1967)

on some external object when the head is often in motion? The vestibular system supplies immediate information concerning head movements. This information is transmitted directly to the oculomotor nucleus, which controls the muscles of the eyes. Thus, movement of the head to the right results in an automatic countermovement of the eyes to the left. This reflexive circuitry explains the apparent whirling of the visual word when children spin around and suddenly stop. The after-motion of the fluid in the horizontal semicircular canal (probably including neural after-effects from adaptation) causes the eyes to scan in a compensatory horizontal movement. Between scans, the eyes snap back to a new "fixation point" and continue the scan. The resulting sweep of the image across the retina is "seen" as a movement of the outside world.

Resting bipolar fibers in the vestibular nerve have a relatively constant level of activity when the organism is at rest. Movement of the hair cells in one direction causes the neurons to increase their rate of firing, while movement in the opposite direction inhibits the activity. Since the vestibular apparatus is bilaterally duplicated (one in each side of the head), combining the excitatory and inhibitory information for a specific movement could result in precise determination of the movement characteristics.

PAIN

Pain presents a number of problems in the discussion of the senses. There seems little doubt that there is a distinct perception of pain. Occasionally, pain may result from overstimulation of the normal receptor cells. We may experience a painfully bright light if we are dark adapted, for example. There is considerable evidence to suggest that there are also pain receptors.

The free nerve endings appear to be the likely candidates for the pain receptors. Free nerve endings are a primitive version of a sensory cell, and pain is a primitive sensory quality! Evidence indicates that the pain pathways in the body are the relatively diffuse networks of the unmyelinated cells, with no obvious direct cortical projections. In other words, the pain system seems to be handled by the more primitive neuronal circuits in the nervous system.

Pain is usually the result of a stimulus that creates tissue damage, which is usually accomplished by cutting, crushing, burning, or freezing the cells. It is hypothesized that the damaged cells release a chemical substance that stimulates the free nerve endings. **Ischemic pain,** which is caused by depriving tissue of the normal supply of blood, may trigger the release of the chemical or directly stimulate activity in the free nerve ending cell as a result of the anoxia. Neurons that respond to a painful stimulus exhibit a different type of activity than the normal sensory-evoked potentials. The typical response to pain is relatively slow at onset and then builds to a crescendo rather than the more precise "on-off" type of coding of the typical sensory neuron. Many neurons appear to carry pain messages exclusively, while others may also respond to nondestructive stimulation.

While pain appears to be a distinct sensory dimension, the response to a painful stimulus varies greatly from one individual to another. Apparently, this difference is not the result of differences in the peripheral sensory apparatus, but is more the result of sensory processing by the CNS. Many regions of the cortex and brain stem appear to be involved in the pain-appreciation system. Localized lesions as well as stimulation have been employed to alleviate the symptoms of otherwise intractable pain. Often, the relief is not one of reduced sensory input. The patient may report, "It still hurts, it just does not bother me any more." The fact that the human response to painful stimulation varies in different cultures suggests how complex the pain response really is.

The complexity and diffuseness of the pain-appreciation system makes the occurrence of a pain center unlikely. Just as the pain neurons code the painful stimulus in a manner quite unlike the precision coding of the other sensory systems, the system that deals with pain information appears less linear and less precise than the other sensory systems.

Examples of mistaken painful information illustrate some of the problems. Amputees report a distinct impression of sensory input—usually painful —from the absent limb: the **phantom limb phenomenon.** It does no good to explain that the aching toe is not there; the pain is real! It is interesting to note that phantom limb pain occurs in adult amputees, but is not known in young children. Apparently, the pain system requires some ontogenetic development time to establish the needed sensory circuits. Another response to pain is exhibited by dogs raised in isolation. The dogs may lack the normal pain response and repeatedly extinguish lighted matches with their noses.

If the nerve serving an area of the skin is severed, pain is a distinct facet of the nerve-regeneration process. As the area reacquires sensation, a nondestructive stimulus (such as a light touch) may result in an intensely painful sensation. The regenerating nerves seem to lack some important mechanism for attenuating the pain message. This could be due to the operation of the more sophisticated nonpain sensory systems or to balancing mechanisms within the pain network. Fortunately for the victim, as the healing process continues, the pain-attenuating function of the nerves also regenerates.

Referred pain is a phenomenon that occurs when the pain source is an internal organ, but the pain is perceived to originate on the skin surface. Sometimes the perceived location lies directly over the affected organ, but sometimes the locus is considerably displaced. Heart attack victims, for example, frequently report the pain in the left shoulder or left arm. Doctors learn to identify internal symptoms from the associated referred pain location. When referred pain occurs, the perceived skin area and the internal organ that is the source have pain fibers that share a common peripheral nerve. For some reason, the activity of the pain fibers leading from the internal organ activate and/or intermingle with the fibers from the surface, and the source is mislocated.

The CNS is devoid of pain receptors. Most brain surgery is conducted under local anesthetic to block the pain of incision, but brain tissue itself is devoid of pain. The blood vessels and meninges that serve and protect the CNS are supplied with pain receptors. Migraine headaches are the result of swelling in the pain-sensitive blood vessels serving the cortex. The headache associated with a "hangover" has a similar source. The same mechanism that dilates the blood vessels in the eyes probably dilates the internal meningeal blood vessels. You can see the bloodshot eyes in the mirror; you can feel the bloodshot vessels in the head.

Pain not only appears when and where it should not, it can also be concealed when it ought to be present. Disruption of the normal CNS activities can be accomplished by existing sensory channels. **Audio analgesia** has been successfully employed by dentists for several years. The practice involves providing the patient with earphones that deliver white noise, which blocks the pain of the dental work. The patient can adjust the volume of the audio signal to match the level of stimulation being blocked.

Two possible mechanisms have been suggested to explain the pain phenomenon. One is a type of "gating mechanism." Many sensory nerves do not carry pain information. Perhaps the activity of a "nonpain" channel somehow blocks the transmission of the pain message. This could account for the audio analgesia effect. It might also account for the analgesic effects of the acupuncture procedure.

A more complicated mechanism suggests that within the diffuse network comprising the pain system is a carefully balanced system of excitatory and inhibitory connections. The primitive sensory information is that of pain, which is appropriate for pure survival. The more sophisticated specialized senses inhibit this basically avoidance response by their more specialized sensory activity. Since the specialized sensory systems conduct faster than the pain network, we usually experience only the sensory activity. In the case of the phantom limb and reinnervated area, the balance is disrupted and the pain sensation is recognized.

AUTHOR'S COMMENTS   The bodily senses are primarily intended to encode and transmit information regarding the internal state of the organism. Because the body also interacts directly with the outside environment, these senses also are used to detect the external world. The skin senses and pain are obvious examples, but even the vestibular sense has become important in these days of modern transportation.

The problem of interfacing the natural reponse with the appropriate response is particularly evident in the case of an airplane pilot. The vestibular system is simply not capable of keeping up with the forces created by the high acceleration forces that can be produced. Experienced pilots, however, can learn to select the appropriate sensory channels and ignore the inaccurate sensory input.

The perception of pain appears to contain significant learned aspects. A number of research findings indicate that the painfulness of a damaging stimulus is related to the early experience and/or expectations of the individual almost as much as the stimulus itself.

Accumulating the varied bodily senses into a single chapter illustrates an important characteristic of the perceptual process. Only in rare cases is the perception of the environment accomplished by means of a single sensory channel. The process of perception involves the accumulation of many separate sensory "impressions." Perhaps the artificial division into five (or more or less) senses is misleading for the student attempting to understand the perceptual process.

Part

VI

Response Systems

The sensory systems provide an elaborate data-extraction network for optimal interaction with the environment. This information extraction is accomplished in a series of "levels," which become increasingly complicated and sophisticated in function. The feature detectors found in the visual system illustrate this progressively complicated data-analysis system. Important stimulus dimensions are being extracted and distributed to various parts of the nervous system to coordinate a total response pattern appropriate to the incoming stimulation.

An elaborate sensory evaluation system would be relatively useless without a complimentary response capacity. The transition from the "input" to the "output" side of the system is very important. Many of the organizational characteristics of the afferent sensory systems may be found in the efferent response networks. If we simplify the organization of a sensory system as a sequence of increasingly sophisticated feature detectors, we can similarly describe the response systems as a series of increasingly sophisticated "response programs."

The more peripheral spinal reflexes provide immediate control for a limited muscular response. More elaborate reflexive circuits coordinate two or more muscles for efficient movement of a single limb. Still more complicated circuits simultaneously manipulate the movement of the limbs on the right and left sides of the body. The spinal cord is finally interconnected throughout the length of the body to provide total bodily coordination in the form of reflexive bodily postures.

These reflexive circuits serve two important functions for the organism. First, they provide a capacity for immediate escape from an injurious stimulus. When damage is being incurred, the response need not be elaborate, but it should be immediate. Second, they provide prefabricated "building blocks" for more elaborate sequences of behavior. A significant portion of the fine control of a voluntary movement is accomplished by means of the automatic functioning of the spinal reflexes. "Higher behavior" is the sequential combination of these more primitive components.

Thus, we find that the nervous system is organized into a hierarchy of functions that become increasingly complex. In the sensory systems, it is the feature-extraction process that increases in sophistication. In the motor system, it is the motor program that becomes increasingly elaborate. In each case, the "higher functions" are built on combinations of "lower functions."

The organization and origin of these feature and program portions of the nervous system are important matters in understanding the functional characteristics of the nervous system. American psychology is strongly committed to the idea that the behavior of an organism plays a large role in learning, and an impressive body of evidence supports this nurture side of the nature-nurture question. Yet interest is growing in reopening the genetic side of this question. Behavior genetics is the study of the genetic components of behavior. Although this approach is relatively new, the physiological ramifications in terms of the organization of the nervous system are important.

Since the nervous system develops in close conjunction with environmental stimulation, the ontogenetic patterns of neural development provide important cues to understanding the adult CNS. The data appear fairly clear that the nature-nurture question is misleading because both heredity and environment are important contributors to the adult nervous system. This epigenetic hypothesis is explored in terms of some of the ramifications for increasing the capacity of the individual.

SUGGESTED READINGS

The material discussed in Part VI represents an interface with "other disciplines." In many cases, the areas covered in these chapters are expanded into semester-long courses. The texts for these courses are organized exclusively around the topic, with a tangential overlap into the physiological area. The relevance of the references suggested below may be total or partial, depending on the perspective of the reader.

Bermant, G. (Ed.) *Perspectives on animal behavior: A first course.* Glenview, Ill.: Scott, Foresman, 1973.

Denny, M. R. & Ratner, S. C. *Comparative psychology: Research in animal behavior.* (Rev. ed.) Homewood, Ill.: Dorsey Press, 1970.

Hirsch, J. (Ed.) *Behavior-genetic analysis.* New York: McGraw-Hill, 1967.

Kuo, Z. Y. *The dynamics of behavior development: An epigenetic approach.* New York: Random House, 1967.

Laughlin, W. S. & Osborne, R. H. *Human variation and origins: An introduction to human biology and evolution.* (Readings from *Scientific American.*) San Francisco: Freeman, 1967.

Lerner, M. I. *Heredity, evolution, and society.* San Francisco: Freeman, 1968.

McClearn, G. E. & DeFries, J. C. *Introduction to behavioral genetics.* San Francisco: Freeman, 1973.

Smith, D. W. & Bierman, E. L. *The biologic ages of man: From conception through old age.* Philadelphia: Saunders, 1973.

Watson, J. B. *Behaviorism.* New York: Norton, 1924.

Winchester, A. M. *Heredity: An introduction to genetics.* (2d ed.) New York: Barnes & Noble, 1966.

Chapter

19

Movement Systems

Once information is transmitted from the transducers to the brain, the organism must usually accomplish an appropriate response. It is generally recognized that the available response units are the movement of a muscle or the secretion of a gland. The glandular system appears to be primarily involved with the adjustment of internal states in the body—with a few spectacular exceptions such as in the skunk—and will not be given extensive treatment. The movement of a muscle, on the other hand, is the major constituent of the behavior that is of interest to psychologists.

THE CORTICAL AREA

The **primary motor cortical area** lies on the precentral gyrus of the frontal lobes. Careful stimulation along the gyrus reveals a motor homunculus corresponding to the parts of the body controlled by the cortical cells in that region (Figure 19.1). The cortical area on each hemisphere controls the contralateral side of the body. Comparison of the motor homunculus and the sensory homunculus (see Figure 18.6) just across the intervening central sulcus shows a similar topical organization. As one progresses down the gyrus, the locus of movement controlled by the cortex proceeds from the feet to the head. The proportions of the motor homunculus and the sensory

257

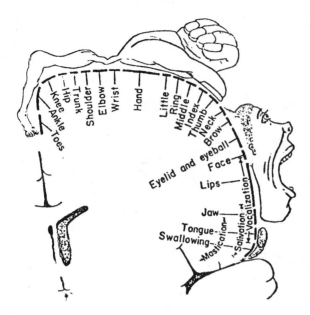

Figure 19.1 Motor cortex homunculus. A coronal section of the human cortex with a sketch of the part of the body which gives a muscular response to stimulation applied to the cortex at that point. (Penfield & Rasmussen, 1950, via Guyton, 1974, p. 326)

homunculus are not identical, with the disparity probably due to phylogenetic changes in the distribution of sensory fields and muscle groups. Many association fibers connect the primary sensory with the primary motor regions of the cortex.

Immediately anterior to the primary motor area is a less specific region of motor control known as the **premotor area.** This area appears to serve a function analogous to that of the sensory association areas. Recorded activity in the premotor area shows that many neurons are active prior to the actual response, and it is suggested that the premotor area selects the response to be accomplished. This choice is then transmitted to the primary motor area, which translates the information into a specific sequence of muscle movements.

MOTOR PATHWAYS

As with the sensory systems, there are two major efferent pathways between the cortex and the muscles. The **pyramidal motor system** consists of large fibers extending from the motor cortex all the way down the spinal cord to the neuron innervating the muscle (Figure 19.2). The pyramidal system is so named because all of the fibers lead through the **pyramids** in the midbrain region. The pyramidal shape is due to the convergence of the fibers in the medulla, where 80 percent of the fibers cross to the contralateral side. The fibers that cross then lead down the spinal cord to synapse with the efferent nerves that lead out of the spinal cord. The 20 percent that do not cross over in the pyramids extend down the ipsilateral side of the spinal cord and then cross to the contralateral side within the terminal spinal segment for that

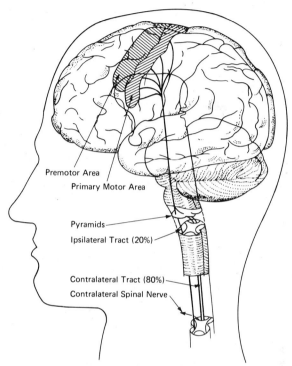

Premotor Area
Primary Motor Area
Pyramids
Ipsilateral Tract (20%)
Contralateral Tract (80%)
Contralateral Spinal Nerve

Figure 19.2 The pyramidal motor system.

fiber. The spinal cord neurons synapse with the efferent neurons leaving the cord. Thus, the pyramidal system control is totally contralateral, although it is accomplished by two different routes.

The **extrapyramidal motor system,** which is bilateral in organization, consists of about one fifth of the motor nerves that are not routed through the pyramids. In general, these neurons are smaller in diameter and, consequently, slower conducting. Extrapryramidal pathways include a number of synaptic connections along the way, with many collateral branches leaving or joining the system (Figure 19.3). The reticular activating system is richly supplied with fibers from the extrapyramidal motor system. The cerebellum also receives information from, and adds information to, the extrapyramidal network. The fibers from the extrapyramidal system proceed down the spinal cord through columns other than either branch of the pyramidal system.

The extrapyramidal system appears to function as a fine-adjustment mechanism for motor control. Destruction of various nuclei in the extrapyramidal system results in exaggerated and jerky movement of the limbs. The tremor of the resting limbs seen in victims of Parkinson's disease is

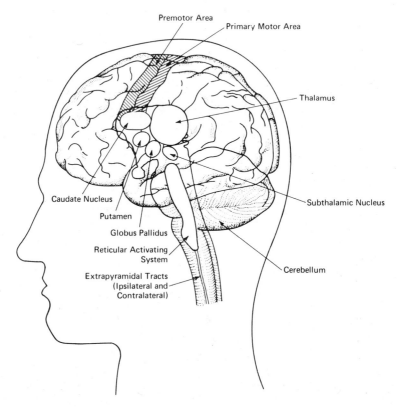

Figure 19.3   The extrapyramidal motor system.

probably due to damage to an inhibitory part of the extrapyramidal system. Parkinson's disease also results in a muscular reflex that actively resists externally induced movement. This symptom is also noted when extrapyramidal nuclei are lesioned. The extrapyramidal system is capable of compensating for loss of the direct pyramidal fibers, although the muscular movement is slow and prolonged rather than rapid and precise.

MUSCLE CONTROL

The motor fibers leading from the spinal cord exit through the ventral root of the spinal nerve and wend their way through the plexus system and the appropriate peripheral nerve to form a synaptic junction on the muscle fiber. Each motor neuron forms a synaptic connection with from 3 to 100 muscle cells. Synaptic activity at the bouton of the motor neuron creates an electrical event in a specialized postsynaptic receiver area of the muscle cell. This **end plate potential** apparently triggers the contraction of the muscle cell. The transmitter chemical for the neuromuscular junction is acetylcholine.

The movement of the muscle is accomplished by interlocked fibers sliding past one another. Each muscle cell is made up of many of these fiber systems. Each fiber has tiny rachetlike extensions that interlock with the neighboring fibers. Activating the rachet mechanism causes the fibers to be pulled past one another. The mechanism is such that active movement can be accomplished only in one direction, so movement in the opposite direction occurs only by releasing the rachet mechanism. Since there is no "reverse rachet" to move the fibers in the opposite direction, muscles can only pull.

Muscles are actually bundles of individual muscle cells attached to the skeleton by means of tendons. The tendons have special "stretch" transducers as a part of their structure. Similarly, the muscles themselves also have a kind of stretch receptor. Both of these transducers contribute to the effective operation of the muscle and the survival of the organism.

Mixed among the larger, more powerful striped muscle cells are special sensory units. These **muscle spindles** consist of a tiny **intrafusal muscle** combined with the sensory **spindle cell.** The spindle cell is a stretch transducer that responds to elongation of the unit with a burst of neuronal activity. The intrafusal muscle is a smooth muscle cell that responds more slowly, steadily, and weakly than the striped muscles. The muscle spindle unit is attached to the fibers of the muscle cell, so contraction or stretching of the muscle results in activation of the stretch receptor.

The peripheral neurons leading to a muscle are of three types. The neurons that synapse directly on the large and powerful striped muscle cells are relatively large, heavily myelinated fibers known as **"A" fibers.** The afferent and efferent fibers leading to the two parts of the muscle spindle are relatively small, lightly myelinated fibers called **"gamma" fibers.** Thus, the size and conduction speed of the associated neurons match the characteristics of the types of muscle cells involved.

The afferent fiber from the spindle cell leads through the dorsal root of the spinal cord to synapse directly on the "A" fiber leading to the motor end plates of the same muscle. This feedback loop explains how the muscles reflexively resist being stretched by an external source (Figure 19.4). Stretching of the muscle causes the muscle spindle to become active. This activity is conducted directly to the "A" fibers, which activate a contraction of the powerful striped muscle cells. Thus, the muscle actively compensates for any stretching motion. The magnitude of the muscle response is directly related to the magnitude of the external force applied to the muscle. If the external force is suddenly released, the muscle begins to contract, resulting in a sharp decrease in spindle activity and a compensating relaxation of the striped muscle cells.

Since the entire circuit is found within the spinal cord and its peripheral connections, this compensatory muscular response is known as a spinal reflex.

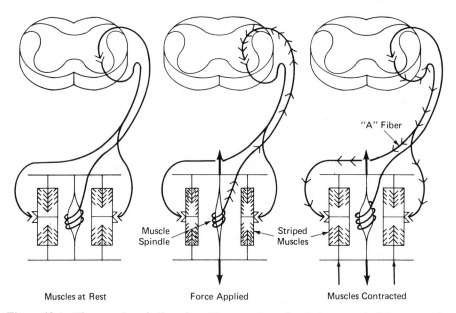

Muscles at Rest   Force Applied   Muscles Contracted

Figure 19.4 The muscle spindle reflex. The muscle resists being stretched because of activity of the muscle spindle.

Spinal animals, or animals in which all fibers have been severed between the spinal cord and the higher brain centers, exhibit this reflexive movement resistance. Apparently, the intact extrapyramidal system includes circuits that inhibit overt expression of the reflex in intact animals because limbs can usually be moved without this resistance.

The intrafusal muscle is a relatively weak muscle cell and contributes nothing to the total strength of the muscle. Instead, the intrafusal muscle pulls only on the spindle receptor cell, which directly controls the entire muscle. This mechanism allows the muscle to maintain a steady position of a limb. If the muscle is to be held in a highly contracted state, a prolonged contraction of the intrafusal muscle will result in a corresponding positioning of the striped muscle cells through the feedback loop. If, on the other hand, the muscle should be held in an extended position, the smooth muscle can establish the necessary level of activity of the spindle cell.

In a totally intact motor system, the movement of a limb is initially accomplished through stimulation of the peripheral "A" fibers by the fast-conducting pyramidal system (Figure 19.5). Following the initial movement is a slower message sent to the intrafusal muscles through the extrapyramidal network. The consequent activity of the spindle cell essentially holds the muscle in the desired position. Without this fine-tuning feedback system, the isolated pyramidal system causes movements that are rough and jerky, or there is a noticeable tremor when an attempt is made to hold the limb in a steady position. Since the extrapyramidal system is closely interconnected with the

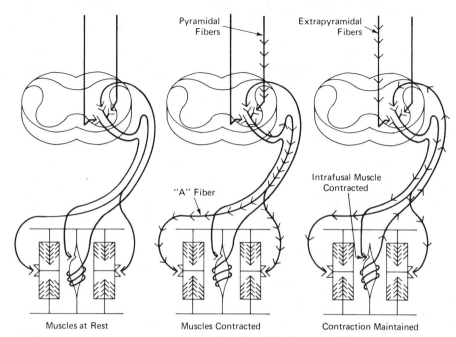

Figure 19.5   Muscle spindle adjustment. The motor system can move the muscle to a new position which is then maintained by the muscle spindle mechanism. The intrafusal muscle in turn adjusts the response level of the muscle spindle, which maintains the new muscle position.

reticular activating system, events that increase activity of the reticular system can alter the muscle spindle adjustments. Thus, we may find that our hands shake when we are nervous or excited; stimulating drugs such as caffeine may cause similar symptoms. The motor control observed in patients after the pyramidal system is destroyed is probably accomplished through the muscle spindle mechanism. By contracting the smooth muscle, the associated striped muscles will respond. Since the extrapyramidal network is diffuse, the neurons are slower conducting, and the smooth muscle is slower to respond, the resulting movement of the limb is correspondingly slowed. The slow, poorly coordinated movements of an animal in a light anesthetic state are of this type.

The patellar, or knee jerk, reflex is a test of the muscle spindle reflexive circuit. Striking the tendon just below the kneecap causes a brief stretch in the muscles that kick the leg forward. This stretch creates a burst of spindle activity, which creates a corresponding "twitch" in the muscle through the spinal feedback circuit.

The muscle spindle system is a purely excitatory system. That is, the muscle is contracted or relaxed depending on the level of activity of the spindle cell. Stretch receptors located in the tendons attaching the muscle to the bone being moved are inhibitory in their action. The **Golgi organs** located in the tendons respond to the tendon being stretched. If all of the muscle cells in a muscle are simultaneously contracted, the total pull exerted is sufficient to damage the muscle, tendon, or sketetal joint. The Golgi apparatus prevents this occurrence by inhibiting the activity of the "A" fibers when the damage level is approached (Figure 19.6).

Each muscle is a self-contained behavioral unit. The muscle spindles adjust the response level of the muscle, while the Golgi apparatus prevents damage from too much activity. If we were to look at individual muscle cells, we would find that each is in a state of continuing flux, although the total muscle is maintaining a constant tension. Fatigue, adaptation, and other localized conditions alter the response capacity of each individual cell, but the total organ consistently gives a uniform and reliable response by automatically making fine adjustments among the component units.

MUSCLE COORDINATION

Because the muscles are incapable of "pushing," the muscles in the body are arranged in reciprocal pairs. That is, movements of the limb are accomplished by opposing pairs of muscles, each "pulling" the limb in an opposite direction. For example, the biceps, in the arm, pulls the forearm toward the body. The triceps, on the back side of the upper arm, pulls on an extension of the

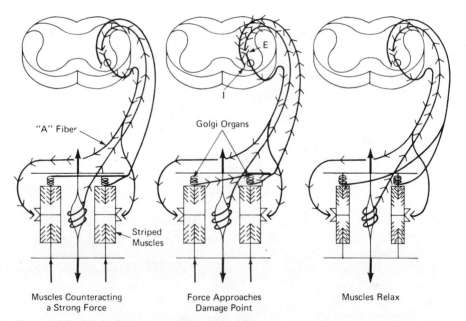

Figure 19.6 Limitations on a spinal reflex. When the force versus counterforce of the muscle spindle reflex approaches the point of damaging the muscle, the reflexive circuit activity is inhibited by the activity of the Golgi organs in the muscle tendons.

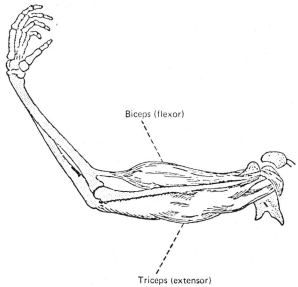

Biceps (flexor)

Triceps (extensor)

Figure 19.7 The flexor-extensor arrangement of the muscles in the arm. (Wenger, Jones, & Jones, 1956, p. 57)

forearm to move the limb away from the body by using the hinged bone joint as a level point. Muscles that close the joint are known as **flexors,** while those that open the joint are called **extensors** (Figure 19.7).

Simultaneous activity of the flexor and extensor muscles is both inefficient and potentially damaging to the joints of the skeleton. If movement of the limb is to be accomplished when one member of the opposing pair of muscles is contracted, the opposing muscle should be relaxed. The **flexor-extensor reflex** is such a mechanism. Excitation in one muscle inhibits the activity of the other. This is accomplished by internuncial neurons that extend excitatory synapses to the "A" fibers of one muscle and inhibitory synapses to the "A" fibers of the opposing muscle. This **reciprocal innervation** is a basic characteristic in the coordination of movement in muscular systems.

Application of a painful stimulus to the limb of a spinal animal results in the immediate withdrawal of the limb from the stimulus. This **withdrawal reflex** involves a reciprocally innervating internuncial neuron (Figure 19.8). Thus, instead of a monosynaptic circuit, this reflex involves two synapses. Simultaneous with the activation of the reflexive circuitry, there is a branching of the information in the normal animal that sends the sensory information to the brain. In this case, however, if the stimulus is strong enough, the command to withdraw the limb from the painful stimulus is on its way to the appropriate muscles before the brain has received the pain information.

Reflexes are basically prewired responses between sensory cells and appropriate motor cells. The functional utility of the muscle spindle, Golgi apparatus, flexor-extensor, and withdrawal reflex are relatively obvious. In

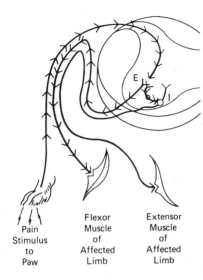

Pain
Stimulus
to
Paw

Flexor
Muscle
of
Affected
Limb

Extensor
Muscle
of
Affected
Limb

Figure 19.8 A diagram of the flexor-extensor circuitry involved in the reflexive withdrawal from a painful stimulus. Activation of the flexor muscle simultaneously inhibits (relaxes) the opposed extensor muscle.

addition, there are known reflexes in human infants that seem less obvious in their utility. The **Babinski reflex** involves a spreading of the toes when a finger tip is drawn across the bottom of the foot. The **Darwinian reflex** is the automatic grasping of the hand to a finger placed across the palm of a baby. The Darwinian reflex is so strong that a human infant may be able to hang by one hand if the grasped finger is raised.

In addition to the coordination of the musculature in a single limb, an organism must coordinate movement between the left and right sides of the body. For example, the reflexive withdrawal of a paw from a thorn would throw a sudden load on the contralateral paw. Since the brain is just receiving the message regarding the painful stimulus, it cannot accomplish a compensatory response for the other leg. The sudden flexion of one paw results in the reflexive extension of the contralateral limb (Figure 19.9). Experiments with dogs have shown that even if the animal were suspended in a sling, only one paw will be raised to avoid a painful stimulus delivered to both. The other paw, in fact, is extended into the stimulus! The determination of which paw is flexed is apparently determined by the side that reports the greatest pain. Obviously, there is some survival value in preventing the organism from toppling to the ground in an effort to minimize damage to a single limb.

Research on spinal cats shows that there is reflexive coordination of entire body units (Figure 19.10). Manually raising the head of a spinal cat results in an automatic extension of the forepaws and flexion of the hind legs, while lowering the head stimulates the opposite limb movements. Thus, the body has internal circuits to enhance the movements and orientation of the head. A normal cat, when lowering its head for a drink of water, drops slightly at the shoulders while raising the hind quarters. A cat looking up lowers the rear; in fact, often the cat looking at a bird in a tree will sit down.

The spinal reflex is a valuable basic survival type of behavior. There are

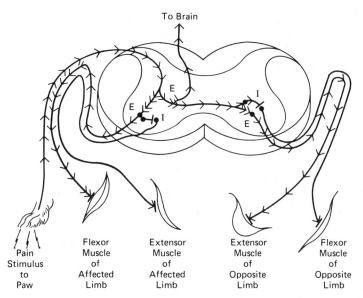

To Brain

| Pain Stimulus to Paw | Flexor Muscle of Affected Limb | Extensor Muscle of Affected Limb | Extensor Muscle of Opposite Limb | Flexor Muscle of Opposite Limb |

Figure 19.9 Reflexive coordination across the body. In four-footed animals, the reflexive withdrawal of one limb causes the simultaneous extension of the contralateral limb.

times, however, when the reflex may not be appropriate. If the muscle spindle system were operative under all conditions, the motor cortex would be resisted in its attempts to initiate any limb movement. Some reflexes must be inhibited by higher coordination centers. The existence of such inhibition is found in a characteristic response of an animal after the spinal cord is severed from the rest of the CNS.

Decerebrate rigidity is a characteristic bodily response following spinal cord transection. The muscular systems go into a prolonged period of rigid contraction, with the limbs typically in an extended position. Apparently, the condition is the result of interrupting the inhibitory signals from higher centers. Eventually, the rigidity disappears and investigation of the spinal reflexes can be initiated. Animals high on the phylogenetic scale have a prolonged period of decerebrate rigidity, while lower animals may not show it at all. Similarly, there is a phylogenetic difference in the functional movements accomplished by the spinal cord. Animals low on the scale may accomplish fairly complex sequences of activity with only an intact spinal cord. Higher animals, however, are typically restricted to spinal reflexive fragments of behavior.

At least in the rat, segments of sexual behavior seem to be reflexive. Penile erection in the male and lordosis (assuming a copulatory position) in the female can be observed with the application of the appropriate stimulation. Copulatory movements and ejaculation may also be observed in the spinal male if positioned appropriately on the female. Apparently, accomplishing the right position involves higher centers.

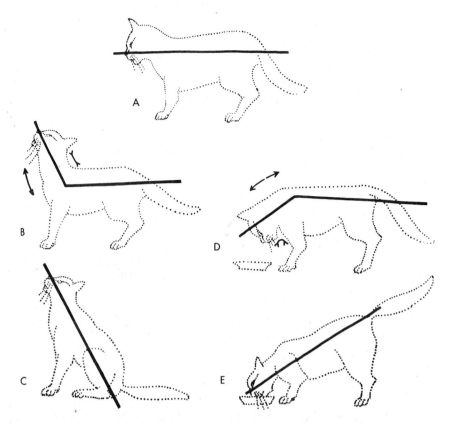

Figure 19.10 Tonic neck reflexes in the spinal cat. Upward (B) or downward (D) movement of the head results in reflexive adjustments of the entire body (C & E). (Elliot, 1963, via Altman, 1966, p. 273)

In addition to the control of the bodily movement muscles, the internal smooth muscles also are coordinated by the spinal cord. The appropriate movement responses of the digestive organs are dependent on feedback concerning fullness of the organs involved. Spinal animals are capable of appropriately accomplishing these vegetative activities. Fecal matter is expelled when the large intestines are filled. Micturation occurs when the bladder is full. The peristaltic movements of the stomach and intestines occurs if food is introduced into the stomach. Swallowing can be accomplished, but efficient eating behavior requires higher coordination centers.

THE BRAIN STEM

Transecting the nervous system so that portions of the brain stem are still functionally attached to the spinal cord produces a set of more complicated behavioral capacities. If we allow the animal to retain the medulla as well as the spinal cord, we find that a number of well-coordinated activities may be accomplished. The control of breathing is a particularly illuminating example. The spinal animal is capable of maintaining a breathing pattern, although it appears to be a very primitive lack of oxygen response. The breathing pattern is irregular and appears to occur only when a carbon dioxide receptor responds to high CO_2 levels in the blood. The medullary animal accomplishes a more regular breathing pattern. Interestingly, transection through the middle of the medulla causes the animal to stop breathing! Apparently, breathing is controlled by two different nuclei in the medulla. The lower center is an "inhale" center. Activity of this center causes an inhale response. The "exhale" nucleus is located higher in the medulla and operates by inhibiting the activity of the lower "inhale" center. Thus, breathing is accomplished by the sequential contraction and relaxation of the muscles controlled by the "inhale" center in the medulla. The relaxation is the result of periodic inhibition by the "exhale" center. Transection between the two centers causes the animal to inhale until the center fails for lack of oxygen.

The medullary "inhale" center is essentially a reflexive response to high CO_2 levels. There is reason to implicate the failure of this center in some infant "crib deaths." Some infants experience short periods of not breathing during sleep. Such stoppages do not occur when the infant is awake, nor during sleep periods of high CNS activity, such as dreaming. Apparently, the "higher breathing centers" successfully control the breathing pattern. It is possible, however, that total control is given the medullary reflexive center when the rest of the CNS is "shut down." If the reflex fails, the lack of oxygen (and saturation of CO_2) would rapidly disable the higher centers before they could become alert and respond.

The medulla includes a number of centers that control and coordinate other vegetative functions of the body. Thus, we find that medullary animals are more adaptive in their digestive processes than spinal animals. Heart functioning and blood flow to various parts of the body are also manipulated in a well-coordinated manner in animals with an intact medulla. Other basic "behaviors" can be observed in the medullary dog or cat. Chewing and swallowing will occur when food is introduced into the mouth, and gagging and/or vomiting are also observed.

Medullary animals also demonstrate more complicated "reflexive" activity. The medulla receives input from the vestibular organs of the middle ear. The medullary animal shows a tendency to maintain the head in the "normal" upright position. The movement of the head results in activity of the rest of the body to establish the "normal" orientation with the head. Thus, the "righting" reflex involves a predictable sequence of motor activities, beginning with the upright orientation of the head and followed by righting activities of the rest of the body.

Motor coordination at the brain stem level has become highly specialized in the structure of the cerebellum. In discussions of the relative development of the cerebral hemispheres, the significant growth of the cerebeller hemispheres is frequently overlooked. The highly complicated, obviously specialized cerebellar structures are very important to motor coordination. Cerebellar damage results in poor control of individual muscles and a debilitating loss of total bodily movement coordination. The cerebellum receives sensory information from all of the senses and utilizes this information to program movements that are adjusted to environmental conditions. The cerebellum interacts with both the pyramidal and extrapyramidal motor systems to modify and coordinate the motor messages originating in the motor cortex.

The reticular activating system is sometimes divided into two functional units. The dorsal portions of the RAS are known as the ascending reticular system and typically alter the level of activity of the cortex and other higher centers. The ventral descending reticular fibers extend into the motor pathways entering the spinal cord. Stimulation of the descending reticular system results in an enhanced reflexive response to a given stimulus. Thus, the reticular system contributes some fine adjustments to the magnitude of the reflexive response.

The reflexive behaviors observed in the spinal and medullary animal are typically immediate and correspond to the magnitude of the initiating stimulus. This behavior is typically labeled apsychic, since it most closely resembles the mechanical response of an automaton rather than the behavior of a conscious animal. When the thalamus and hypothalamus are added to the functional units of the brain stem, the available behaviors become both complicated and multifaceted. Relatively complete patterns of eating, drinking, sexual behavior, aggressiveness, and so on, can be observed. These behaviors typically include an "emotional component," although brain stem behavior may appear compulsive or automatic. The eating behavior may be directed at nonfood objects; the rage may be out of proportion to the triggering stimulus; the sexual behavior may be expressed without an appropriate partner.

Two research examples support the notion that the higher centers may contribute an inhibitory control over the lower reflexive units. The medullary cat may be able to accomplish walking behavior. When subjected to a tail pinch, the animal might respond with a sequence of unsteady steps. If the thalamus and hypothalamus are intact, walking is improved greatly. By lesioning one of the centers in the hypothalamus, it is possible to produce an obstinate walking behavior. A cat with such a bilateral lesion will commence walking and continue walking in spite of any obstacles encountered. Such an animal may literally butt its head into a wall and continue attempts to walk forward in a well-coordinated sequence of leg movements. Apparently, the hypothalamic nucleus (the caudate nucleus) must inhibit a lower center that activates the "walking program."

The possible inhibitory role of the cortex has been discovered in electroencephalogram recordings of cortical activity during a delayed response task. If the stimulus is given but the response must be delayed for a couple of seconds, the EEG will show a pronounced negative electrical potential during the delay period. The negative potential disappears with the response, or if the subject decides not to respond. It is suggested that the sustained negative potential reflects the activity of an inhibitory "clamp" on the response program. When the delay interval is completed, the inhibited response is allowed to be expressed.

The different levels of the CNS seem to contribute different levels of motor behavior. The spinal cord is capable of simple, immediate, but relatively nonadjustable reflexes. The lower brain stem enhances adaptiveness by adjusting the intensity of the reflex and coordinating several "simple" reflexes into a more complicated response. The upper portions of the brain stem choreograph the simpler units into response programs that involve the whole body, a sequence over some period of time, and an "emotional" component. The cortex is probably responsible for "consciousness," but much of the complicated behavior associated with that term may be a carefully orchestrated sequence of the basic behavioral units. An important aspect of this escalation of control undoubtedly involves inhibitory processes.

AUTHOR'S COMMENTS   There is a marked similarity in the organization of the mammalian sensory and motor systems. Both systems have two significant components—a system of large, rapid-conduction fibers that conduct precise information to or from the cortex (the pyramidal and the lemniscal pathways) and a slower-conducting, less precision-oriented supplementary system involving lower brain structures (the extrapyramidal system and the extralemniscal system).

Both the stimulus and the response systems are composed of many levels, all intercoordinated to provide a unitary function. This hierarchial organization allows the cortex the "luxury" of dealing with major features of the program, with the remainder of the CNS cooperating in providing necessary "minor details."

20

Species Differences

At various times the phylogenetic scale has been mentioned in discussing the structures or functions of the nervous system. The phylogenetic scale is based on the theory of evolution. The different species to be seen in today's world are the result of a long series of evolutionary events. Each species constitutes a pool of characteristics which are coded on the genetic material for that species. The combination of characteristics in this total **gene pool** constitutes the variation to be seen in individuals in the species.

Certain combinations of characteristics make some individuals better suited for survival in a particular environment. Those individuals with a less adaptive combination of traits will be less likely to survive than those with a superior genetic endowment. The individuals that survive long enough to bear offspring pass on their genetic traits to the offspring. The characteristics of sexual reproduction are such that the characteristics of each parent are combined, rearranged, and transmitted to the succeeding generation. Thus, each generation constitutes a sort of genetic "experiment" with new combinations of traits. The criterion for success in this experiment is the ability of the individual to survive and reproduce, thereby contributing its traits to the next experiment. Each new generation receives a compliment of traits of proven survival value—or at least does not receive the obvious failures!

EVOLUTION

An animal species over millions of years continually adapts to its environment. This adaptation is accomplished by the process of "survival of the fittest," where individual failures are eliminated, thereby eliminating those failing traits from the gene pool. Thus, the choice of "appropriate traits" is determined by a natural selection process. The traits that work are continued; the traits that do not work are eliminated.

If a species is widespread, individuals of the species may be attempting to survive in two different, isolated environments. The criteria for "survival" will differ in the two environments, so the collection of successful traits will diverge. Eventually, the differences will be so great that the individuals can no longer be considered the same. Not only are they no longer competitive in the "other" environment, but neither are intermediary offspring. The result is two different species, each suited for a particular environment.

Each species continues to contribute generations to the continuous selection process. Mutations introduce sudden radical new traits which are field tested for survival. Changes in climate, migration, overpopulation, competing species, and predators, all may introduce new criteria for the test of survival. Some species may develop, flourish, and disappear, while others may remain essentially unchanged over millions of years.

The genetic code is usually considered a way to pass on characteristics from parents to offspring. From the point of view of the total gene pool, each individual of the species is simply the temporary custodian of a certain combination of the traits in the total species pool. If certain traits place the individual at a disadvantage, that portion of the gene pool is eventually lost. Each individual organism is a unique test mechanism for the continual selection of traits in the gene pool.

Most descriptions of the theory of evolution show the process to be one of producing increasingly sophisticated and complicated organisms (Figure 20.1). Humans are generally accepted (by humans at least) to represent the evolutionary pinnacle of this survival of the fittest contest. The assumed direction is from single cells to clusters of cells to differentiated cells. The term "simple" is usually used synonymously with "primitive" or "lower"; the words "high" or "low" for position on the phylogenetic scale reflect this orientation. Even the term "subhuman" reflects the evolutionary assumption. The fact is, simple mechanisms can also be effective in the survival of the species. There is even evidence of "retrogressive" evolutionary steps. Thus, the "lower" animals that have survived to today may represent just as much of an improvement over their ancestral stock as the more complicated "higher" animals evolving from the same original pool of traits.

There is no such thing as a phylogenetic scale in the way the term is usually used. Every contemporary species represents the current status of an evolutionary process that is ever-changing. In general, the longer the time period since any two species shared the same pool of characteristics, the less

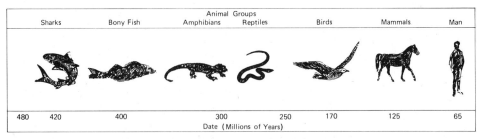

| | | Animal Groups | | | | |
| Sharks | Bony Fish | Amphibians | Reptiles | Birds | Mammals | Man |

| 480 | 420 | 400 | 300 | 250 | 170 | 125 | 65 |

Date (Millions of Years)

Figure 20.1 An evolutionary sequence showing the estimated time of appearance of different classes of animal.

similar they will be. By cataloging the traits of the various species, it is possible to estimate the historical events leading to the present distribution of species.

Increasing knowledge about the characteristics and mechanisms of the genetic code have helped us understand the evolutionary process. It is possible to estimate the number of separating generations by the number and types of traits that differ between two species. Consequently, we can use existing animal species as living history books of their branch of the evolutionary process.

PHYLOGENETIC DISTANCE

The genetic code is found on the DNA molecules found in the nucleus of the cell. Since the DNA molecule is essentially a code for the production of proteins by the cell, evolution consists of changes in the protein-production capacity of the cells. To the physiological psychologist, changes in protein production mean changes in structures and/or changes in behavior. In fact, these three dimensions—structure, chemistry, and behavior—are the basic criteria for determining phylogenetic position.

The earliest phylogenetic categories were established on the basis of morphological characteristics. On a simple level, birds, fish, and mammals can be sorted according to the presence of feathers, fins, or fur. With more closely related species finer structural differences must be employed. Eventually, structures become so similar that they are no longer a reliable discriminator.

Because the DNA code involves chemical production, the degree of chemical similarity between species provides a finer measure of genetic distance. Thus, blood types, amino acid assays, and protein analyses provide measurements of close genetic proximity.

Another indicator of genetic proximity is obtained by comparing the behavioral characteristics of two species. There is no question of the preprogrammed behavior resulting from the reflexive circuitry in the spinal cord. There is considerable evidence that more complex behaviors are also preprogrammed into different species. These species-specific behaviors are another indicator of genetic proximity.

Recognizing that the phylogenetic scale represents only a crude approximation of the genetic route between a single-celled organism and the human CNS, we have useful clues from comparative physiology and psychology concerning the functions of various structures in the nervous system. Comparisons of major classes of animals, the significant nervous system structures possessed, and the behavioral capacities provide an indication of the functional significance of the structures.

INDEPENDENT CELLS

The earliest living organisms were single cells, each accomplishing all of the actions for survival. Such a single-celled organism is the amoeba, moving here and there, enveloping food particles, reproducing daughter cells, avoiding or retreating from noxious stimuli (Figure 20.2). If total time of existence were the criterion, the amoeba is a most adaptive organism.

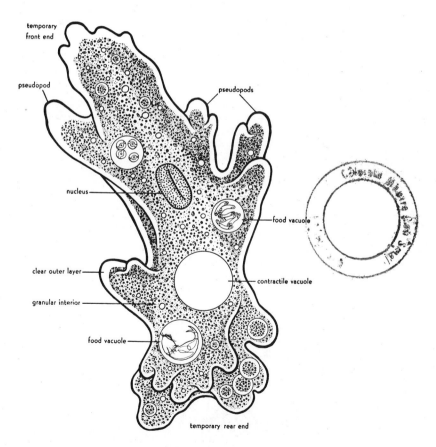

Figure 20.2   An amoeba. An example of a single-celled organism. (Buchsbaum, 1948)

For some single-celled organisms, survival is enhanced by clustering together in "colonies" of similar cells. Some single-celled organisms can survive higher concentrations of poisons in their water environment when in a colony than as individuals. Each of the cells continues to function independently, but there is an inadvertent "cooperative" advantage. Whatever the advantage is, the colonization trait is in the genetic code and will be "selected" as long as it is an advantage.

The "colonial" advantage may be elaborated into a tightly packed cluster of cells. When the cluster becomes large enough, different cells will be obliged to interact differently with the environment, depending on whether they lie on the outside surface or comprise part of the internal mass. This functional difference evolving through the process of natural selection results in specialized cells which can serve one function well. The genetic information for both specialties is coded genetically, but the portion of the code used by each individual cell depends on its location in the now-multicelled organism.

The specialization of cells in a multicelled organism is a mixed blessing for the individual cell. The cell becomes more efficient in its special function but at the sacrifice of its other abilities. Each necessary function is provided by specialized cells in the organism. The total organism can effectively encounter a wider variety of environmental situations than can a single nonspecialized cell, but the specialized cells are now reliant on the smooth and efficient operation of every specialized component. Thus, specialization enhances the survival chances of a cell as long as it is a member of the intact organism, but the cell is less likely to survive on its own.

NERVE NETS

Highly specialized organisms must transmit information from one group of cells to another for coordinated behavior. The jellyfish exemplifies the functioning of such a nerve net (Figure 20.3). A **nerve net** is a loosely interconnected network of nerve cells extending throughout an organism. The component nerves conduct in all directions, and the transmission appears to

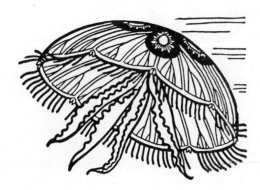

Figure 20.3 A jellyfish. An example of a nerve net system. (Buchsbaum, 1948)

be a generalized activity throughout the network rather than any sort of specific pathway. Feeding into the nerve net are rudimentary transducer cells activated by external stimuli. Thus, the jellyfish exhibits a generalized data-transmission capacity along with a rudimentary set of receptor cells.

Jellyfish exhibit coordinated, though undirected, motor behavior. The rhythmic, pulsing, swimming movements of jellyfish are the result of waves of activity flowing through the nerve net. The muscle responses throughout the entire organism are coordinated through this "nervous system." The effect of sensory input appears to be similarly general. The frequency or strength of the response may increase or be inhibited by stimulation, but there seems to be little directionality of response to stimulation. The lack of response directionality is largely due to the fact that the sensory spots are evenly distributed over the surface of the organism. The nerve net system seems to encode the presence or absence of a stimulus without attempting the finer task of locating the stimulus source.

There is considerable adaptability available in even this primitive "stimulus-response" system. For example, while an organism may respond to a mildly noxious stimulus only by increased activity, the resulting behavior contains the rudiments of an adaptive escape response. Even if the movement is random, the organism will be active in the presence of the noxious stimulus. If the moving animal encounters a "better" (less noxious) environment, the movement activity slows down. This simple "speed up-slow down" mechanism results in an animal that spends most of its time in an appropriate environment by actively escaping the noxious situations. Such an organism can also be described as "seeking" the optimal environment.

A TRUE NERVOUS SYSTEM

Planaria represent the next level of nervous system sophistication. Planaria are small "flatworms" which resemble snails without shells. They are bilaterally symmetrical with the spinal cord located on the axis of symmetry (Figure 20.4). The planarian has a concentration of a few ganglion cells at its "head" end. The "spinal cord" consists of two parallel bundles of nerve cords extending the length of the body. Branches from these bundles collect and distribute information along the body. The ganglion and the nerve cords, along with the ladderlike network of nerve fibers between the two cords, provide a rudimentary nervous system. The fibers in the "spinal cords" are the first appearance of axons for data transmission. The planarian has two light-sensitive spots on each side of the head.

Planaria present a number of significant improvements in behavioral capacity. The directional eye spots allow the planarian to locate a source of light. With receptor cells concentrated on the front, the animal can explore or detect objects that are likely to be encountered when moving forward. The "brain," consisting of a few ganglion cells, processes the sensory informa-

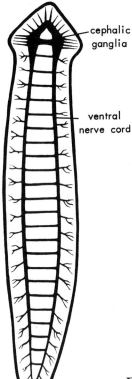

cephalic
ganglia

ventral
nerve cord

Figure 20.4   A planarian. A primitive CNS with cephalic ganglia and nerve cord. (Buchsbaum, 1948)

tion and transmits the product along the double nerve cords. The existence of axons means that the neural-transmission process is greatly improved over the primitive nerve net arrangement. There is evidence to suggest that the planarian is capable of learning a conditioned response. Research into the "memory molecule" has utilized planaria among other animal species.

THE BRAIN

Fish represent an elaborate modification from the simple nerve cord organization of the planaria. Fish have a skeletal cell system to support the larger number of cells in the total organism coupled with muscle cells highly specialized for rapid and powerful movement. Whereas the muscles of the less elaborate animals are like the smooth visceral muscles in humans, the propulsion muscles in fish are highly specialized for strong, efficient movement, more like the human voluntary muscles. To coordinate this complicated organism, the fish has a structure that can legitimately be called a brain (Figure 20.5). Although it is possible to identify cells that correspond to the human cortex,

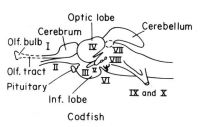

Figure 20.5 The CNS of a codfish. Major structures are labeled. Roman numerals identify cranial nerves. (Isaacson, Douglas, Lubar, & Schmaltz, 1971, p. 94)

there is really no cortex in the fish brain. Basically, the fish has structures corresponding to the human brain stem and spinal cord. In addition, the fish has well-defined special transducer cells combined with other elaborate auxiliary structures. The improved sensory information is refined in the brain, and then well-coordinated efferent messages are sent to the muscles.

Fish are capable of learning, and many behavioral laboratories include goldfish as laboratory animals. Both classical and operant conditioning are within the capacity of a fish; however, fish are limited in learning more complicated tasks. Goldfish can be taught to discriminate a circle from a triangle but have great difficulty learning to reverse this discrimination. Fish must essentially learn a new response as though the first response had never occurred. Mammals, on the other hand, learn a reversal task relatively easily by switching the "rules." Fish are also supplied with a number of elaborate genetically determined behavior sequences. The automatic "threat and attack" behavior in Siamese fighting fish is an example. The mere presence of another male results in immediate combat. Even a mirror which allows the fish to see its own reflection will trigger the fighting behavior. This stereotypical pattern of behavior is probably not learned, but is an automatic response to specific stimuli, perhaps like an elaborate spinal reflex. Most of the known species-specific behaviors are concerned with courtship and/or mating behaviors which could be efficiently selected by means of a genetic mechanism.

Amphibians (frogs, toads, salamanders) represent the phylogenetic expansion of animal life from water to dry land. The break is not total, for amphibians still require a water environment during part or all of their life cycles, including reproduction and embryological development. Amphibians represent a substantial elaboration over fish. The control of limbs for walking on dry land is considerably more complex than that required for the swimming motions of fish. Correspondingly, the cerebellum of amphibians is structurally more elaborate (Figure 20.6).

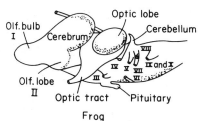

Figure 20.6 The CNS of a frog. (Isaacson, Douglas, Lubar, & Schmaltz, 1971, p. 94)

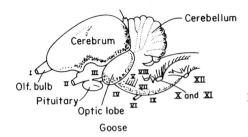

Figure **20.7** The CNS of a goose. (Isaacson, Douglas, Lubar, & Schmaltz, 1971, p. 94)

The sensory organs in amphibians are modified considerably over the water-oriented transducers of fish. The olfactory mechanism is very elaborate, with additional brain structure devoted to processing this information. These new structures can be identified as the beginnings of the limbic system. Similarly, the eyes and the ears are substantially modified for perceiving stimuli through the air. The tectal areas of the thalamus are expanded to process the improved sensory information.

Birds and reptiles represent two branches toward a permanent existence free from the water. The elaborate differences in each of these groups of animals is partially a result of the tremendous range of environments suddenly opened for habitation when the "tie to the sea" was successfully severed. From dinosaurs to snakes and lizards, from eagles and ostriches to hummingbirds and penguins, the variety is impressive. In terms of neural structures, the variety is similarly panoramic. Some snakes have developed special infrared sensors especially tuned to mammalian body temperature. There is some evidence that the photoreceptors in the visual system of the owl are shifting toward infrared sensitivity to accomplish a similar function. The motor coordination of a snake is a symphony of muscular activity, while the slow motion of a soaring eagle exhibits elaborate fine adjustments and movements of individual feathers which contribute to the "effortless flight."

In birds and reptiles, we find an elaboration of limbic system structures with only a hint of the neocortical structures found in mammals (Figures 20.7 and 20.8). The behavioral repertoire of these animals is sufficiently varied and interesting that many species are found in pet stores. Birds exhibit a wide variety of behaviors, although much may fall into the species-specific category. There is little research on the learning capacity in reptiles, but birds show significant capacity for learning. Pigeons are popular laboratory animals for the study of operant learning.

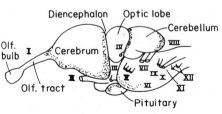

Figure **20.8** The CNS of an alligator. (Isaacson, Douglas, Lubar, & Schmaltz, 1971, p. 94)

THE NEOCORTEX

The marsupials represent a bridge between birds and reptiles and later-evolved mammals. Marsupials demonstrate a pronounced growth of neo-cortical structures. An interesting feature of the marsupial brain is that there is no corpus callosum providing communication between the right and left hemispheres (Figure 20.9). The right-left coordination is accomplished by the anterior and posterior commisural fibers associated with the underlying limbic system. Marsupial behavior is interesting to behavioral scientists in terms of some unique behavioral patterns, but data are scarce in terms of variety or upper limit. One could predict from the neurological structures that marsupials fall short of the more elaborately endowed mammals. The mammalian CNS is most distinct in terms of neocortical development (Figure 20.10). In the "higher" mammals, the mass of cortical material is so great that it must be convoluted to fit into the skull. Mammals also have a distinct corpus callosum to provide intercommunication among the elaborate cortical structures. Mammals can learn more complicated tasks than "lower" animals. "Learning to learn" is an example. Mammals required to learn a series of similar tasks can profit from learning the previous task, so each successive task is solved more rapidly. Thus, the mammals are capable of learning a process rather than being bound to the specific cues of the learning situation.

Primates represent a relatively complicated example of the mammalian nervous system (Figure 20.11). Of particular interest is the substantial expansion of the prefrontal cortex along with the pronounced expansion of the

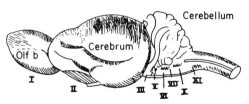

Figure 20.9 The CNS of an opossum. (Isaacson, Douglas, Lubar, & Schmaltz, 1971, p. 95)

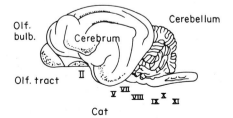

Figure 20.10 The CNS of a cat. (Isaacson, Douglas, Lubar, & Schmaltz, 1971, p. 95)

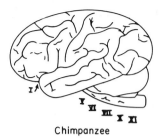

Chimpanzee

Figure 20.11 The CNS of a chimpanzee. (Isaacson, Douglas, Lubar, & Schmaltz, 1971, p. 95)

tips of the temporal lobes. Another feature of the primate nervous system is the further specialization in the visual system. The eyes are located in the front of the skull so that binocular vision is represented in almost the entire visual field. Possibly related to this sensory development, but definitely a facet of primate behavior, is very fine hand-eye coordination.

Observations of primates in the wild show that they are capable of tool-making. Research involving primates has chimpanzees learning to play tic-tac-toe and other "intellectual" games. Of special interest at the present time is the attempt to teach chimpanzees to use a language. By using a variety of mediums to make up for the chimp's lack of speech apparatus, experimenters have demonstrated that there is little doubt that chimpanzees are capable of learning and effectively using a form of speech.

The human nervous system represents the epitome of complexity—to the present—in the evolutionary process (Figure 20.12). The total area of the cortex is greater (for body size) than in any other animal. Although often overshadowed by the elaborate cortical development, the human brain stem (particularly the cerebellum) and limbic system are larger and more complicated than in the "lower" species.

Bilateral symmetry, which evolved relatively early in the evolutionary sequence, has been generally described as a mirror image organization. Although each side is occasionally specialized to handle ipsilateral or contralateral functions, the corresponding structures on each side do essentially the same thing. In the higher centers of the infrahuman cortex and brain stem, the structures are typically not only corresponding but redundant. Lesions to

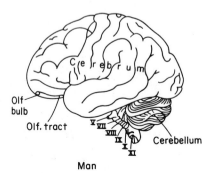

Man

Figure 20.12 The CNS of a human. (Isaacson, Douglas, Lubar, & Schmaltz, 1971, p. 95)

one structure usually result in no behavioral change, since the intact contra-lateral structure appears to handle the functions without a "partner."

Broca's functional "mapping" of the human cortex indicated one important exception to this bilateral redundancy. The "speech center" is usually located on the left hemisphere. Recent evidence suggests that the two hemispheres are specialized for other "thinking" functions. As a general rule, the left hemisphere seems to specialize in the "logical" and "rational" thinking tasks, while the right hemisphere is devoted to the "intuitive" and "emotional" types of thinking.

Phylogenetic comparisons between CNS structures and behavior can lead to a cumulative "building block" conception of the increasing complexity of the systems. It is true that the corresponding neurological structures have a common functional orientation at different phylogenetic levels. For example, the optic tectum in birds is analogous to the superior colliculi in the human visual system. The human colliculi, however, do not accomplish the same wide range of visual data processing observed in the bird tectum, which has no visual cortex. The human cortex has assumed many of the visual-analysis functions, while the colliculi are specialized for fine oculomotor tasks. Thus, the colliculi are responsible for eye movement to maximize the visual information for the sophisticated analysis by the cortex.

Although it is seductive to think of each additional CNS structure as a simple "add-on" unit to the already existing system, the dynamic interplay between the units in the total system cannot be ignored. Phylogentic comparisons of species existing today is not a repeat of the evolutionary process. Species differences are created not only by the selection process, which initially separated two species, but by the selection process, which has continued within each species to the present.

AUTHOR'S COMMENTS The phylogenetic scale represents an approximation of the evolutionary sequence of development leading to the human animal. One trend in this development is the increased complexity of the total organism. A second trend is the increased specialization of the individual cells which jointly comprise the organism. The result of this increased specialization of the individual components is an organism that is more adaptive to a wider range of environmental challenges.

Study of present-day animals that represent various significant phylogenetic stages provide a clue to the functional capacity of several CNS structures. Such comparisons must be tempered, however, with the recognition that the additional structures found in higher animals interact and alter the functions of the existing structures. Thus, mammals have a greater functional capacity because of their neocortex, but the neocortex is enhanced by redistributing the "work load" among brain stem structures. Thus, the lower structures do not serve the identical function in nervous systems at different stages in the phylogenetic sequence.

Chapter

21

Behavioral Genetics

The concept of inherited behaviors has a checkered history in American psychology. Darwin, in his statement of the theory of evolution, almost certainly included, as traits, behaviors that are subject to selective pressure. His book, *The Expression of Emotions in Man and Animals,* which has been lightly regarded when compared with his other publications, is emerging as an important scientific contribution in its own right.

Two events in the 1920s conspired to cause psychologists to avoid looking for genetic components in behavior. First was the problem caused by "instincts" early in the history of psychology. The concept of instincts was so overused that it had become nothing more than a labeling device without contributing any understanding to the behavior so labeled. Any behavior that appeared to be common to most people was suggested as a "human instinct." Thus, there were serious proposals of human instincts for "stealing ripe apples from trees" or "driving on the right side of the road." John Watson's revolutionary statement of an adamant Behaviorism placed the study of behavior on a solid scientific basis. The thrust of the Behaviorist declaration was to reject such "introspective" data as reports by individuals concerning their own internal processes and to accept only publically observable behavior as the raw material for a science of psychology. By rejecting the "unseen and unseeable," Watson moved American psychology from a philosophical endeavor to a scientific discipline. Behaviorism soon permeated

American psychology. Although instinctive behavior would qualify as a legitimate source of data to a Behaviorist, Watson also happened to be a staunch environmentalist. Watson attacked the concept of innate fear with his classic study involving Albert and the rabbit. Albert was a young child who was not afraid of rabbits but showed a pronounced fear response to a loud sound. Watson showed Albert the rabbit and simultaneously frightened him with a loud sound. Albert soon exhibited a strong fear response to the rabbit. His fear generalized to other white furry animals, and rumors are that Albert found Santa Claus to be an aversive stimulus the following Christmas. Thus, fear can be acquired through conditioning, and similar experiments indicate that existing fears can be extinguished with appropriate conditioning procedures. Watson suggested that "instinctive fear" was an inappropriate explanatory device.

In a more extreme attack on hereditary behavior, Watson said: "Give me a dozen healthy infants, well-formed, and my own specialized worlds to bring them up in and I'll guarantee to take any one at random and train him to become any type of specialist I might select—doctor, lawyer, artist, merchant, chief, and, yes, even begger-man and thief, regardless of his talents, penchants, tendencies, abilities, vocations, and the race of his ancestors" (1924, p. 104). Thus, heredity was acceptable for explaining eye color, height, and other structural characteristics—including some inherited intellectual defects—but behavior was entirely learned from the environment.

The infamous Lysenko affair in Russia was a second factor that made investigators hesitate to invoke hereditary factors to explain behavior. Lysenko, while minister of science in the USSR, insisted that Russian scientists embrace the Lamarckian version of evolution. According to this view, offspring inherit the changes that occur during the lifetime of the parent. For example, a giraffe stretches its neck reaching for leaves high in trees. This longer neck is then inherited by the animal's offspring. Darwinian evolution, on the other hand, argues that the parents that have genetically inherited longer necks are more likely to survive in a tall tree environment; therefore, the "long neck" gene is more likely to be retained in the gene pool.

The data support the Darwinian version, but Lysenko's insistence on a "science" based on Lamarck's theory lent credence to certain Communist policies. Such a deliberate attempt to legislate a science because of political ideology and in spite of accumulated data represents a classic example of the prostitution of a science. Behavior is definitely affected by the environment, therefore it is acquired. Consequently, the term "inherited behaviors" has Lysenko-type overtones.

For these reasons, American psychology has been committed to the nurture side of the nature-nurture question. The genetic contribution to behavior is to provide the physiological structures that will enhance the organism in its necessary interaction with the environment. Inherited structural defects such as color blindness or even brain anomalies will restrict the extent to which the organism can succeed in the environment. Thus, genetics provides the computer components necessary for behavior to occur, but the programming of the computer is accomplished through learning. Even though American psychology has had a pronounced environmental emphasis, a number of articles have appeared since Watson's time suggesting that genetic factors must be considered in order to understand behavior.

It is relatively easy to see how behavioral traits and capacities may contribute to the survival chances of individuals in a species, and thus become a factor in the gene pool of the species. Thus, behaviors peculiar to a species could represent the selection for high-survival behavior for that species. Many such behaviors are involved with intraspecies interactions. Courtship, mating, parental behavior, threat displays, and/or fighting often are examples of such genetically stereotyped behavior.

The genetic component of mating behavior illustrates a particularly telling example of the role of behavior in gene pool selection. Some subspecies are biologically capable of interbreeding if the males from one subspecies mated with the females from the other. The problem is that the courtship behaviors of the two subspecies have diverged to the extent that the males of one subspecies are no longer attractive to the females of the other, and vice versa. In other words, the two subspecies are kept separate not on geographic or morphological grounds, but because of a genetically determined behavioral mechanism. Any mechanism that prevents the exchange of genetic information contributes an ever-widening difference in the gene pools involved. Eventually, the genetic information becomes so disparate that it is no longer compatible even if interbreeding were to occur. The result is the evolution of an additional species. Biologists frequently use behavioral criteria to determine fine distinctions in the phylogenetic scale.

The science of ethology, which branched from biology in Europe, has been a major force in insisting that behavior might be genetically determined. The ethologists observed complex sequences of behavior which seem to occur without any environmental opportunities for learning. These behavior patterns are so replicable between members of the same species that the term **species-specific behavior** is used to describe them.

The strong environmental bias of American psychology has led to the discovery of a number of principles that contribute to our understanding of behavior. Now, growing awareness of genetic contributions is opening new areas of research.

GENETIC PRINCIPLES

In order to understand how behavior can be "inherited," certain basic principles of genetics need to be understood. Gregor Mendel's classic studies of inheritance in garden peas provides the basic information. Mendel systematically observed and recorded a number of identifiable traits in the peas. He then carefully cross-pollinated plants with different characteristics and re-

TABLE 21.1   Mendel's Monohybrid Crosses with Peas. (Winchester, 1966, p. 43)

Characteristic	Second Generation Results		Ratio
Form of seed	5474 round	1850 wrinkled	2.96:1
Color of albumen	6022 yellow	2001 green	3.01:1
Color of seed-coats	705 gray-brown	224 white	3.15:1
Form of pods	882 inflated	299 constricted	2.95:1
Color of pods	428 green	152 yellow	2.82:1
Position of flowers	651 axial	207 terminal	3.14:1
Length of stem	787 long	277 short	2.84:1
All combined	14,889 dominant	5010 recessive	2.98:1

corded the characteristics of the offspring. Mendel continued his studies over several plant generations, always noting the characteristics expressed along with the expression of the ancestors. He found that the characteristics seemed to occur in a ratio of approximately 3 to 1 (Table 21.1). The dominant, or more frequent, characteristic usually resulted in offspring with a mixed set of characteristics, whereas the recessive characteristic invariably bred "true." On the basis of his careful experimentation, Mendel concluded that each trait was determined by a pair of "genes." One gene of each pair came from each parent. If both genes specified the "recessive trait," then the recessive trait was observed in the offspring. If, on the other hand, either or both of the genes carried the information for the dominant trait, then the offspring inherited the dominant trait. Parents with the dominant trait would breed "true" if both parental genes were the same, but would yield mixed offspring if one parent had a recessive gene.

We find, then, that the genetic characteristics of an individual can be deciphered by two factors: the characteristics expressed in the individual and the characteristics expressed in the offspring and/or ancestors of the individual. Because genes are found in pairs, a recessive trait may be concealed by a dominant gene. Thus, we find that the same characteristic can result from different genetic combinations. The characteristics observed in the individual summarize that individual's **phenotype,** while a description of the genetic pairs that led to that phenotype is known as the individual's **genotype** (Figure 21.1).

A genotype of recessive characteristics will yield a phenotype of that characteristic. Interbreeding of recessive phenotypes results in a unform set of offspring all showing the recessive trait. **Albinism** is caused by a recessive gene which cannot produce normal pigmentation in the individual. Thus, the albino's skin and hair are white, while the eyes are pink. The pink eyes are due to the color provided by the blood distributed through the colorless tissue of the iris of the eye. Many animal colonies select for the recessive albinism trait because genetic variation or contamination is often spotted immediately in the form of pigmented individuals. Laboratory experiments also breed for this trait because of the cleaner appearance of the white animals, especially in a laboratory setting.

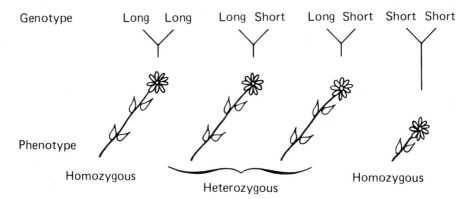

Figure 21.1 Diagram of Mendelian terms. Two genotypic traits contribute to each phenotype. If the traits are the same, the phenotype is homozygous; if different, heterozygous.

A dominant phenotypic trait is not so reliable in determining the traits of the offspring. A dominant trait may occur if both of the relevant genes are coded for that trait, but may also occur if either one of the genes is coded for the recessive trait. Thus, a **homozygous** individual, with both genes the same, would breed true, while a phenotypically identical **heterozygous** individual, with one gene dominant and one recessive, would produce a mixture of offspring.

Since each parent contributes one gene in the pair, the characteristics of an individual—both phenotypic and genotypic—are the result of a combination of the genotypes of the parents. Conversely, to determine the genotype of an individual, one needs to analyze the phenotypic traits of many offspring and/or ancestors. In plants and animals, such genetic data may be generated by controlled breeding experiments. While such experimental control is not possible in human research, a number of human traits have been observed that follow the Mendelian dominant-recessive inheritance patterns. Eye color is the most frequently cited example, with brown eyes dominant and blue recessive.

Mendel's work was ignored for a number of years before the importance of his conclusions was recognized and acknowledged. Many researchers believed that the simple dominant-recessive model was inadequate to explain most traits. Instead of falling into Mendel's convenient either-or category, it seemed that most inherited characteristics were distributed along a continuum. Even human eye color is not cleanly divided into brown and blue, for there are additional shades such as hazel, green, or gray.

Such continuous traits are determined by the cumulative effect of more than a single pair of genes. Height appears to be one of these phenotypic traits. If the individual receives mostly "tall" genes, his height will be toward the tall end of the scale. If the genetic code specifies mostly "short," then the individual will be relatively short. Most individuals receive a relatively even mixture of "tall" and "short" genes and, therefore, are of average height.

The height trait illustrates two important problems with any simple genetic explanation of behavior. First, height cannot be measured with the precise analysis used by Mendel because multiple genes contribute to the trait. Second, height is not a purely genetically determined trait. Nutrition, especially during childhood, plays an important role in the eventual height of the adult. We find, then, that the picture is obscured by environmental events.

The genetic basis for behavior is singularly difficult to measure. Behavior is much more difficult to categorize than the color of peas. The whole nature-nurture issue is obscured because the parents usually provide both the genetic material and the early environment to the offspring. Any "family characteristics" can be used as evidence for the importance of either factor. Thus, it is nearly impossible to point to an unambiguous behavioral genotype.

Even with the single-gene traits so fortuitously selected by Mendel, thousands of observations with carefully controlled interbreeding were required to determine the laws of inheritance. A single-gene source of a behavioral trait has not been located. Since behavior is the result of a complicated neuronal network, and the operation of each subcomponent in that network is probably determined by different genes, a single gene for any behavior is unlikely.

Despite the problems associated with measuring genetic determiners for behavior, a number of approaches provide hints into this area. The research approaches used to establish the laws of genetic inheritance are applied with behavior as the phenotypic trait. Fortunately, the rules for genetic inheritance are relatively well established in the inheritance of structures, so the behavioral geneticist can concentrate on applying these known rules to observed behavior patterns.

GENEALOGIES

A standard method for identifying genetic traits is to trace the genealogical lineage of an individual. Tracing characteristics through "family trees" constitutes making a collection of phenotypically expressed characteristics. The pattern of inheritance through several generations can sometimes be analyzed to establish classic dominant or recessive traits. Tracing the genealogy of the descendants of Queen Victoria, for example, has yielded strong evidence that the monarch carried the recessive gene for hemophilia, an inability of the blood to clot in the normal manner. Such individuals may literally bleed to death from a "minor" cut or abrasion. Since this trait is on the X chromosome, it is a **sex-linked trait.** Only males have a single X chromosome, so if the recessive trait is on the X chromosome, that is the phenotype. Females have two X chromosomes, so to be expressed a recessive trait must be on both chromosomes. Thus, for characteristics genetically coded on the X chromosome, males are more likely to show the recessive characteristics than females. Color blindness is another sex-linked trait (Figure 21.2).

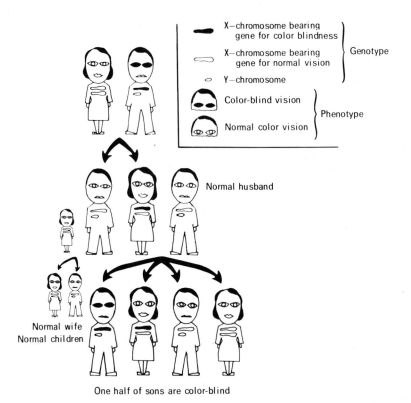

Figure 21.2 Inheritance patterns for color blindness in humans. This sex-linked trait is found on the X chromosome, causing a skipped-generation phenotypic expression. (Winchester, 1966, p. 105)

A well-known behavioral genealogical study was that of a family named Kallikak. A Civil War soldier fictitiously named Martin Kallikak established one family tree through a liaison with a barmaid. Upon returning home at the end of the war, Martin married a local girl, and their offspring led to the other Kallikak family tree. Whereas the legitimate Kallikaks show a lineage of upstanding, solid citizens, the other family tree is burdened with criminals, prostitutes, and other socially unacceptable characters. The difference is attributed to the different genetic contributions of the maternal source of each branch of the tree. An example of a more positive behavioral pattern emerges in the genealogical table for the relatives of Johann Sebastian Bach. Here an unusual number of musically talented individuals are recorded over a brief number of generations.

In the case of both the Bach family and the Kallikaks, the point has often been made that the behavioral genealogy is contaminated by environmental factors. Children in the Bach family were almost certainly given massive doses of musical experience during their early years. As for the Kallikaks, it could be said that the differences in social acceptability and milieu encountered by the offspring of a legitimate marriage and individuals born out of wedlock provide many viable environmental reasons for observed behavioral differences.

Twins provide a naturally occurring genetic "experiment" for comparing the effects of heredity and environment. **Identical twins** look exactly alike because they have the same genotype. **Fraternal twins,** on the other hand, represent different genotypes that happened to be conceived and born in the same time period. According to the laws of Mendelian inheritance, fraternal twins should share approximately 50 percent of their genotypes, just as in the case with other siblings. By comparing the traits of twins, siblings, and unrelated children, reared together and raised separately, it is possible to estimate the relative contribution of genes and upbringing. While many traits have been measured in this manner, "intelligence" has received the most attention in behavioral studies. As would be expected, identical twins raised together are uncannily similar in IQ test performance, while unrelated children raised in different family situations are essentially dissimilar (Figure 21.3). Data from fraternal twins reared together and apart resemble the data derived from siblings rather than identical twins. On the basis of these twin studies, behavioral geneticists claim that the genetic component is two to four times as important as the environmental component as a determinant of IQ. The staunch environmentalists remain unconvinced, while the general conclusion is that both factors interact so strongly as to make an either-or argument unlikely.

As knowledge increases and new techniques are developed, we discover more about the genetic process. It is possible to count and categorize the chromosomes in human blood cells. The normal human cell contains 46 chromosomes which occur in 23 pairs. Some of the chromosomes are very large, while others are relatively tiny. In some cases, an individual might have

Genetic and Nongenetic relationships studied		Genetic Correlation	Range of Correlations	Studies Included
Unrelated Persons	Reared Apart	0.00		4
	Reared Together	0.00		5
Foster-Parent-Child		0.00		3
Parent-Child		0.50		12
Siblings	Reared Apart	0.50		2
	Reared Together	0.50		35
Twins — Two-Egg	Opposite Sex	0.50		9
	Like Sex	0.50		11
Twins — One-Egg	Reared Apart	1.00		4
	Reared Together	1.00		14

Figure 21.3 Summary of correlations observed between genetic distance and IQ. (Lerner & Libby, 1976)

an "extra" chromosome. **Down's syndrome,** or mongolism, is the phenotypic result of a specific extra chromosome. Generally speaking, the larger the chromosome, the less likely the individual is to be able to survive. Thus, most of the extra chromosome abnormalities involve the smaller chromosomes.

The Y chromosome found in the male of the species is an interesting anomaly in the genetic picture. Whereas the rest of the chromosomes appear in matched pairs, the X and Y chromosomes in the male are completely mismatched. Since the Y chromosome is so small, the genetic information must be supplied by the single X chromosome from the mother; thus, the occurrence of sex-linked characteristics like color blindness and hemophilia.

The X and Y chromosomes are also anomalous in the fact that an extra X or Y chromosome has less impact on the phenotype than other chromosomes. It is quite possible to have one or even two additional X or Y chromosomes without fatal consequences to the individual. The XYY syndrome created much excitement when it was first discovered. Early indications were that there was a disproportionate number of XYY males in prison populations. There soon developed a phenotypic description of individuals with the extra Y chromosome. These males were characterized as being larger than the "normal" male, and there seemed to be a typical psychological profile which included a "tendency to be short-tempered." There were hints of a genetically caused "criminal personality." Outstanding examples such as the Texas tower sniper who began shooting at anyone he could see from his tower vantage point helped the stereotype. Richard Speck, the killer of eight in Chicago, is another example. In the case of the Texas tower killer, a brain tumor was found in the limbic system, which probably better accounts for the rage behavior. Speck's lawyer mentioned the XYY syndrome in his legal defense. Subsequent data indicate that the XYY syndrome is not so spectacular as first suspected and needs additional study before any definite conclusions are drawn.

Genealogical evidence suggests that two contemporary human behavioral problems may have a genetic basis. For years it has been suspected that there is a genetic component to schizophrenic behavior (Figure 21.4). The usual summary statement has suggested that there may be a hereditary "predisposition" to schizophrenia, but that the environment creates the situation that precipitates the psychosis, if it is to occur. Improved government record-keeping today makes the task of tracing the genealogies of individuals easier than it once was. Denmark, with its comprehensive national health program, keeps very complete records on Danish citizens which provide important supportive evidence for the genetic basis for schizophrenia. These records show, for example, that the offspring of psychotic mothers diagnosed as schizophrenic are much more likely to develop schizophrenia—even when they were placed in foster homes years before the mother demonstrated psychotic symptoms.

Genealogical studies of alcoholism suggest a similar line of evidence pointing to an important genetic component (see Table 21.2). Although de-

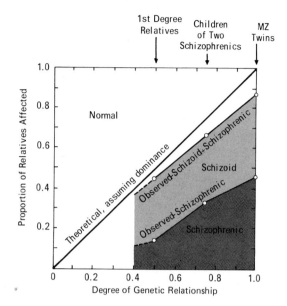

Figure 21.4 Graph of inheritability of schizophrenia. The observed data fall closer to an ideal 100 percent inheritance line than a zero inheritance line. (Heston, 1970, p. 252)

finitive evidence is scarce, it may be that an individual is susceptible to alcohol not because of an inherited personality type but because of some metabolic inefficiency in breaking down the alcohol molecule into harmless by-products.

POPULATION STUDIES

Rather than trace the genealogy of each individual, geneticists can study the characteristics of an entire population to establish the constituents of the gene pool. When examing genetic processes, it seems impossible not to include behavior patterns in conjunction with the evolution and selection of physiological structures. For example, the spectacularly colored tail feathers of the peacock would not attract many hens unless the cock were also provided with the ability to spread the tail and make use of the other elements in

TABLE 21.2   Morbidity Risks for Various Relatives of Alcoholic Individuals and for Controls in a Swedish Population (After Amark, 1951, p. 90)

Relationship	Morbidity Risk (Percentage)
Brother	21
Father	26
Sister	0.9
Mother	2
None—male controls	3.4
None—female controls	0.1

courtship display. The persistent display of the male guppy in the home aquarium is probably more related to a genetic behavior pattern than to the male's color pattern. It is possible to speculate a situation where the male's persistence might lead to greater breeding success than bright colors. In this case, the behavior would be preferentially selected over the pattern.

The evolutionary diversity is not irreversible if the related subspecies have not diverged too far. An interesting situation has occurred in Europe, where two subspecies of mice are now competing for the same ecological niche. The original stock which led to each subspecies evolved in Asia approximately 10,000 years ago and began spreading outward from this source. Some of the descendants moved into the increasingly cold environments of the Russian steppes, while others occupied the relatively balmy areas of southern Asia. Each group was subjected to different environmental pressures, selecting for survival features from the common gene pool. During the 10,000 years of evolution, this different selection pressure has resulted in mice that look different. The "northern" variety has longer extremities, "pointed" facial features, and white paws and underbelly. The "southern" variety is more "roly-poly" and is a uniform gray color.

The southern variety expanded westward along the warm shores of the Mediterranean and colonized the European continent through the southern regions of France. The northern variety moved across the Russian steppes to colonize Europe from the east. At the present time, there is a relatively sharp line of demarcation between the two subspecies (Figure 21.5). The line is, coincidentally, approximate to the political boundaries of the Iron Curtain— although no political ideology has been observed. The two subspecies can successfully interbreed, although the hybrid offspring appear to be less competitive than either pure strain, since the band of hybridization remains relatively narrow and restricted.

The two subspecies of mice can also be discriminated in terms of behavior. The northern mice will voluntarily use an exercise wheel if given the opportunity, and will also readily swim across water. The southern mice tend to hoard large supplies of food (or other objects) and to be highly responsive to light changes in the environment. The respective behavior patterns are distinct and reliable for members within either subspecies. Hybrids tend to run in wheels *and* hoard, which might reflect the relative dominant characteristic of each behavior. Thus, we find that two discriminably different subspecies on morphological characteristics also demonstrate reliable behavioral differences.

In recent years, the question of race and intelligence quotient (IQ) has been the subject of considerable attention on the part of psychologists and educators. Research in this area has utilized studies of an entire population to focus on the IQ trait. Arthur Jensen, a major spokesman for the genetic hypothesis, points to the observed difference between the black and white races on IQ test performance and states that IQ is, therefore, genetically determined. Jensen has been strongly attacked for his conclusions, first, because

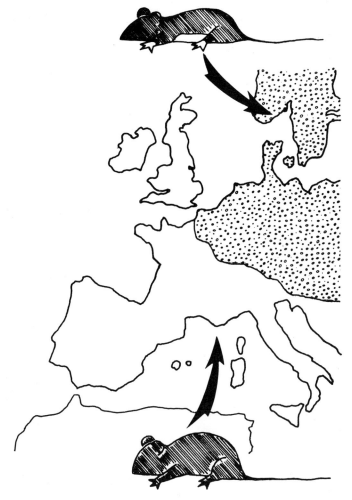

Figure 21.5 Two types of European mice.

he does not take into account the known environmental inequalities between the races, and, second, because of the social implications of his conclusion. Another dimension has been injected into the furor by those who question the accuracy, relevancy, or necessity of a score on an arbitrary test such as the IQ test.

With so many factors clouding both the data and interpretations derived from those data, a definitive conclusion cannot be drawn at this time. To the physiological psychologist, the problem can be translated into a somewhat different format. IQ test performance, however arbitrary, is probably related to differences in the structures and functioning of the nervous system. The crucial question becomes, "How are neurological differences established?" If there is the equivalent of species-specific behaviors in humans, then we must entertain the possibility of a genetic impact on neurological connections. If, on the other hand, the human nervous system makes all of its connections according to information received from the environment, the genetic argument is rejected.

If we decide that human behavior includes some genetically coded elements, the race and IQ argument may be restated. If the gene pools that contribute to each race are different enough to create reliable morphological differences such as skin color, and biochemical differences such as blood types, we would expect to find a corresponding difference in behaviors or behavioral capacities.

SELECTIVE BREEDING

Genealogies and population studies are contaminated by a number of uncontrolled variables. The possible role of environmental factors is particularly vexing. In order to establish the genetic contribution in an unambiguous manner, it is necessary selectively to breed for a particular trait. Humans selectively bred domestic animals long before they knew the rules they were following. Although we are aware of the physical characteristics that mark a "pure-bred" dog or cat, certain behavioral characteristics are associated with particular breeds. Pointers or setters may be observed "automatically" to freeze in the appropriate position the first time they encounter wild game. Shepherd dogs which have been house pets all of their lives may show a remarkable degree of "correct" herding behavior upon first exposure to cows or sheep.

Many dogs seem to manage the "wrong" behavior with equal aplomb. To a behavioral geneticist, this depends on the traits that were selectively bred in the animal's ancestry. Most dogs that are bred to be shown are bred for bodily characteristics without regard to behavioral traits. Hunters, on the other hand, may prize blood lines for hunting ability, even though the dog's show appearance is flawed.

The two different European mouse subspecies have been studied in the laboratory setting with some illuminating results. After two generations in laboratory cages, the two subspecies still exhibit the behavioral differences observed in the wild animals. Thus, after two generations of essentially identical environments, the behavioral differences of the respective strains are retained.

The drosophila, or fruit fly, has been extensively used in genetic studies. Since these flies need an extremely short time period between successive generations (15 days) and are remarkably productive (100 offspring per batch), it is possible in a relatively short time to breed selectively through many generations for a given trait. Another distinct advantage is that the drosophila has only two pairs of easily observed chromosomes. By correlating phenotypic traits with stained bands on the two chromosomes, geneticists can "map" the genes in terms of their location on the chromosomes.

Behavioral geneticists have found that it is possible to breed drosophilas for certain behaviors. For example, by arranging a vertical maze (one with "up and down" choice points), it is possible to sort out "high-flying" fruit flies from "low-flying" ones (see Figure 3.2). Since the flies tend to fly toward light, one can release them on the dark side of a vertical multiple-unit maze and collect the individuals that make their way to the top or bottom "goal bottle" on the lighted side. These can be interbred and the offspring selected again in the maze. Within two or three generations, there are two strains of fruit fly that differ according to their tendency to fly upward or downward. Cross-breeding a high-flying strain with a low-flying strain results in flies that are almost randomly distributed between the two extremes. This result reflects the polygenetic factors that contribute to the flying behavior.

Tryon (1929) attempted a more ambitious selective breeding project by selecting for maze-learning ability in rats. He selected the fastest-learning animals and interbred them, and he also interbred the animals that took longest to learn the maze. Tryon then repeated the procedure by selecting the "fastest of the fast" offspring for further interbreeding as well as the "slowest of the slow." After two generations, there was a distinct dichotomy in terms of the number of errors made by each strain to learn a standard maze-learning task (Figure 21.6).

Tryon's strains have been retained and carefully interbred, although without further maze-learning selective pressure. Thus, it is possible to purchase animals that are maze bright or maze dull according to the needs of

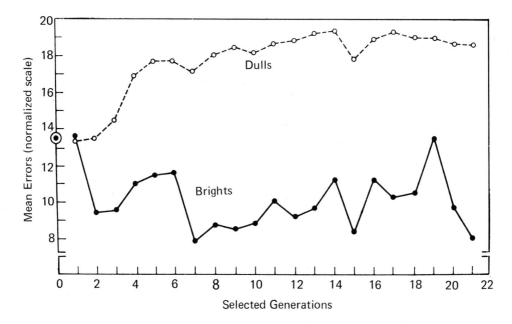

Figure 21.6 Maze performance of rat generations selected for maze brightness and maze dullness. (Tryon, 1940, p. 115)

the researcher. An interesting sidelight to the "maze dull-maze bright" description is that the animals appear to differ in learning abilities specific to the maze-learning task. There is no consistent difference in the learning performance of the two strains when required to learn to press a bar in a Skinner box.

In England rats have been selectively bred for their "emotional behavior" in selective breeding paradigms similar to that used by Tryon. "Nervous" rats tend to crouch and freeze rather than explore a new environment. "Nervous" rats also require the experimenter to spend much time cleaning the apparatus after each animal. By using exploratory behavior and fecal output as the selection criteria, researchers have produced emotionally reactive and nonreactive strains of rats (Figure 21.7).

Offspring from the two strains follow the typical genetic inheritance pattern. If both parents are reactive, the offspring are reactive, and so on. In an exhaustive study of the genes versus environment question, Joffe (1963) experimented with pure-bred and cross-bred rats in various environmental rearing conditions. Part of the study involved switching some litters with nonreactive foster mothers. As expected, the genetic history as well as the environment (reactive versus nonreactive mother) had an effect on the eventual behavior of the pups. An unexpected result was that the behavior of the foster mothers was found to change according to the genotype of their foster pups! Not only does the parent provide the genetic and environmental conditions, but the parent also adjusts to the environment provided by the offspring. Thus, the interaction between heredity and environment is not linear from generation to generation but is in a constant state of interactive flux.

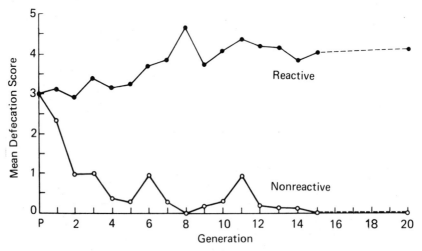

Figure 21.7 Defecation rate of rat generations selected for emotional reactivity. (Broadhurst, 1967, p. 125)

THE GENETIC CODE AND BEHAVIOR

Although the data are obscured by the multiple factors that affect any behavior, it seems that at least some components of behavior are the phenotypic expression of genetic factors. Since the genetic code consists of amino acid sequences coded on the DNA molecule, the "genes" must be the code for certain proteins, enzymes, or other chemical products of the cell. A few of the chemical-neuronal steps between the DNA and "behavior" are now being explored, and a few glimpses of the process are available.

Most of the genetic defects known to occur in humans involve the failure in one step of a metabolic sequence. For example, the urine of newborn babies is normally tested for the presence of phenylpyruvic acid. Presence of this acid indicates a dangerous condition called phenylketonuria (PKU). Phenylpyruvic acid is toxic to the CNS and results in permanent brain damage. The condition occurs because the acid cannot be metabolized into less dangerous by-products. Apparently, the necessary enzyme for this metabolic step is not produced by the cells because there is an error in the DNA genetic code. Fortunately, the damage can be prevented by early diagnosis and a special diet that is devoid of phenylalenines, which would otherwise be metabolized into the harmful phenylpyruvic acid.

The damage to the CNS by PKU is not directly coded on the DNA, but the inability to produce the appropriate enzyme has profound side effects on the CNS. The recessive trait albinism may also be traced to the absence of a crucial enzyme in a metabolic sequence. In this case, the missing enzyme fails to convert a substance into the precursor for the production of melanin (cell pigments). Coincidentally, the albinism metabolic chain is a part of the phenylalanine sequence. The difference in the phenotypic expression reflects the different points of disruption in the entire metabolic sequence. Since in some cases the metabolic defect impairs life-sustaining functions, the term "lethal gene" is sometimes used to describe the genetic error (Figure 21.8).

Many human diseases and disorders will eventually be traced to a disruption in one of the many metabolic sequences that normally occur. If the disruption is caused by a genetic mistake in specifying a needed enzyme, it will be labeled a hereditary disease. Hemophilia is undoubtedly the inability to complete the chain, which leads to the production of blood-clotting compounds. Color blindness is the result of a "mistake" in the production of one of the three visual pigments normally found in the cones of the eye. Gout, the painful accumulation of uric acid in the lower extremities, appears to be the result of an overproduction of uric acid. Whether this excess is the result of an overly efficient enzyme that produces uric acid or the absence of the enzyme needed to futher metabolize the uric acid remains to be seen.

Both alcoholism and schizophrenia have been mentioned as candidates for genetically caused malfunctions. The alcoholic may have a metabolic abnormality similar to the PKU condition. Alcohol itself is relatively harmless in the system, but some of the intermediary compounds in the metabolic

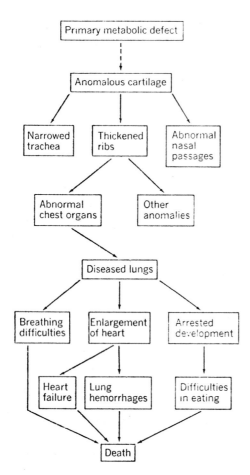

Figure 21.8 Diagram of a lethal gene in the rat. The metabolic defect inherited in the genetic code is expressed in a number of physical abnormalities which prove fatal to the animal. (Grüneberg, via Lerner & Libby, 1976)

sequence are quite toxic to the nervous system. The differential tolerance to alcohol between an alcoholic and a nonalcoholic could well be due to differences in the ability to produce and/or destroy these toxic intermediary products. The conditions that result in schizophrenic behavior are not well established by supportive data, so it is difficult to argue a simple metabolic malfunction. The fact that schizophrenia responds to chemotherapy does lend credence to a chemical theory of its cause.

The entire transmission process at the synaptic cleft between neurons involves the production of a number of chemicals. The normal synapse involves a delicate chemical balance between transmitter and inhibitory substances. A change in the concentration of any of these chemicals would have a profound effect on the efficiency of transmission across the synapse. Since the genetic code is basically one of chemical production, the synapse is a likely site for the genetic manipulation of behavior.

Biochemical study of the Tryon selectivity bred rats suggests that the maze-bright animals may have a higher concentration of acetylcholine than the maze dulls. Since cholinergic fibers appear to be specialized for rapid and efficient data transmission and processing, it is reasonable to associate the changes in learning ability with chemical changes in the data-processing circuits.

Maudsley's reactive and nonreactive rats, on the other hand, appear to differ in concentration of serotonin. Serotonin is an important transmitter in the autonomic nervous system, and chemical changes in the "emotional" nervous system would be expected to lead to changes in the "reactivity" of the animal. Although the data are fragmentary, the genetic code–chemical change–behavioral effect chain appears to be supported.

AUTHOR'S The field of behavioral genetics is rapidly growing in both
COMMENTS knowledge and acceptability. From the total rejection of the nature side of the nature-nurture question which has typified American psychology for 50 years, there is growing acceptance of the importance of inherited contributions. Behavioral genetics is complicated by two significant factors. First, both the genetic inheritance process and behavior are so complicated that unambiguous data are not easily obtained. A second significant factor is that there are profound social and political implications if the behavorial genetics argument is applied to human behavior.

22

Developmental Changes

The functioning of the CNS is typically considered with reference to the adult organism, with the component structures established, organized, and functioning. Occasional reference is made to the effects of early environment on some of the characteristics of the system, but frequently the ontogenetic contributions are ignored. The nervous system, like the entire organism, undergoes an orderly growth and development. The sequence and rate of this growth account for many of the capacities and limitations in the growing child. Recognition of these ontogenetic opportunities and limitations could contribute to our understanding of the adult CNS as well as provide the ability to choreograph optimal environmental experience for the growing system.

The catchy phrase "ontogeny recapitulates phylogeny" suggests that the ontogenetic development of the organism is a rough and abbreviated historical sketch of the phylogentic sequence that resulted in that particular organism. As is the case with such sayings, it hints at a basic truth, but in doing so leads to a number of false conceptions. Since the phylogenetic tree began with a single-celled organism which eventually evolved to include all of the organisms that now exist, including humans, the source and eventual product of each process is certainly analogous. Even some of the mid-point steps in the process seem to lend credence to the comparison. At one stage in its development, the human embryo exhibits distinctly gill-like structures which later become the middle ear structures more appropriate to the human animal. In their early stages, the embryos of a wide variety of animals bear a startling resemblance (Figure 22.1). As the embryos continue to develop, they acquire the characteristics unique to their own genetic heritage.

The misleading part of the ontogeny-phylogeny analogy is that the genetic material for the developing embryonic cells is precoded to establish the adult characteristics of the organism. To oversimplify the difference, ontogeny "knows" where it is going, while phylogeny is a continuing trip.

In the ontogenetic development of the organism, we find a surprising degree of purposiveness in the growth of each individual cell. At the same time, we find that the individual cells are capable of making some rather remarkable adjustments in order to fulfill their role in the growing organism.

STRUCTURES IN THE CNS

The line of cells that will eventually become the brain and spinal cord of the adult is one of the earliest distinguishable features in the developing organism (Figure 22.2). This line of specialized neural cells continues to grow until it forms a "plate" which eventually curls to form the neural tube. The CNS generally follows a cephalo-caudal development, which describes development of most structures in the organisms.

The neural tube continues to grow and to thicken around the central ventricular space. The cells that are dividing to form the ever-increasing mass of neural tissue are the cells at the ventricular surface (and, later, some special "growth" tissue which develops from the ventricular lining and migrates to other positions). The fact that cell growth is localized at specific regions means that the new cells must migrate within the neural tissue in order to arrive at their eventual location in the CNS.

Some regions at the anterior end of the neural tube undergo spectacular growth "bursts" which result in pronounced structural prominences. As was described in an earlier chapter, at first there are three such prominences, with five becoming identifiable as the nervous system continues to develop. It is largely on the basis of these ontogenetic prominences that the major regions of the CNS are identified (see Figure 4.1).

NEURONAL PROLIFERATION AND GROWTH

Different neurons in the CNS seem to develop in a specific sequence (Figure 22.3). Studies of the ontogenetic development of the spinal cord in monkeys show that the efferent neurons leading from the spinal cord to the muscles are the first to develop completely. Next to develop are the afferent neurons between the sensory organs and the spinal cord. Only after the peripheral afferent and efferent fibers are established do the internuncial neurons appear to form the rudimentary spinal reflex. This initial reflex is a direct excitatory connection between the sensory and motor neurons.

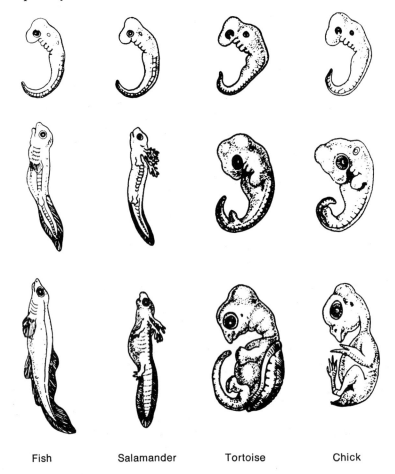

Fish   Salamander   Tortoise   Chick

During growth of the initial reflexive circuit, more complicated inter-nuncial cells are also growing in the spinal cord. These relatively complicated internuncials make a variety of connections between the peripheral afferent and efferent nuerons and form more complicated reflexive circuits. Inhibitory cells are observed that provide additional control over the simple excitatory circuits. Interneurons develop to carry information between the two sides of the cord, establishing the basis for coordinated movement of opposing limbs. Other interneurons are formed to carry information up and down the spinal cord. Some of these fibers synapse in other segments of the spinal cord to provide coordinated reflexive activity along the length of the body. Still others carry information into and out of the developing brain. The first identifiable tract to develop in the spinal cord is a motor tract. It appears to be a general rule that development of the response circuitry precedes that of the associated sensory network. In terms of survival priorities, this sequence seems most reasonable. It also explains why nervous systems generally have the

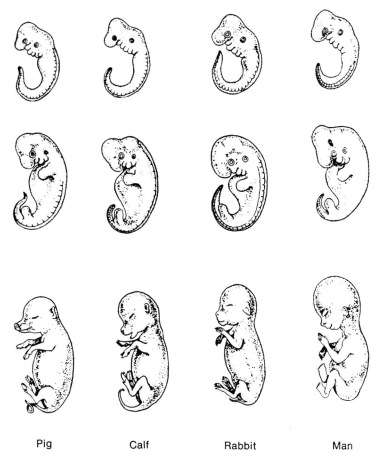

Pig	Calf	Rabbit	Man

Figure 22.1 Embryological development in several different species. The embryos are nearly indistinguishable in the early stages but develop distinct characteristics according to the genetic code they carry. (Hardin, 1966)

motor systems located medially, while the sensory systems are often laterally positioned.

By the time the human infant is born, the major structures of the CNS are well established. The nervous system as a whole undergoes physical growth concomitant with the physical growth of the individual. Thus, the total size of the CNS increases during the growth of the individual to adulthood. This growth is not exclusively genetically determined. Experiments with animals reared in enriched and impoverished environments show that the weight of the adult brains correlate with the degree of environmental stimulation encountered. The "enriched" animals are correspondingly superior in learning tasks as adults. Thus, on a global scale, the data are clear that structural characteristics and behavioral capacities of the CNS are directly related.

The increase in dimensions is not seen to be concentrated in any spe-

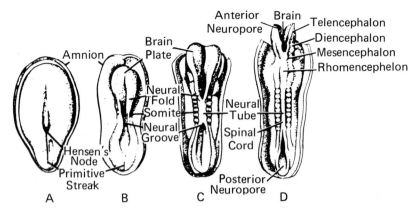

Figure 22.2 Early ontogenetic development of the human embryo with major CNS structures identified. (Curtis, Jacobson, & Marcus, 1972, p. 21)

cific structures of the CNS. With the exception of some tumors or obvious genetic abnormalities, there is no reliable predictor of intelligence or accomplishment on the basis of the appearance of the brain structures. The changes that must be occurring are apparently on a relatively fine scale compared with the changes that can be observed with today's techniques. An increase in the size and/or number of neurons may be a part of the brain changes that

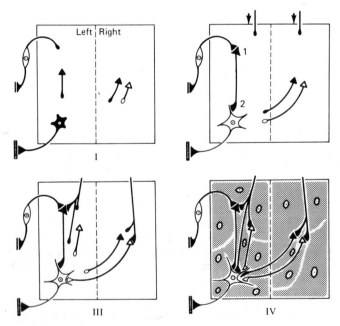

Figure 22.3 Schematic diagram of the development of synaptic circuits in the spinal motor system. (Bodian, 1970, p. 132)

occur with increased stimulation, but it seems likely that the most important changes are in the connections between the existing neurons. Observing or counting synapses in the CNS will require considerable technological advancement.

At the neuronal level, there is growing evidence for CNS adjustments to the environment. Kittens reared in horizontally or vertically striped environments develop a high proportion of the appropriately oriented "straight-line" detector in their visual system. It seems fairly clear that the organization of the growing sensory system is partially determined by the incoming stimulation provided by the environment. Observations of the growth of different types of neurons in the developing CNS provide a clue to the adaptive mechanism.

The developing nervous system in the spinal cord consists of efferent, afferent, and interneurons connected apparently by some genetically coded mechanism. As the various circuits are established, corresponding reflexive behaviors may be observed in the developing animal. Stimulation of these circuits appears to play an important part in the development of the nervous system. It has been recently noted that the ontogenetic process is not merely one of cellular growth and proliferation. Many areas of the growing nervous system generate more neuronal cells than can be found in the mature organism. Cellular death appears to be an important part of the development process. The nervous system apparently develops more neurons than it will ultimately use.

One hypothesis explaining the functional significance of the death of the cells proposes that this allows for last-minute adjustments in the neural circuitry. The genetic code provides only the "general" scheme for neural connections within the nervous system. Thus, we may find many different interneurons interconnecting many sensory neurons and motor neurons. Some of these connections may be more functional to the organism than others. During development, the "useful" circuits are likely to be activated more often than the "less useful" circuits. Some circuits could be redundant and/or useless and serve no function. Hypothesizing that the circuits that are used become "stronger" while the unused circuits weaken and fade away might explain the loss of some neurons during the development process.

Recall the experiment in which chimpanzees reared in visually deprived conditions eventually lost normal visual capacities. Significantly, there was a measurable loss of ganglion cells (feature detectors) in the unused visual system.

If this hypothesized mechanism for fine adjustment of the final circuits in the CNS is correct, we can begin to appreciate the complexity of the nature-nurture problem. The genetic code is responsible for providing the circuits in case they are needed. The environment provides the necessary stimulation to "cement" the connections and/or prevent their disappearance. The circuits to be found in the mature organism are the product of the contribution of each.

After the neuronal circuitry is well developed, glial cells associated with the neurons begin to develop. The formation of myelin sheaths around the axons and the interstitching of other nonneuronal cells between the established neurons proceeds. These glial cells apparently enhance and/or adjust the neural circuits in the nervous system. The myelin sheath improves the rapid conduction of messages along the axons. Glial cells found near the synaptic clefts are suspected to participate in the synaptic events, thus further altering neuronal connections.

ONTOGENETIC EXPERIMENTS

Amphibians possess a unique trait which affords the researcher a powerful tool for investigating the developing nervous system. The frog and salamander can tolerate radical tissue transplants, and the transplanted tissue will grow and remain healthy. A number of interesting phenomena are seen in the transplant experiments.

As the organism develops from a single cell to a multicelled organism, there are distinct growth stages. After the neural tube is formed, it is possible to predict which of the multiplying cells will eventually become specific body parts of the adult animal. For example, in the salamander, it is possible to transplant the cells that would normally become the "left front leg" to the area of the "right rib" of the animal. If this tissue transplant is done very early in the blastular stage of development, the salamander develops with no misplaced parts. The transplanted tissue is assimilated where it has been transplanted, and neighboring cells accommodate the gap created by the removed tissue.

If performed slightly later in the development sequence, the identical surgical procedure results in a "left front leg" growing out of the right side of the animal (Figure 22.4). The results from cell transplant studies show that each cell contains all of the genetic information to form any portion of the body. At some development point, however, the cells specialize and can form only specific parts according to their location in the whole organism. This specialization must be a restriction of the information available from the DNA molecule. Something occurs that causes the cells which are destined to become "left front leg" to lose the ability to become anything else. Thus, there is a critical period after which the cell has become specialized. Once the specialization occurs, the cell follows its special genetic instructions, no matter where it has been moved!

Surgically altered salamanders not only provide the bizarre appearance of a limb in the wrong place, but the transplanted limb shows movement! The developing nervous system has successfully innervated the displaced appendage. The nature of the movement of the displaced leg indicates the degree of specialization in the nervous system. If the displaced "left front leg" shows movement that would be expected from a normally placed "left front

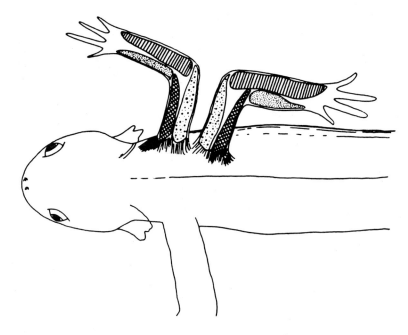

Figure 22.4 Growth of a transplanted limb in the salamander. Identical muscles are indicated by shading. The growing nerves connect to the "appropriate" muscle. (Weiss, 1952, p. 18)

leg," the nervous system must contain an elaborate "search and identify" mechanism for every muscle in the body. If, on the other hand, the transplanted leg responds more like the nearest normal leg or some other response scheme, the specificity of the neuronal circuits is not quite so rigid.

The transplanted leg shows the movement of its normally located neighbor. Whenever the normal leg extends to take a step, the adjacent transplanted leg responds with a similar flexor-extensor pattern of muscular movements. Apparently, the growing nervous system simply incorporates the transplanted limb within the network that is developing to innervate the normal limb. The unique feature of this innervation is that it is appropriately coordinated in the transplanted leg. The nerves that control the flexor muscles for the normal limb also connect to the flexor muscles in the transplanted limb. The same is true with the extensors. Since the salamander leg involves the coordinated movement of two pairs of muscles for the movement of the limb, this means that four different neuron types successfully locate and establish contact with the appropriate four muscles.

This could be the result of an extraordinarily generalized nervous proliferation out into the new limb, with the subsequent selection and rejection of the connections according to the functional uses of the circuits. It may also indicate a "target" mechanism which attracts specific types of nerves to their appropriate destination. There is some evidence for either of these interpretations, but the ability of the nervous system to make this type of adjustment is remarkable.

In the case of the salamander, this neuronal connecting mechanism is a distinct inconvenience with certain leg transplants. In the example used, the transplanted limb is essentially a normal "front leg" but is pointed in the opposite direction. For every movement of the normal limb that would result in forward motion, the transplanted limb works to move the animal backward. If all of the limbs were transplanted contralaterally, the salamander would be totally reversed. Forward commands from the nervous system result in "forward" movement of the rearward-facing limbs. Therefore, the animal moves in the opposite direction of the desired movement with a well-coordinated sequence of limb movements. The salamander brain lacks the learning capacity to overcome the remarkable developmental adaptability of the peripheral nervous system. Such surgically altered animals are "locked in reverse gear."

Mammals cannot adapt to the massive transplant procedures inflicted on amphibians. It is possible, however, to exchange the attachment point of the flexor and extensor muscles in the leg of the cat. When this is done, contraction of the flexor muscle pulls on the extensor part of the limb, and vice versa. The net effect of this muscle reversal is that the cat will push down on a paw that it wishes to lift. This motor reversing causes a certain amount of distress as the cat tries to use the altered limb. Eventually, the cat will learn to appropriately control the reversed muscles and can successfully walk using altered legs. If, however, the animal is subjected to a painful stimulus which normally triggers a spinal reflexive withdrawal, the paw is driven forcefully onto the painful stimulus. The cat also may revert to the wrong movement if startled. The ability to reorganize motor neuronal patterns is probably found in the mammal's well-developed cortex, but does not replace the permanent circuitry of lower CNS centers.

Reliable behavioral differences may be observed between rats of different sexes. These differences are most obviously expressed in courtship and mating behavior, but more subtle differences are observable in other situations. Adult rats can be caused to express some of the behavior patterns of the opposite sex if they are injected with hormones from the opposite sex. This chemical masculinization or feminization is never total; that is, some components of the "appropriate" behavior are still observed, and the animal reverts to normal response patterns after the injected chemicals are metabolized. It seems that some behavioral programs are available in the rat nervous system which are expressed only in the presence of a specific hormone.

The programming of the developing nervous system is subject to hormonal influences of a more permanent nature. If hormones are administered to the animal during the first few weeks of infancy, corresponding behavioral differences are observed in the adult animal. Thus, if a female rat is injected with male hormones during infancy, its adult behavior is much like that of a typical male rat. Similarly, male rats can be feminized by early injections of female hormones. The artificially programmed behavior often occurs in spite of the normal sex hormones provided by the animal's own endocrine system. In this situation, apparently, certain circuits are preferentially established according to the prevailing hormone concentration in the system during certain developmental stages.

EPIGENESIS

The developing nervous system is the product of a close interplay of genetic and environmental factors. To argue an either-or interpretation conflicts with the known data. An **epigenetic theory,** which assumes a close interaction between hereditary and environmental contributions, is a more appropriate model. Several of the known characteristics of the nervous system can be combined into a feasible epigenetic model.

During the prenatal period, the development of the organism is almost exclusively genetic. The intrauterine environment is protected and constant, and except for occasional invasions by injury, disease, or chemical insult, the environment plays a strictly supportive role for the genetically determined patterns of growth.

Neural growth continues after birth, however, and the contribution of the environment becomes very important. The data suggest that neural circuits will atrophy and disappear with disuse. Thus, "horizontal" feature detectors are not maintained if the visual world consists of only vertically oriented stripes. If the animals is raised in a world of total sensory deprivation, the entire brain is smaller due to spontaneous destruction of the unused cells.

As the nervous system continues to develop and more complex circuitry appears, the sensory and motor capacities of the individual also change. Newborn infants are capable of only rudimentary responses. More important, the infant is also limited in the range of stimulation it can process with the rudimentary afferent system.

As growth continues, capabilities become more varied and simultaneously more precise. Presentation of a stimulus before the nervous system can effectively encode it would not be useful to the organism. Similarly, withholding a stimulus too long when the circuitry is being selected might result in the destruction of the appropriate circuits. Baby chicks, if not allowed to peck at food for the first two weeks of life, will starve to death if the force feeding is discontinued, even though they are surrounded with palatable grain. The epigenetic view argues that environmental stimulation must be carefully arranged to coincide with the optimal developmental stage of the nervous system.

Studies of the positive effects of enriched early environment are the basis for a number of educational and/or social enrichment programs in the United States for the benefit of impoverished children. The epigenetic view suggests that an important variable is the developmental stage at which the child experiences the enrichment. There is considerable reason to believe that many of the developing neuronal circuits require environmental stimulation in order to be permanently established. Thus, such programs ought to be offered while the circuits are still being established. In the human infant, the "critical period" for a number of social skills may be before the age of 2 years. As we learn more about the ontogenetic sequence in the development of the nervous system, we will be able to identify more specific mechanisms involved in this process.

MAINTENANCE, REPAIR, AND AGING

During the period of expanding growth, new neurons are being produced in the mammalian nervous system, and the system is capable of repairing damage by generating replacement neurons. This capacity is retained in the peripheral adult nervous system, so that damage to a sensory nerve results in a localized area of anesthesia which gradually closes as the neurons regenerate into the affected area.

The CNS, on the other hand, appears to lose the ability to produce new neurons with the cessation of ontogenetic growth. For this reason, damage to structures of the CNS has serious and permanent consequences. Since cellular death is inevitable, the nervous system must be sufficiently redundant in its organization to tolerate the loss of individual neurons. Only in the case of a massive insult to a large number of neurons sharing a common function is a significant loss to be observed.

The adult nervous system is undoubtedly capable of some kind of change, since learning is not restricted to the growth period of the CNS. The capacity to learn, whatever the mechanism, provides the phylogenetically "higher" animals with a powerful alternative to neuron regeneration as a means of adjusting to component failure. The experiment that reversed the action of the flexor and extensor muscles in the cat showed that the cortex was capable of reorganizing the motor control patterns to compensate for the novel muscular arrangement. Although the reflexive response was never reorganized, the cat was eventually capable of using the leg for normal walking movements. Experiments with altered sensory input suggest that the sensory systems are also capable of remarkable reorganization with relative ease.

Prefrontal lobotomy surgery is a massive destruction of neural tissue. A rationale for prefrontal lobotomy is that the patient is less difficult to control, which could be a direct function of the loss of neocortical functioning. The "improved personality" benefits of the surgery are somewhat transitory. If the patient does not respond to psychotherapy during the months following the surgery, the symptoms that led to the surgery are generally reacquired. Other brain structures seem to "learn" the functions once under the control of the structures that were surgically isolated. Thus, the learning capacity frees the organism from a slavish dependence on each individual component.

As the individual becomes older, the continuing irreparable damage has a cumulative effect. Many of the symptoms of old age are probably due to the gradual erosion of the individual parts, and the redundancy feature can no longer adequately compensate for the damage.

Two distinct features mark the aging nervous system. The first is that the entire nervous system seems to operate more slowly. Although not an obvious difference, the EEG rhythms in the older person are typically approximately one cycle per second slower than the equivalent wave in a younger person. Another indication of this slowed functioning is the gradual erosion in reaction time observed with advancing age.

A possible contributing factor in the slowed reaction time is the gradual failure of the sensory systems. All of the sensory systems seem to undergo a gradual increase in threshold sensitivity as the individual becomes older. One hypothesis for the "pain" of old age may be the creeping anesthesia produced by progressive failure of the normal senses. In the carefully balanced afferent system, the pain messages may normally be masked by other sensory activity.

The other peculiar effect of old age is a marked deficit in learning ability and short-term memory. Since the physiological mechanisms for these functions are not well established, it is difficult to tell whether this deficit represents the failure of a particularly vulnerable structure in the CNS or is the most sensitive function to show the effects of a general nervous system deterioration.

The cumulative effects of injuries, infections, or natural attrition could be sufficient to explain the eventual breakdown of CNS functions. The problem is undoubtedly more complex than this, since the symptoms of senility usually show a sharp onset, more often than not precipitated by a specific event or stress. Although the physiologist tends to focus on the physical causes of malfunctions in the nervous system, psychological stress has a physically measurable impact on CNS functioning.

AUTHOR'S COMMENTS   The nature-nurture controversy will undoubtedly be resolved by a general acceptance of both components. The term "epigenesis" describes the dynamic interaction between the developing organism and the environmental stimulation received during growth. The nature of the adult organism is very much dependent on events that transpire during the early developmental period.

One possible effect of the environment is to "select" the "appropriate" neural circuits from a larger number of genetically determined possibilities. In some ways, this process might be considered an extension of the component specialization pattern which marks the evolution process.

Most of the data concerning the nervous system relate to the intact and developed adult system. Much interest has also centered on the developmental changes and/or the changes that occur with learning in the nervous system. Surprisingly little is known concerning the maintenance and/or breakdown of nervous system structures which lead to the symptoms of senility.

VII

Adaptive Behavior

A static structure, even if it is a complex one, cannot provide the adaptive behavior accomplished by the nervous system. The fascination of physiological psychology is in explaining the remarkable adjustments the organism can make in response to environmental challenges. For the most part, the neurological functions described thus far have been relatively fixed behavioral mechanisms. Reflexes, species-specific behavior, feature detectors, and critical periods, all describe almost automatic responses to stimuli in the environment. Each of these mechanisms contributes distinctly adaptive capacities to the organism's behavior in terms of survival value, but each is the rigid "background" to even more adaptive dynamic behaviors.

Animals high on the phylogentic scale exhibit a wide range of totally integrated responses to novel, extreme, or unique environmental situations. Each individual organism is capable of fabricating a set of behaviors unique to the environmental challenges it alone experiences. It is this level of behavioral adaptiveness that is most interesting and at the same time most puzzling to the physiological psychologist.

On a relatively simple level, the ability merely to adjust the total activity level of the entire organism to match the demands of the environment provides a very useful response mechanism. The CNS contains an "activating center" which adjusts the level of responsiveness of the entire CNS. This allows the nervous system to be "mobilized" for situations that require rapid evaluation and response. The opposite capacity is also very important. The ability to reduce activity level when the environment is not presenting a challenge allows the conservation of resources during these quiescent periods. The periodic need for sleep suggests that the quiescent periods are not only convenient but necessary. Sleep research indicates that CNS "rest" is only a part of the sleep benefit; apparently, sleep also allows the CNS to accomplish some regenerating activity. The mechanism of this "recharge" activity is not completely clear.

Motivation and emotion are closely intertwined psychologically and also in terms of the neurological structures that mediate these behaviors. Affective tone provides two significant advances in adaptability of the organism. First, part of the emotional response is an extension of the simpler activating response for mobilization of all of the bodily organs. Thus, all systems are alerted to meet the emotion-producing situation. The second adaptive advantage of emotional behavior is that behavior is sustained beyond the precipitating stimulus. This prolonged behavior, after the termination of a threatening stimulus, provides a sustained and more effective escape from danger. It also maintains "seeking" behaviors when an internal drive is produced.

"Learning" represents an extraordinary capacity for adaptation on the part of the individual organism. Learning not only allows for the "correction" of existing inappropriate responses, but it also allows the animal to fabricate a totally original stimulus-response unit. The structures and mechanisms involved in the learning process are not definitely established, but there are some feasible hypotheses that are compatible with the known characteristics of the nervous system structures.

SUGGESTED READINGS

The topics in Part VII are the essence of physiological psychology. The assignment of specific behavioral functions to specific CNS structures and/or mechanisms is the goal of the discipline. To a great extent, the information available represents the "leading edge" of the advance of scientific knowledge. New data are being collected and published in the research journals. The discovery of a new phenomenon or the refinement in the interpretation of a known phenomenon keeps the status of contemporary theories in a constant state of flux. Special symposia are frequently held to enhance the information exchange among workers in a special area.

With the current explosion of information, it is difficult to offer a comprehensive list of suggested readings to meet the interests of each student. The following list is most appropriately described as a sample of the kind of information available and the sources where it may be found. The references suggested in Part I are also relevant to these topics.

Ax, A. F. The physiological differentiation between fear and anger in humans. *Psychosomatic Medicine,* 1953, **15,** 433–442.

Bullock, T. H. Simple systems for the study of learning. *Neurosciences Research Program Bulletin,* 1966, **4**(2).

Delgado, J. *Physical control of the mind.* New York: Harper & Row, 1969.

Dement, W. C. *Some must watch while some must sleep.* New York: Macmillan, 1972.

Dement, W. C. & Kleitman, N. Cyclical variations in EEG during sleep and their relation to eye movements, body motility, and dreaming. *Electroencephalography and Clinical Neurophysiology,* 1957, **9,** 673–690.

Ebert, J. D. Gene expression. *Neurosciences Research Program Bulletin,* 1967, **5**(3).

Eccles, J. C. *The neurophysiological basis of mind.* Baltimore, Md.: The Johns Hopkins Press, 1953.

Garcia, J., McGowan, B. K. & Green, K. F. Biological constraints on conditioning. In A. H. Black & W. F. Prokasy. *Classical conditioning II: Current theory and research.* New York: Appleton, 1972.

Heath, R. G. Electrical self-stimulation of the brain in man. *American Journal of Psychiatry,* 1963, **120,** 571–577.

Livingston, R. B. Brain mechanisms in conditioning and learning. *Neurosciences Research Program Bulletin,* 1966, **4**(3).

Moruzzi, G. & Magoun, H. Brain stem reticular formation and activation of the EEG. *Electroencephalography and Clinical Neurophysiology,* 1949, **1,** 455–473.

Nauta, W. S. H. Some brain structures and functions related to memory. *Neurosciences Research Program Bulletin,* 1964, **2**(5).

Nauta, W. S. H., Koella, W. P. & Quarton, G. C. Sleep, wakefulness, dreams, and memory. *Neurosciences Research Program Bulletin,* 1966, **4**(1).

Olds, J. & Milner, P. Positive reinforcement produced by electrical stimulation of the septal area and other regions of the rat brain. *Journal of Comparative and Physiological Psychology,* 1954, 419–427.

Penfield, W. & Roberts, L. *Speech and brain mechanisms.* Princeton, N.J.: Princeton University Press, 1959.

Pribram, K. H. (Ed.) *On the biology of learning.* New York: Harcourt, 1969.

Quarton, G. C., Melnechunk, I. & Schmitt, T. O. (Eds.) *The neurosciences: A study program.* New York: Rockefeller University Press, 1967.
Since two sections of this volume are unusually appropriate, the page, title, and author of individual articles are given in the following list.

BRAIN CORRELATES OF FUNCTIONAL BEHAVIORAL STATES

BRAIN CORRELATES OF LEARNING

Schachter, S. & Singer, J. Cognitive, social, and physiological determinants of emotional state. *Psychological Review,* 1962, **69,** 379–399.

Selye, H. *The physiology and pathology of exposure to stress.* Montreal: Acta, Inc., 1950.

Sperry, R. W. Physiological plasticity and brain circuit theory. In H. Harlow and C. N. Woolsey (Eds.), *Biological and biochemical bases of behavior.* Madison, Wisc.: University of Wisconsin, 1958.

Teyler, T. J. Altered states of awareness. In *Readings from Scientific American.* San Francisco: Freeman, 1972.

Valenstein, E. S. Biology of drives. *Neurosciences Research Program Bulletin,* 1968, **6**(1).

The final chapter in a study of the structural-functional operation of the human CNS should involve the mechanisms of thinking, cognition, creativity, and so on. The complexity of both the neocortex and the behavior described by these labels successfully conceals most of the mechanisms that operate at this functional level. There are, however, sufficient data for some speculations on the probable organization of the neocortical connections.

23

Arousal and Sleep

Control of rate of activity is one of the first adaptive capacities found in a primitive nervous system. The ability to speed up or slow down behavior provides a surprisingly purposive quality. Let us hypothesize a simple organism that is capable of only random movement. Since the movement will cause the organism to encounter either noxious or friendly environments, controling the rate of movement will maximize the time spent in the compatible environment. If the organism simply increases the rate of movements in the noxious environment, it will "escape" from the noxious situation sooner. If it slows down its rate of behavior in the friendly environment, it will "avoid" reentering the noxious situation. This avoidance or escape process can also be described as "seeking" the friendly situation. Even though the behavior itself is random, the organism can adjust effectively to its environment.

Human behavior is much more directive than the random behavior in the hypothesized primitive animal. Control of activity level even in the complex behavior available to humans is still an important adaptive function. The ability to deal effectively with a situation often depends on the organism's state of arousal or alertness. Situations that demand prolonged periods of alertness indicate that the human CNS is limited in its ability to operate at maximum capacity. Fatigue, sleep, or inattention will inevitably overtake a person. Typically, human behavior is marked by alternating periods of activity and rest. The ability of the CNS to adjust the activity level to the demands of the situation allows the total facilities of the system to be available if needed, but also prevents unnecessary expenditure of energy when it is not warranted.

Although the capacity to control general level of activity is a relatively crude mechanism compared to some of the highly specific human capacities, two facts illustrate its importance to human behavior. There are occasions when arousal level is not directly responsive to the situation at hand. Dozing during a speech or lecture may be embarrassing, but drowsiness while driving may have fatal consequences. The opposite situation, insomnia, illustrates an inappropriate level of activity in the opposite direction.

A second phenomenon illustrating the importance of CNS arousal level is that many drugs, particularly of the nonprescriptive variety, are used to mildly stimulate or depress general activity level. Some people are only occasional users, while for others such drugs are a daily ritual. Considerable commercial investment is based on our need to artifically manipulate the general activity of the CNS.

THE RETICULAR ACTIVATING SYSTEM

Interspersed among the predominant ascending and descending tracts in the brain stem is a reticulum of interconnected neurons without sharply delineated nuclei or tracts. As was mentioned in Chapter 4, the reticular formation extends through the medial aspects of the medulla, pons, midbrain, and thalamus (see Figure 4.3) and appears to interact with all information entering or leaving the CNS. Every significant sensory pathway (except olfaction) has a major collateral branch extending to the reticular structures. The pyramidal motor fibers also branch into the reticular formation. Much of the diffuse network of the extrapyramidal motor system involves the structures of the reticular formation.

The reticular formation is often divided into two subunits according to the direction of the tracts leading from it. The dorsal regions of the reticular formation send tracts that project to all regions of the cortex. Sensory information appears to be processed through this **ascending reticular system** (Figure 23.1). The **descending reticular system** is located in the ventral regions of the reticular formation, and tracts from this region join the efferent motor tracts entering the spinal cord (Figure 23.2).

Early attempts to establish the function of this network of cells indicated that this region of the CNS seemed to be as diffuse in activity as it is in structure. Cells seemed to respond to everything in general and to nothing in particular. Partly because of its location in a primitive portion of the CNS, investigators were not expecting the equivalent of "consciousness" or "attention." It turns out, however, that the reticular formation serves this function. Stimulation of the reticular region in a sleeping cat will awaken the animal. Stimulation while the animal is awake frequently results in an alertness-type

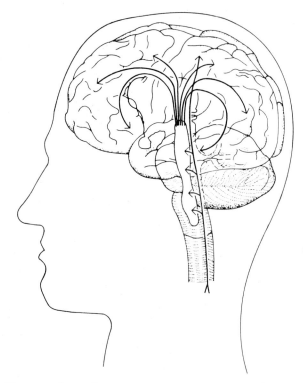

Figure 23.1 The ascending reticular system.

of response which might best be described as a "what was that?" response. Destruction of reticular formation areas often results in a lowering of the animal's alertness level ranging from lethargy to coma. On the basis of these data, the former structural descriptive name of the reticular formation has been replaced by the functional name "reticular activating system" (RAS). The functional unit known as the RAS includes structures that are not found within the morphological boundaries of the reticular formation. The activity of several thalamic nuclei indicate that they are intimately involved with RAS activity even though they are geographically separated.

The alerting or activating function of the RAS helps to explain the wide variety of information that is fed into this system. The sensory pathways conduct precise sensory information directly to the primary sensory area of the cortex. The feature detectors in the primary visual pathway to the occipital lobe include "lines," "angles," and other information necessary to organize and recognize the stimulus object. The visual information that branches to the RAS seems to involve features like "change," "movement," or "newness." The resulting activity of the ascending RAS appears to alert the visual cortex to attend to this new and potentially threatening environmental situation.

The descending RAS has direct access to the efferent fibers leading from the brain to the body. The function of these connections seems to be to

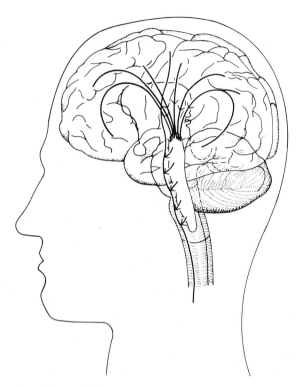

Figure 23.2 The descending reticular system.

control the level of muscular response. Stimulation of the RAS even affects the more peripheral synapses involved in the spinal reflexes. Reflex responses can be enhanced or inhibited by RAS activity. Thus, the alert animal is literally more responsive to all aspects of the environment.

The connections between the RAS and the higher CNS regions are again relatively diffuse. Fibers from the RAS appear to extend through the thalamus to all regions of the cortex. In addition, the RAS receives information from many cortical regions. Thus, cortical activity can trigger RAS activity. It is this mechanism that allows us to anticipate a potential danger even though the environment provides no alerting information.

The RAS represents an important exception to the usual model of "lower" and "higher" CNS structures. Most CNS models assume that the higher centers have superseded and/or taken over the functions of the more primitive CNS structures. The RAS, located in the brain stem, would qualify from its location as a primitive structure, yet the RAS determines the level of activity of the entire nervous system. EEG recordings show cortical activity changes similar to those observed in behavior. Stimulation of the RAS results in a typically "awake" EEG pattern, while lesions result in a "sleep" EEG pattern.

Intense stimuli, such as a loud sound, lead to a distinct alerting response. In addition to the obvious motor startle response, we find that an unexpected loud sound is followed by a period of enhanced mental alertness. Many stimuli have characteristics that trigger RAS activity. Neon signs, flashing lights, wailing sirens, and raucous alarm clocks are examples of stimuli that are specifically utilized because of their relatively direct access to the RAS.

We have all had the experience of attempting to fall asleep in an unusually noisy environment and suffered from an activated RAS. Stimulus intensity or special features, however, will not account for all of the known characteristics of the RAS. Some individuals can become accustomed to sleep under extremely noisy conditions. In fact, these people may find that it is impossible to fall asleep when they go camping because it is too quiet. The driver of an automobile may not attend to the noises of the car until there is a strange sound that makes him or her suddenly alert. Sometimes the strange "sound" is actually the silence caused by the failure of a normally noise-producing component. Although there are obvious stimuli that will activate the RAS, it also appears that the RAS is responsive to a missing stimulus. The alerting mechanism even involves a more complicated process than merely attending to a single stimulus, for the RAS is simultaneously processing all of the information coming in on all of the sensory channels. Since RAS activity is a prerequisite for the brain to be alert, it must be the RAS that "decides" which stimuli are important enough to activate the cortex for finer perceptual analysis. How can a structure located in the primitive brain stem accomplish this difficult discrimination task?

Although the product of RAS activity could lead to the conclusion that some highly sophisticated data analysis must be occurring, a single simple mechanism may explain both the location and function of the RAS. The sensory branches leading to the RAS give only a profile of the external stimulus situation. The actual perceptual processing occurs in the primary sensory areas of the cortex. If the cortical evaluation is uninteresting, there is little need for the cortex to continue to process the same stimuli. Any environmental change, on the other hand, should be immediately processed by the cortex. If the RAS could form a neurological "template" to match the profile of the incoming sensory information, then the CNS would not need to be alerted so long as the afferent sensory profile remained unchanged and matched the template. With a change in the environment, the sensory profile would change, the template would not match, and the cortex would be alerted to the mismatch. The new stimulus configuration could be evaluated by the cortex, action would be taken with RAS participation, or a new template would be created to match the current environment.

A template-matching model resolves most of the paradoxes associated with the RAS. It is a simple mechanism that is compatible with its brain stem location. In many ways, the alerting response is a sophisticated version of the spinal reflex mechanisms. Any change, either upward or downward, in stimulus intensity would result in a template mismatch; thus, the RAS is capable of responding to either loud sounds or silence. An RAS template explains why we are alerted by novelty and become bored or inattentive if the environment is unchanging. In addition, the RAS is responsive to the activity of the cortical regions that feed into it. Many of the symptoms of anxiety are due to the diffuse activity created by an active RAS that is responding to internal signals rather than environmental events.

The communication between the cortex and the RAS undoubtedly explains another unique feature of the RAS. Certain very specific but very subtle cues in the environment are highly meaningful to each individual. A person may awaken to the sounds made by a prowler in the house while sleeping through the sounds made by a family member. A student who must deal with frequent emergencies may be instantly awakened by the sound of a telephone while sleeping through the alarm clock set by a roommate. The roommate, on the other hand, may be unaware of the phone while the alarm clock is highly effective. The role occupied by each individual determines the salient cues in the environment. The RAS must be capable of being programmed to respond to certain highly unique stimulus cues.

A template model is compatible with the known characteristics of neuronal connections. By hypothesizing an equilibrium state of excitation and inhibition between the sensory input and the "template" neurons, RAS cells could show an immediate change in activity if the balance were altered. In many ways the RAS template is an extension of the feature detectors found in the sensory systems. The RAS is much more complicated in terms of input characteristics and is adjustable rather than prewired. Feature detectors, motor reflexes, and individual neurons are all essentially "go"–"no go" systems. That is, when the incoming information is "right," the system is active. When the incoming information is insufficient, the system does not respond. These systems are essentially "prewired" by genetic and/or environmental events and constitute an "automatic" response to the environment. The RAS extends this basic "go"–"no go" mechanism to include an adjustment to contemporary environmental conditions.

The name and function of the RAS emphasize the activating aspects of the system. Equally important is the ability to lower or reduce CNS activity level. The RAS provides a valuable integrative function for the entire CNS. The functioning of the CNS accounts for more than 20 percent of the body's total energy expenditure. During periods of physical rest and high mental activity, the CNS may be consuming more than half of the energy being expended by the body. The RAS undoubtedly contributes an energy "thermostat" by adjusting the activity level to match the demands of the environment.

Concomitant with this important ability to lower activity level, the RAS may be divided into two functionally separate units. The majority of the RAS structures are activating (excitatory) and are found in the anterior two thirds of the RAS. The posterior RAS structures are typically inhibitory and lower the responsiveness of the organism (Figure 23.3).

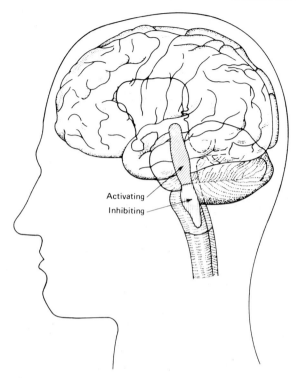

Figure 23.3   Activating and inhibiting sections of the reticular system.

SLEEP

The need to undergo periods of lowered activity is most obviously exemplified in the phenomenon of sleep. In some ways, the benefits of sleep periods are obvious. Both the accumulating fatigue that develops over prolonged sleepless periods and the well-rested feeling that results from sufficient sleep indicate the restorative qualities accomplished during a sleep period. Since sleep involves a substantially reduced physical activity level, the benefits could be exclusively muscular. Research indicates, however, that the muscles can recover from fatigue during periods of rest without the unconscious state of sleep. It appears that sleep episodes are primarily beneficial to the functioning of the CNS.

Research involving EEG records of brain activity, however, shows that the brain can hardly be considered quiescent during sleep periods. In other words, the restorative value is not accomplished through a simple rest phenomenon. Sleep seems to signal a special type of CNS activity.

Sleep research frequently involves the use of an EEG machine to monitor brain activity. Analysis of EEG patterns during sleep shows that there are several different stages or types of sleep according to the prevailing brain activity. A simplified two-way table establishes four levels of consciousness,

TABLE 23.1   Levels of Consciousness as Determined by EEG and Behavioral Criteria[a]

		EEG	
		Active	*Quiet*
	Awake	Alert	Drowsy
Behavior	*Asleep*	Deep (paradoxical) sleep	Light sleep

[a] Sleep cycles are typically clockwise in direction.

which provide a rough description of important stages in an underlying continuum (Table 23.1).

Behaviorally speaking, an individual may be classified as awake or asleep. The criterion for each is essentially responsiveness or unresponsiveness to the environment. The awake individual is aware of environmental events, while the sleeping individual is not.

In terms of EEG activity, the brain may be described as electrically active or quiet. The typical active brain wave pattern is fast and small. The quiet brain wave pattern is slow and large. Most prominent of these slower-frequency EEG waves is the alpha (so named because it was the first discovered), which is centered in the occipital lobes. The awake person with an active EEG pattern may be described as an alert person. Muscle tone is high, and the person attends to relatively small changes in the environment. The awake individual with a quiet EEG pattern is either relaxed or drowsy. Muscle tone is somewhat lower, and small stimuli may not be responded to, although the person is still aware of environmental events.

From the relaxed waking state, it is a relatively small step to the first sleep stage. **Light sleep** is typified by sleeping behavior accompanied by a quiet EEG pattern. Muscle tone is maintained, but responsiveness to environmental events is substantially lowered. Breathing and heart rates are slower than in the waking state. Although the individual is less responsive to the environment, it is relatively easy to awaken a person in the light sleep stage.

Deep sleep is characterized by sleeping behavior combined with an active EEG pattern (Figure 23.4). Because the EEG pattern is essentially that of an alert organism, this sleep stage is also known as **paradoxical sleep.** Muscle tone is essentially absent, and the breathing pattern changes from the long, slow breathing of light sleep to a faster, irregular rate. Although the loss of total muscle tone persists throughout paradoxical sleep, the later segment of the paradoxical sleep period is marked by considerable uncoordinated muscular activity in the form of small twitches. This muscular activity coincides with the occurrence of rapid eye movements (REM) behind the closed eyelids. For this reason, this stage of sleep is also called **REM sleep.**

Care should be taken in understanding the use of the terms "light sleep" and "deep sleep." In this text, the terms are keyed to behavioral characteristics.

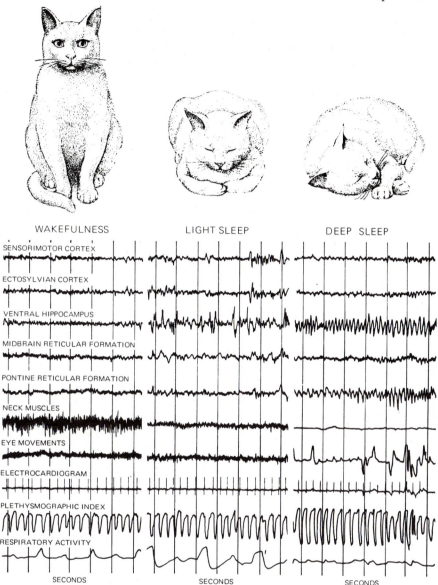

WAKEFULNESS   LIGHT SLEEP   DEEP SLEEP

SENSORIMOTOR CORTEX

ECTOSYLVIAN CORTEX

VENTRAL HIPPOCAMPUS

MIDBRAIN RETICULAR FORMATION

PONTINE RETICULAR FORMATION

NECK MUSCLES

EYE MOVEMENTS

ELECTROCARDIOGRAM

PLETHYSMOGRAPHIC INDEX

RESPIRATORY ACTIVITY

SECONDS   SECONDS   SECONDS

Figure 23.4 Physiological rhythms observed in the cat during different stages of consciousness. (Jouvet, 1967, p. 63)

Thus, deep sleep indicates the stage of minimum muscle tone and least responsiveness to environmental stimulation. If the EEG pattern is used as the criterion, the terms are reversed. This difference in usage can cause confusion when reading different authors' reports on sleep research.

Sleep research data indicate that the stages follow each other in a predictable order. The person moves from alert to relaxed to light sleep to deep sleep. If slumber continues, the person moves from the REM activity of deep sleep to a nearly awake state, and the cycle is then repeated. The transition from awake to deep sleep always traverses the light sleep stage, and the person often naturally awakens after deep sleep.

A number of sleep behaviors correlate with the characteristics of light and deep sleep. Snoring most commonly occurs during the heavy breathing pattern associated with light sleep. The light sleep stage is also the period of coordinated muscular activity. Thus, tossing and turning, as well as sleepwalking, are observed during the light sleep periods. Dreaming, on the other hand, appears to be associated with the REM activity of deep sleep. Individuals awakened during REM activity usually report a dream episode. There is some evidence to indicate that the eye movements are related to the visual display of the dream. Deep sleep is a time of high brain activity with minimum responsiveness to the environment. The brain seems to be generated from within rather than in response to environmental stimulation.

Experiments that deprive an animal of REM sleep indicate that there is a deep sleep "debt" which accrues during the deprivation. Animals (including human volunteers) that are awakened whenever REM activity occurs will exhibit an excess of REM sleep the following night. Cats deprived of REM sleep for several days show a correspondingly lengthy recovery period of increased REM sleep.

One function of the sleep period may be to reestablish a chemical balance in the CNS. The injection of chemicals that affect the enzymatic digestion of monoamines (neurotransmitters) can substantially alter the normal patterns of both light sleep and paradoxical sleep.

Recent evidence suggests that two systems found in the pons may serve as "sleep centers" (Figure 23.5). These systems are often considered part of the structures comprising the posterior inhibitory structures of the RAS, but there is reason to separate them into a unique "sleep system." The **Raphé** ("seam") **system** is composed of a scattered collection of nuclei along the ventral midline of the pons. Stimulation of the Raphé structures triggers the onset of light sleep. The Raphé structures are extraordinarily rich in the transmitter chemical serotonin.

Positioned like saddle bags astride the RAS, the locus coeruleus is a pair of nuclei located in the dorsal-lateral region of the pons. The **locus coeruleus** appears to be the major components of a deep sleep system. Stimulation of this region triggers deep sleep, while ablation prevents the occurrence of the deep sleep stage. The locus coeruleus is extremely rich in the transmitter noradrenalin.

The alternate occurrence of the two types of sleep in the normal individual seems to be the alternate predominant activity of these two sleep systems in the pons. Both appear to inhibit the ability of the RAS to awaken, but the serotonin from the Raphé system and the noradrenalin from the locus coeruleus have different effects on the CNS and the muscles. Since both of these transmitters are monoamines, and both the serotonergic and adrenergic

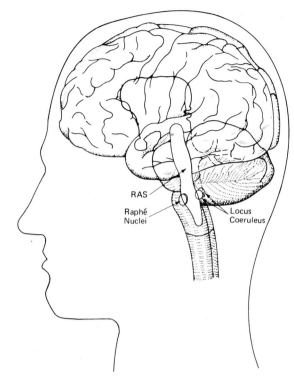

Figure 23.5 "Sleep centers" in the CNS.

neurons are probably fine-tuning mechanisms for the functioning of the CNS, it could well be that these substances become exhausted with prolonged waking activity. All animals show periodic episodes of light sleep, but deep sleep seems to be correlated with the amount of neocortex in the CNS.

BIOLOGICAL RHYTHMS

The stages of sleep show an interesting cyclical pattern throughout the sleep session. Although the human adult may sleep for an eight-hour period, the sleep alternates between light sleep and paradoxical sleep. About an hour and a half after falling asleep, the individual has gone from light sleep into a deep sleep and back to a light sleep stage. This cycle repeats itself through the rest of the night except that succeeding deep sleep stages are not as pronounced as the initial cycle. The individual may even spontaneously awaken emerging from the deep sleep phase, often to then doze and go into another sleep cycle.

This cycle of approximately an hour and a half is seen most obviously in a new born infant. A baby tends to spend much of its time asleep, separated by brief periods of wakefulness spaced approximately every hour and a half.

Eventually, these evenly spaced periods of sleep are entrained to the 24-hour cycle, so that the sleep periods are deeper and tend to merge together during the night; the cycles during the day may be observed only as fluctuations in activity level. Even adults show a remnant of the original hour and a half activity cycle of the infant.

The rhythmic nature of behavior has been largely ignored or considered primarily to be only a novel feature of some behaviors. Modern technology has led to the reliance on the alarm clock and other arbitrary constraints on the sleep pattern. If the alarm happens to sound early in a light sleep phase, the individual awakens relatively easily. If the alarm sounds during a deep sleep phase, the individual often experiences considerable difficulty in waking. Many people have reported the phenomenon of naturally awaking less than an hour prior to the alarm and seriously considering getting up. Instead, they doze into another cycle and then find the alarm (and the morning) a heavy burden. Since the early sleep cycles are the deepest sleep stages, perhaps the feeling we have on awakening is less related to the total number of hours we have slept than to the sleep phase we were in just prior to waking. Since individual sleep cycles differ slightly, the optimal total sleep period would have to be individually determined.

The hour and a half sleep cycle is only one example of a biological rhythm. The **circadian** (*circa* = "approximately"; *dies* = "day") **rhythm** approximates a 24-hour cycle. Experiments have shown that most organisms exhibit a circadian cycle of activity. Experiments conducted deep in caves or under highly controlled laboratory conditions show that these daily cycles are self-sustaining. Such "free-running" circadian rhythms typically deviate slightly from a precise 24-hour reference. By altering the constant conditions, for example, light level, the cycle may drift ahead or behind real time, but the circadian behavioral fluctuations do not disappear.

Longer rhythms are also shown to affect behavior, although the physiological mechanisms are not well understood. The estrous cycle in the female of most mammalian species is relatively constant, ranging from days to months in length. The periodic emotional swings of a manic-depressive psychotic represent another long-term cyclical fluctuation in behavior. Many behaviors vary with the season of the year. Some are undoubtedly triggered by environmental seasonal changes, but there is also reason to suggest a biological rhythm.

There has been considerable recent interest in the hypothesis that human behavior might be controlled by the simultaneous operation of several internal rhythms. As each of these cycles waxes and wanes, the capacities and potentials of the individual rise and fall. Although the data available at the present time place this theory closer to astrology than physiology, research into biological rhythm mechanisms is yielding some interesting information.

The circadian rhythm is the most thoroughly studied of the biological clock mechanisms. Although the free-running circadian rhythm only approximates the 24-hour day, this same device is remarkably accurate if provided a single temporal reference each day. Apparently, the "internal clock" is reset each day to coincide with the environmental day-night cycle. Experiments conducted in deep caves with artificially lengthened or shortened "days" indicate that the circadian "clock" has a certain degree of latitude (possibly up to 2 hours), but it is basically a 24-hour device.

Jet lag is the result of having to reset this internal clock. If a jet traveler traverses several time zones, it will take about three days to "get back in phase" with the local time of day. Difficulty in coordinating sleep, eating, or activity periods is typically experienced during the readjustment period.

The ability to judge the length of day requires a fairly accurate biological clock combined with sensory input telling the span of daylight. The visual system is not the channel for detecting the daylight, since blinded birds respond to the lengthening days in the spring with increased activity on the day migration usually occurs. The pineal body seems to be the daylight detector. Activity changes can be recorded from the pineal body when a light stimulus is used. In addition, removal of the pineal body seems to disrupt the normal circadian rhythm (Figure 23.6). In the case of the sexual receptivity of the mink, the normal activity of the pineal seems to suppress the release of the sexual hormones. Prolonged light stimulation inhibits the pineal body, which in turn releases the hormones, which results in sexual receptivity. The

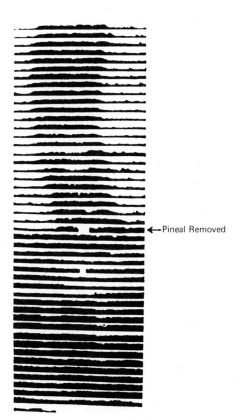

←Pineal Removed

Figure 23.6 Circadian rhythm in body temperature of the sparrow. Removal of the pineal body disrupts the internal clock. (Binkley, Kluth, & Menaker, 1972, p. 313)

location of the pineal body on the dorsal surface of the brain stem, almost literally in the middle of the CNS, seems an unlikely location for a photosensitive structure. There is speculation that the human pineal body may need supplementary light-level information from the visual system, since it is buried under much more opaque material than in the "lower" animals.

The circadian rhythm is probably responsible for several known behavioral phenomena. Hospitals are discovering that the efficiency of prescribed drugs may differ in the same patient depending on the time of day they are administered. Research has indicated that the body is maximally tolerant of alcohol during the late afternoon and evening. At the present time, it is not known whether this biological response resulted from, or resulted in, the timing of the traditional cocktail hour. Knowing about the cyclical responsiveness of the body also tells us how to maximize our liquor expenditures. Alcohol has the greatest impact from 3 to 5 A.M.

The internal biological clock serves as a reference for initiating behaviors based on the length of the day. Migratory birds begin their migrations according to the lengthening and shortening of daylight in the spring and fall. Most mammals breed only in the spring, which results in the young being born and developing during the warm summer months. The mechanism for this breeding season is that the lengthening day triggers the release of hormones in the female, and she becomes behaviorally receptive at a critical day length in the spring. Mink ranchers have discovered that these animals can be kept in a continuous breeding state year round by maintaining a 24-hour artificially lighted environment.

In order for a biological clock to keep accurate time, it must have an accurate reference frequency. A number of possible mechanisms could serve this basic time-keeping function. The constant temperature maintained in the mammalian body means that chemical reactions will progress at a constant rate. Thus, any number of chemical reactions could serve as a time constant. Some neurons in the CNS appear to maintain a constant firing rate independent of stimulation or motor activity. Neural circuits that literally form a loop of activity could also provide a constant repetitive time reference. The basic EEG rhythms of the resting brain could be expression of such timing circuits. Although many of the basic mechanisms are not yet known, biological rhythms are an important factor in the study of behavior.

AUTHOR'S COMMENTS   The RAS is the "accelerator pedal" of the nervous system. This structure adjusts the activity level of the nervous structures to match the environmental situation. Internally, such adjustments provide an efficient conservation and/or expenditure of energy resources. Externally, the resulting behavior increases the proportion of time the organism spends in a "friendly" environment.

Control of activity level apparently involves more than an improvement in environmental interaction. Sleep involves both a decrease in and an alternate type of CNS activity than that observed during waking behavior. Each different stage, or type, of sleep seems to contribute an important facet to the overall restorative effects of sleep.

A number of internal biological clocks appear to have an effect on an animal's behavior. The most thoroughly studied is the circadian rhythm, which approximates the 24-hour daily cycle. The internal clock mechanism seems to provide supplementary internal information to control the daily activities of the animal. Such internal timing mechanisms definitely slow down and speed up behavior, but it is not clear how this function is utilized or established.

Chapter

24

Motivation and Gratification

The hypothalamus is a complicated interconnected matrix of nuclei (Figure 24.1). Constituting the ventral portion of the top of the brain stem, the hypothalamus is a major relay center for efferent messages emanating from the cortex. Projection fibers from all regions of the cortex converge on hypothalamic nuclei. The rich interconnections with the paleocortical limbic structures cause many researchers to include the hypothalamus as an integral unit of the limbic system. The "master gland," the pituitary, hangs from a stalk extending from the ventral surface of the hypothalamus. CNS control of the endocrine system is accomplished through neural and chemical messages sent along the pituitary stalk.

In many ways, the hypothalamus is an "action center." Information from many sources converges on the nuclei in the hypothalamus. These nuclei cumulate and synthesize this information into coherent response programs. Each nucleus appears to have specialized into processing a special category of behavior. Stimulation (or ablation) of a specific nucleus often alters drive-reducing activities such as hunger, thirst, and sex. Other hypothalamic areas affect emotional tone, such as rage or passivity. In general, the hypothalamic nuclei seem to involve behaviors that provide an affective or gratificational quality for the organism. Activity of these nuclei usually creates a shift along the dimensions of "pleasure-pain," "good-bad," "positive-negative," and so on.

The hypothalamus is a complicated interconnected matrix of nuclei (Figure 24.1). Constituting the ventral portion of the top of the brain stem, the hypothalamus is a major relay center for efferent messages emanating from the cortex. Projection fibers from all regions of the cortex converge on hypothalamic nuclei. The rich interconnections with the paleocortical limbic structures cause many researchers to include the hypothalamus as an integral unit of the limbic system. The "master gland," the pituitary, hangs from a stalk extending from the ventral surface of the hypothalamus. CNS control of the endocrine system is accomplished through neural and chemical messages sent along the pituitary stalk.

    In many ways, the hypothalamus is an "action center." Information from many sources converges on the nuclei in the hypothalamus. These nuclei cumulate and synthesize this information into coherent response programs. Each nucleus appears to have specialized into processing a special category of behavior. Stimulation (or ablation) of a specific nucleus often alters drive-reducing activities such as hunger, thirst, and sex. Other hypothalamic areas affect emotional tone, such as rage or passivity. In general, the hypothalamic nuclei seem to involve behaviors that provide an affective or gratificational quality for the organism. Activity of these nuclei usually creates a shift along the dimensions of "pleasure-pain," "good-bad," "positive-negative," and so on.

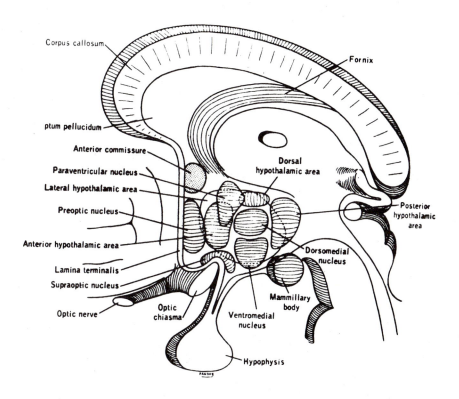

Figure 24.1 Three-dimensional reconstruction of the hypothalamus. (House & Pansky, 1960)

The ability to localize an affective quality into a specific hypothalamic nucleus has important pragmatic and theoretical consequences. Manipulation of the level of activity within a specific nucleus will directly alter the affective state of the animal. With an electrode placed in the appropriate location, it is possible electrically to "turn on" and "turn off" specific behaviors. This ability to directly manipulate a behavior such as eating leads to the logical description of the nucleus as a "hunger center."

CENTERS AND SYSTEMS

The term "hunger center" is simultaneously highly descriptive and highly misleading. Stimulation of a **hunger center** does trigger eating behavior. Such a center must be a focal point for information regarding the internal nutritional state as well as for sensory information regarding the availability of food. When the pattern of impinging activity reaches a certain level, the center becomes active, initiating food-seeking and/or eating behavior. This model for the operation of a hunger center is analogous to that for the operation of the feature detectors in the sensory system.

The misleading aspect of the term "hunger center" is that no nucleus has exclusive control over any single affective dimension. There are many different hunger centers, each with its own unique contribution to normal hunger behavior. Stimulation of some centers causes chewing and swallowing movements even though there is nothing to be consumed in the mouth. Other centers may precipitate eating behavior even though the behavior is directed to normally inedible objects. Stimulation of these regions may cause the animal to eat plastic or wood. If nothing more appropriate is available, the animal may gnaw on the metal bars of the cage, sometimes with disastrous impact on the teeth. Still other hunger centers will produce eating behavior only if real food is available. These centers are actually components of a more comprehensive "hunger system." Thus, the behavior resulting from the stimulation of a hunger center is probably the result of disrupting the delicate balance of many such centers within the system rather than of a simple triggering of programs stored in that nucleus. The collection of many centers into a system may be analogous to combining the information from many feature detectors into a parallel conduction network.

It is important to note that the hypothalamic affective systems do not wrest motor control from the cortex. The RAS could regulate the arousal and/or total reactivity of the ongoing behavior, but the actual sequence of motor messages leading to the muscles is determined by the motor cortex. The food-seeking behavior exhibited by a hungry animal simultaneously drives the animal toward the food and adjusts the animal to the presence of intervening environmental barriers. The general selection of a "goal" appears to be the result of the hypothalamic hunger system, while the choice of specific behaviors is a cortical function.

DRIVE SYSTEMS

The various centers constituting a system appear to be organized into a network of excitatory and inhibitory structures. Stimulation in an excitatory center produces the related activity. A similar stimulation delivered to an inhibitory nucleus will stop or suppress the activity. Thus, it is possible to cause a satiated animal to eat by stimulating a hunger center. Conversely, it is possible to stop the eating behavior of a hungry animal by delivering a stimulus to an inhibitory **satiety center.** Ablation of a satiety center may create an animal that literally cannot stop eating because the activating centers in the system are now unchecked in their activity.

As a general rule, nuclei located in the lateral and dorsal portions of the hypothalamus appear to function as drive-producing or motivating centers. Stimulation of these structures typically activates the animal. Nuclei found in the ventral and medial portions of the hypothalamus seem to contain a concentration of satiety or drive-reducing structures. This generalization also applies to the location and function of the Raphé nuclei and the locus coerulei in generating an "active" or "quiet" sleep EEG.

The general model to account for these gratificational systems uses a basic excitation-inhibition mechanism. In the case of a hunger system, the transducers that monitor blood sugar level, the quantity of food in the stomach, and other indicators of nutritional imbalance converge on centers in the lateral hypothalamus. Simultaneous activity of a sufficient number of these hunger-related cues results in activity in the nuclei. Activity in these excitatory nuclei results in the animal's searching for food in the environment and/or eating edible material available. When enough food has been consumed, receptors which indicate that blood sugar is adequate, the stomach is full, and so on, send information to a satiety center in the medial hypothalamus. The satiety centers connect to the hunger center by inhibitory synaptic connections. Thus, the behavior ceases through inhibition of the hunger center.

Similar phenomena may be observed with thirst centers and drinking behavior. The thirst-drive system appears to be organized much like the hunger system, including the general location of the drive and satiety centers. It is quite likely that the hunger and thirst systems are interrelated. Chemical stimulation of certain hypothalamic nuclei by injecting adrenergic drugs alters eating behavior, while injections of cholinergic drugs in the same nucleus alter drinking behavior.

The cues that control hunger or thirst behavior are subtle and complex. An experiment with dogs illustrates one detail of the thirst mechanism. If a dog is deprived of water for several hours and then given access to water, it will drink a certain quantity of water. The thirst system can monitor the amount of water needed and also measure the amount of water consumed.

A relatively minor surgical procedure involves interrupting the esophagus in the animal's throat. A fistula may be attached to each of the severed ends. Now anything the animal swallows goes only as far as the throat where it exits through the fistula. Nutrition can be introduced into the stomach through the second fistula.

A fistulated dog deprived of water the same length of time as an intact animal will begin drinking when water is made available. Surprisingly, the animal will drink only the same quantity as the intact dog, even though no water reaches the stomach. Apparently, some type of metering system in the mouth and/or throat measures the quantity of water being consumed. Thus, the shut-off mechanism is not the amount of water in the stomach.

If we offered the same two animals another opportunity to drink a few minutes after the first, the intact animal would drink little, if at all. The fistulated animal, on the other hand, would drink the same quantity taken the first time. Despite the presence of the "mouth meter," the fistulated animal still responds to a need for water. If the appropriate quantity of water is injected into the stomach through the other fistula, the animal becomes un-interested in voluntarily drinking available water. If adequate water is periodically introduced through the fistula to the stomach, the dog may take only an occasional brief drink, probably to alleviate mouth dryness.

The ability to manipulate basic drive behavior by altering the activity of hypothalamic centers provides a powerful tool to the physiological psy-chologist. It localizes a specific component of behavior to certain neurological structures. This means that the many structures of the nervous system cooperate to provide the multiple components of behavior. Even without fully understanding the contributing neuronal network, it is possible to utilize the known centers to manipulate behavior. Electrode technology is advanced to the point that integrated circuits less than the size of a small coin may incorporate a radio-controlled stimulator which can deliver a current through an electrode placed in the center. With such a device, it is possible to manipu-late the animal by electronic remote control. Eating, drinking, sexual behavior, or abstinence can be imposed on the animal at the whim of the person at the radio controls. Essentially, one can create a rudimentary robot which is al-ready programmed for coordinated movement.

Research indicates that corresponding nuclei in animals and humans ac-complish similar functions. Knowledge of the location and function of the various CNS centers allows us to consider psychological "plastic surgery." Obesity could be controlled by controlled lesions in hunger centers. Of par-ticular clinical interest is the fact that there are also rage centers and passivity centers. Results somewhat akin to those obtained by prefrontal lobotomies might be accomplished with substantially less tissue destruction.

PLEASURE CENTERS

The inhibitory centers in any drive system provide the equivalent of a reward or reinforcement. That is, activity in these structures moves the ani-mal toward the pleasant end of the affective scale. Under most circumstances, such a center in the hunger system would be activated by the afferent activity accompanying the consumption of food. By placing an electrode in such a center, it would be possible to activate the center directly (Figure 24.2). Thus, these nuclei can be used as a generalized reward or reinforcer in a typical learning situation. Animals will work to deliver an electric stimulus to these centers. Because of the reinforcing properties, these structures are described as pleasure centers.

The discovery of nuclei in the CNS that provide pleasure to the animal led to a flurry of speculation and research. It was believed initially that the drive mechanism was the equivalent of neurological activity and that drive reduction occurred with neurological quiescence. The fact that an animal would voluntarily introduce an electrical stimulus to its own brain did not fit the hypothesis.

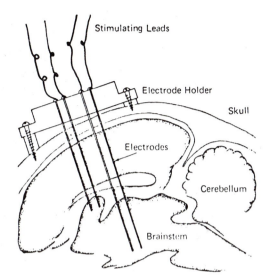

Figure 24.2 An electrode holder screwed to the skull, which allows electrical stimulation of brain structures. (Hess, Koella, & Akert, 1953, p. 78; via Milner, 1970, p. 45)

The mechanism of inhibition in the nervous system provides a plausible explanation for the action of the pleasure centers. Increased activity of these inhibitory centers results in decreased activity in the excitatory portion of the system. Evidence supports this interpretation of the satiety centers. Some of the pleasure centers seem to act precisely like satiety centers. In the case of the hunger system, the stimulation might not act as a reward unless the organism were hungry. Other pleasure center implants appear to be rewarding, no matter what the drive condition of the animal. Animals have been known to starve in the presence of food because they will not leave the lever that activates the electrical stimulus long enough to eat. Rather than a simple excitation-inhibition process, the gratificational systems seem to be a balanced network of nuclei. Activity of some nuclei creates a drive state, or motivated state, while activity of the other nuclei produces reduction of drive, satiation, or pleasure. This balanced system is apparently similar to the mutual interaction between the RAS and the sleep centers.

Pleasure centers are defined by strictly objective criteria. The usual paradigm is to implant the tip of a stimulating electrode in the target area and then allow the animal to control the stimulator in some fashion. If the animal does work in order to deliver a stimulus, the stimulated region is a pleasure center. A punishment center would be a region that resulted in avoidance behavior if the animal were to have control over the delivery system.

Systematic placement of electrodes throughout the entire CNS shows that pleasure centers appear to be concentrated in the **medial forebrain bundle (MFB)** (Figure 24.3). The MFB is a major tract interconnecting the hypothalamus and the higher limbic system structures. Other pleasure areas are found scattered in the brain stem and in the limbic structures. No portion of the neocortex has been found to provide a pleasure center-type of response when stimulated.

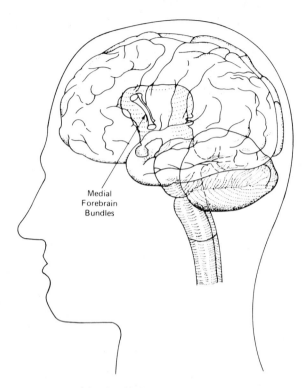

Medial
Forebrain
Bundles

Figure 24.3   Pleasure centers in the CNS.

Pleasure centers appear to outnumber punishment centers by a sub-stantial margin. Stimulation in the MFB probably involves the simultaneous activation of a number of widely scattered pleasure centers. The MFB inter-connects the nuclei of the hypothalamus with the limbic system with both afferent and efferent fibers. Thus, stimulation will be conducted through the activated tracts to a number of widely scattered nuclei. Many MFB pleasure electrodes also stimulate motivational components which assist in maintaining a high rate of responding. Thus, the term "pleasure centers" may describe the fortuitous placement of the electrode to produce a reinforcing pattern of electrical activity throughout the brain.

THE LIMBIC SYSTEM

The limbic system consists of the paleocortical and mesocortical structures in the CNS. Geographically, the limbic system structures surround the brain stem and are in turn enveloped by the neocortical hemispheres. Perhaps a geographical coincidence, the limbic structures essentially line the chambers of the lateral ventricles. The limbic system consists of four structures—the septal area, the amygdala, the hippocampus, and the cingulate cortex (Figure 24.4).

The septal area and the amygdala appear to be major communication

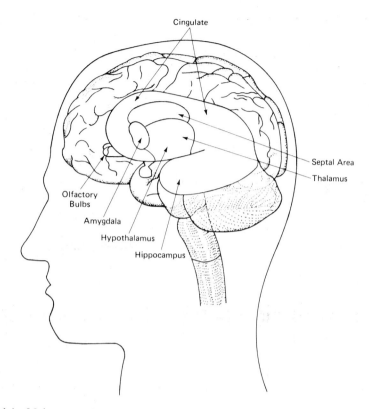

Figure 24.4   Major components of the limbic system.

centers, and together are described as the **internal capsule** (see Figure 4.7). The MFB provides substantial afferent and efferent communication with the brain stem structures, particularly the thalamus and hypothalamus. The extensive intercommunication between the thalamus and hypothalamus and the known limbic system structures leads some people to include these diencephalic structures as functional components of the limbic system. The internal capsule also communicates directly with the overlying neocortical hemispheres through an impressive group of radiating projection fibers. The major communication tracts from the hippocampus and cingulate lead into the internal capsule.

The hippocampus and cingulate structures are made up of both paleocortical and mesocortical material. The substantial amount of mesocortex explains why these structures are sometimes called the hippocampal gyrus and the cingulate gyrus. Because of the obvious cortical nature of these limbic system structures, the limbic system is generally assumed to be responsible for relatively complicated behaviors.

The complexity of the limbic system is probably not yet fully appreciated. In addition to the major tracts converging on the internal capsule, several other tracts interconnect components of the limbic system structures. The limbic system is also traversed by major tracts providing information to the neocortical hemispheres. There is some evidence now that these tracts do not simply carry information through the limbic system structures, but some of the fibers deliver information into limbic structures. Despite the complications, research into limbic functions is providing some exciting and provocative information regarding the operation of this primitive cortical system.

MacLean (1958) suggested that the internal capsule could be divided into two basic survival mechanisms. The amygdala processes the information and behavior involved with survival of the individual, while the septal area is the center for behaviors that assure the survival of the species. Swallowing, chewing, drinking, eating, seeking, self-protection, fighting, freezing, fleeing, territoriality, and other self-preservation behaviors are affected by activity of the amygdala. Courtship, sexual behavior, grooming, care and protection of progeny, and other acts conducive to survival of the species are assigned to the septal system. Since many of these behaviors overlap, it seems obvious that there is considerable interaction between these two structures in the limbic system.

Speculation and research into the functions of the hippocampus and cingulate are more enigmatic. An initial problem is that they are identified as structures primarily on the basis of anatomical characteristics. Probably each structure has a number of functional subareas, each serving its own unique function. This is certainly the case with the neocortex, and it seems logical that the primitive cortical structures would be similarly organized. The overriding neocortex provides an additional problem for discerning limbic functions, since many limbic functions are concealed by neocortical activity.

The hippocampus and cingulate are essentially the equivalent of lobes of a primitive cortex, but most research effort has been concentrated on the functions of the hippocampus. Lesions of the hippocampus provide a number of effects, but one seems predominant in importance. Hippocampal-lesioned animals lose the ability to learn new tasks. Tasks learned prior to the lesion are unaffected, but new material cannot be acquired. Two possible mechanisms have been suggested to explain this effect. The hippocampus might be the site of the short-term memory. Basically, new material must be temporarily stored while it is being permanently recorded by the cortex. If the material cannot be put in temporary storage, there is no opportunity to transfer the information to the permanent circuits. The second hypothesis suggests that the hippocampus simply recognizes a new, or novel, situation. If the situation is one that has already been encountered, existing circuitry should adequately deal with the situation. If, on the other hand, the situation is one never before encountered, the learning machinery should be engaged in order to establish an appropriate response. The hippocampus may recognize novelty and activate the learning mechanism. There are cells in the hippocampus that seem to serve as novelty detectors.

Disruption of limbic structures in general seems to alter the animal's "contact with reality." The inability to learn a new response is one example. Monkeys with limbic lesions may repeatedly burn themselves exploring a lighted match. This could be strictly due to the learning deficit; however, the animals act as though they also cannot appreciate the meaning of pain. The **Kluver-Bucy syndrome** is noted after substantial lesions to the temporal lobes, which include lesioning the limbic system, particularly the amygdala. Animals with such lesions typically demonstrate a wide range of inappropriate behaviors. They attempt to eat inedible material, attempt to copulate with inanimate objects, fail to avoid injurious stimuli, lose their normal fear of man, in the case of wild animals, and even fail to respond to a hissing snake. This latter stimulus seems to be a universal fear-producing stimulus in normal animals, even in those that have never before seen a snake.

The behaviors ascribed to the limbic system have two important characteristics. First, the behaviors are complicated and goal oriented in order to accomplish a specific survival function. Probably the drive centers in the hypothalamus are components of this limbic circuitry. A second characteristic of limbic activity is that there is a distinct affective quality to the behaviors. Many of the survival traits have distinct emotional qualities, and some of the behaviors are best described in terms of the emotional content. "Fear," "rage," "terror" are terms that are less descriptive of the behavior than of the associated feelings.

The behaviors attributed to limbic activity range from digestive processes to basic learning skills. Most of the survival skills, however, fall within a pattern of behaviors unique to a particular species. The choice among "fight, freeze, or flight" is largely dependent on the type of animal making this choice. Similarly, courtship, copulation, and care of offspring must incorporate species-unique situations. The chances are very high that the limbic system is the neurological substrate for these species-specific behaviors.

AUTHOR'S COMMENTS   The limbic system, including the thalamus and hypothalamus, is the "emotional center" of the CNS. It is also called the survival system because of the close relation between survival responses and affective tone. Life-threatening situations are an obvious case of the close association between emotions and life preservation. The food-seeking activity of a hungry animal is an example of affective behavior that also enhances the organism's survival chances. This motivational-gratificational-emotional complex may be seen to center around the hedonistic behavior that assures the survival of the individual.

Animals are also capable of altruistic behavior, sometimes to the potential detriment of the individual. Usually when this occurs, the animal is behaving in a way that enhances the survival potential of the species. Altruism and hedonism need not always be in opposition, as evidenced by sexual behavior.

The limbic system controls the various survival-emotional behaviors. Many of these behaviors are complicated, multifaceted, and elaborately sequential. At the same time, the behaviors are relatively reliable and responsive to environmental stimuli. If the word were socially acceptable in psychology, many of these behaviors might be called "instinctive."

25

Emotion

Emotional behavior involves much more than limbic system activity. In order to meet the challenges of a life-threatening situation, the organism should be able to mobilize the entire body to meet the threat. The bodily response associated with emotional experience has been known for a long time. The descriptive term to "feel" an emotion is largely a statement of the bodily feedback from the various systems that have suddenly altered their activity. The cardiovascular system, the respiratory system, the digestive system, the endocrine system, and the muscular system all respond with measurable changes to an emotion-producing situation. To accomplish the coordinated response of the entire body, a special distributional system of peripheral nerve fibers communicates emotionally related information throughout the body. In many ways, this special system is an extension of the limbic system throughout the body.

THE AUTONOMIC NERVOUS SYSTEM

As described in Chapter 5, the autonomic nervous system (ANS) is a distributional system of peripheral fibers, primarily carrying information from the CNS to most of the major organs throughout the body. The activity of the ANS appears to be largely automatic (thus, the name) in that we are usually unaware of its operation. Although the ANS is made up of many different efferent pathways, each leading to a different organ, the ANS appears to respond as a unitary whole, with the individual pathways assuring that each of the target organs receives the message.

The ANS is divided into two subcomponent systems—the sympathetic and the parasympathetic nervous systems (see Figure 5.11). The total ANS can be called a "survival system," with the two components each contributing a unique aspect of the total survival function. The two components of the ANS are reciprocally active, which means they are mutually inhibitory, much like many other systems encountered thus far. The sympathetic and parasympathetic branches of the ANS each extend fibers to the major organs of the body. The fibers extending to the same organ originate from different portions of the CNS and take different peripheral routes to arrive at the target organ. The neurons associated with each component system differ in reliable ways, apparently consonant with their differing functions. The combination of the sympathetic and parasympathetic activity provides a highly adaptive mechanism in the survival of the individual. The parasympathetic system accomplishes long-term survival functions for the organism by storing vital supplies and keeping the body machinery in good repair. The sympathetic system, on the other hand, totally reverses the priorities if a situation is encountered that threatens to shorten the life of the organism. In an emergency, available resources are mobilized to deal with the imminent threat. It is as if the parasympathetic system were involved with the well-being of the organism tomorrow, while the sympathetic system is involved with being sure there is a tomorrow for the organism.

The parasympathetic system controls the digestive process, adjusts respiration for most efficient oxygen and carbon dioxide transport, monitors heart rate for optimal performance, distributes the blood flow among the CNS, the muscles, and internal organs, supervises the collection and disposal of waste by-products, and so on. Parasympathetic activity monitors and directs the efficient utilization, production, and storage of materials needed by the organism. The parasympathetic system maintains the ongoing activity of the organism for optimal efficiency, assists in maintenance and repair activities of injured or overused tissue, and provides for the storage of potentially useful material not immediately needed.

Parasympathetic fibers extend from the CNS through the cranial nerves on the sacral portion of the spinal cord. From this location, at each end of the CNS, the parasympathetic neurons extend to the major internal organs in the body. Each pathway consists of two neurons. The synaptic junction is located in a ganglion near the target organ. The long preganglionic fiber is large and heavily myelinated, while the postganglionic neuron is short and unmyelinated. The synaptic chemical for the parasympathetic fibers is acetylcholine. This combination most resembles the fast-conducting, fine-coordination pathways of the voluntary muscle system. The fine adjustments necessary to maintain the many homeostatic balances in the organism probably require precise control circuits.

The sympathetic nervous system, on the other hand, appears to be the functional antithesis of the parasympathetic system. Sympathetic activity stops the ongoing homeostatic process and mobilizes the body to meet an emergency situation. The physiological symptoms of fear illustrate many of these effects. The dry mouth, "butterflies in the stomach," and frequent need to urinate or defecate are all indicative of the disruption of the normal digestive processes. Heart rate increases, and the contraction of each beat becomes stronger, with the result that there is an enhanced blood flow throughout the body. Simultaneously, peripheral capillaries contract, resulting in three adaptive functions. The skin becomes pale (which also reduces bleeding from surface injuries), the air passage linings shrink (enhancing airflow into the lungs), and the displaced blood volume is diverted to the voluntary muscles and the CNS. Sympathetic activity also alters the sensory channels. Stimulation of the muscles in the iris of the eye to dilate the pupils and the enhanced air flow through the nasal passages both increase the level of available stimulation. In addition, hormones are released into the bloodstream that enhance the metabolic rate and total capacity of cells throughout the body, particularly neurons and muscles. In the case of the striped muscles, the cells are more responsive to innervation and respond with stronger force, and the limiting circuitry from the Golgi organs in the tendons is partially disabled. This combination allows a muscular response that is beyond the "limits" established in nonemergency situations.

Sympathetic nerve fibers extend from the thoracic and lumbar portions of the spinal cord. Although connecting at different parts of the CNS, the sympathetic nervous system extends to most of the same organs as the parasympathetic fibers. The myelinated fibers form a synaptic junction almost immediately after leaving the spinal cord. Lying on each side of the spinal cord are two long chains of spinal ganglia which include the sympathetic synaptic junctions. The small unmyelinated postganglionic fibers then conduct the information to the target organ. The synaptic connections in the spinal ganglia are relatively diffuse when compared with the peripheral ganglia of the parasympathetic system. One indicator of the lowered precision is the fact that there is a much higher ratio of postganglionic to preganglionic neurons in the parasympathetic system. The preganglionic neurons in the sympathetic system are cholinergic, while the postganglionic cells are adrenergic (activated by epinephrine and norepinephrine). The type of neuron, choice of transmitter chemical, and general organization suggest that the sympathetic nervous system is designed for a "mass action" type of control as opposed to precise adjustment.

One important internal organ is innervated by the sympathetic nervous system but not the parasympathetic. The adrenal glands are stimulated to release their hormones only during sympathetic activity. The adrenal glands produce two important hormones, adrenaline and noradrenaline (also known as epinephrine and norepinephrine). The norepinephrine released by the adrenal glands is exactly the same as the synaptic transmitter chemical produced by the adrenergic neurons. Thus, activity of the sympathetic nervous system floods the bloodstream with the transmitter chemical for adrenergic neuronal circuits. This sudden flood of norepinephrine undoubtedly alters the activity of certain CNS circuits.

Adrenaline may be injected to stimulate directly the muscles of a failing heart. The increased emergency responsiveness of the muscles is largely due to the released adrenaline. Individuals under extreme emotion, such as in a disaster situation, have been known to accomplish physical feats that would be impossible under normal circumstances. It is interesting to note that simultaneously certain higher intellectual functions seem to be less efficient. One example of this is the failure to analyze a task as being physically impossible, but just doing it. After the crisis, the individual often cannot remember the precise details involved.

The reciprocal activity of the sympathetic and parasympathetic systems is frequently observed after the emergency is over. After a period of intense sympathetic activity, there is frequently a **parasympathetic rebound.** This period of behavioral hyporesponsiveness may be called the "between semester blues," "promotion shock," or "postpartum depression," depending on the precipitating situation. Whatever the label, it probably indicates a situation where the parasympathetic system must reestablish some of the resources expended by the sympathetic activity during the emergency.

PHYSIOLOGICAL RESPONSES

The activity of the ANS is directed at the control of many organs distributed throughout the body. Under calm conditions, the parasympathetic system provides minute adjustments in the activity of many different organs as it maintains an optimal homeostatic state. This activity is expressed in many different ways, depending on the present state of the individual. Hunger, thirst, and other basic drives may occur sequentially or simultaneously. Similarly, the activity of each organ may require individual fine adjustments throughout the day.

One example of the fine-tuning capacity of the parasympathetic system is the occurrence of **specific hungers.** Animals deprived of a specific vitamin or mineral will learn to select the food containing the missing chemical when allowed to feed from a "cafeteria" of several foods. Human children, if allowed a cafeteria-feeding situation, will eventually voluntarily select spinach if spinach is the only available source of iron. Interestingly, the child is still selecting food that tastes best, since spinach begins to taste good if it contains a needed substance.

The taste preference mechanism can be misled, however. For example, artificial sweeteners like saccharine and sodium cyclamate may be selected by animals that require the nutrition available in sugar.

Taste preferences can be acquired, so the homeostatic mechanism is not completely innate. Animals in a cafeteria-feeding situation will learn to prefer an artificial flavor if it is associated with a needed dietary substance (normally tasteless). Later, if again deprived of the substance, the animal will pick the same flavor, although the substance is no longer present.

The Garcia effect illustrates a similar example. Predaters (coyotes) that eat meat (sheep) laced with an emetic poison will stop preying on that specific prey. Apparently, the nausea response transfers to the food that "caused" it. Such one-trial taste aversion has obvious survival value but also demonstrates a remarkable degree of adaptability for a supposedly automatic system.

This orchestration of homeostatic activity is cancelled by the activity of the sympathetic system in response to an emergency situation. The simultaneous shift in activity of many internal organs is detectable by the individual as a true "feeling" component of the emotional response. Because the massive physiological change produced by the sympathetic system is so obvious, it is this activity that has received the most attention in the physiological study of emotion.

The **lie detector** (or **polygraph**) is basically a machine that can measure the bodily responses concomitant with sympathetic activity. The individual who is lying usually exhibits an accompanying emotional response. This emotional response is transmitted through sympathetic activity to the organs of the body and can be measured in the form of changes in breathing and pulse rates, blood pressure, and electrical resistance of the skin.

The psychological experience of a strong emotion, such as fear or anger, is obviously correlated with sympathetic physiological changes. This relation leads to the rather interesting question of which leads to which. Around the turn of the century, two distinct theories emerged. The Cannon-Bard theory states that the psychological response occurs and then activates the sympathetic system for the physiological response. The mechanism for this theory might be the activity of the "fear" or "rage" centers in the limbic system. The James-Lange theory states that the physiological response occurs first, and the emotion is actually the cognitive processing of the physiological changes. A common example is the experience of an emergency situation in an automobile. We may skillfully avert the accident only to find that we must pull over to the side of the road until the delayed fear response subsides.

Increased knowledge about the CNS and especially the limbic system suggests that both are components in a closely interrelated emergency system. Injecting adrenaline into the bloodstream of human volunteers produces many of the physiological symptoms of a sympathetic response (heart pounding, sweaty palms, and so on). Subjects who experience this bodily response without knowing it is due to the injection report experiencing an emotional state. The actual emotion experienced, however, is usually modeled on the behavior of others in the same situation. Subjects reported euphoria or anger consonant with the model provided by another "subject" (who was actually an actor for the experiment). Thus, the internal physiological state is capable of triggering an emotional response, but external cues are important in interpreting the state. Adrenaline-injected subjects who were forewarned that there might be physiological symptoms experienced the same bodily responses but correctly attributed them to the injection and experienced no affective overtones.

Individuals who do not show "normal" physiological activity or who are deprived of sensory feedback regarding the physiological response report feeling definite emotions. Thus, it seems that neither activity is a necessary condition, but both probably facilitate and supplement one another as components of a total emergency response.

The adrenal glands secrete two different compounds with stimulation by sympathetic activity. Both epinephrine and norepinephrine are released into the bloodstream. The mass action response of the sympathetic system seems to include the capacity to release these two substances differentially. According to the preponderant substances, the emotional reaction is subtly different.

Epinephrine and norepinephrine are sufficiently similar in chemical properties to have a largely overlapping effect on most organs. Norepinephrine increases blood flow and releases glucose into the bloodstream. This activity seems to prepare the organism for a "fight or flight" activity. Epinephrine generally contracts blood vessels providing the valuable function of minimizing bleeding in case of injury.

Research indicates that norepinephrine is released into the bloodstream when a situation is ambiguous, but an immediate physical response might be necessary, either fight or flight. If the situation is unambiguous, however, and there is no escaping the threatening stimulus, epinephrine is released. Thus, the sympathetic response consists of a two-phased physiological reaction. When a potential emergency is encountered, the body is mobilized for an efficient physical response. If the response does not alleviate the threat, the system is adjusted to minimize or repair the damage.

The psychological emotion that is experienced with each of these physiological states is subject to considerable interpretation by the cortex, but seems to fall into the general categories of "anger" or "fear." The behavior typically observed with each of these emotions can be summarized as outwardly directed activity as opposed to withdrawal. Research which exposes a person to a fear- or anger-provoking situation shows that the anger situation produces a noradrenaline type of physiological response, while fear (being trapped in a life-threatening situation) produces an adrenaline type of physiological response.

The withdrawal-attack dichotomy can be applied to many of the psychotic syndromes, as well as to the behavior to be expected from certain wild animals. The data indicate that the relative level of epinephrine and norepinephrine found in the bloodstream matches the behavior pattern.

GENERAL ADAPTATION SYNDROME

Hans Selye (1956) coined the term **general adaptation syndrome (GAS)** to describe the universal features of the bodily response to stress. Selye, while in medical school, noted that it was possible (and necessary) for doctors to learn the unique symptoms of the various diseases, but he also noted that there was little difficulty in determining that a patient was not feeling well. This universal "not well" response of the body represents a general bodily response to illness. The GAS can be triggered by physical stress, such as cold, noise, or lack of sleep; but the same GAS response will occur with psychological stress (such as the threat of a physical stress) without the actual physical trauma. In other words, the GAS appears to be the universal response to a stressful situation.

The GAS occurs in four distinct stages (Figure 25.1). The first stage is the **alarm** or **shock stage.** The alarm stage is when the organism first recognizes the stress and initiates a response to deal with it. This initial response is immediate but nonspecific. The system is alerted so that an appropriate response can follow. This stage probably involves the activity of the RAS as well as the release of nonrepinephrine by the sympathetic system.

The second stage of the GAS is the **adjustment** or **countershock stage** when the nature of the stress is evaluated and appropriate countermeasures are initiated. The adjustment stage involves going from a generalized alert to specific action. If the "fight or flight" mechanism effectively terminates the threat, the emergency is ended. If the threat is inescapable, then epinephrine is released, which prepares for impending injury.

If the stress is prolonged, the organism then enters the **resistance stage.** The adrenal glands appear to be instrumental in this prolonged stage. The adrenal glands are actually two different endocrine glands. The medulla ("middle") secretes epinephrine and norepinephrine in response to sympa-

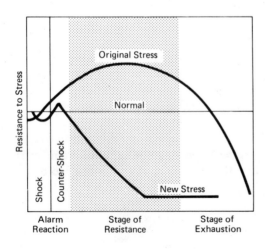

Figure 25.1 The general adaptation syndrome. Graph of the sequence of bodily responses to stress. (Selye, 1950; via Gray, 1971)

thetic nervous activity. The cortex ("shell") secretes a number of hormones that control life-sustaining activities usually ascribed to the parasympathetic system. These hormones (corticosteroids) are indirectly controlled by the pituitary gland. The pituitary releases adrenocorticotrophic hormone (ACTH) into the bloodstream, which then triggers the release of the hormones by the adrenal cortex.

In the GAS sequence, the epinephrine released into the bloodstream by the adrenal glands triggers the release of ACTH by the pituitary, which in turn stimulates the release of the corticosteroids by the adrenal cortex. The ACTH apparently enhances the normal life-sustaining and repair capacities of the organism. If the GAS is a response to a real stress, such as disease or injury, the sequence is highly adaptive to sustain and repair the organism. If the stress is prolonged, the sustained resistance stage keeps the life-sustaining systems functioning at an enhanced level.

The enhanced activity during the resistance stage may involve the utilization of vital materials faster than they can be produced by the body. If the stress is prolonged, the supply of vital materials is finally exhausted, and the organism enters the **exhaustion stage** of the GAS. The adaptation response can no longer be sustained, and the animal will show symptoms of collapse, frequently by dying.

The sequence of the internal physiological responses in the GAS parallels that of the behavioral adjustments made by an animal to a new external threat. The animal first becomes aware of the threat (alarm) and responds to the threat in some way (adjustment); if that response fails, the animal tries to learn an appropirate response that is effective (resistance), but finally succumbs (exhaustion) if no response is developed.

If the stress is terminated prior to the exhaustion stage of the GAS, the organism will survive and reestablish an equilibrium state. In addition, during the resistance stage, the organism is developing an enhanced ability to cope with that particular stress. Thus, if the stress is successfully met, the organism will be better equipped to deal with that same stress in the future. Selye first proposed the GAS to explain the bodily response to disease or infection. The development of the immunization response through contracting the disease or being inoculated with a facsimile of the disease is an example of the modification that is accomplished during the stage of resistance. Learning a new behavior to cope with a novel environment is a similar adaptive device.

PSYCHOSOMATIC ILLNESSES

Several physical symptoms are related to the occurrence of psychological stress. Ulcers, high blood pressure, migraine headaches, blood serum cholesterol, asthma, certain skin problems, and fainting are just a few of the known examples. Many of these symptoms are directly attributable to the exhaustion of certain components of the emergency system. Selye (1956) found that specific failures can be produced by programming the length, type, and severity of the stress that causes the GAS.

The GAS seems to be primarily a physical emergency system. Many of the components are highly appropriate to injurious incidents or disease. The GAS is also triggered by psychological stress. For example, the cholesterol level in the blood is substantially elevated in persons placed in a cold room. The same rise in cholesterol level is seen in subjects who are kept warm but are required to watch the cold-stressed subjects—thinking their turn will be next.

Modern society (and/or the development of the cortex in humans) creates many opportunities for prolonged psychological stress to occur. For this reason, the GAS may be kept in a relatively constant stage of resistance. If some of the bodily organs cannot sustain the prolonged elevated activity, they may fail, and a psychosomatic "disease" is the result. There is also reason to believe that overly frequent mobilization of the GAS is harmful, leading to such conditions as ulcers.

It has been shown that monkeys that can avoid a painful shock by pressing a lever will develop ulcers. Monkeys that are shown the same warning light and are connected to the same shock-delivery circuit but have no lever to press do not develop ulcers. The only difference is that the "executive" monkeys have a "choice" as to whether they get the shock, while the "employees" have no such choice. There is a marked similarity in this laboratory situation and the human environment known to produce ulcers. Since ulceration results from excessive stomach acids, measures have been made as to when the acidity occurs. Surprisingly, there is not an excess of acid during the time the monkey is avoiding the shock. The acidity occurs during the hour or so after the monkey is removed from the apparatus. This parasympathetic rebound (possibly enhanced by high ACTH levels) appears to be the destructive element.

AUTHOR'S   The autonomic nervous system provides an elaborate ex-
COMMENTS   tension of the survival functions of the limbic system. The total mobilization of the body to meet the life-threatening situation is highly adaptive so long as the threat can be met with a physical response. One price of higher cortical functioning may be that this elaborate emergency response may also be triggered by psychological stimuli without the physical threat. Psychosomatic disorders are probably an expression of this miscued emergency reaction.

Chapter

26

Learning

The capacity to learn represents a significant improvement over the survival mechanisms available to the individual animal. The behavioral capacities discussed thus far are primarily the result of many generations of Darwinian selection for behavior patterns that have survival value. These "preprogrammed" behaviors, appropriate to specific environmental conditions, provide the animal with a storehouse of adaptive responses to frequently encountered situations by the species. A major difficulty with preprogrammed behaviors is that a peculiar environmental situation encountered by an individual member of the species may make the preprogrammed behavior inappropriate. For example, the "food washing reflex" of the raccoon works well with natural foods, but creates problems with cookies or sugar cubes.

Learning allows the individual animal to fabricate responses that are appropriate to the unique environment it occupies. The preprogrammed behaviors provide broad survival capacities, and learning can modify these behaviors to be especially appropriate for each individual situation. A raccoon will learn not to wash certain foods which degrade in water. In addition, the learning capacity equips the individual with the ability to completely adjust to environments never before encountered.

The usual definition of "learning" requires a relatively permanent change in behavior that occurs by nondestructive means through interaction with the environment. There are many adjustment mechanisms, however, that are frequently excluded from the category because they do not meet one or more of the criteria. The material in this chapter encompasses a broad range of environmental adjustments, some of which count as "learning" only in the most general use of the term.

The phenomena presented here span a time scale ranging from seconds to the lifetime of the organism. The common denominator is the capacity of the individual to adjust to the particular environmental demands unique to it. This adjustment to the environment is assumed to be an enabling type of mechanism rather than a disabling one. Thus, we can dismiss immediately the behavioral changes that occur as a result of disease, injury, or genetic error. There may be cases where these mechanisms have proved favorable to the victim, but they usually prove to be destructive "adjustments."

SHORT-TERM PHENOMENA

Adaptation is the process by which the nervous system adjusts to the existing levels of stimulation in the environment. Dark adaptation is the physical, chemical, and neurological adjustment of the visual system to low light levels. Adaptation represents an adjustment by the nervous system to the ambient stimulation level of the immediate environment, but it is not a permanent change. When the environmental conditions change, the sensory system typically shifts to a new adaptation level. Adaptation is typical of the operation of most of the sensory systems and possibly the CNS in general. It deemphasizes constant or unchanging features in the environment and enhances responsiveness to changes. Adaptation typically involves a time scale ranging from seconds to hours and can be observed in the neurons found in the perpiheral circuitry.

Habituation is another example of a relatively short-lived adjustment to the environment. Habituation is the ability to adjust to repetitious (as opposed to constant) stimuli. An animal may be subjected to the repeated calls of other species which contain no information for the individual animal. In our modern technological age, we are usually unaware of the repetitious clatter of factory or office machinery. Even within the confines of our own homes, we may not attend to the automated noises of the furnace, air conditioner, or other automatic appliances.

Lie detector research indicates that there is a distinct physiological response **(orienting reflex)** that can be observed at the introduction of a noval stimulus. With repeated representations, however, this orienting reflex will fade and disappear. Any change in the stimulus parameters—intensity, quality, extent, duration, interstimulus interval, a skipped presentation, and so on —will trigger a new orienting reflex. Habituation is a more complicated level of the adaptation process in that it allows the system to deemphasize innocuous changes in the environment and preferentially to respond to novelty. The hippocampus is known to contain "novelty detectors," so habituation may be a limbic system function. To some people, habituation is "learning not to respond" to repetitive cues and therefore qualifies as a learning phenomenon. Others argue that since habituation is dependent on the sustaining input from the environment and must be reestablished each time the environment is re-entered, it is not "relatively permanent" enough to be called learning.

ONTOGENETIC ADJUSTMENTS

The early experience of an organism has a profound impact on the growth, development, and eventual capacity of the adult nervous system. Ontogeny dictates genetic growth, but this process interacts with environmental input to provide an epigenetic development of the nervous system.

In the case of intellectual development, the research comparing the performance of animals raised in "enriched" and "impoverished" environments is relatively clear. Animals reared for prolonged periods of time in total darkness, or in some other situation that lacks normal environmental features, are characteristically inferior to animals reared in a normal environment. Similarly, animals reared in an enriched environment with an unusually high stimulation value are typically superior. The difference is seen in ability to learn new skills in the laboratory, but also seems to extend to health, physique, and temperament. The difference is sufficiently large that many behavioral laboratories have added "handling" to the rearing procedures for the laboratory colony. The act of picking up and stroking baby rats appears to provide the necessary enriched early environment. The investment in effort is justified by the superior experimental animal that is available for behavioral research when it is an adult.

Careful measurement of the brains of the enriched and impoverished animals shows that there are corresponding changes in the brain structures. Most obvious is the fact that the enriched animals have heavier and larger brains. That is, the amount of cortical material is greater. The increased cortical material appears to reflect an increased number of synaptic connections and dendritic extensions of the neurons in the CNS. Rather than an increase in the total number of cells, the enhanced capacity seems to be derived from an elaboration of the connections between existing cells.

The data concerning enriched early environment are parallel to the observations made by Selye about the GAS. If the organism can successfully survive a stress situation, the organism is better equipped to cope with subsequent occurrences of the same kind of stress. The GAS deals with disease and injury, and a similar mechanism operates for environmental stimulation.

The debilitating effects of an impoverished environment on the adult organism are as apparent as the positive effects of enrichment. The mechanism in either ontogenetic adjustment appears to be the environmental contribution in the selection or development of appropriate neural circuits. Like other structures throughout the body, unused structures are not maintained, but are allowed to atrophy. In the case of the muscles, this process is reversible. Lack of exercise will result in a sharply reduced muscular capacity, while an exercise program greatly enhances muscular potential. The data indicate that the epigenetic development of the CNS is less forgiving and that the early environmental impact may have permanent ramifications.

The effect of early environmental experience on the developing nervous system is not usually considered an example of learning. The term "learning" is usually applied to the acquisition of a specific response. Basically, the nervous system selects the circuitry that is relevant to the environment of that specific individual. The behavioral capacity of the adult organism is directly related to the environmental situation during early CNS development.

IMPRINTING

Not all species-specific behaviors are genetically precoded. Certain species-specific responses are established according to critical early interactions with the environment. The phenomenon of **imprinting** is a clear example of this special case of learning (Figure 26.1). Goslings have a species-specific tendency to follow a moving object during the first few hours they hatch. The visual cues provided by the mother goose as she walks away from the nest are a **releaser stimulus** for the following response. If an object is followed, the following response then becomes a permanent part of the gosling's behavioral repertoire. It happens, however, that a person walking past the gosling will also trigger the following response. In this case, the gosling develops a permanent tendency to follow people rather than geese. In other words, the gosling has a species-specific tendency to follow a certain class of visual stimuli. If the gosling follows a specific object, the following response is then focused on that particular object for that gosling.

In the case of geese, the following response will occur only during the first 16 hours after hatching. During this time, a wide range of objects can imprint the animal. If no releaser stimulus occurs during this crucial time period, however, the gosling "outgrows" the following response. The gosling will then flee from the stimulus and, consequently, will not imprint. Ethologists have introduced the phrase **critical period** to describe the period of time when imprinting can occur.

Figure 26.1 An apparatus for imprinting ducklings. (Blough & Blough, 1964, p. 149)

Imprinting, or some similar process, has been observed in most flock and herd animals. In most cases, the imprinting occurs to form a bond between the baby and the mother. Occasionally, the baby becomes imprinted on an inappropriate object, but the system is usually remarkably efficient.

Harry Harlow's (1969) research involving surrogate mothers for baby monkeys points to the importance of "contact comfort" (touching experience) in the development of certain adult behaviors. Additional research by Harlow suggests that baby monkeys require the play activity of interacting with other baby monkeys if they are to show normal adult social behaviors. There appears to be a critical period for certain environmental social experiences that if missed profoundly handicaps the adult animal. There is speculation that the first two years in the human infant are a critical period for social development. The close personal contact between parent and child during this time may be vital to the eventual capacities of the infant.

Imprinting involves two important phenomena. First, a specific releaser stimulus can be learned from the environment even though the basic behavior is genetically precoded to a range of stimuli. Imprinting is more than a simple mechanism for getting goslings to follow in a line behind the mother. Goslings that have been imprinted on humans tend to direct their adult courtship behaviors toward humans rather than toward geese! Thus, the imprinted object shows a demonstrable permanent behavioral effect.

The second important aspect of imprinting is the occurrence of the critical period. Apparently, the ontogenetic development in the nervous system retains the behavioral capacity only for a limited period of time. If a releaser stimulus is not encountered soon enough, the circuitry is not maintained.

The phenomenon of critical periods may not result only from ontogenetic changes in the nervous system but might apply to certain adult behaviors. A mother sheep will reject the approach of a strange lamb, although she will be very accepting of her own offspring. Sheepherders have discovered two tricks to circumvent this rejection and provide foster mothers for orphaned lambs. One is to introduce the new lamb immediately after the prospective mother has given birth. The odor cues of the orphan are accepted (along with those of the newborn legitimate offspring) during a brief period of time after the birth process. In the case of an older lamb and a mother that has lost a lamb, the mother can be tricked into accepting the orphan if the orphan is covered with the skin of the legitimate offspring. The odor of the lamb is apparently the cue to the mother sheep. This odor cue is apparently "imprinted" during a brief critical period immediately after birth, and any lambs that nurse during this period will be accepted. The skin of an "acceptable lamb" seems to provide enough cues after the critical period. The acceptance response seems to generalize over time, since the adopted lamb will be accepted without the disguise after a few days.

The neural mechanism that accounts for imprinting may be the selective atrophy of unused circuits, as was hypothesized for the detrimental effects of an impoverished early environment. In this case, it is a highly special type of environmental impoverishment. Another possibility is that the ontogenetic development of the CNS generates more sophisticated behaviors which override the earlier response. In the case of the following response on geese, a growing "fear" response may obliterate any tendency to follow a strange object. In either case, the ontogenetic growth of the CNS establishes a sharply defined period of time when the animal is highly receptive to certain environmental events. If the appropriate stimulation does not occur during this critical period, significant behavioral costs may be incurred later in the life of the animal.

CLASSICAL CONDITIONING

Pavlov's classic experiments involving dogs, bells, and meat powder illustrate the phenomenon of **classical conditioning.** If a stimulus reliably causes a response in an organism, it can be used to establish that same response to another stimulus. Pavlov used meat powder to produce a flow of saliva in dogs. By ringing a bell just prior to giving the meat, the dogs learned to salivate to the sound of a bell (Figure 26.2).

The neurophysiological events that lead to a classical conditioned response could be quite simple. The flow of saliva is controlled by one or more "centers" in the brain-stem–hypothalamus–limbic system. The sensory activity evoked by placing meat powder in the mouth activates the "salivary center." The simultaneous afferent activity of the auditory system merges with the meat powder activity in various locations in the CNS. This "cross talk" most likely occurs in one of the structures that responds to stimulation of more than one sensory channel. With repeated occurrence of this activity pattern caused by the paired presentation of the stimuli, the pattern acquires a

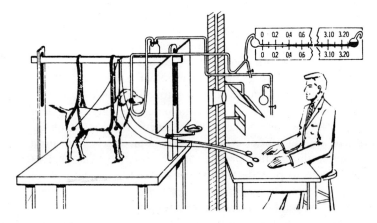

Figure 26.2 An apparatus for measuring the classically conditioned salivary response in dogs. (Blough & Blough, 1964, p. 22)

unitary quality of its own, so that the complete stimulus array is no longer necessary to trigger the response. In this way, the sensory pattern of activity created in response to the bell becomes sufficient to activate the salivation center and trigger the response.

Classical conditioning represents yet another improvement in the adjustment capacity of the organism. Classical conditioning is essentially a customized spinal reflex. A totally new stimulus can be wired into the CNS circuitry that will trigger the response.

The classical conditioning procedure can also work in reverse. If the bell is repeatedly rung without the presentation of the meat powder, the salivation response becomes weaker. This process, known as extinction, demonstrates the plasticity of the nervous system. New responses can be acquired and inappropriate responses can be extinguished. It is not yet clear whether the extinction is the result of "unlearning" (the destruction of established neural circuits), of "learning a new response" (the establishment of even stronger circuits that override the old response), or of the combination of a new response with inhibitory control of the previous response circuitry.

OPERANT CONDITIONING

The study of operant conditioning is most frequently associated with American psychology. It is typified in the Skinner box paradigm, where the hungry animal learns a bar-press response which results in the delivery of a food reinforcer (Figure 26.3). The basic ingredient for **operant conditioning** is that the response in some way is instrumental in the delivery of a reinforcement.

Classical conditioning consists of connecting a new stimulus pattern to an already established response circuit. Operant conditioning is much more of a trial and error process. The organism basically attempts a number of different

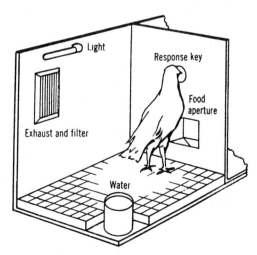

Figure 26.3 An apparatus for instrumental conditioning in pigeons. (Blough & Blough, 1964, p. 43)

responses to a given situation. Those responses that are followed by a painful or negative effect or by no change of any kind are extinguished, while those that lead to a positive effect become "learned." Operant conditioning is the selection of the most appropriate available response for a particular situation. The means of selection seems to be the shift in affective tone as a result of the response. In its simplest form, a neurophysiologist might describe operant conditioning as follows: "During a specific pattern of afferent activity (stimulus), there is generated a certain pattern of efferent neural activity (response). If the response is followed by activity in pleasure centers in the limbic system (reinforcement), changes occur in the pathways between the ongoing sensory and motor activity."

When phrased in these terms, both classical and operant conditioning consist of establishing the connection between a sensory neurological pattern and a motor neurological pattern. The difference appears to be the method by which the connection is established. Classical conditioning emphasizes the role of repetition, pairing the conditioned stimulus and conditioned response many times. Operant conditioning seems to rely on an affective shift mechanism to "reinforce" the connections. The difference between these two types of conditioning may be artificial, since the presentation of meat powder certainly involves an affective shift to a hungry dog, and animals usually require many repeated reinforced trials in the Skinner box before the learning is completed.

The ability to program a response to stimuli that are frequently encountered and/or may have an affective impact on the organism provides a highly adaptive device for the individual. The mechanism for this learning process appears to be an extension of the epigenetic process. The organism has the capacity to give many responses to any situation. Learning consists of selecting which of the available responses are to be used. Instead of making this selection a part of the ontogenetic growth process, learning seems to be accomplished by the phylogenetically advanced circuitry found in the cortex.

The mechanism that selects the appropriate circuits also would seem to discard valuable alternative circuits. The organism becomes increasingly specialized for an ever-narrowing set of environmental challenges. To some extent this is true, but specialization in components leads to an increased capacity in the total system. Specialization and progress seem to be highly related, whether we are talking about cells, behavior, or societies. As is the case with each of these "systems," adaptive responses are accomplished by combining many highly specialized components into a unique and appropriate pattern. Behavior modifiers can "build" complicated behaviors by combining individual operant conditioned responses.

LEARNING CIRCUITRY

Learning probably requires some sort of permanent change in the underlying neural circuitry. The connections between the afferent and efferent components are somehow altered. If we consider a learned response to be a very elaborate neuronal pathway, learning consists of the changes in this pathway that make it easier to use on subsequent occasions.

Learning is a cumulative process, usually involving repeated trials, so that the neuronal changes must progress in a cumulative manner each time the circuit is activated. Much of the learning that is related to school performance is based on a repetition principle. Television advertisers seem also to have discovered the cumulative effect of repetition. If a particularly irritating advertisement comes to mind, this is evidence for how well that pathway has become established through repetition—certainly not because you wanted to learn that brand name.

Not all information is learned through repeated trials. Under certain circumstances, the individual appears to be able to remember in a single trial. Most of us are able to recall with considerable clarity certain outstanding incidents in our lives. Usually the remembered event is one that had a strong emotional impact. We were very likely happy, scared, or angry or experienced some other strong emotion. There is some evidence to suggest that the emotional activity of the limbic system somehow keeps active circuits in a state of continued activity. This amounts to an artificially produced repetition. Each repetition contributes to the cumulative change. If the repeated television ad makes you angry, the advertiser has both conditions working to be sure the brand is remembered! This affective mechanism is similar to that suggested for operant learning when a reinforcement is given.

Research indicates that the permanent changes take some time to be accomplished in the circuit. This **consolidation period** ranges from 15 minutes to over an hour. If the activity of the nervous system is disrupted during the consolidation period, learning is lost. The **retrograde amnesia** suffered by victims of a head injury is one example of the disruption of the consolidation process. Often the victim has total amnesia for the accident that produced the injury. In addition, the amnesia may extend for a time period prior to the occurrence of the accident. The head injury apparently disrupts the ongoing activity that is necessary for "learning." The victim's memory for incidents occurring more than an hour prior to the accident is usually unimpaired. Once the neural change is accomplished, it appears to be permanent.

Several lines of evidence suggest that the change is indeed permanent. Accurate recall of facts under drugs, hypnosis, cortical stimulation, or even senility suggests that the storage mechanism holds the learned information in spite of lack of use. Forgetting seems to entail an inability to locate the appropirate circuit rather than a significant deterioration in circuitry.

The consolidation period can be explained by the necessary maintenance of neural activity until sufficient learning changes are accumulated. In some cases, however, the reinforcement is not encountered until after the stimulus and response are over. The nervous system seems to maintain an activity "trace" for some period of time after the event has occurred. This **short-term memory** provides a temporary storage of incoming information until a decision is made whether it should be "learned" (transferred into **long-term memory**) or forgotten. It is the short-term memory that holds a telephone number long enough to dial it. It is also the short-term memory that allows one's mind to wander during a conversation or lecture and still extract important details of what is said. Short-term memory is only a temporary mechanism but seems to be necessary for the permanent memory mechanism. The information is held on the short-term memory and transferred over to the long-term memory if the material is to be learned.

Some computers have an electronic equivalent of the short-term–long-term memory mechanism. Engineers can feed a complicated problem into the computer and display the solution on a television screen. The engineers then systematically change the input variables while watching the effect of these changes on the display. When a desired result is obtained, the engineer presses a "Now Print" button on the computer. The computer then prints out a permanent copy of the desired problem parameters and the solution. In many ways the hypothesized limbic-affective mechanism for sustaining neural circuit activity is analogous to the "Now Print" mechanism of the computer.

The two memory types could be located in different structures in the CNS, or they could represent a temporary long-term circuit that can be modified to be permanent. It is generally agreed that the location for the long-term memory circuit process is in the cortex. The known characteristics of the long-term process are that there is some sort of permanent change that must occur and that there is a consolidation period required to accomplish this permanent change. There are literally dozens of theories that attempt to name the neurophysiological mechanism that explains learning. A neuronal circuit can be permanently changed in many different ways. The search for the engram, as the quest for the physiological learning mechanism is called, is one of the more active fields in physiological psychology.

AUTHOR'S COMMENTS   The CNS exhibits a remarkable capacity to make adjustments for the environment it encounters. Some of these phenomena, like adaptation and habituation, are relatively short lived, but provide the organism with a valuable facility to selectively ignore nonthreatening dimensions of the existing environment. These short-lived phenomena can be easily explained by some of the known activity characteristics of neurons. Even short-term memory is not too difficult to handle with some clever neuronal circuitry.

The mystery of the nervous system is the apparently permanent neurological changes that account for the "real learning." The structural changes that accompany the learning capacity are sufficiently subtle to elude direct observation with present methods. Whatever the changes are, they seem to require a definite period of brain activity in order to be accomplished. After the changes are accomplished, there is good reason to believe that they are permanent, irrespective of use or disuse of the storage mechanism.

27

Learning and Memory

In many ways, Descartes' search for the "seat of the soul" has been transformed into a modern-day search for the engram. To many behavioral scientists, the learning process holds the key to understanding the nature of man. The physiological learning mechanism must be plastic enough to encode rapidly a new response and yet permanent enough to retain that response for the remainder of the individual's life. Since the neuron is the basic building block for the necessary neuronal circuitry, the activity must be accomplished within the known limitations of the neuron. The most obvious limitation is the short time any activity is observed on each neuron.

D. O. Hebb has offered a plausible solution to the problem of neuronal capacity to hold information despite the short-lived activity of the neurons. Hebb has hypothesized that the neuronal circuits in the brain form a loop so that activity is continuously recycled in a **reverberatory circuit** (Figure 27.1). The activity of one neuron in the circuit then is passed on to the next in a continuous chain, and the activity is kept circulating as long as needed (Figure 27.2). A simple model for learning is that the continuous activity of the reverberatory circuit gradually creates a permanent change in the cells or connections in the circuit. This permanent change then makes that particular circuit more conductive, which results in the change in behavior we call learning. Hebb calls these altered circuits **cell assemblies.**

If each cell assembly constituted a "memory," it should be possible to

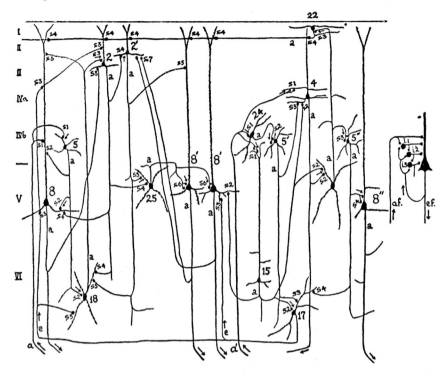

Figure 27.1 Diagram of reverberatory neural pathways in the human cortex. (De No; via Hebb, 1966, p. 76)

locate specific "memory centers" by artifically activating the cell assembly. Penfield & Rasmussen (1950) have elicited highly specific recall by stimulating the surface of the human brain. There is no indication, however, that the memory cell assemblies are all concentrated into a specified cortical region which would qualify as a cortical memory area. The secondary sensory areas appear to be involved with the recognition and/or identification of incoming stimuli. Thus, specific types of memory can be localized on the cortex, according to sensory origin. As brain research continues, areas of the cortex that were believed not to be involved with sensory activity are found to have cells which give sensory-evoked potentials. Thus, even sensory functions are more widely distributed on the cortex than previously believed.

With a reverberatory circuit hypothesis as the mechanism for temporarily holding a pattern of activity, the circuit is converted into a permanent cell assembly by some sort of cumulative permanent alteration in the reverberatory circuit. There are a myriad of possible sites in a reverberatory circuit for the permanent change to take place. Three major possibilities can be loosely categorized. These involve (1) a change in the connections between the cells in the circuit; (2) a change in the characteristics of each cell in the circuit; or (3) some alteration in the area surrounding the circuit which changes the

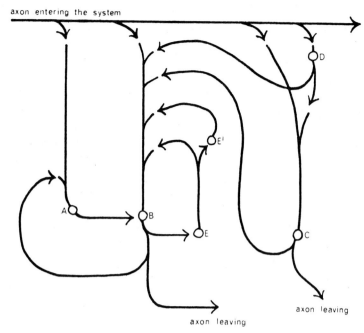

Figure 27.2   A reverberatory system. (Beach, 1960; via Hebb, 1966, p. 77)

activity in the circuit. Since these possible sites differ primarily in terms of neuronal characteristics, we can label them interneuronal, intraneuronal, and extraneuronal theories for learning and memory.

INTERNEURONAL THEORIES

The synapse is the most frequently cited candidate for learning and memory functions. If a concept or skill is accomplished by a specific reverberatory circuit, the connections between the components in that circuit are extremely important to the functioning of the circuit. The role of these connections is similar to those in an electrical appliance. In troubleshooting a faulty appliance, we often find that the problem is not a component but a broken or faulty connection. The connections in the nervous system provide a rich source of possibilities in the search for the engram.

The characteristics of the synaptic cleft have been of great interest to neurophysiologists. Although there is the problem of accidental distortion during the histological process, it is fairly well established that the synaptic cleft is a distinct gap between the sending and receiving cell. If this gap were to become narrower with repeated usage, the synapse would transmit more easily. Test tube nerve cells, or neurons maintained in an artificial growing medium, may be seen to grow synaptic connections, and the gap may be observed to fluctuate. Perhaps the fluctuation under artificial conditions is a sample of a permanent-change mechanism in the CNS.

The synaptic cleft has been found to contain a lattice structure between the bouton and the postsynaptic membrane (Figure 27.3). The lattice structure could determine the intercellular distance as well as the alignment of the bouton releaser sites with the postsynaptic receptor sites. The lattice matrix might even form special channels for more efficient transportation of the transmitter chemical.

The size of the transmitting bouton could have a direct bearing on the characteristics of the synapse. Some evidence suggests that the bouton grows in size with frequent usage. The growth of the bouton could provide increased capacity for production and release of the transmitter chemical. The bouton growth idea is directly analogous to the phenomenon of muscle growth resulting from exercise. The growth could result in increased transmitter chemical production, higher-capacity storage facilities, additional transmitter release mechanisms, or a better transmitter recycling mechanism for material salvaged from the synaptic cleft. Simultaneously, of course, the physical growth of the bouton could affect a number of other operating characteristics of the synaptic cleft.

Changes in the postsynaptic receptor sites could similarly alter the functional characteristics of the synapse. An increase in the number and/or extent of receptor sites for a given synapse might improve transmission efficiency.

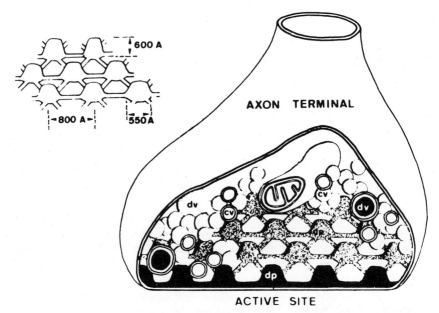

Figure 27.3 Organization of the presynaptic bouton. Structural or chemical changes could result in learning. (Pfenninger, Sandri, Albert, & Eugeter, 1969, pp. 12–18)

Qualitative change in the responsiveness of each receptor site in generating a postsynaptic potential upon arrival of the transmitter chemical represents another possibility.

The chemical characteristics of the fluids in the synaptic gap may also hold a key to the learning mechanism. Strychnine acts on the cholinergic synapse by altering the cholinesterase normally found in the gap. A permanent change in the concentration of such eraser chemicals would make it easier to transmit information across the synapse. Many other chemicals contribute to the complicated balance of chemicals in the synaptic junction. Each one affects the transmission characteristics of the synaptic junction, so that the physiological mechanism of learning could be accounted for by the change in the level of a number of synaptically related chemicals.

INTRANEURONAL THEORIES

Each neuron in a circuit must collect, summarize, conduct, and transmit information. Changes in the characteristics of each neuron in the circuit could also make the total circuit more efficient. Just as conduction between the cells is important, conduction between the synapses is important in the operational characteristics of the total circuit.

The neuronal membrane could radically change the transmission characteristics of the neuron. The axon might have the capacity to change and become a more efficient conductor with repeated usage. The improved performance could be merely an increase in axon size, since larger axons conduct faster. In terms of the total activity of the neuron, changes in the characteristics of the cell membrane on the soma and dendrites would probably have an even greater effect than changes on the axon. A significant information delay point in a neuron is the initiation of the axon spike at the axon hillock. Changes in the formation and transmission of the postsynaptic potential could result in a significant change in the generation of axon spikes.

The electrotonic spread of the postsynaptic potential across the cell membrane could be changed by a number of metabolic alterations in the cell. Changes in the operation of the sodium pump mechanism or the semipermeable characteristics of the membrane itself could account for the learning mechanism. Since the neuron is a cell specialized for the task of electrotonic conduction, the activity of a neuron represents the "work" of such a special cell. Thus, the efficiency of the neuron is related to the metabolic activity of the neuron. By increasing the energy-converting capacity of the neuron, the cell may be able to do its work more effectively. Thus, learning may be accomplished by a simple increase in the metabolic efficiency of the neuron.

Increased metabolic activity means increased chemical production in the interior of the cell. Increased chemical production is accomplished by a chain of chemical events beginning with the genetic code in the nucleus of the cell. The genetic code is primarily the specification for protein synthesis which is necessary for the efficient functioning of the cell. The relevant portions of the DNA-coded information are transcribed onto RNA molecules which act as messengers to the production components of the cell. Other types of RNA help in the actual production of the specified compounds. The result is the production of a complicated molecule known as an enzyme or a protein, which is used in the normal functioning of the cell. A change anywhere along this chemical chain of events could alter the overall efficiency of the cell. Thus, any of the steps in the internal chemical production capacity of the neuron could affect the transmission characteristics of that neuron and be the key to understanding the learning phenomenon.

Considerable experimental evidence suggests that the chemical capacity of the neuron has an important impact on the learning process. For example, chemicals that are known to block protein synthesis are known to disrupt the learning and retention process. Actinomycin and puromycin both block protein synthesis in the cells. If goldfish are administered an injection of either of these chemicals immediately after a learning session (during the consolidation period), the following day the animals show no retention of the task. If, however, the same chemical is injected several hours after the learning session, the goldfish suffer no retention deficit. Protein synthesis may account for the learning mechanism. Once the protein is produced, learning is permanent in terms of permanent chemical changes inside the cell. The time it takes to produce the protein is the consolidation period for learning. Thus, learning is the production of proteins, while memory is the presence of the proteins in the cell.

Protein synthesis may improve the overall operating characteristics of the neuron, which would account for the improved performance we call learning. There are, however, some provocative alternative chemical hypotheses for the improved performance. The DNA molecule contains all of the genetic information in the nucleus of the cell. This genetic code is a set of specifications for the production of certain proteins or enzymes by the cell. The proteins and/or enzymes produced by the cell in turn determine the "behavioral" capacity of the cell. Between the DNA in the nucleus and the protein synthesis sites in the ribosomes, at least two types of RNA are involved in the production process. RNA is similar to the DNA molecule and is capable of encoding similarly complex information in the same way that DNA does.

Thus, it is possible that RNA represents a sort of "environmental code" in much the same way that DNA is the genetic code. There are two ways that this might be accomplished. The conservative view is that the RNA encodes only the relevant information from the DNA according to the demands from the environment. RNA is known to follow this principle in selecting only the appropriate genetic information for each specialized cell, and this mechanism could also be expanded to include environmental conditions. In fact, the "right front leg cells" of the salamander become so identified because of their location (environment) in the early development of the organism.

A more radical position is that the RNA is able to directly encode environmental information. Since the RNA in the cell serves several different functions, one of them could be that of a "memory molecule." The memory molecule hyopthesis has aroused a considerable controversy among researchers. Some cite evidence suggesting that learning may actually depend on the formation of a specially encoded RNA molecule. Chemical transfer of learning has been claimed by extraction of the RNA from the brain of a trained animal and injection of it into the brain of a naive animal. Some workers even claim that such transfers can be accomplished between different species, which suggests a common information code. The possibilities presented by this hypothesis are startling, to say the least. Theoretically, it would be possible to prefabricate knowledge by artificially manufacturing an appropriately coded RNA molecule. It might be possible to replace a four-year college education experience with a series of chemical injections directly into the brain!

The relation between protein synthesis and learning could be a variant of this same memory molecule hypothesis. Proteins are also sufficiently complex to serve as a chemical molecular code for environmental information. Thus, the production of proteins might actually be the production of memory molecules at a different level than that suggested by the RNA memory molecule hypothesis.

The memory molecule hypothesis is greeted with disdain and/or skepticism by many physiological psychologists. Some even question the data which are cited to support the hypothesis. Most tend to give alternative explanations for the reason RNA changes and protein synthesis seem to be closely related to the behavioral learning process. There is little doubt, however, that some facet of the chemical production capacity in the neuron is important to the learning process.

EXTRANEURONAL THEORIES

Neurons are not the only cells in the nervous system. A large number of cells, known as glial ("glue") cells, are found associated with neuronal tissue. Many investigators have attributed passive roles to the wide variety of glial cells. Thus, structural support, electrical insulation, and nutritional support functions have been assigned to the glial cells.

Other researchers have suggested that the glial cells might play an important role in the electrical activity of the CNS. The discovery that glial cells demonstrate long, slow electrical potentials allows the possibility that the glial cells may provide an electrical field within which the neuron functions. The electrical response of the cell membrane can be manipulated by placing them in electrical fields. Glial cells, which totally envelop the neuron, could move the cell membrane nearer or farther from the $-55mV$ trigger potential. Thus, an electrical bias provided by the glial cells could excite or inhibit the activity of the adajcent neurons. Although this mechanism is unlikely as a permanent storage mechanism, it does provide a possible mechanism for maintaining the reverberatory circuit during the cell assembly formation process.

Other evidence suggests that the interaction between neurons and glial cells involves a chemical interchange. Even the exchange of RNA between the two types of cells is a possibility. If, as some data suggest, there is a reciprocal shift in chemical levels during the learning process, then the real "cause" of learning might not be found in the neuron but in the changes in the associated glial. The extraneuronal hypotheses illustrate an important oversight in most discussions of the functioning of the nervous system. Attention is usually concentrated on neuronal characteristics and neuronal circuitry. The observed neuronal activity may be the most easily observed expression of a multicelled "unit." The "quiet" cells may be contributing in ways not observable with present methods.

AUTHOR'S COMMENTS   The potential number of mechanisms that might accomplish the permanent neurological change that explains learning is nearly limitless. These possibilities can be loosely categorized into three general classes: (1) those involving changes in the neuron, (2) those having to do with changes in the connections between the neurons, and (3) those associated with changes in the neuronal environment. The basic assumption concerning the neurophysiological mechanism for learning is that there is some alteration in the neural pathway so that information transmission is more effective.

Most of the neurological explanations for learning are based on a reverberatory circuit notion. A reverberatory circuit is not the only way neurons could be combined for the hypothesized engram. The reverberatory circuit hypothesis is an elegant way to provide neural circuitry with a storage capability, which is impossible for the individual neuron. Once again, we find that the characteristics of a system exceed the capacity of any of the components. The contribution of glial cells to the system may be far greater than is suggested by the passive role now assigned them.

Chapter
28

The Brain
and Behavior

The phylogenetic, ontogenetic, and epigenetic development of the nervous system all show a trend of increased specialization of components combined with increased complexity of the total system. As the system becomes more complicated, it becomes increasingly difficult to locate and measure all of the factors that contribute to the operation of that system. The human neocortex presents such a challenge to the neurophysiological researcher (Figure 28.1). Higher behaviors such as thinking, imagination, and creativity are multiplex and subtle to the observer. The human neocortex, which is assumed to be the structure responsible for these higher behaviors, is a correspondingly sophisticated area of neuronal interconnections.

Even the relatively simple problem of explaining learning is largely an accumulation of theoretical possibilities with fragmentary data supporting various alternatives. The reverberatory circuit hypothesis is attractive because it provides a way for neuronal activity to be maintained without exceeding the known limitations of individual neurons. Histological examination of the nervous system shows a number of possibilities for reverberating circuits, and simple feedback loops are known to exist for fine motor control and various homeostatic functions. The existence of cell assemblies is based largely on theoretical conviction rather than specific confirmatory data. The variety of hypothesized mechanisms that might produce such an assembly also reflects the elusive character of the engram.

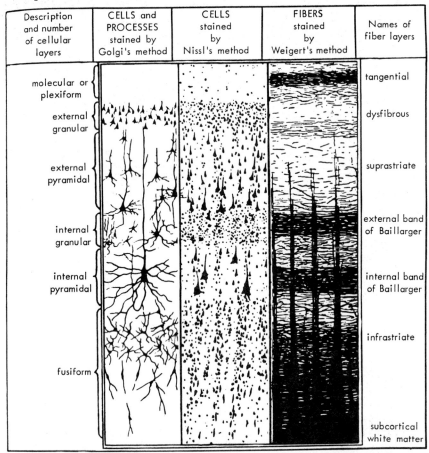

Description and number of cellular layers	CELLS and PROCESSES stained by Golgi's method	CELLS stained by Nissl's method	FIBERS stained by Weigert's method	Names of fiber layers
molecular or plexiform				tangential
external granular				dysfibrous
external pyramidal				suprastriate
internal granular				external band of Baillarger
internal pyramidal				internal band of Baillarger
				infrastriate
fusiform				subcortical white matter

Figure 28.1 The six layers of the human cerebral cortex stained by different techniques. (Altman, 1966, p. 221)

ORGANIZATIONAL HIERARCHY

The structures in the human nervous system represent the progressive accumulation of increasingly specialized capacities. In this progression, it appears that each successive improvement is accomplished by the modification and improvement of a more primitive mechanism. Thus, it is possible to trace a trend of successive modifications as the newer structures appear in the developing nervous system. This comparative approach allows some glimpses into the probable neurological mechanisms that contribute to higher thought processes. Altman (1966) has summarized the relation between behavioral capacity and CNS structures by identifying three key categories of behavioral capacities (Table 28.1). On the basis of this tripartite scheme, he then identifies behavioral, affective, and structural concomitants that exemplify the cumulative improvements.

TABLE 28.1 Tripartite Organization of Animative Activities and of the Mammalian Central Nervous System (Altman, 1966, p. 267)

STRUCTURAL SUBDIVISIONS	Specific Components	Phylogenetic Origin	Subjective Concomitants	Mode of Organization	Specific Functions	Activity Classification	FUNCTIONAL SUBDIVISIONS
SPINOMEDULLARY	Segmental parts of spinal cord and medulla	Protochordate (Amphioxus)	Apsychic (None) ("Reflex")	Stereotype Innate Impervious to modification	Respiratory Alimentary Circulatory Postural (Locomotor)	Persistent Routine	MAINTENANCE
PALEOCEPHALIC	Tectum Reticular formation Tegmentum Hypothalamus Rhinencephalon Limbic system	Protovertebrate (Cyclostomes Elasmobranchs Teleosts Amphibia)	Affective-emotional ("Instinctive")	Species-specific Modifable	Appetitive Consummatory Agonistic Affiliative	Recurrent Frequent	CATERING
NEENCEPHALIC	Lemniscal pathway Neothalamus Neocortex Pyramidal tract	Protomammalian (Mammals)	Cognitive-volitional ("Intelligent")	Personal Unique Acquired	Discriminatory Skilled Exploratory	Singular Occasional	INSTRUMENTAL

The most primitive level of behavior is the vegetative and reflexive functions served by the spinal cord and posterior brain stem (below the midbrain). This level of behavior allows the organism to react to immediate stimuli in the environment with responses that are controlled by the incoming stimulus. The reflexive circuitry in the spinal cord illustrates how this level of behavior is organized. The afferent neural activity created by the stimulus is conducted directly to the efferent motor fibers which precipitate the movement. The reflexive circuitry includes a network of interconnections which distribute the activity to a number of muscle groups. Thus, a pattern of simultaneous activity is distributed throughout the body which results in the coordination of many components into a unitary movement response. The coordination of vegetative homeostatic activities by the small nuclei in the lower portions of the brain stem appear to be slight elaborations of the reflexive network. Internal transducers signal the status of various compounds in the bloodstream, and appropriate adjustments are made in the circulatory system, breathing, and digestion to maintain an optimal homeostatic balance. These homeostatic adjustments involve the simultaneous maintenance and fine control of many ongoing activities.

The second level of behavior in the tripartite scheme involves instinctive or species-specific behaviors that include a significant emotional component. The arousal functions of the RAS, the drive systems in the brain stem, and the emotional systems in the limbic system control this middle level of behavior. The CNS structures are essentially the brain structures above the midbrain but below the neocortex. Most of the "centers" found in this region of the CNS appear to be extensions of the vegetative centers in the medulla. A unique pattern of afferent cells converges onto a single structure, and when a sufficient number of the incoming cells are active, the center reports. In the superior colliculi in the thalamus, a large number of visual feature detectors are found. These special cells select for particular features ("on-off," "movement," "direction," and so on) primarily to coordinate an appropriate oculomotor response to aim the eyes for more exact processing by the visual cortex. The colliculi are more complicated than vegetative centers in that they house a large number of individually unique visual features and possible response patterns. Thus, the nuclei found in the upper brain stem are actually a collection of many different centers. Apparently, concentrating cells into a cluster or nucleus with some common function provides economies in information transmission and/or integration. The centers for emotional behavior appear to be a similar concentration of cells with common functional characteristics. Here again, we find that each nucleus controls a number of separate but related behaviors. Although stimulation of one of these nuclei will produce drive-related or emotional behavior, mass activation of an entire structure is probably accomplished only by artificial means. Each center probably functions in subtle, different ways according to the combination or pattern of afferant activity. Instead of the fixed motor pattern of the reflex, or even the fine adjustments made on the vegetative functions, these higher centers provide the organism with the capacity to select from several different options, all of which are programmed and available.

Different options are probably connected to specific sensory patterns, much like an elaborate spinal reflex. These stimuli are the ones that act as automatic "releasers" to a particular behavior pattern. Most of these stimuli (and automatic behaviors) involve characteristics involving survival of the individual or survival of the species. Preprogramming these behaviors provides a common set of responses for members of a species to environmental situations frequently encountered by the species. Although much of this level of behavior is preprogrammed by the gene pool information of the species, there is allowance for modifying the behavior according to the specific situation each individual encounters. Thus, social responses in a pecking order depend on the social position of the individual. Similarly, feeding behavior may adjust to the food available or to the food preferences developed from past experiences.

The feature detectors and centers of this middle region of the CNS are collections of behavioral response units coordinated into a unitary response pattern that includes distinctly affective components. The emotional component enhances and prolongs the behavior beyond immediate stimulus control. In addition to providing the organism with a greater variety of behavioral responses than the reflex mechanisms, this level of CNS development is capable of making a number of adjustments to accommodate the environment of the individual. Early environmental events as well as the immediate situation have a measurable impact on the behavioral responses of the adult organism.

If we examine the structures in the limbic-system–brain-stem complex as individual centers, it is possible to describe each as an elaborate and adjustable spinal reflex. In fact, each of these complicated centers is a component of a still more elaborate system. The systems in this region are comprised of structures distributed through the thalamus, hypothalamus, amygdala, septal area, cingulate, and hippocampus. Each of the individual centers probably controls separate functional components of the total response. The system, however, provides an elaborate coordination network among these components. An important characteristic of many of these activities is that they are sustained over a considerable period of time, with different components appearing or receding, depending on the stage attained. Most animals, for example, engage in a prolonged and elaborate mating ritual which requires a very precisely controlled sequence of appropriate behaviors. The systems seem to provide the sequence and timing for the sustained and sequential activity of the various centers.

The third and highest level of behavior consists of activities termed "learning," "memory," "thinking," "imagining," "creating," and so on. The neurological structure primarily responsible for this kind of activity is the neocortex. If we extend the elaborateness and modifiability of the systems in the limbic system, we could arrive at the capacity to fabricate a connection between a unique pattern of sensory activity to a unique program of motor responses. Learning appears to be the result of just this capacity and leads to the ability of the organism to program a truly individual pattern of behavior to the particular environment encountered. This capacity not only frees the individual from the constraints of a species-specific pattern but it also gives the organism the capacity to interact with totally novel environments. In humans, this capacity is demonstrated in the ability to anticipate and prepare for totally novel environments (space and deep sea environments), and even to contemplate environments that never will exist (science fiction and fairy tale worlds).

THE NEOCORTEX

The neocortex is a structure of elaborate neuronal synaptic connections with six identifiable layers which vary slightly in different locations. In the center of each gyrus is a concentration of afferent and efferent axons carrying information to and from that cortical region to other areas of the CNS. The appearance of the cortex is relatively uniform, without the nuclear concentrations found in lower CNS structures. It is almost as though the entire cortex were one elaborate nucleus. The cortex can be divided into general functional regions. The primary sensory areas appear to accomplish the process of "sensation"—that is, the processing of the basic stimulus characteristics of an incoming stimulus. The association sensory areas appear to be involved with the "perception" process of recognition and evaluation of the stimulus array. Obviously, the sensory association areas are likely areas for learning circuits, since recognition involves comparison of the incoming stimulus with past experience.

Similarly, the primary and association motor areas are specialized, with the primary motor area controlling particular parts of the body and the association areas involved with learned motor programs. The training and drills of a skilled athlete not only condition the muscles but also provide the needed repetition for the motor circuits to "learn" how to respond appropriately.

The frontal lobes and the tips of the temporal lobes are the newest phylogenetic features of the human brain. These two cortical regions are also the most enigmatic in terms of establishing specific functions. Concomitant with their "higher" structural status, the frontal and temporal lobes are probably involved with higher mental functions. Destruction of the temporal lobes is typically associated with significant memory impairment. The resultant amnesia following temporal lobe damage significantly reduces the behavioral adaptiveness of the afflicted individual.

The frontal lobes, on the other hand, seem to process different memory functions. Destruction of the frontal lobes creates an inability to replace an already learned response with newer behavior. "Frontal" individuals can learn a task when first exposed to the situation. They will obstinately continue the first-learned response even though the rules are changed and another response becomes appropriate.

Prefrontal lobotomized patients frequently exhibit this syndrome or the somewhat similar trait of "cheating" on tasks. The patient may be able to verbalize the rule being violated but has considerable trouble actually following the rule. It is almost as if the patient were so totally preoccupied with succeeding at the task that it is impossible to recognize the illegitimate ways to accomplish success. Prefrontal lobotomized mental patients also show a marked drop in the ability to be deliberately devious. Such patients are relatively tractable in therapy and are easier to maintain in an institutional setting.

INTERACTIONS

The structures of the CNS are bilaterally symmetrical, with the left and right sides essentially mirror images of one another. In the brain stem, this bilateral symmetry is assumed to reflect a redundant or overlapping function of the corresponding areas. When lesioning a center in the lateral hypothalamus, the nuclei or tract on both sides typically must be destroyed or the behavior will not be altered. At the brain stem level, it appears inconsequential whether the left or right structure is left intact, since either seems to be capable of the same function.

Research on the cortex, however, suggests that the two hemispheres are not totally redundant. Total sensory processing appears to be distributed equally between the two hemispheres. There is considerable overlap in the form of sensory information which is shared by both hemispheres. At the same time, there is an obvious contralateral feature in the sensory processing. That is, the right hemisphere processes sensory information coming from the left region of the body, and vice versa.

By severing the commissural fibers which provide interhemispheric communication, it is possible to create a "split-brain" individual in which the right hand literally may not know what the left hand is doing. One extreme therapy for certain types of epilepsy involves split-brain surgery in humans. In these cases, the epileptic attack begins in one hemisphere, recruiting activity in the corresponding region of the opposite hemisphere. The recruited activity is fed back to the original hemisphere, causing the original activity to spread. This "ping-pong effect" can be disrupted by severing the fibers of the corpus callosum, thereby preventing the runaway exchange of neural activity.

Patients that have undergone split-brain surgery give evidence that each hemisphere is a relatively complete brain by itself. The right hand can accurately signal with finger signals a numeral presented to the right part of the visual field or the number of taps on the right side of the body. The left hand, however, will randomly guess at the number, although it can accurately provide the appropriate response if the information has been presented to the left side of the body.

Broca's numerical map of the cortex was based on the observation of a tumor in the speech area of an individual which resulted in aphasia. The speech area has been a curious exception to the bilateral symmetry hypothesis because it seems to be located only on the left hemisphere. The location of Broca's area relates to some interesting verbal reports from split-brain patients. The patient can accurately name objects placed in the right hand, but has literally no verbal connection for information supplied to the left hand. Occasionally, the patient may report with considerable bemusement the behavior of his own left hand. The independence of the operation of the two hemispheres is seen most obviously in the case of the patient who found his left hand selecting an item from a grocery store shelf. The right hand (the verbal left hemisphere) reported that it had decided not to buy that item ("too fattening"), so the right hand took it from the market basket and placed it on the shelf—only to have the left hand grab it off the shelf and put it in the basket again!

Although it lacks a language area, recent evidence suggests that the right hemisphere has considerable potential language capacity. The right hemisphere is capable of understanding spoken language. This may occasionally result in some vigorous response when it hears incorrect information. For example, a split-brain individual can verbally distinguish whether a hairbrush or a tennis ball has been placed in the left hand. The left hemisphere, which must give the verbal answer, can only guess because the tracts carrying that information have been severed. The right hemisphere, however, can hear and understand the guess. If the answer is correct, the answer stands. If the answer is wrong, the right hemisphere begins to shake the head, which is detected by the left hemisphere, which immediately changes to the correct response. The entire process is so rapid that the verbal response sounds like a natural error in a normal person. "A tennis ball. No, I mean a hairbrush!"

Experiments with split-brain patients show that each hemisphere is indeed capable of relatively complete functioning without the assistance of the other. There are even situations where the split-brain condition is superior. Each hemisphere can function without the competing interference of the other. The well-known trick of simultaneously rubbing your head and patting your stomach is not a problem to a split-brain patient.

There are, of course, significant costs. Although the unsplit cerebellum coordinates the walking motor patterns fairly efficiently, most tasks involving the cooperative activity of both hands are a significant challenge. The simple action of tying a shoelace becomes the equivalent of using your right hand and somebody else's left hand (or vice versa). By using the eyes (which transmit information to both hemispheres), each hemisphere can watch what the ipsilateral hand is doing and provide a response for the (contralateral) hand it controls. With sufficient practice, the patient can tie a shoelace quickly and efficiently, although it is definitely the result of a team effort. The other significant cost is that each hemisphere receives only a fraction of the total sensory input. Even though this fraction is more than a half, because of the shared information, it is very difficult for a split-brain person to evaluate and integrate messages from both the right and left sides.

Split-brain research indicates that the speech function is not the only example of specialization of functions in one or the other hemisphere. In addition to the speech function, the left hemisphere appears to excel in tasks involving logical analysis and mathematical reasoning. The reasoning process is primarily inductive, where the individual parts are examined and assembled into a final product. The right hemisphere, on the other hand, appears to be more adept at tasks involving visualization and intuition. The reasoning process for the right hemisphere is primarily deductive, beginning with an overall organization which determines the mode of analyzing the individual components.

Some psychologists have suggested that the right brain and left brain represent two alternative thinking modes. Left brain thinking is typical of the scientist, while right brain thinking is more typical of artistic endeavors. There is some evidence to suggest that the eyes may provide a hint as to which hemisphere is being utilized at a given moment. Since each hemisphere processes the contralateral visual field, the eyes may shift to provide information to the most active hemisphere. Thus, when confronted with a question, if an individual's eyes shift to the left, the answer is likely to be an intuitive, or "feeling," type of response, while a glance to the right signals a logical, or "thinking," analysis.

The functional characteristics of the cortex appear to have become so specialized that bilateral redundancy is being replaced for increased functional variety. A significant amount of human "thinking" may be identified as either a logical or an intuitive response to a given situation. If the data on left brain thinking and right brain thinking hold true, the left and right hemispheres might both process the information in their own unique program with the choice being made from the solution with the most satisfactory results.

The impressive size and structural complexity of the neocortex create a tendency to attribute all of the unique aspects of human behavior to the CNS, which is most prominent in man. It is true that the human CNS is dominated by the neocortical structures, but the human brain also has the most complicated limbic system and brain stem structures found along the phylogenetic scale. Although the phylogenetic sequence seems to involve adding on new, more specialized neural structures, the existing structures have also been modified and improved. Thus, humans not only have the advantage of a neocortex over animals with only limbic system structures but also have a superior limbic system. To compound this advantage, most of the systems identified in the CNS actually consist of interconnected activity of structures at many levels in the CNS. Thus, the human cortex with its superior specific data-processing capacity has better communication with an improved model of the affective limbic structures.

ADJUSTMENTS

While the cortex appears to be histologically homogeneous, there is obvious evidence for the notion that specific parts of the cortex are extremely specialized. The "right brain–left brain" difference, the relatively precisely defined cortical sensory and motor areas, the discovery of highly specific feature detector cells, all argue for functional specialization. In most lower areas of the CNS, functionally discriminable areas exhibit corresponding structural differences. The neocortex does not. There is some reason to argue that the highly adaptive capacity of the neocortical circuitry, which is capable of learning a unique response to a unique situation, is a potentially universal information-processing device.

Neurophysiologists are often impressed with the remarkable resilience of the structures in the CNS. Although tumors, strokes, and injuries can result in obvious losses of function corresponding to the cortical area involved, severe damage can be sustained without obvious debilitation. Lashley's experiments in the 1930s demonstrated that the brain worked on a concept of "mass action." Lashley claimed that destruction of 10 precent of the cortical tissue resulted in approximately a 10 percent loss of function, irrespective of the site of destruction. With regard to most of the cortical regions which are not "primary" areas, Lashley's statement appears accurate.

Lashley also argued for the concept of equipotentiality. According to this concept, any area of the cortex is as capable of handling a given function as any other. The equipotentiality concept is exactly the opposite of Broca's notion of a "speech area." The speech area in humans is not always necessary for efficient human speech. Certainly destruction of this area in the adult results in the classic aphasiac syndrome. Similar destruction in an infant under one year of age does not impair the normal speech capacity as the child matures. It appears that there is a critical period for the specialization of functions in the human CNS. If the speech area is removed prior to the critical period, other regions of the CNS can take over the functions without difficulty. At a certain developmental point, however, the neurons seem to lose their generalized capabilities and to specialize into particular functions.

Although it appears to be limited to a relatively early development period in CNS development, the fact that other regions of the cortex can take over the functions for removed tissue hints at the universal potential of the neocortical circuitry. Apparently, this generality becomes restricted to a special function at an early developmental stage. In the normal (both neurologically and environmentally) individual, there are some genetic predispositions to assign certain functions to certain cortical regions.

Even the adult brain is capable of remarkable adjustments. The adaptiveness of split-brain patients is one example. Although the normal interhemispheric communication is blocked by the severing of the corpus callosum, the individual hemispheres utilize alternate ways to communicate. By head shake, gestures, visual cues, and so on, the two hemispheres can monitor each other's activity and respond accordingly. Cats with reversed flexor-extensor muscle attachments can learn to readjust the motor "programs" to accomplish efficient walking movements. The more primitive spinal reflex circuits cannot adjust.

Experiments with human subjects wearing prism goggles which shift the entire visual world to the right show that this visual displacement can be accommodated relatively rapidly. Within minutes, the individual will show considerable improvement in responding to a visual world that is suddenly shifted laterally. When the displacing goggles are removed, the subject must then relearn to interact with a visual world now shifted to the left!

OVERVIEW

In functional organization, the CNS is analogous to the feature detectors. It is unlikely that a single feature detector is the only cell responsible for a particular feature. To restrict a specific memory to a single cell assembly or a certain intellectual function to a few circuits in the cortex is similarly implausible, in spite of neurophysiological evidence suggesting that such specialized functional units exist. To entrust a unique function to a single structure places extreme demands on the neural circuitry. A minor failure in any component can destroy the capacity to perform a particular task. The major reason for the emphasis on the one structure, one function view is that our recording devices are primarily single channel. Thus, the information we have about the operation of the nervous system primarily concerns the activity of one unit at a time. Because the units seem to provide a remarkably complete response, there is a tendency to ignore the possibility that each unit is simply one note in an entire symphony of neural activity.

It is most likely that the engram is not a single locatable neuron or cell assembly. Lashley's notion of the involvement of the entire cortex for any information processing is probably very appropriate. The advantage of parallel transmission and redundancy, as was suggested for the feature detectors of the visual system (Chapter 14), are even more applicable to intellectual processing. Such a mechanism successfully eludes the problem of a numerical limit since each cortical neuron could be involved with many different cell assemblies, and the theoretical upper numerical boundary is the total combination of synaptic connections the CNS could accomplish. The known functional cortical regions are probably areas where this total cortical activity pattern is collected and summarized for further action, if necessary. Rather than a single engram structure which must record, retain, and reproduce its stored information absolutely perfectly, the engram is probably a collection of widely scattered but related neural activity. Each component in this widely scattered system could provide a rather crude estimate of the stored information. If each of these estimates were transmitted to a common center, the average of all of these estimates could be very accurate. Thus, we return to a parallel processing model where the real information in the nervous system is not the activity of a single cell, but is really found in the pattern of activity generated by a unique combination of cells.

The "right brain-left brain" difference suggests that the CNS may be a parallel processing structure, but that the parallel units are not completely redundant. Each channel in the parallel organization may emphasize a slightly different aspect of the total information. The feature detectors that have been identified in the visual system frequently overlap with similar feature detectors in terms of stimulus information. There is even some evidence that the bilateral nuclei in the brain stem are not identical in terms of their contribution to the operation of the "system." Thus, the pattern of activity that marks the processing in the system is established by the relative activity of many different components, each providing a unique response profile. Memory and intellect circuits probably involve patterned activity of many unique cell assemblies.

The problems of observing and decoding a neural pattern are formidable. Analysis of the components provides hints, but the scope and capacity of the entire system has not been recognized. It would be necessary to record from many components and simultaneously analyze the activity at each site in order to understand the interactions. If the system contains many components, it is difficult to locate and identify the contribution of each component.

If the system is linear and static—if it transmits information in a line and the characteristics are unchanging—even complicated systems can be decoded. The more complicated spinal reflexes have been traced and decoded in this manner. If the system includes feedback and is dynamic—uses information about its own activity to readjust the same activity—the problem is compounded considerably. The variable nature of a learned response over the rigid spinal reflexes argues that the higher systems contain considerable dynamic, or changing, capacities.

Several lines of evidence provide clues that the cortical systems work on a dynamic patterning system. Recording of the visual fields of "on-off" cells shows that the size of the visual field changes with changes in the brightness of the target light. Such changes in the size of the field are difficult to explain by hypothesizing that the field is determined only by the synaptic connections with a certain population of rods and cones. There appears to be a much more flexible system in operation in providing information to the "on-off" cell. Similarly, there would have to be a sophisticated system for analyzing the information coming from such a dynamic cell. Neither location nor brightness information are available from the "on-off" cell without simultaneous evaluation of the other dimension.

The remarkable recovery in right- and left-hand coordination by split-brain patients is another possible example of the dynamic nature of the cortical mechanisms. Although such patients have been deprived of the normal interhemispheric communication provided by the commissural tracts of the corpus collosum, they are not reduced to one-handed tasks. By utilizing the eyes, ears, and proprioceptive senses, the two hemispheres reestablish an effective means of communication. It might be argued that this is simply an example of the resourcefulness of the nervous system in making the best of a bad situation, but the normal brain also uses these alternative information channels. It is easier to touch the fingertips of both hands with the eyes open than to close the eyes and depend only on the corpus callosum!

These data indicate that the normal nervous system simultaneously utilizes many different data-processing strategies. Thus, it is probably inappropriate to slip into an either-or way of analyzing functions. If such a choice is possible, the appropriate conclusion is probably "both." This has proved to be the case with color vision and pitch perception.

Pribram has suggested a hologram model for describing the brain's functioning. A **hologram** is a special type of photographic record accomplished by recording the interference fringes produced by light reflected from an object. If the object is illuminated by a pure single wavelength source of light, the reflected light from the object will appear as a pattern of light and dark ripples on a photographic plate. Nothing other than a pretty pattern may be seen if the plate is examined in normal light. If the plate is illuminated by the same wavelength light as the original exposure, however, the image of the object reappears. A holographic image is quite different from a standard photograph, for the holographic image looks exactly like the original object! It is as though the object were actually present except one cannot touch it.

The pattern of interference fringes on the holographic plate is uniquely produced by the interaction between the light and that particular object. Even a nick in the same object would cause a change in the interference patterns over the entire holographic plate. The information stored in this unique pattern is recovered by illuminating the plate with the original wavelength of light. The light passing through the pattern of fringes reverses the process and appears to converge on a particular object. Thus, the holographic pattern contains all of the information transmittable by light.

The hologram stores the information across its entire surface. Thus, if you cut a hologram in half, the entire object is still reconstructed. The reduced information is seen as a less precise reproduction; in other words, the object may appear a little out of focus. It is possible to reconstruct a crude image of the object by using any small section of any part of the holographic plate. Conversely, one can remove any segment of the holographic plate and still reconstruct the image with the remainder of the plate.

The hologram summarizes all of the visual information about the object at all points on the plate. Each individual point is relatively light or dark and, consequently, relatively useless in reconstructing the image. The unique pattern of light and dark spots distributed over the surface reconstructs the image. By using two different wavelength light sources, it is possible to store two images on the same hologram. The holographic plate has a new unique pattern of fringes; however, when illuminated with the appropriate light source, one or the other images appears. The nonappearing image is lost because the change in wavelength is not appropriate to the pattern contributed by that object.

Pribram argues that the cortex is a neurological equivalent to a hologram. Each neuron (or cell assembly) is analogous to a point on the holographic plate. The information is stored at each point, but the real data are the patterns of activity of many different points. Different "thoughts" are created by different electrical patterns, but the same neurons may be involved.

The holographic model is attractive, since it would account for Lashley's observation that the cortex appeared relatively impervious to localized destruction. If certain patterns converge on certain centers, it might be possible to show how the hologram is an extension of the lower brain centers. At the present time, the operation of the human cortex is largely speculative, although knowledge and technology have moved us away from Descartes' fluid model, which placed the "seat of the soul" in the pineal body.

AUTHOR'S COMMENTS   It is possible to deduce some of the simpler functions of the neocortex. The discovery of feature detectors is one example of a relatively well-measured component. The more complicated functions, however, are elusive and enigmatic. The cortex does not show the distinct segregation into tracts and nuclei that mark the centers in the brain stem. There is evidence for a definite localization of functions, such as the primary sensory areas, but there is no obvious structural demarcation of each functional region. At the same time, however, there is evidence to suggest that specific functions are scattered widely throughout the cortical tissue.

It is possible to extrapolate some possible cortical mechanisms by tracing the progressive changes in structures and functions in different levels of the CNS. On the basis of such an extrapolation, it is suggested that the important unit of behavior is not individual circuits or neurons but the patterning of activity among a large number of these individual components. Such a suggestion would explain why specific functional units can be found in the cortex and yet the cortex is so impervious to localized damage.

A patterning mechanism, whether it is called parallel conduction or a hologram, exceeds the known limitations of the components by combining them into a system. This solves some of the theoretical problems of the obvious capacity of the CNS. At the same time, however, it establishes a significant problem in attempting to measure and observe the functioning of this system. It will be interesting to observe how the research data develop.

References

Adey, W. R. The sense of smell. In J. Field (Ed.), *Handbook of physiology. Neurophysiology*, 1959, *1*. Washington D.C.: American Physiological Society, 535–548.

Altman, J. *Organic foundations of animal behavior*. New York: Holt, Rinehart and Winston, 1966.

Amark, C. A. A Study in alcoholism. *Acta Psychiatrica et Neurologica Scandinavica*, 1951, *70*.

Amoore, J. E. Current status of the steric theory of odor. *Annals of the New York Academy of Sciences*, 1964, *116* (2), 457–476.

Ax, A. F. The physiological differentiation between fear and anger in humans. *Psychosomatic Medicine*, 1953, *15*, 433–442.

Ban, T. *Psychopharmacology*. Baltimore: Williams & Wilkins, 1969.

Bannister, R. *Brain's clinical neurology*. London: Oxford University Press, 1969.

Barlow, H. B. & Hill, R. M. Selective sensitivity to direction of movement in ganglion cells of the rabbit retina. *Science*, 1963, *139*.

Barondes, S. H. Axoplasmic transport. *Neurosciences Research Program Bulletin*, 1967, *5* (4).

Beach, L. A. *et al.*(Eds.). *The neuropsychology of Lashley*. New York: McGraw-Hill, 1960.

Beatty, J. *Introduction to physiological psychology*. Monterey, Calif.: Brooks/Cole, 1975.

Beidler, L. M. & Reichardt, W. E. Sensory transduction. *Neurosciences Research Program Bulletin*, 1970, *8* (5).

Békésy, G. von. *Experiments in hearing.* New York: McGraw-Hill, 1960.

Békésy, G. von. *Sensory inhibition.* Princeton. Princeton University Press, 1967.

Bell, C. C. & Dow, R. S. Cerebellar circuitry. *Neurosciences Research Program Bulletin,* 1967, *5* (2).

Bermant, G. (Ed.). *Perspectives on animal behavior: A first course.* Glenview, Ill.: Scott, Foresman, 1973.

Binkley, S., Kluth, E. & Menaker, M. Pineal function in sparrows: Circadian rhythms and body temperature. *Science,* 1972, *174,* 311–315.

Bishop, M. P., Elder, S. T. & Heath, R. G. Intracranial self-stimulation in man. *Science,* 1963, *140,* 394–395.

Black, P. (Ed.). *Drugs and the brain.* Baltimore: The Johns Hopkins Press, 1969.

Bloom, W. and Fawcett, D. *A textbook of histology* (9th ed.). Philadelphia: Saunders, 1968.

Blough, D. S. & Blough, P. M. *Experiments in psychology laboratory studies of animal behavior.* New York: Holt, Rinehart and Winston, 1964.

Bodian, D. The generalized vertebrate neuron. *Science,* 1962, *137,* 323–326.

Bodian, D. Neurons, circuits and neuroglia. In G. C. Quarton, T. Melnechuk & F. O. Schmitt (Eds.), *The neurosciences: A study program.* New York: Rockefeller University Press, 1967.

Bodian, D. A model of synaptic and behavioral ontogeny. In G. C. Quarton, T. Melnechuk & F. O. Schmitt (Eds.), *The neurosciences: A study program.* New York: Rockefeller University Press, 1970.

Boren, J. The study of drugs with operant techniques. In W. K. Honig (Ed.), *Operant behavior: Areas of research and application.* New York: Appleton, 1950.

Boring, E. G. *A history of experimental psychology.* New York: Appleton, 1950.

Brachet, J. The living cell. *Scientific American,* 1961, *205* (3), 2–12.

Brindley, G. S. *Physiology of the retina and visual pathway.* London: E. Arnold, 1970.

Brinkley, S. "Pineal function in sparrows: Circadian rhythms and temperature," *Science,* 1971, *174,* 311–314.

Broadhurst, P. L. The biometrical analysis of behavioral inheritance. *Science Progress,* 1967.

Brodman, K. *Vergleichende Lakalisations lehre der Grosshirnrinde.* Munich: Barth, 1909.

Brown, P. B., Maxfield, B. W. & Moraff, H. *Electronics for neurobiologists.* Cambridge: MIT Press, 1973.

Bullock, T. H. Simple systems for the study of learning. *Neurosciences Research Program Bulletin,* 1966, *4* (2).

Bunch, C. C. Age variations in auditory acuity. *Archives of Otolaryngology,* 1929, *9.*

Burkhardt, D., Schleidt, W. & Altner, H. *Signals in the animal world.* New York: McGraw-Hill, 1967.

Cannon, W. B. and Washburn, A. C. An explanation of hunger. *American Journal of Physiology,* 1912, *29,* 441–454.

Chaplin, J. P. & Kraweic, T. S. *Systems and theories of psychology.* New York: Holt, Rinehart and Winston, 1960.

Christian, J. & Davis, D. Endocrines, behavior and population. *Science,* 1964, *146,* 1550–1560.

Christman, R. J. *Sensory experience.* Scranton, Pa.: Intext Educational, 1971.

Clark, W. & delGuidice, J. *Principles of psychopharmacology.* New York: Academic Press, 1970.

Coons, E. E. & Miller, N. E. Conflict versus consolidation of memory traces to explain "retrograde amnesia" produced by ECS. *Journal of Comparative Physiological Psychology,* 1960, *53,* 524-531.

Cornsweet, T. N. *Visual perception.* New York: Holt, Rinehart and Winston, 1967.

Corso, J. F. *The experimental psychology of sensory behavior.* New York: Holt, Rinehart and Winston, 1967.

Curtis, B. A., Jacobson, S. & Marcus, E. M. *An introduction to the neurosciences.* Philadelphia: Saunders, 1972.

Davis, H. Psychophysiology of hearing and deafness, In S. S. Stevens (Ed.), *Handbook of experimental psychology.* New York: Wiley, 1951.

Davis, H. Acoustic trauma in the guinea pig. *Journal of the Acoustical Society of America,* 1953, *25.*

Deagle, J. *Study guide and workbook in physiological psychology.* Englewood Cliffs, N.J.: Prentice-Hall, 1973.

Delafresnaye, J. F. Fessard, A. Gerard, R. W. & Konorski, J. (Ed.), *Brain mechanisms and learning.* Oxford: Blackwell Scientific, 1961.

Delgado, J. *Physical control of the mind.* New York: Harper & Row, 1969.

Dement, W. C. *Some must watch, while some must sleep.* New York: Macmillan, 1972.

Dement, W. C. & Kleitman, N. Cyclical variations in EEC during sleep and their relation to eye movements, body motility and dreaming. *Electroencephalography and Clinical Neurophysiology,* 1957, *9,* 673–690.

Denny, M. R. & Ratner, S. C. *Comparative psychology: Research in animal behavior* (Rev. ed.). Homewood, Ill.: Dorsey Press, 1970.

de Nó, L. In J. F. Fulton, *Physiology of the nervous system.* New York: Oxford University Press.

Deutsch, J. A. & Deutsch, D. *Physiological psychology.* Homewood, Ill.: Dorsey Press, 1966.

Dowling, J. E. & Boycott, B. B. Organization of the primate retina: Electron microscopy. *Proceedings of the Royal Society,* 1966, Series 13.

Ebert, J. D. Gene expression. *Neurosciences Research Program Bulletin,* 1967, *5* (3).

Eccles, J. C. *The neurophysiological basis of mind.* Baltimore: The Johns Hopkins Press, 1953.

Eccles, J. C. *Physiology of nerve cells.* Baltimore: The Johns Hopkins Press, 1957.

Eccles, J. C. *The physiology of synapses.* New York: Academic Press, 1964.

Efron, D. H. (Ed.). *Psychopharmacology: A review of progress.* Washington, D.C.: Department of Health, Education and Welfare, 1968.

Field, J. Mayoun, H. W. & Hall, V. E. (Eds.). *Handbook of physiology.* (Vols. 1, 2, & 3). Washington, D.C.: American Physiological Society, 1959, 1960

Fisher, A. E. & Coury, J. N. Cholinergic tracing of a central neural circuit underlying the thirst drive. *Science,* 1962, *138,* 691–693.

Flexner, J. B., Flexner, L. & Stellar, E. Memory in mice as affected by intracerebral puromycin. *Science,* 1963, *141,* 57–59.

Foulkes, D. *The psychology of sleep.* New York: Scribner, 1966.

Galambos, R. Glial cells. *Neurosciences Research Program Bulletin*, 1964, *2* (6).

Garcia, J., McGowan, B. K. & Green, K. F. Biological constraints on conditioning. In A. H. Black & W. F. Prokasy, *Classical conditioning II: Current theory and research*. New York: Appleton, 1972.

Gardner, E. *Fundamentals of neurology* (4th ed.). Philadelphia: Saunders, 1963.

Gardner, E. *Fundamentals of neurology* (6th ed.). Philadelphia: Saunders, 1975.

Geldard, F. A. *The human senses*. New York: Wiley, 1953.

Gibson, J. J. *The senses considered as perceptual systems*. Boston: Houghton Mifflin, 1966.

Gibson, W., Reid L., Sakai, M. & Porter, P. Intracranial reinforcement compared with sugar-water reinforcement. *Science*, 1965, *148*, 1357–1359.

Goodman, L. & Gilman, A. *The pharmacological basis of therapeutics*. New York: Macmillan, 1970.

Graham, C. H. (Ed.). *Vision and visual perception*. New York: Wiley, 1965.

Granit, R. *Receptors and sensory perception*. New Haven: Yale University Press, 1955.

Gray, J. *The psychology of fear and stress*. New York: McGraw-Hill, 1971.

Gregory, R. L. *The eye and the brain*. New York: McGraw-Hill, 1971.

Grossman, S. P. *A textbook of physiological psychology*. New York: Wiley, 1967.

Grossman, S. P. *Essentials of physiological psychology*. New York: Wiley, 1973.

Grundfest, H. Synaptic and ephaptic transmission. In G. C. Quarton, T. Melnechuk & F. O. Schmitt (Eds.), *The neurosciences: A study program*. New York: Rockefeller University Press, 1967.

Gulick, W. L. *Hearing: Physiology and psychophysics*. New York: Oxford University Press, 1971.

Guyton, A. C. *Function of the human body*. Philadelphia: Saunders, 1974.

Haber, R. & Fried, A. H. *Introduction to psychology*. New York: Holt, Rinehart and Winston, 1975.

Hammes, G. G., Molinott, P. B. & Bloom, F. E. Receptor biophysics and biochemistry. *Neurosciences Research Program Bulletin*, 1973, *11* (3).

Hardin, G. *Biology: Its human implications*. San Francisco: Freeman, 1949.

Hart, B. J. *Experimental neuropsychology*. San Francisco: Freeman, 1969.

Harvey, J. (Ed.) *Behavioral analysis of drug action*. Glenview, Ill.: Scott, Foresman, 1971.

Heath, R. G. Electrical self-stimulation of the brain in man. *American Journal of Psychiatry*, 1963, *120*, 571–577.

Hebb, D. O. *A textbook of psychology*. Philadelphia: Saunders, 1966.

Hect, S. The development of Thomas Young's theory of color vision. *Journal of the Optical Society of America*, 1930, *20, 5*, 231–270.

Hect, S., Haig, C. & Chase, A. M. Influence of light adaptation on subsequent dark adaptation of the eye. *Journal of General Physiology*, 1937, *30*, 831–850.

Held, R., & Freeman, S. Plasticity in human sensorimotor control. *Science*, 1963, *142*, 455–462.

Held, R. & Richards, W. *Perception: Mechanisms and models*. (Readings from *Scientific American*.) San Francisco: Freeman, 1972.

Hernández-Peón, R., Scherrer, H. & Jouvet, M. Modification of electrical activity in cochlear nucleus during "attention" in unanesthetized cats. *Science*, 1956, *123*, 331–332.

Hess, R., Jr., Koella, W. P. & Akert, K. Cortical and subcortical recordings in natural and artificially induced sleep in cats. *Electroencephalography and Clinical Neurophysiology*, 1953, *5*, 75–90.

Heston, L. L. The genetics of schizophrenic and schizoid disease. *Science*, 1970, *167*.

Hirsch, J. (Ed.). *Behavior-genetics analysis*. New York: McGraw-Hill, 1967.

Hoffman, R. & Reiter, R. Pineal gland: Influence on gonads of male hamsters. *Science*, 1965, *148*, 1609–1610.

House, E. L. & Pansky, B. *A functional approach to neuroanatomy*. New York: McGraw-Hill, 1967.

Hubel, D. H. The visual cortex of the brain. *Scientific American,* 1963, *209* (5), 54–62.

Hubel, D. H. & Wiesel, T. N. Receptive fields, binocular interaction and functional architecture in the cat's visual cortex. *Journal of Physiology*, 1962, *160* (1).

Hurvich, L. M. & Jameson, D. An opponent process theory of color vision. *Psychological Review*, 1957, *64*, 384–390; 397–404.

Hyden, H. Biomedical changes accompanying learning. In G. C. Quarton, T. Melnechuk & F. O. Schmitt (Eds.), *The neurosciences: A study program*. New York: Rockefeller University Press, 1967.

Isaacson, R. L., Douglas, R. J., Lubar, J. F. & Schmaltz, L. W. *A primer of physiological psychology*. New York: Harper & Row, 1971.

Iversen, L. L. & Schmitt, F. O. Synaptic function. *Neurosciences Research Program Bulletin*, 1970, *8* (4).

Jacobson, M. Development of specific neural connections. *Science*, 1969, *163*, 543–547.

Jacobson, M. & Baker, R. Neuronal specifications of cutaneous nerves through connections with skin grafts in the frog. *Science*, 1968, *160*, 543–545.

Jarvik, M. The psychopharmacological revolution. *Psychology Today*, 1967, *1* (1), 51–59.

Jasper, H. H., Procter, L. D., Knighton, R. E., Noshay, W. C. & Costello, R. T. (Eds.). *The reticular formation of the brain*. Boston: Little, Brown, 1958.

Joffe, J. M. *Prenatal determinants of behavior*. Oxford: Pergamon, 1969.

Johnson, W. H., DeLanney, L. E., Cole, T. A. and Brooks, A. E. *General biology* (4th ed.). New York: Holt, Rinehart and Winston, 1972.

Jouvet, M. Neurophysiology of the states of sleep. In G. C. Quarton, T. Melnechuk & F. O. Schmitt (Eds.), *The neurosciences: A study program*. New York: Rockefeller University Press, 1967.

Jouvet, M. The states of sleep, *Scientific American*, 1967, *216* (2) 60–69.

Julien, R. M. *A primer of drug action*. San Francisco: Freeman, 1975.

Kandel, E. R. Cellular studies of learning. In G. C. Quarton, T. Melnechuk & F. O. Schmitt (Eds.), *The neurosciences: A study program*. New York: Rockefeller University Press, 1967.

Kety, S. S. & Matthysse, S. Prospects for research on schizophrenia. *Neurosciences Research Program Bulletin*, 1972, *10* (4).

Kling, J. W. & Riggs, L. A. *Woodworth and Schlossberg's experimental psychology* (3rd ed.). New York: Holt, Rinehart and Winston, 1971.

Kluver, H. & Bucy, P. Preliminary analysis of functions of the temporal lobes in monkeys. *Archives of Neurological Psychiatry*, 1939, *42*, 979–1000.

Kopin, I. J. The mode of action of psychotometric drugs. In J. R. Smythies (Ed.), *Neurosciences Research Program Bulletin*, 1970, *8* (1).

Kretch, D., Crutchfield, R. S. & Livson, N. *Elements of psychology*. New York: Knopf, 1974.

Kreig, W. J. S. *Brain mechanisms in diachrome* (2nd ed.). Evanston, Ill.: Brain Books, 1957.

Kuffler, S. W. Discharge patterns and functional organization of mammalian retina. *Journal of Neurophysiology*, 1953, *16*.

Kuffler, S. W. Excitation and inhibition in single nerve cells. In *The Harvey Lecture Series, 54*. New York: Academic Press, 1960.

Kuo, Z. Y. *The dynamics of behavior development: An epigenetic approach*. New York: McGraw-Hill, 1967.

Ladaur, T. K. (Ed.). *Readings in physiological psychology*. New York: McGraw-Hill, 1967.

Laughlin, W. S. & Osborne, R. H. *Human variation and origins: An introduction to human biology and evolution*. (Readings from *Scientific American*.) San Francisco: Freeman, 1967.

Leavitt, F. *Drugs and behavior*. Philadelphia: Saunders, 1974.

Lehninger, A. L. How cells transform energy. *Scientific American*, 1961, *205* (3), 62–73.

Lehninger, A. L. Cell membranes. *Neurosciences Research Program Bulletin*, 1964, *2* (2).

Lerner, I. M. & Libby, W. J. *Heredity, evolution, and society* (2nd ed.). San Francisco: Freeman, 1976.

Lettvin, J. Y., Maturna, H. R., McCullock, W. S. & Pitts, W. H. What the frog's eye tells the frog's brain. *Proceedings of the Institute of Radio Engineers*, 1959, *47*.

Leukel, F. *Introduction to physiological psychology* (2nd ed.). St. Louis: Mosby, 1972.

Livingston, R. B. Brain mechanisms in conditioning and learning. *Neurosciences Research Program Bulletin*, 1966, *4* (3).

Longo, V. C. *Neuropharmacology and behavior*. San Francisco: Freeman, 1972.

Lubar, J. F. (Ed.). *A first reader in physiological psychology*. New York: Harper & Row, 1972.

MacKay, D. M. Evoked brain potential as indicators of sensory information processing. *Neurosciences Research Program Bulletin*, 1969, *1* (3).

McClearn, G. E. & DeFries, J. C. *Introduction to behavioral genetics*. San Francisco: Freeman, 1973.

MacLean, P. D. The limbic system with respect to self-preservation and the species. *Journal of Nervous Mental Disease*, 1958, *127*, 1–11.

McConnell, J. Memory transfer through cannibalism in planarians. *Journal of Neuropsychiatry*, 1962, *3*, Suppl. 1, 542–548.

McGaugh, J. L., Weinberger, N. M. & Whaler, R. E. (Eds.). *Psychobiology*. San Francisco: Freeman, 1966.

Matheson, D. & Davidson, M. (Eds.). *The behavioral effects of drugs*. New York: Holt, Rinehart and Winston, 1972.

Medical Economics Incorporated. *Physicians' desk reference to pharmaceutical specialities and biologicals* (25th ed.). Oradell, N.J.: Litton Publications, 1971.

Melzack, R., & Scott, T. The effects of early experience on the response to pain. *Journal of Comparative Physiological Psychology*, 1957, *50*, 155–161.

Mercer, E. H. *Cells, their structure and function*. Garden City, N.Y.: Doubleday, 1962.

Michael, R. Estrogen-sensitive neurons and sexual behavior in female cats. *Science*, 1962, *136*, 322–323.

Michael, C. R. Receptive fields of single optic nerve fibers in a mammal with an all-cone retina. *Journal of Neurophysiology*, 1968, *31* (2).

Michael, C. R. Retinal processing of visual images. *Scientific American*, May 1969, *220* (5), 104–114.

Miller, N. E. Certain facts of learning relevant to the search for its physical basis. In G. C. Quarton, T. Melnechuk & F. O. Schmitt (Eds.), *The neurosciences: A study program*. New York: Rockefeller University Press, 1967.

Miller, N. & Kessen, M. Reward effects of food via stomach fistula compared with those of food via mouth. *Journal of Comparative Physiological Psychology*, 1952, *45*, 555–564.

Milner, P. *Physiological psychology*. New York: Holt, Rinehart and Winston, 1970.

Mokrasch, L. C., Bear, R. S. & Schmitt, F. O. Myelin. *Neurosciences Research Program Bulletin*, 1971, *9* (4).

Montagna, W. The skin. *Scientific American*, February 1965, *22* (2).

Morgan, C. T. *Physiological psychology* (3rd ed.). New York: McGraw-Hill, 1965.

Morgan, C. T. & King, R. A. *Introduction to psychology* (4th ed.). New York: McGraw-Hill, 1971.

Moruzzi, G. & Magoun, H. Brain stem reticular formation and activation of the EEG. *Electroencephalography and Clinical Neurophysiology*, 1949, *1*, 455–473.

Nauta, W. S. H. Some brain structure and functions related to memory. *Neurosciences Research Program Bulletin*, 1964, *2* (5).

Nauta, W. S. H., Koella, W. P. & Quarton, G. C. Sleep, wakefulness, dreams, and memory. *Neurosciences Research Program Bulletin*, 1966, *4* (1).

Netter, F. *The CIBA collection of medical illustrations. 1. Nervous system*. New York: CIBA, 1968.

Olds, J., & Milner, P. Positive reinforcement produced by electrical stimulation of the septal area and other regions of the rat brain. *Journal of Comparative Physiological Psychology*, 1954, *47*, 419–427.

Olds, J. & Olds, M. Interference and learning in paleocortical systems. In J. F. Delafresnaye, A. Fessard, R. W. Gerard & J. Konorski (Eds.), *Brain mechanisms and learning*. Oxford: Blackwell Scientific, 1961.

Osgood, C. E. *Method and theory in experimental psychology*. New York: Oxford University Press, 1953.

Patten, B. M. *Human embryology* (2nd Ed.). New York: McGraw-Hill, 1953.

Penfield, W. & Rasmussen, A. T. *The cerebral cortex of man*. New York: Macmillan, 1950.

Penfield, W. & Roberts, L. *Speech and brain mechanisms*. Princeton: Princeton University Press, 1959.

Perkel, D. H. & Bullock, T. H. Neural coding. *Neurosciences Research Program Bulletin*, 1968, *6* (3).

Pfaffman, C. Gustatory nerve impulses in rat, cat and rabbit. *Journal of Neuro-physiology,* 1955, *18,* pp. 429–440.

Pfenninger, K., Sandri, C., Albert, K. & Eugster, C. H. Contribution to the problem of structural organization of the presynaptic area. *Brain Research,* 1969, *12.*

Pirenne, M. H. *Vision and the eye.* London: Chapman and Hall, 1967.

Polly, E. H., Apple, D. J., Bizzel, J. W. The laser as a research tool in the visual system investigation. *American Psychologist,* 1975, *30* (3).

Polyak, S. *The retina.* Chicago: University of Chicago Press, 1957.

Pribram, K. H. (Ed.). *On the biology of learning.* New York: Harcourt, Brace Jovanovich, 1969.

Quarton, G. C. The enhancement of learning by drugs and the transfer of learning by macromolecules. In G. C. Quarton, T. Melnechuk & F. O. Schmitt (Eds.), *The neurosciences: A study program.* New York: Rockefeller University Press, 1967.

Quarton, G. C., Melnechuk, T. & Schmitt, F. O. (Eds.) *The neurosciences: A study program.* New York: Rockefeller University Press, 1967.

Quastler, H. (Ed.). *Information theory in psychology: Problems and methods.* New York: Free Press, 1955.

Ray, O. *Drugs, society and human behavior.* St. Louis: Mosby, 1972.

Rasmussen, A. T. *Outlines of neuroanatomy.* (3rd ed.). Debuque, Iowa: William C. Brown Company, 1943.

Robertson, J. D. The synapse, morphological and chemical correlates of function. *Neurosciences Research Program Bulletin,* 1965, *3* (4).

Rosenblith, W. A. *Sensory communication.* Cambridge: MIT Press, 1961.

Selye, H. *The physiology and pathology of exposure to stress.* Montreal: Acta, Inc., 1950.

Schachter, S., and Singer, J. Cognitive, social and physiological determinants of emotional state. *Psychological Review,* 1962, *69,* 379–399.

Schneibel, M. E. & Scheibel, A. B. Anatomical basis of attention mechanisms in vertebrate brains. In G. C. Quarton, T. Melnechuk, and T. O. Schmitt (Eds.), *The neurosciences: A study program.* New York: Rockefeller University Press, 1967.

Schmitt, F. O. The neurosciences: Second study program. New York: Rockfeller University Press, 1970.

Schmitt, F. O. & Worden, F. G. *The neurosciences: Third study program.* Cambridge, Mass.: MIT Press, 1974.

Schneider, M. *Einfuhrung in die physiologie,* Berlin: Springer-Verlag, 1964.

Schwartz, M. *Physiological psychology.* New York: Appleton, 1973.

Selye, H. *The stress of life.* New York: McGraw-Hill, 1956.

Sheer, D. E. (Ed.) *Electrical stimulation of the brain.* Austin: University of Texas Press, 1961.

Sheridan, C. L. *Fundamentals of experimental psychology.* New York: Holt, Rinehart and Winston, 1976.

Sidowski, J. B. *Experimental methods and instrumentation in psychology.* New York: McGraw-Hill, 1966.

Skinner, J. E. *Neuroscience: A laboratory manual.* Philadelphia: Saunders, 1971.

Smith, C. U. M. *The brain: Towards an understanding.* New York: Putnam, 1970.

Smith, D. W. & Bierman, E. L. *The biologic ages of man: From conception through old age.* Philadelphia: Saunders, 1973.

Smythies, J. R. The mode of action of psychotominetic drugs. *Neurosciences Research Program Bulletin,* 1970, *8* (1).

Sperry, R. W. Physiological plasticity and brain circuit theory. In H. Harlow and C. N. Woolsey (Eds.), *Biological and biochemical bases of behavior.* Madison, Wis.: University of Wisconsin Press, 1958.

Sperry, R. W. Split-brain approach to learning problems. In G. C. Quarton, T. Melnechuk & F. O. Smith (Eds.), *The neurosciences: A study program.* New York: Rockefeller University Press, 1967.

Spinelli, D. N. Visual receptive fields in the cat's retina: Complications. *Science,* 1966, *152.*

Strange, J. R. & Foster, R. (Eds.) *Readings in physiological psychology.* Belmont, California, Wadsworth, 1966.

Stevens, S. S. *Handbook of experimental psychology.* New York: Wiley, 1951.

Strumwasser, F. Neurophysiological aspects of rhythms. In G. C. Quarton, T. Melnechuk & F. O. Schmitt (Eds.), *The neurosciences: A study program.* New York: Rockefeller University Press, 1967.

Sutton, *Genes, enzymes, and inherited diseases.* New York: Holt, Rinehart and Winston, 1962.

Teevan, R. & Birney, R. C. *Color vision.* Princeton, N.J.: Van Nostrand, 1961.

Teitelbaum, P. The biology of drive. In C. G. Quarton, T. Melnechuk & F. O. Schmitt (Eds.), *The neurosciences: A study program.* New York: Rockefeller University Press, 1967.

Teitelbaum, P. & Epstein, A. N. The lateral hypothalamic syndrome: Recovery of feeding and drinking after lateral hypothalamic lesions. *Psychological Review,* 1962, *69,* 74–90.

Teyler, T. J. (Ed.). Altered states of awareness. (Readings from *Scientific American.*) San Francisco: Freeman, 1972.

Teyler, T. J. *A primer of psychobiology: Brain and behavior.* San Francisco: Freeman, 1975.

Thompson, R. F. *Foundations of physiological psychology.* New York: Harper & Row, 1967.

Thompson, R. F. (Ed.). *Physiological psychology.* San Francisco: Freeman, 1971.

Thompson, R. F. *Introduction to biopsychology.* San Francisco: Albion, 1973.

Thompson, T. & Shuster, C. *Behavioral pharmacology.* Englewood Cliffs, N.J.: Prentice-Hall, 1968.

Tryon, R. Genetic differences in maze learning in rats. In *National Society for the Study of Education, Thirty-ninth Yearbook.* Bloomington, Indiana: Public School Publishing, 1940.

Valenstein, E. S. Biology of drives. *Neurosciences Research Program Bulletin,* 1968, *6* (1).

Vallecalle, E. & Svactichin, G. The retina as model for the functional organization of the nervous system. In R. Jung and H. Kornhuber (Eds.), *The visual system: Neurophysiology and psychophysics.* Berlin: Springer-Verlag, 1961.

Wagner, H. G. & Wolbarsht, M. L. Studies on the functional organization of the vertebrate retina. *American Journal of Ophthalmology,* 1958, *46.*

Wagner, H. G., MacNichol, E. F., Jr. & Wolbarsht, M. L. Functional basis for "on"-center and "off"-center receptive fields in the retina. *Journal of the Optical Society of America*, 1963, *53*.

Wagner, H. G., MacNichol, E. F., Jr. & Wolbarsht, M. L. The response properties of single ganglion cells in the goldfish retina. *Journal of General Physiology*, 1960, *43*.

Walls, G. L. *The vertebrate eye and its adaptive radiations.* New York: Hafner, 1963.

Walton, J. *Essentials of neurology* (2nd ed.). London: Pitman Medical Publishing Co., 1966.

Watson, J. B. *Behaviorism.* New York: Norton, 1924.

Webster, W. G. *Principles of research methodology in physiological psychology.* New York: Harper & Row, 1975.

Weiss, W. Patterns of organization of the central nervous system. *Research Publications Association in Nervous Mental Disease*, 1952, *30*, 3–23.

Wenger, M. A., Jones, F. N. & Jones, M. H. *Physiological psychology*, New York: Holt, Rinehart and Winston, 1956.

Whitfield, I. C. *The auditory pathway.* (Monographs of the Physiological Society, No. 17.) London: E. Arnold, 1967.

Wiesel, T. & Hubel, D. Comparison of the effects of unilateral and bilateral eye closure on cortical unit responses in the kitten. *Journal of Neurophysiology*, 1965, *28*, 1029–1040.

Wilson, A. & Schild, H. *Applied pharmacology* (10th ed.).Boston: Little, Brown, 1968.

Winchester, A. M. *Heredity: An introduction to genetics* (2nd ed.). New York: Barnes & Noble, 1966.

Wolman, B. B. *Contemporary theories and systems in psychology.* New York: Harper & Row, 1960.

Wolstenholme, G. E. W. & O'Connor, M. (Eds.). *CIBA foundation symposium on the nature of sleep.* Boston: Little, Brown, 1961.

Woodward, L. E. Strengthening family life by educating for family living. *Journal of Social Casework*, December 1947. In H. W. Hepner, *Psychology applied to life and work* (5th ed.). Englewood Cliffs, N.J.: Prentice-Hall, 1975.

Woolridge, D. E. *The machinery of the brain.* New York: McGraw-Hill, 1963.

Woodworth, R. S. & Schlosberg, H. *Experimental psychology* (Rev. ed.). New York: Holt, Rinehart and Winston, 1965.

Worden, F. G. & Galambos, R. Auditory processing of biologically significant sounds. *Neurosciences Research Program Bulletin*, 1972, *10* (1).

Zanchetti, A. Subcortical and cortical mechanisms in arousal and emotional behavior. In G. C. Quarton, T. Melnechuk & F. O. Schmitt (Eds.), *The neurosciences: A study program.* New York: Rockefeller University Press, 1967.

Zucker, M. H. *Electronic circuits for the behavior and biomedical sciences.* San Francisco: Freeman, 1969.

(Continued from p. iv)

American Psychological Association for Figure 15.3 from Polly, E. H., D. J. Apple, and J. W. Bizzel: "The laser as a research tool in visual system investigation." *American Psychologist, 30*(3):340–348, 1975. Copyright © 1975 by the American Psychological Association. Figure 15.9 from Hurvich, L. M., and D. Jameson: "An opponent process theory of color vision." *Psychological Review, 64,* 1957. Copyright © 1957 by the American Psychological Association. Reprinted by permission.

ASP Biological and Medical Press for Figure 24.2 from Hess, R. Jr., W. P. Koella, and K. Akert: "Cortical and subcortical responses in natural and artificially induced sleep in cats." *Electroencephalography and Clinical Neurophysiology, 5*:75–90, 1953. Figure 27.3 from Pfenninger, K., C. Sandri, K. Albert, and C. H. Eugster: "Contribution to the problem of structural organization of the presynaptic area." *Brain Research, 12*:10–18. Reprinted by permission.

Association for Research in Nervous and Mental Disease, Inc., for Figure 22.4 from Weiss, R.: "Patterns of organization of the central nervous system." *Proceedings of the Association of Nervous and Mental Disease, 30*:3–23, 1952.

Blackwell School Publications for Figure 21.7 from Broadhurst, P. L.: "The biometrical analysis of behavioral inheritance." *Science Progress,* 1967. Reprinted by permission.

Chapman and Hall, Ltd., for Figure 15.4 from Pirenne, M. H. (as plotted from the numerical data of Osterberg, 1935): *Vision and the eye.* Copyright © 1967 by Chapman and Hall, Ltd. Reprinted by permission.

Cranbrook Institute of Science for Figure 15.2 from Walls, G. L.: *Vertebrate eye and its adaptive radiation,* 1963.

Thomas Y. Crowell, Company, Inc., for Table 16.1 and Figures 17.7, 18.3, and 18.8 from Christman, R. J.: *Sensory experience.* Copyright © 1971 by International Textbook Company. Reprinted by permission of Thomas Y. Crowell Company.

Doubleday & Company for Figure 6.4 from Mercer, E. H.: *Cells: Their structure and their function.* Copyright © 1961 by E. H. Mercer. Reprinted by permission of Doubleday & Company, Inc.

W. H. Freeman and Company for Figure 22.1 from *Biology: Its human implications,* 2d ed., by Garrett Hardin. W. H. Freeman Company. Copyright © 1966. Figure 3.8 from *Experimental neuropsychology* by Benjamin L. Hart. W. H. Freeman and Company. Copyright © 1969. Figure 5.3 from *A primer of drug action* by Robert M. Julien. W. H. Freeman and Company. Copyright © 1975. Figures 21.3 and 21.8 from *Heredity, evaluation, and society,* 2d ed., by I. Michael Lerner and William J. Libby. W. H. Freeman and Company. Copyright © 1976. Figure 10.2 from *Neuropharmacology and behavior* by V. G. Longo. W. H. Freeman and Company. Copyright © 1972. Reprinted by permission of W. H. Freeman and Company.

Harper & Row, Publishers, Inc., for Figures 20.5–20.12 from *A primer of physiological psychology* by Robert L. Isaacson et al. (portions of Fig. 4-1, p. 93, Fig. 4-2, p. 94, Fig. 4-3, p. 95, as adapted from C. J. Connolly, *External morphology of the primate brain,* Charles C Thomas, 1950; R. J. Truex and M. B. Carpenter, *Human neuroanatomy,* 5th ed., Williams & Wilkins, 1959; and J. W. Papez, *Comparative neurology,* Thomas Y. Crowell, 1929). Copyright © 1971 by Harper & Row, Publishers, Inc. Reprinted by permission. Figure 3.6 from *Foundations of physiological psychology* by Richard F. Thompson, 1967. Copyright © 1967 by Harper & Row, Publishers, Inc. Reprinted by permission. Figure 4.1 from *Introduction to physiological psychology* by Richard F. Thompson, 1975 (Fig. 2.9, p. 56, as adapted from B. M. Patten, *Human embryology,* 2d ed., McGraw-Hill, 1953). Copyright © 1975 by Harper & Row, Publishers. Reprinted by permission.

Holt, Rinehart and Winston for Figure 8.5, Figure 28.1, and Table 28.1 from *Organic foundations of animal behavior* by Joseph Altman. Copyright © 1966 by Holt, Rinehart and Winston, Inc. Figures 26.1–26.3 from *Experiments in psychology: Laboratory studies of animal behavior* by Donald S. Blough and Patricia McBride Blough. Copyright © 1964 by Holt, Rinehart and Winston, Inc. Figure 15.7 from *An introduction to psychology* by Ralph Norman Haber and Aharon H. Fried. Copyright © 1975 by Holt, Rinehart and Winston, Inc. Figure 5.12 from *Biology,* 4th ed., by Willis H. Johnson, Louis E. DeLanney, Thomas A. Cole, and Austin E. Brooks. Copyright © 1956, 1961 by Holt, Rinehart and Winston, Inc., under the title *General biology.* Copyright © 1966, 1972 by Holt, Rinehart and Winston, Inc. Figures 2.1, 16.2, 16.4, 17.4, 17.6, 17.8, 18.4, 18.7, 18.11, and 18.12 from *Physiological psychology* by Peter M. Milner. Copyright © 1970 by Holt, Rinehart and Winston, Inc. Figure 3.9 from *Fundamentals of experimental psychology*, 2d ed., by Charles L. Sheridan. Copyright © 1976 by Holt, Rinehart and Winston. Figure 6.6 from *Genes, enzymes, and inherited disease* by H. Eldon Sutton. Copyright © 1961 by Holt, Rinehart and Winston, Inc. Figure 19.7 and Tables 5.1, 5.2, and 14.1 from *Physiological psychology* by M. A. Wenger, F. N. Jones, and M. H. Jones. Copyright © 1956 by Holt, Rinehart and Winston, Inc. Reprinted by permission of Holt, Rinehart and Winston.

Journal of the Optical Society of America for Figures 15.8 and 15.10 from Hecht, S.: "The development of Thomas Young's theory of color vision." *Journal of the Optical Society of America,* 20(5):231–270, 1930. Copyright © 1930 by the Journal of the Optical Society of America. Reprinted by permission.

Alfred A. Knopf, Inc., for Figure 3.2 from Kretch, D., R. S. Crutchfield, and N. Livson: *Elements of psychology,* 3d ed. Copyright © 1974 by Alfred A. Knopf, Inc. Reprinted by permission.

J. B. Lippincott for Figure 19.10 from Elliott, C.: *Textbook of neuroanatomy.* Copyright © 1963 by J. B. Lippincott Company. Table 10.1 from Koelle, G. B.: "Functional anatomy of synaptic transmission." *Anesthesiology,* 29:643–653, 1968. Copyright © 1968 by J. B. Lippincott Company. Reprinted by permission.

Macmillan Publishing Company, Inc., for Figures 18.6 and 19.1 from Penfield, W., and A. T. Rasmussen, *The cerebral cortex of man.* Copyright © 1950 by Macmillan Publishing Company, Inc.

McGraw-Hill Book Company for Figure 4.1 from *Human embryology,* 2d ed., by B. M. Patten. Copyright © 1953 by McGraw-Hill Book Company. Reprinted by permission of McGraw-Hill Book Company (as adapted in R. F. Thomson, *Introduction to physiological psychology,* Harper & Row, Publishers, 1975). Figure 18.13 from *A functional approach to neuroanatomy* by E. L. House and B. Pansky. Copyright © 1967 by McGraw-Hill Book Company. Figure 24.1 from *Neuroanatomy* by E. L. House and B. Pansky. Copyright © by McGraw-Hill Book Company. Figure 25.1 from *The Psychology of fear and stress* by J. Gray. Copyright © 1971 by McGraw-Hill Book Company. Figure 27.2 from *The neuropsychology of Lashley* by F. A. Beach et al. (eds.). Copyright © 1960 by McGraw-Hill Book Company. Reprinted by permission of McGraw-Hill Book Company.

The C. V. Mosby Company for Figure 6.3 from Leukel, Francis: *Introduction to physiological psychology,* 3d ed. Copyright © 1976 by The C. V. Mosby Company, St. Louis.

Neurosciences Research Program for Figures 9.6 and 10.4 from Kopin, I. J.: "The mode of action of psychotominetic drugs." *Neurosciences Research Program Bulletin,* 8(1), 1970. Copyright © 1970 by the Neurosciences Research Program. Reprinted by permission.

New York Academy of Sciences for Figure 17.9 from Amoore, J. E.: "Current status of the stereochemical theory of odor." *Annals of the New York Academy of Sciences,* 116:457–476, 1964.

Oxford University Press for Figure 27.1 from Lorente de Nó: "Cerebral cortex," in J. F. Fulton: *Physiology of the nervous system.* Copyright © 1949 by Oxford University Press.

Prentice-Hall, Inc., for Figure 1.2 from Luther E. Woodward, "Strengthening family life by educating for family living." *Journal of Social Casework,* December 1947, reproduced in Harry Walker Hepner, *Psychology* applied to life and work, 5th ed. Copyright © 1975, p. 234. Reprinted by permission of Prentice-Hall, Inc., Englewood Cliffs, N.J.

Princeton University Press for permission to adapt Figure 3.5 from data in Penfield, W., and Roberts: *Speech and brain mechanisms.* Copyright © 1959 by Princeton University Press. Used by permission.

Psychology Today for Figure 10.3 from Jarvik, M.: "The psychopharmacological revolution." *Psychology Today,* 1(1):51–59, 1967. Reprinted by permission.

The Rockefeller University Press for Figure 4.7 by R. B. Livingston in Quarton, G. C., T. Melnechuk, and F. O. Schmitt (eds.): *The neurosciences: A study program,* Vol. 1. Copyright © 1967 by The Rockefeller University Press. Figures 9.1 and 9.5 from H.

Grundfest, "Synaptic and ephaptic transmission," in Quarton, G. C., T. Melnechuk, and F. O. Schmitt (eds.): *The neurosciences: A study program,* Vol. 1. Copyright © 1967 by The Rockefeller University Press. Reprinted by permission of The Rockefeller University Press. Figure 7.1 from D. Bodian, "Neurons, circuits and neuroglia," in Quarton, G. C., T. Melnechuk, and F. O. Schmitt (eds.): *The neurosciences: A study program,* Vol. 1. Copyright © 1967 by Cold Spring Harbor Laboratory, Cold Spring Harbor, N.Y. Reprinted by permission of The Rockefeller University Press. Figure 15.5 from Hecht, S., C. Haig, and A. M. Chase: "Influence of light adaptation on subsequent dark adaptation of the eye." *The Journal of General Physiology, 30*:831–850, 1937. Copyright © 1937 by The Rockefeller University Press. Reprinted by permission of The Rockefeller University Press.

The Royal Society, London, for Figure 15.6 from Dowling, J. E., and B. B. Boycott: "Organization of the primate retina." *Proceedings B of The Royal Society,* 1966, p. 80. Copyright © 1966 by the Royal Society. Reprinted by permission.

W. B. Saunders Company for Figure 9.2 from Bloom, W., and D. W. Fawcett: *A textbook of histology,* 9th ed. Copyright © 1968 by W. B. Saunders Company. Figures 4.5, 5.2 (bottom), 16.3, 16.6, and 22.2 from Curtis, B. A., S. Jacobson, and E. M. Marcus: *An introduction to neurosciences.* Copyright © 1972 by W. B. Saunders Company. Figures 5.1, 5.4, 5.5, 5.7, 5.8, 5.9, 5.10, 7.8, and Table 9.1 from Gardner, E.: *Fundamentals of neurology,* 4th ed., 6th ed. Copyright © 1963, 1975 by W. B. Saunders Company. Figures 6.2, 6.7, 7.3 from Guyton, A. C.: *The function of the human body.* Copyright © 1974 by W. B. Saunders Company. Table 10.2 from Leavitt, F.: *Drugs and behavior.* Copyright © 1974 by W. B. Saunders Company. Reprinted by permission.

Scientific American, Inc., for Figure 6.1 from Lehninger, A. L.: "How cells transform energy." *Scientific American,* September 1961. Copyright © 1961 by Scientific American, Inc. Figure 6.5 from Brachet, J.: "The living cell." *Scientific American,* September 1961. Figure 9.4 from Eccles, Sir John: "The synapse." *Scientific American,* January 1965. Copyright © 1965 by Scientific American, Inc. Figure 18.2 from Montagna, W.: "The skin." *Scientific American,* February 1965. Copyright © 1965 by Scientific American, Inc. Figure 23.4 from Jouvet, M.: "The states of sleep." *Scientific American,* February 1967. Copyright © 1967 by Scientific American, Inc. Reprinted by permission of W. H. Freeman and Company.

Springer-Verlag, Heidelberg, for Figure 17.2 from Schneider, M.: *Einfuhrung in die physiologie.* Copyright © 1964 by Springer-Verlag.

University of Chicago Press for Figures 20.2, 20.3, 20.4 from Buchsbaum, R.: *Animals without backbones.* Copyright © 1948 by the University of Chicago Press. Reprinted by permission.

Van Nostrand Reinhold Company for Table 21.1 and Figure 21.2 from *Biology and its relation to man* by A. M. Winchester. Copyright © 1975 by Litton Educational Publishing, Inc. Reprinted by permission of Van Nostrand Reinhold Company.

John Wiley & Sons, Inc., for Figure 16.5 from Davis, H.: "Psychophysiology of hearing and deafness," in Stevens, S. S. (ed.): *Handbook of experimental psychology.* Copyright © 1951 by John Wiley & Sons, Inc. Figure 18.10 from Geldard, F. A.: *The human senses.* Copyright © 1953 by John Wiley & Sons, Inc. Reprinted by permission.

Index/Glossary

"A" fibers, a group of heavily myelinated efferent fibers, **261**

Ablation, the removal of tissue, **32,** 55

Absolute refractory period, the refractory period in which no stimulus, however strong, can elicit a response, **110**

Absolute threshold, the lowest intensity,
as measured under optimal experimental conditions, at which a stimulus is
perceived, **151**

ACh (acetylcholine), the transmitter
chemical of cholinergic nerve impulses, **120,** 261, 300, 345.

Adaptation, a decline in the frequency
of nerve impulses to a constant stimulus, **161,** 172, 205, 354

Adenosine diphosphate (ADP), the "discharged" state of the energy molecule
in the cell, **93**

Adenosine triphosphate (ATP), the
"charged" state of the energy molecule in the cell, **93**

Adjustment stage, the second stage of
the GAS in which measures are taken
to reduce stress through a fight or
flight response, **350**

Adrenergic, neural circuits that use E or
NE as the transmitter chemical.
Usually involved with the autonomic
nervous system and/or emotional
tone, **121,** 139, 328, 346

Afferent nerves, sensory or "input"
fibers for the CNS, **24,** 159, 303,
360, 374

Alarm stage, the first stage of the GAS
in which the organism is alerted to
the onset of stress, **350**

Albinism, hereditary inability to produce
pigment from the skin, hair, and
eyes, **287**

Allocortex, older portion of the cerebral
cortex, component of the limbic
system, **56**

Amine theory of mood, the direct relationship between transmitter amine
level and mood, **135**

Ampulla, the location of the transducers
in the semicircular canals, **246**

nently altered into a memory circuit, **363,** 370, 381

Cell body, that portion of the neurons which contains the nucleus and associated structures, and from which extend the dendrites and axon, **22,** 96

Cell membrane, the outer boundary of the cell, **89,** 93, 367, 369.

Central nervous system (CNS), the brain and the spinal cord, **24,** 47, 63, 127, 145, 159, 197, 207, 231, 250, 299, 302, 319, 340, 356, 376

Central sulcus, the sulcus that divides each cerebral hemisphere between the frontal and parietal lobes, **58**

Cephalo-caudal, directional terminology indicating a trend from head to tail, **20**

Cerebellum, a central nervous system structure lying dorsal to the pons and beneath the cerebrum, involved in coordinating muscular activity, **25,** 51, 200, 213, 238, 247, 270, 279, 378

Cerebral aqueduct, the canal in the midbrain that connects the third and fourth ventricles, **65**

Cerebrospinal fluid, the fluid surrounding the brain and spinal cord and contained in the ventricles, **65**

Cerebrum, another term for "cortex," **24**

Chemotransducers, receptors that respond to chemical stimulation as in the olfactory and gustatory sensors and the chemical homeostatic sensors, **146**

Chloral hydrate, an alcohol utilized as a "truth serum," **128**

Cholinergic, neural circuits that use ACh as the transmitter chemical; usually involved with precise information and/or rapid transmission, **121,** 139, 367

Cholinesterase, an enzyme that neutralizes acetylcholine, **123**

Choroid coat, middle lining of the eye containing blood vessels, **192**

Chromosomes, structures in the nucleus that contain genetic information, **90**

Ciliary cells, hair cells that are frequently special transducer cells, **147**

Cingulate cortex, a gyrus of the limbic system lying beneath the frontal and parietal lobes, **57**

Circadian rhythm, a recurring sequence of behaviors of an approximately 24-hour cycle, **57,** 340, 375

Classical conditioning, the process by which an originally neutral stimulus, when paired repeatedly with a reinforcing stimulus, comes to elicit a response, **279,** 358

Cochlea, a spiral-shaped structure of the inner ear which contains the transducers for sound vibrations, **208,** 215, 243

Cochlear microphonic, an electrical response of the cochlea closely matching the sound stimulus, **214**

Commissural fibers, tracts that transmit information from one side of the CNS to the corresponding area of the opposite side, **61,** 377

Complex cortical cells, cells that respond to a stimulus of a particular orientation and moving across the visual field in a preferred direction, **173**

Cones (visual receptors), visual transducers responsible for the perception of color, **148,** 153, 196, 203

Consolidation period, the time required for permanent neurological changes to develop in the learning process, **361**

Contralateral control, the control of one side of the body by the opposing hemisphere of the brain, **51**

Convergence (neural), the channeling of neuronal impulses from several neurons to a single neuron, **182**

Convergence (visual), the crossing of two eyes so as to focus on a nearby subject, **202**

Cornea, the transparent outer tissue at the front of the eye, **192**

Coronal section, a slice of the brain taken vertically, dividing the brain into anterior and posterior portions, **40**

Corpus callosum, a large bundle of nerve fibers that transmits information between hemispheres, **62,** 280, 380

Cortex, the gray matter composing the outer layer of the brain responsible for higher-order processes, **24,** 28, 35, 56, 60, 66, 134, 167, 172, 181, 200, 214, 270, 281, 323, 364, 377

Retina, the layer of neurons and transducers lining the inside of the eye, **192**

Retinal disparity, the different image on the retina of each eye due to the difference in eye location, **202**

Retrograde amnesia, the loss of memory for events occurring just prior to the disruption of CNS activity, **361**

Reverberatory circuit, a neuronal system of inner connections which forms a loop through which activity can be recycled, **115,** 363, 371

Rhodopsin, the photopigment of the rods, **196**

Rhombencephalon, the posterior of the three structures in the embryonic development of the brain, **48**

Ribonucleic acid (RNA), a chemical which carries information in the cell and might be a "memory molecule," **92,** 368

Ribosomes, a cellular structure that is the site of protein synthesis, **93**

Rods, transducers in the retina of the eye producing achromatic vision, **148,** 153, 196, 205

Rostral, directional terminology indicating "toward the head," **20**

Round window, a membrane-covered opening in the cochlea which allows fluid movement due to sound waves, **211**

Saccule, an otolithic chamber in the vestibular apparatus, **244**

Saggital section, a vertical slice showing a lengthwise view of the brain, **40**

Saltatory conduction, the skipping of an axon spike from one node to the next as it passes down the myeinated axon, **105**

Satiety center, a nucleus (usually in the brain stem) which halts consummatory behavior, **337**

Sclera, the relatively tough exterior layer of the eye, **192**

Scopalamine, an anticholinergic psychedelic drug, **139**

Semicircular canals, the sensory apparatus for detecting rotary movements of the head; located in the inner ear, **244**

Semipermeable membrane, a membrane that selectively admits substances into or out of the cell, **89**

Sensory nerve, a bundle of nerve fibers which transmit afferent impulses from sensory receptors to the CNS, **24**

Sensory system, the transducers, neural network, and auxiliary structures which comprise the apparatus to process a certain class of external stimuli, **189–251**

Septal area, a structure in the limbic system involved in motivation and emotions, **57, 340,** 375

Serotoninergic, neural circuits that use 5-HT as the transmitter chemical; usually involved with emotional tone, **139,** 301, 338

Sex-linked trait, characteristics transferred to the male by the genetic information supplied by the X chromosome, **289**

Shock stage, the stage in the GAS when the stress is first encountered, **350**

Short-term memory, the temporary preservation of a memory trace before learning occurs, **361**

Simple cortical cells, visual neurons that are activated at the onset of a stationary straight line of a particular orientation across the visual field, **173**

Single-unit recording, the recording of the spike activity of a single axon, **38,** 203, 231, 238

Sodium pump, the mechanism in the membrane of the neuron that transports sodium and potassium ions against the normal osmotic flow, **93,** 98, 367

Soma (cell body), the part of the nerve cell containing the nucleus, **97,** 106

Spatial summation, the combination of activity (EPSP's) from different locations on the neuronal membrane, **108**

Species-specific behavior, complex, genetically determined sequences of behavior peculiar to a species, **274,** 356, 374

Specific energies of nerves, the law that different functions are served by different nerves, **13**

Specific hungers, a taste-preference mechanism by which an animal will select foods which contain vitamins

Trichromatic theory, the statement that there are three different cones in the retina that respond to red, green, and blue, respectively, **202**

Tricyclic antidepressants, drugs that prevent the reabsorption of the transmitter amines by the presynaptic bouton, **135**

Ventral root, the motor branch of the spinal nerves, **260**

Ventricles, hollow spaces throughout the middle of the CNS filled with cerebrospinal fluid, **147**, 340

Vitreous humor, a gelatinous substance in the posterior cavity of the eye, **194**

Withdrawal reflex, a spinal reflex through which a painful stimulus to a limb results in its immediate withdrawal before the sensory information reaches the brain, **265**

X chromosome, the chromosome that contributes to the sex of the individual and also carries sex-linked genotypic traits, **289**